WESTWARD IN EDEN

WESTWARD

The Public Lands and

UNIVERSITY OF CALIFORNIA PRESS

BERKELEY LOS ANGELES LONDON

IN EDEN

the Conservation Movement

BY WILLIAM K. WYANT

Illustration on jacket and title page: Jim Aycock's photograph of a wall mural in Department of Interior building, Washington, D.C., painted by well-known American artist John Steuart Curry in 1939.

University of California Press
Berkeley and Los Angeles, California
University of California Press, Ltd.
London, England
Copyright © 1982 by The Regents of the University of California

Library of Congress Cataloging in Publication Data

Wyant, William K.
　Westward in Eden.

　Bibliography: p. 499
　Includes index.
　1. United States—Public lands.　2. Land use—
Environmental aspects—United States.　3. Land use—
Law and legislation—United States.　I. Title.
HD205 1982.W9　　　333.1'0973　　　81-7519
ISBN 0-520-04377-4　　　　　AACR2

Printed in the United States of America
1 2 3 4 5 6 7 8 9

To my wife Carita Laurence

CONTENTS

ACKNOWLEDGMENTS

The principal debt owed by the author of this book is to Paul W. Gates, professor of history, emeritus, at Cornell University. I have leaned heavily upon Professor Gates's writings on the public lands. His *History of Public Land Law Development*, which has a chapter on mineral law by Robert W. Swenson of the University of Utah, has been a valued ally. It was written for the Public Land Law Review Commission and published in 1968. Irving Senzel of the Bureau of Land Management lent me his copy some years ago. I am afraid I have not yet returned it.

I have also benefited greatly from numerous other books, some of them scholarly and others of popular interest, that are listed at the back of this volume. I have a special debt to the works of Wallace Stegner and Bernard DeVoto, to Walter Prescott Webb for his *Great Plains*, to Vernon Louis Parrington for his *Main Currents in American Thought*, and to A. M. Sakolski for his *Great American Land Bubble*. In the realm of American history, I am grateful to Samuel Eliot Morison and Henry Steele Commager for *The Growth of the American Republic*. I have an obligation to many an anonymous staff person or researcher, on Capitol Hill or somewhere in the federal labyrinth, for reports and studies that were illuminating.

Among the onerous burdens falling on public officials and those who are or have been in public life is the task of reading drafts of a prospective book at the author's request. I have been guilty of asking people to do this. I am very grateful for the cheerful and helpful response I have had. John Mattoon of the Fish and Wildlife Service, formerly of the Bureau of Land Management, waded through the whole of an early draft and later looked at several revised chapters. I have had assistance of this kind from former Secretary of the Interior Stewart L. Udall; Representative Morris K. Udall (Dem.) of Arizona; former Interior Department Solicitor Frank J. Barry; Jerry A. O'Callaghan, historian of the Bureau of Land Management; former Assistant Attorney General James W. Moorman; Brock Evans of the Sierra Club; Edward B. Danson, former director of the Museum of Northern Arizona; and others. Patricia Hass of Washington, D.C., a writer, read the text and gave useful counsel.

Along the way, I have had the pleasure of interviewing and talking with all of the above people as well as with former Secretary of the Interior Cecil D. Andrus; former Interior Department Solicitor Edward Weinberg; former BLM Directors Marion Clawson, Burton Silcock, Curtis J. Berklund, and Frank Gregg; former Assistant Secretaries of the Interior Nathaniel Reed and Jack Horton; S. Dillon Ripley, secretary of the Smithsonian Institution; Russell E. Train, former chairman of the Council on Environmental Quality and director of the Environmental Protection Agency; William Van Ness, former chief counsel of the Senate Interior Committee; Harry B. Crandell, staff director of the House Interior Subcommittee on Public Lands; Stewart N. Brandborg and James G. Deane of the Wilderness Society; and many others.

Federal information officials were of major help in responding to inquiries, arranging interviews, and rounding up essential documents. I want to acknowledge particularly the assistance of Harmon Kallman, Charles Wallace, and their colleagues in the Interior Department and that of George Castillo in the Forest Service. In the assembling of photographs, I am indebted for help received from the Interior and Agriculture departments, the National Park Service, the Bureau of Land Management, the Fish and Wildlife Service, the Geological Survey, and the Library of Congress.

I owe thanks to the *St. Louis Post-Dispatch*, particularly to former Managing Editor Evarts Graham, Jr., and Washington Bu-

Acknowledgments

reau Chief Richard Dudman, for moral support and for a series
of assignments that enabled me to gather material in the field,
notably the West and Alaska. My interest in the subject matter of
this book—the public lands and the environmental movement—was heightened by a 1969 foray into Alaska, made in
company with my wife and with *P-D* colleagues Al Delugach
and Robert Holt. I made another visit in 1978.

The Library of Congress made a research desk available to me
for several months. I am grateful for the cheerful assistance of
Stanley Holwitz and his colleagues at the University of California Press.

Needless to say, nobody but myself is responsible for what is
in this book, and any sins of omission or commission are my
own.

PROLOGUE:
FROM SEA TO SEA

Not love of beauty, but love of gold with its good and evil is the grand force that pulls and pushes people into such wilds as these.
— JOHN MUIR, about 1872

I t is easy to overstate things in the battle over conservation. The clashing battalions give little quarter. What can be said truly is that much of the pristine quality of what was once an immense and beautiful land is now gone and that although some attrition was inevitable as the nation filled out, there has been disgraceful waste. Fortunately, a great deal of the heritage has not been spoiled beyond redemption, although its fate is in doubt.

We are not a nation of people given to lingering over dusty mementos in the attic or to weeping over what might have been. Americans may love their country deeply and passionately, but they are accustomed to moving along. For many of us, the United States is a kind of glorious panorama, a montage seen in the pages of a magazine or on television. We seldom hunker down, grab up a handful of soil, and sift it through our fingers. We are air-conditioned and mobile.

Thomas Jefferson had his Monticello in the soft countryside of Virginia, and Gilbert White, the eighteenth-century parson-turned-naturalist, had his tiny village of Selborne and its green environs west of London.[1] Living in more quiet times, they each made studies of what was around them—the hills, the trees, the animals, the earth itself. For such observers, the felling of a familiar clump of trees was a momentous event.

In contrast to this careful and concerned scrutiny, the American has usually seen real estate as expendable. It is something of which there is assumed to be plenty more, somewhere else. Most of us will mow our lawns, wage fitful war against the jimsonweed and crabgrass, and keep up our property values, but in our souls we are wayfaring strangers, ready to travel on. They have been telling us for more than a century that the frontier is no more, but we do not believe it.

The restless mobility and the throw-it-away-and-get-a-new-one attitude of the national population as a whole have not been unmixed blessings. Granted that the American standard of living is the envy of the world, it is nonetheless accurate to say that

1

we have achieved the standard by running through domestic and global resources at a clip that cannot be sustained. Not only are we beginning to see the bottom of our own flour barrel in terms of resources available at home but we have set an example that, if widely and successfully imitated by less advanced countries, would quickly exhaust the world cornucopia.[2]

As we attempt to make midcourse corrections—and in our case, fortunately, there is still opportunity for doing that—we can see that we might have done better with what we had. We might also have done worse. In addition to the harm that has come from waste, the evidence of which is everywhere to be seen, much damage has been done by the myopic view, rooted deep in our history, that there is something wrong and inappropriate about federal ownership of land. Better that the Devil own it than Uncle Sam, who is seen as a meddlesome interloper. Better the local, regional, state, or private interest than the national interest. But why?

Even more harmful, as we look back, has been the notion that the private owner of land—its proper and rightful lord and master and caretaker—has a property right that is sacrosanct and may do with his land whatever may please him or bring him profit, regardless of the transience of his tenure and the claims of the yet unborn. Such an uncluttered right has never existed in fact, in this or any other country, but nonetheless it is solemnly asserted. One encounters it at congressional hearings to this day.[3]

In the context of the nation's historical background, which includes the fierce reaction against power vested in the British crown, or "sovereign," as they say in the law, these attitudes are understandable, and some of the consequences have been good. The land had to be divided and distributed. Its resources had to be extracted. Private enterprise and the élan of the entrepreneur, as free as possible from bureaucratic red tape, are what this country is all about. And the federal record as land manager, it must be admitted, is not reassuring. Even so, we have carried the folklore of hostility toward federal intervention to ridiculous lengths. It feeds a Know-Nothing bias against intelligent planning. It is seized upon by selfish interests that exalt and exploit it for their own purposes.

By the 1970s, the wreckage caused by laissez-faire and "local control" —or no control—was impossible to ignore. With dwindling resources and a much larger population, the nation faced the task of rebuilding itself. Almost literally, it was said, the entire physical habitation had to be replaced.[4] There was turmoil over land ownership and planning. Attitudes of the public and the courts were changing rapidly, and public-interest lawyers, young and brave and possessed of brassbound nerve, came to the fore. Assisted by the conservationists, the visionaries, and the aesthetes, people were coming to think about what had happened to their country and what, if anything, could be done to curb further erosion of the quality of life. Some found it self-evident that there had been too little guidance—that the old system, if it could be called a system, had left the development of the United States to its speculators and profiteers.

Who was making the decisions about the federally owned portion of the United States, which was still about one-third, and about the rest? When a farmer sold his pastures and corn-fields to a speculator who sold them to a real estate agent who built suburban houses, whose decision was it? Who benefited, and who suffered loss? Who retired to Florida with the profits, and who stayed behind to deal with the problems? And the ugly but convenient commercial "malls," attached leechlike to suburban beltways and sucking the life from the inner cities while contributing nothing to urban taxes and urban culture—whose decision? The strip developments and "Miracle Miles" on highways passing through nameless, faceless towns, brave with hamburger joints and aflutter with the pennants of automobile dealers—again, whose decision?

Should the owner of property be free to saw down trees that were there before he was born? Not always, apparently. Under what circumstances should a mining company be allowed to invade the lovely and unspoiled places in federal ownership? These questions and others were being asked with persistence, often in the courts of law. It was difficult to find answers that did not upset traditional mores and deeply held beliefs.

A lot was at stake in all this. In the balance was, to begin with, whether government at all levels, acting as the agent of citizens, could and would protect the value of lands that were owned in common. An issue of broader importance was the extent of government's right, under the Constitution, to control use or abuse of land in private ownership. Through the well-recognized power of eminent domain, government clearly had the right to condemn land and pay the owner for it. The Fifth Amendment makes it illegal, however, that "private property be taken for public use without just compensation." Fair enough, but at what point does government's regulation of private property—telling the owner what he can or cannot do with his own land but stopping short of seizure—become a "taking" for which payment must be made? The law's flabbiness on this point, together with the ignorance or timidity of public officials, has blunted the thrust of intelligent planning.[5]

As the chickens of the past came home to roost, there were signs of reform and constructive movement. The National Environmental Policy Act of 1969, signed into law by President Richard M. Nixon, was a miracle in itself.[6] For the first time, federal agencies were put under a mandate to consider the impact of major actions they proposed to take—the issuance of a pipeline permit, for example, or the construction of a dam. Such was the atmosphere that Nixon, no environmentalist but keenly sensitive to the public mood, was persuaded to urge on Congress in February 1971 a sound but ill-starred proposal called the National Land Use Policy Act.[7]

The land-use proposal was essentially mild, a device for federal encouragement of land planning at the state and local level. For a time, all winds seemed to favor its passage. Mild though it was, however, it turned out to be anathema to business, rural, and conservative elements, who assailed it as a threat to private property. Nixon, beleaguered by the Watergate exposures and looking for friends where he could find them, suddenly withdrew his support.[8] The measure failed. Its foes cheered its narrow defeat.

President Jimmy Carter's election brought to high federal office a baker's dozen of known and active conservationists who had, from the outside, been calling on the nation to mend its ways.[9] It was not immediately apparent how effective these Galahads and Joans of Arc would be against the cunning and grizzled old warriors resisting change. Carter himself, blowing an uncertain trumpet at times, undertook to right some wrongs. The climate was improving, but a great many Americans still were reserving judgment about the environmental movement.

This book is concerned chiefly with the federally owned public lands—their history and their prospects as seen from the vantage point of the late 1970s. It is also concerned, though less directly, with privately owned lands, whose fate is intertwined with that of the public lands. If the reader notes a tendency to defend the federal as against the local or private interest when clashes between these occur, it is because in the case of the public lands the federal authority tends to reflect more closely the perceived national or public interest.

Although concerned with energy problems as they relate to the public lands, this book does not attempt to address the complicated and controversial issue of nuclear energy.

Ronald Reagan's stunning victory in the 1980 presidential election brought to power a conservative Republican sworn to reduce the cost and size of the federal establishment and to cut back federal intervention in the affairs of industry and of state and local governments. Prominent among his supporters were advocates of the Sagebrush Rebellion, who felt that states should take over certain federal lands in the West. Whether or not this revival of an ancient struggle had basis in law or fact, the ascent

5

to power of its champions cast a new shadow over the fate of the public lands.

The Reagan sweep and the changing of the guard in the executive branch and in the Senate brought a measure of dismay to some environmentalists, who as a group had taken satisfaction in the election of President Carter in 1976 and had favored his reelection in 1980. Many a fox, it was feared, would now be turned loose in the federal hen roosts where Carter's people had been benign and supportive. There was a perceived danger that the federal structure for protecting the nation's air, land, and water from degradation would be dismantled or else so weakened as to be useless.

Like the fallen angels in John Milton's *Paradise Lost*, the environmentalists picked themselves up from the dust, beat out the flames, and took what comfort they could. The election, they said, had not been a referendum on America's environmental concerns but had been decided chiefly on pocketbook issues. They insisted, as did outgoing Secretary of the Interior Cecil D. Andrus, that notwithstanding the election returns there was evidence of firm public support for such progress as had been made in safeguarding the quality of life.

Be that as it may, even though voters may not have realized that environmental issues were at stake, the 1980 landslide meant a radical and immediate reversal of course in the federal land-managing agencies. Generally speaking, the Reagan White House's nominees for top jobs in these areas were nightmare candidates, from the environmentalists' standpoint. Some solace could be found in the knowledge that the tripartite federal structure is notoriously resistant to abrupt change, whether at the hands of Carter's environmentalists in office or Reagan's industry-oriented foes of Big Government.

"When I walk out the door, I'll do it with my head held high," said Secretary Andrus in an interview before going home to Idaho. "You live by the sword and you die by the sword."

Pounding Pacific surf at Cape Perpetua, Oregon. *Courtesy U.S. Forest Service.*

CHAPTER 1

THE PUBLIC LANDS

And the Lord God took the man, and put him into the Garden of Eden, to dress it and to keep it.

— BOOK OF GENESIS

Mr. Speaker, the land in America is taking a beating.

— Rep. MORRIS K. UDALL addressing the House in 1974.

The United States began life two centuries ago at the eastern rim of a magnificent, vast, and largely unpopulated land area extending more than 2,500 miles from the Atlantic to the Pacific Ocean and more than 1,000 from the Great Lakes to the Gulf of Mexico. Out of this patrimony, with hard work and wisdom, courage and a lot of luck, came the richest and most powerful nation on earth.

We have now pretty much run through the well-watered, easily arable land and the best of the mineral resources. We wasted a great deal, and we made many mistakes, some of which are still being made. We are in a period of soul-searching, knowing as we do that the future reaches beyond the horizon and that so much of what we started with is gone.

There have been many warnings. Not all of them have gone unheeded and ignored.

In June 1952, President Harry S. Truman received a document called *Resources for Freedom* from his Materials Policy Commission, headed by William S. Paley. The famous Paley commission report noted that the United States was using its reserves faster than any other country. And on page 5, after expressing its faith in the principles of growth and free enterprise, the commission made this simple but startling assertion: "There is scarcely a metal or a mineral fuel of which the quantity used in the United States since the outbreak of the first World War did not exceed the total used throughout the world in all the centuries preceding."[1]

This is a nation, the report said in an alliterative passage more than twenty-five years ago, that has always been "more interested in sawmills than in seedlings." In June 1973, President Richard M. Nixon heard from another panel of citizens and experts, this one called the National Commission on Materials Policy.[2] Its findings reflected a growing demand for raw materials and energy together with a mounting anxiety about the impact of these demands on the environment.

9

With the world's population escalating in places where people already could not feed themselves and with global shortages of food and energy being predicted, there was no lack of non-government studies sounding the alarm. In 1972 the Club of Rome, an international research group identified with the Massachusetts Institute of Technology, published *The Limits to Growth*.[3] This small book was widely read and discussed. A major conclusion was that man would continue to exist indefinitely on the earth, but only if limits were imposed on both population growth and the production of material goods.

The Club of Rome's preoccupation with the predicament of mankind at the supranational level was shared by the Worldwatch Institute, a Washington-based effort organized by Lester R. Brown with private foundation support to focus on problems considered worthy of attention. The institute poured out from its offices on Massachusetts Avenue, opposite the Brookings Institution, a series of books and pamphlets on population, food, the loss of good forest and farmland, and other subjects. It spoke of deforestation across the world, the lessons of the American Dust Bowl in the 1930s, the ravages of desertification, the virtues of solar energy. As an official of the Department of Agriculture in the 1960s, Brown had done much to call attention to the possibility of famine in certain less developed countries, notably India.

Quite apart from Sunday-newspaper jeremiads couched in hysterical doomsday terms, serious worry about the adequacy of raw materials over the long haul was widely shared, and it put a sharper focus on the nation's federally owned lands. They are of immense extent, they are what remains after the binge, and they are thought to contain a very significant part of the still-available American reserves.[4]

At the beginning, when the first census was taken fifteen years after the Declaration of Independence, the national population was just under 4 million, and the center of population—so the *World Almanac* tells us—was twenty-three miles east of Baltimore. On the eve of the Bicentennial, with President Gerald R. Ford in the White House, there were about 215 million Americans, and the center had shifted to a point near Mascoutah, Illinois. It was not the size of the population that gave a thoughtful celebrant pause, of course, but the American economy's cormorantlike gobbling of resources in this country and abroad.

The United States had at the outset an incomparable Garden of Eden to dress and keep, as the Old Testament phrases it. Its husbandry has been at some times profligate, greedy, and shortsighted and at other times blessed with extraordinary vision. Closely relevant to that sorry and glorious record is the story of the westward movement—how the broad public lands were acquired and how they were distributed. And how well we are facing up to the struggle for wise and prudent use of the residue.

There is point in recalling the basic events and laws of the nation's settlement, if only hastily and superficially, because the present status of the federally owned lands, and indeed the lands as a whole regardless of ownership, cannot be well understood without some grasp of what has gone before. There was doubtless a much keener understanding of the facts of life about land tenure a hundred years ago, when the United States was largely rural, than there is now that most of us live in urban areas and many millions have never felled a tree or heard a rooster crow.

The country in its springtime was a domain of incredible richness tenanted in human terms only by the outnumbered and wandering Indian tribes and a scattering of Americans, French, British, and Spanish. It had a population density of perhaps one person to five square miles beyond the Alleghenies and was, for practical purposes, an unsettled wilderness. By and large it was a tablet on which the eager young nation would write at will—virgin forests, great rivers, the prairies and high plains, the shining Rockies, the arid and sandy wastes, and then again mountains, forests, and the golden Pacific shore. The early settlers found it majestic and unspoiled, teeming with furred animals,

11

birds, and other wildlife.[5] They plunged into it, defiant of restraints imposed by the crown and later by their own elected government.

It was not just another wilderness to be subdued, and we Americans may be forgiven even at this late date for thinking there was something unusual about those who settled it. The Ohio country seen by Washington was a darkly splendid place, unforgettable, and we have the testimony of such early observers as Thaddeus Mason Harris of Massachusetts that the fabled Northwest Territory was a fair land. Despite his having "long labored under a wasting sickness," as Harris put it, he undertook the journey from New England in the spring of 1803 and saw the town of Marietta and a good deal of the country along the Ohio River.

"The passage down the river was extremely entertaining, exhibiting at every bend a change of scenery," Harris wrote in his *Journal of a Tour into the Territory Northwest of the Alleghany [sic] Mountains.*[6] "Sometimes we were in the vicinity of dark forests, which threw a solemn shade over us as we glided by; sometimes we passed along overhanging banks, decorated with blooming shrubs which timidly bent their light boughs to sweep the passing stream; and sometimes along the shore of an island which tinged the water with a reflected landscape."

Harris was enchanted on his voyage by the lively carols of the birds, which he said "entertained us exceedingly, and gave life and pleasure to the woodland scene. The flocks of wild geese and ducks which swam upon the stream, the vast number of turkies, partridges, and quails we saw upon the shore, and the herds of deer or some other animals of the forest darting through the thickets, afforded us constant amusement."

Without question, Harris had a feeling for nature, but the rising settlements and cultivated plains of the newly settled country also found favor in his sight:

> When we see the land cleared of those enormous trees with which it was overgrown, and the cliffs and quarries converted

12

into materials for building, we cannot help dwelling upon the industry and art of man, which by dint of toil and perseverance can change the desert into a fruitful field, and shape the rough rock to use and elegance. When the solitary waste is peopled, and convenient habitations arise amidst the former retreats of wild beasts; when the silence of nature is succeeded by the buzz of employment, the congratulations of society, and the voice of joy; in fine, when we behold competence and plenty springing from the bosom of dreary forests—what a lesson is afforded of the benevolent intentions of Providence!

Harris's pious raptures offer a not unpleasing contrast to the dank and morbid forebodings that sometimes befogged the national spirit two centuries later. Leaving Marietta, he took horse northeast along the Ohio toward Wheeling, on his way home. He philosophized on a marked difference he perceived between the tidy, thrifty New Englanders he saw on the river's west bank, in Ohio, and the Virginia "back settlers" who lived a hunter's life on the east bank.

"They neglect, of course, the cultivation of the land," Harris said of the latter. "They acquire rough and savage manners. Sloth and independence are prominent traits in their character; to indulge the former is their principal enjoyment; and to protect the latter their chief ambition."

In land matters, the founding fathers demonstrated the genius for compromise and political accommodation that has characterized the nation since. They were not frozen men, and they were, in some respects, more liberal and better educated than their descendants. In the seventeenth and eighteenth centuries, the practice of buying up land and holding it for a profit was a respectable activity for public officials. It was one of the few ways a gentleman could make money. Such speculation was prevalent among the early American leaders—including the splendidly honest George Washington—to a degree that might have dismayed and outraged later generations.[7]

After independence, Americans with capital and foresight organized companies to buy up lands ahead of settlement.

Washington, Benjamin Franklin, and most other persons of substance invested in these ventures. Washington himself had large personal holdings in the country that was opening up west of Pittsburgh. In 1784, three years after he took Cornwallis's sword at Yorktown and five years before he was inaugurated as the first president, Washington rode into the backwoods to inspect his acquisitions, which totaled 32,373 acres on the Ohio and Great Kanawha rivers. He found settlers on his land, claiming it as their own.

"Such is the rage of speculating in, and forestalling of lands on the northwest side of Ohio," Washington wrote from Mount Vernon after a 680-mile journey that consumed more than a month, "that scarcely a valuable spot within any tolerable distance of it is left without a claimant."[8]

He complained that unauthorized persons were roaming into Indian territory, surveying and settling. Such efforts should be nullified, he said, and the culprits regarded as outlaws— "fit subjects for Indian vengeance."[9]

From early times, as Washington's letter suggests, it was never easy to curb the seepage of people along the frontier. The problem disturbed the gentry. When the Confederation Congress sought to bar settlers from Indian lands north of the Ohio, it was vexed by "the increase of feeble, disorderly and dispersed settlements in these remote and widely extended territories ... the depravity of manners which they have a tendency to produce; the endless perplexities in which they must involve the administration of the affairs of the United States."[10]

In western Pennsylvania, an agent of the land-rich Penns found the Scotch-Irish immigrants "bold and indigent strangers." The agent, James Logan, commented in a fashion that reflected the ideas of the great English philosopher John Locke. He noted that the settlers took up land audaciously, considering it, as he put it, "against the laws of God and Nature that so much land should be idle, while so many Christians wanted it to labor on to raise their bread."[11]

14

The Public Lands

During the turmoil of the revolution, the new nation acquired its first public lands through cession of western territories that had been granted to Virginia and certain other states by the British crown. The Continental Congress, seeking to raise troops, offered land bounties before the central authority, such as it was, owned any land. There was friction between the landed and the landless states, particularly involving Maryland, before the extensive backlands finally were ceded and became the common property of all.

The land issue was paramount as the Congress of the Confederation, under the necessity of getting funds to pay the nation's debts, bestirred itself after the war was won to lay down the terms for dividing and selling the federal domain and for the admission of new states. This was done in the Land Ordinance of 1785, which adopted the New England rectangular survey in preference to the less formal metes and bounds system of the South, and in the Northwest Ordinance of 1787, which dealt with the problem of disposing of the Ohio wilderness and the eventual creation of new states on equal terms with the old.

There was spirited debate over these two basic ordinances, which along with the inherited English common law had tremendous influence in shaping the national expansion, for better or worse. In choosing the rectilinear survey over the South's "tomahawk system," Congress chose a method in which the publicly owned vacant lands were divided neatly into townships of 36 square miles, or 23,040 acres, each township to contain mile-square lots, or "sections," each section having 640 acres.

Thus was imposed the familiar survey grid and the smaller divisions, such as the 160-acre "quarter-section" tract enshrined in the Homestead Act of 1862. Of precisely this size, it was ordained, was the classic family farm of the American Republic. It worked well in some places, but as the nation forged farther west into arid country, it became an arbitrary, procrustean number—too large or too small for practical purposes.

15

Federal land policy as shaped in the 1780s stipulated that public lands be surveyed and then sold at auction to the highest bidder at one dollar an acre or more. In every township, one square-mile section—section sixteen—was to be reserved "for the maintenance of public schools." The New England custom of reserving one section also for religion was not perpetuated, although five states wanted it. James Madison of Virginia said it smelled of "antiquated bigotry."[12] There was no limitation on the amount of land a person or a company could buy, no requirement that a purchaser had to improve or settle the land, and no protection for squatters who had jumped the gun and settled where they had no legal title. In the Northwest Territory, at least, there was to be no extension of slavery.

In these circumstances, with frontiersmen pressing across the Alleghenies and into the Indian-held Ohio country, Congress lent itself to several gargantuan land sales while using troops to clear out squatters. For example, New England entrepreneurs organized the Ohio Company, bought about one million acres at eight cents an acre, and made their way through the wilds and down the Ohio River to Marietta. Theirs was genuine settlement. Not so much could be said for the less respectable Scioto Land Company, with which the New Englanders had been induced to join forces in gaining Congress's approval for buying the government's land. The Scioto scheme, involving members of Congress and federal and state officials, was speculation. It lured a band of unfortunate French to Ohio, but it was in time revealed to be a will-o'-the-wisp.[13]

There were other major transactions at roughly the same time, in the period the Northwest Ordinance was approved. War veterans cut a large figure in them. The last cut-rate sale of federal land to private speculators was made in 1787 to a group headed by John Cleve Symmes of New Jersey, who had served in the War of Independence. This involved less than one million acres on the Ohio between the Great and Little Miami rivers. It was by no means, of course, the last disposal of large federal tracts for little or nothing.

The Public Lands

The hazards of life along the periphery of the American advance, in the Ohio country as well as in Tennessee, Kentucky, and elsewhere, were of more immediate concern than the legalities of land title. Pioneers beyond the Ohio River had been demanding federal protection. Indians and their allies, the British, were not pushed back from the path of onrushing settlement until Gen. Anthony Wayne won a decisive victory in 1794 at Fallen Timbers, near what is now Toledo. Peace was still a long time coming to the area in contest, a formidable woodland encompassing the present states of Ohio, Illinois, Indiana, Michigan, Wisconsin, and eastern Minnesota.

American troops in this wilderness found themselves playing a dual role. At times they had the unpopular and onerous chore of defending Indian territory against illegal incursion, rounding up settlers and driving them back, destroying their cabins and crops.[14] At other times, the soldiery was engaged in arduous, dangerous, and not always successful expeditions to find and punish the Indians for border outrages.

The difficult, independent life and rough-and-ready justice of the frontier bred a cheerful contempt for the distant lawgivers which was to manifest itself often as the nation fleshed out its destined space. Although squatters received no protection when the rules were laid down in the 1780s, they had the advantage of real presence on the land, and eventually they and those who succeeded them gained political power.

Even before the American Revolution, the right of preemption—that is, the first-come settler's right to get title to land he had improved—was widely recognized. This tradition did not square with the new nation's policy of selling land for revenue, which dictated intolerance toward squatting. Where the tradition prevailed, it gave the settler a measure of security against remote purchasers and speculators, enabling him at least to obtain payment, if ousted by another claimant, for the value of improvements he had made.

Thomas Jefferson, champion of agrarian democracy, sided with the landless poor. In 1776, he proposed that men who did

17

not own fifty acres should receive free grants. Later, echoing John Locke, he wrote: "Whenever there is in any country un-cultivated lands and unemployed poor, it is clear that the laws of property have been so far extended as to violate natural right. The small landholders are the most precious part of a state."[15] In any event, said Jefferson of the incoming thousands, "they will settle the land in spite of everybody."

Modern Americans, accustomed to thinking of democracy's virtues as unassailable, have trouble recalling that in the eigh-teenth century democracy had a bad name. It sounded good, but where it had been tried it had shown a tendency to degenerate into mob rule or tyranny. The checks and balances set up in the Constitution, designed to guard against an overbearing central authority on the one hand and against anarchy on the other, did not make for neat settlement patterns. Typically, there was little or no respect for the federal writ or for federal property, whether opened to entry or not. Absentee owners got similar treatment. Land sharks swam in these roiled waters from earliest times, buying up veterans' land bounties, finding loopholes, staying a jump ahead of the law.

The brilliant Robert Morris, money raiser for the Revolution, was a tireless speculator in land. Born in England, he was a fi-nancial power in Philadelphia before he reached the age of thirty. He signed the Declaration of Independence, gave invalu-able service in finding funds for Washington's army and for the emerging nation, and became a senator from Pennsylvania. Later in his life, Morris's western land dealings laid him low. He sank into obscurity after imprisonment for debt— "the hotel with the grated doors," Morris called it. When he departed life in 1806, he is said to have owed $12 million, a colossal sum, roughly half what the United States paid France for the Loui-siana Territory.[16]

Of all the land swindles during the Republic's infancy, the boldest and most infamous was the Yazoo fraud, or frauds. The Georgia state legislature in 1795 approved an act that enabled four companies to buy about thirty-five million acres, partly along the Yazoo River, in what later became Alabama and Mississippi. The price worked out to a penny and a half an acre for a wooded satrapy the size of modern Illinois. When it was revealed that most members of the legislature had an interest in the deal, indignation among Georgians ran high. One of the lawmakers narrowly escaped hanging. The next Georgia legislative assembly, in 1796, voided the land grants. This did not settle the matter, because the sale had created a dog's breakfast of far-ranging legal and financial entanglements.[17]

"The frauds practiced in the negotiation and sales of these Georgia lands have been as numerous and complicated as the mind of man could conceive," wrote Abraham Bishop of Connecticut in a brief but blistering contemporary account. He was court clerk in New Haven and a supporter of Jefferson.

"Men who have never added an iota to the wealth or morals of the world," Bishop commented with indignation, "and whose single moment was never devoted to making one being wiser or happier throughout the universe—riding in their chariots—aiming with feathers to cut throats, and on parchments to seal destruction—these are the robbers of modern days."[18]

Gen. James Oglethorpe had given haven to refugees from English debtors' prisons when the Georgia Colony was set up, but the Yazoo affair could not be blamed on immigrants of poor estate or low degree. It involved some of the nation's leading men—prominent citizens, politicians, and land jobbers from all over the country. United States Sen. James Gunn of Georgia led one of the companies. Wade Hampton, wealthy southern planter and grandfather of the Confederate general, had an interest in two companies. The able but ill-starred Morris also took part.

Yazoo and the claims arising from it occupied the country for some time. In 1810 the Supreme Court answered the prayers of investors who had bought Yazoo land. Chief Justice John Marshall ruled in *Fletcher* v. *Peck* that Georgia's sale of the lands was a contract and the state's rescinding act was unconstitutional.

Congress then voted in 1814 to indemnify the holders of grants to the lands, which by then had been ceded by Georgia to the federal government. Most of those sharing in the $4,282,151 paid by the Treasury Department were not the original claimants, but wealthy speculators who had bought out, for a song, those who had been bilked.[19]

Meanwhile, the nation had grown apace. In the acquisition of the immense empire of public-domain lands which ended with the Alaska Purchase in 1867, the first increments were cessions made by states that, as colonies, had been shaped by royal grants. Seven of the original thirteen—New York, Virginia, Massachusetts, Connecticut, and South and North Carolina, in addition to Georgia—turned over large western tracts to the national government in the period between 1781 and 1802. From these early state cessions, totaling 233,415,680 acres, the United States assumed the great Northwest Territory as well as the area that became Alabama and Mississippi in the South.

That, however, was only a preliminary roughing out of a border that was to move westward as inexorably as a cloud shadow drifts eastward across an open sea. From 1802 through the years immediately following the Civil War, the nation made seven additional land acquisitions, by war, international negotiation, and purchase, to round out its holdings and reach the Pacific. Three of them—the Louisiana and Alaska purchases and the extensive concessions wrung from Mexico by conquest— were much larger than the areas ceded by the original states.

Firstly, in 1803, President Jefferson bought the Louisiana Territory from Napoleon of France. The Corsican who had spilled the blood of thousands to win a European field like Marengo gave up, with a scratch of the pen, a fabulous empire he had never seen. At the same moment, he denied that empire to the British. In the transaction, Jefferson obtained 523,446,400 acres of the New World for $23,213,000, doubling the national area at a stroke. The price came to three or four cents an acre. Thus were garnered the port of New Orleans and all or part of what were to become the states of Louisiana, Arkansas, Missouri, Iowa,

Minnesota, North and South Dakota, Nebraska, Kansas, Oklahoma, Colorado, Wyoming, and Montana. With the American flag at New Orleans, western settlers had a safe harbor and outlet for their goods.

President Jefferson in that same year sent Meriwether Lewis and William Clark on the exploration that took them up the Missouri River, across the Rockies, and to the Pacific. The leaders were well chosen. Both were Virginians from families Jefferson had known around Charlottesville, and both were army officers seasoned by campaigning under General Wayne in Ohio. Pushing up the Missouri in a keelboat with a party of less than thirty-five, including many newly enlisted frontiersmen, they made their way across the "Shining Mountains" and down the Columbia. Lewis and Clark got along well with the Indians, whom they treated with kindness, courtesy, and whisky. The mission, completed in 1806, was amazingly successful. It stitched lightly a bond soon to be riveted in iron, copper, and gold.[20]

William Clark, the junior officer on the journey, was a sanguine and outgoing man who lived to a ripe old age in Saint Louis. Captain Lewis, unfortunately, had a raven on his shoulder. He was given to melancholia. He shot himself with a pistol in 1809 at a backwoods inn in the Natchez Trace.

As Jefferson was well aware, the North American continent had already been crossed successfully to the north between 1791 and 1793 by a fur-trading Scottish explorer. This was Alexander Mackenzie of the North West Company, rival to the Hudson's Bay Company. He reached the Pacific north of Vancouver Island, giving substance to British claims to the far Northwest. In 1818, under President James Monroe, the United States and its more powerful neighbor in Canada agreed on a boundary west along the forty-ninth parallel to the Rockies. Added to the public domain thereby was the Red River basin, including parts of what are now North and South Dakota and Minnesota. The national holdings were increased by about twenty-nine million acres of land and half a million of water. West of the Rockies, the boundary remained unsettled until more than a quarter century later.

Far to the southeast, before the Red River basin was enfolded, President Jefferson had claimed West Florida as part of the Louisiana Purchase, and tried to buy both West and East Florida from Spain. Spanish authority in the region was weak. A hawk-visaged young Andrew Jackson, later to become president, led a punitive expedition into Spanish Florida against the Creek Indians. Spain yielded in 1819 during Monroe's administration, giving up all of Florida. The federal domain was increased by 46,144,040 acres, more than 43,000,000 of it dry land. The cost was $6,674,057, of which a substantial part amounted only to payment by the United States of claims its own citizens had against Spain. The acquired territory filled in the heel of Louisiana to the Sabine River at the present eastern border of Texas.

Mexico was next to make its contribution. That country had become independent of Spain in 1821 and had welcomed Americans to Texas, making land available to them on liberal terms. By 1830, in the Jacksonian era, Texas had twenty thousand Yankees and one thousand slaves. The English-speaking newcomers proved intractable under Mexican rule. After the slaughter at the Alamo came the defeat of the brutal Santa Anna at San Jacinto and the birth of the Independent Republic of Texas in 1836. The United States, riven by the dispute over slavery, did not embrace Texas until 1845, and when it did, the federal government acquired no additional public lands—that is, lands owned by the people of the United States as a whole.

Texas was, as always, a special case. In admitting her, Congress provided that Texas would retain both its public debt and more than 200,000,000 acres of state public land that the nine-year-old Republic had not granted away or sold, some of which later turned out to contain a sea of oil. There was talk of the state selling its land to the federal government for $10,000,000, but this was not done. There was some reluctance on the federal side, since along with the land the federal government would have had to take over a tangle of questionable financial dealings the republic had countenanced. In 1850 the federal authority did buy from Texas a disputed tract of 78,842,880 acres, which went to form parts of Oklahoma, New Mexico, Colorado, Wyoming, and Kansas. The price, $15,496,488, helped Texas retire its war debt. The Lone Star State thus was left with its own public domain, which by 1970 produced revenues of more than $1,600,000,000.[21]

President James K. Polk, the North Carolina Democrat and expansionist, prevailed upon Congress to declare war on Mexico in 1846 and finished what the Yankees who moved to Texas had begun. The hard-fought campaign brought a harvest of new territory and served as a training ground for the young West Pointers who were to lead the armies of the North and South in the Civil War. Grant, Lee, Meade, Jackson, McClellan, and Beauregard were among them.

In the year Polk invaded Mexico, he settled with the British by reaching agreement that the nation's northern boundary west of the Rockies would be the forty-ninth parallel, except that the southern end of Vancouver Island, which projects below it, would remain British. The so-called Oregon Compromise averted war by abandoning the American Fifty-four Forty or Fight posture.[22] It gave the federal domain another 180,644,480 acres of land from which the states of Washington, Oregon, and Idaho and parts of Montana and Wyoming emerged.

From a prostrate Mexico, President Polk in 1848 demanded and got an enormous cession in the Treaty of Guadalupe Hidalgo. With American troops in Mexico City, the Mexicans recognized the Rio Grande rather than the Nueces River as the boundary of Texas. In addition, they sold to the victorious invaders for $15 million an area of staggering immensity. It amounted to 334,479,360 acres and encompassed all of what are known today as California and Nevada as well as most of Arizona and segments of New Mexico, Wyoming, and Colorado.

In 1853, when Franklin Pierce was president, the United States returned to the Mexican carcass and bought for $10 million another piece of it for which James Gadsden, a railroad promoter, was the negotiating agent. The Gadsden Purchase involved 18,961,920 acres south of the Gila River, mostly in what is now southern Arizona but extending eastward into New Mexico. The impetus for buying the tract, then regarded as a waste—"utterly desolate, desert, and God-forsaken," Sen. Thomas Hart Benton of Missouri called it—was that rail interests wanted a shorter, all-American Gila River route to the west coast at San Diego.[23] The purchase, arranged three-quarters of a century after the Declaration of Independence, completed the nation's annexation of contiguous areas.

Alaska, then and now a beautiful and largely unknown realm in the icy North, followed in fourteen years as the last addition to the nation's treasure of federally owned public domain. It was also the largest acquisition next to the Louisiana Purchase, amounting to 365,481,600 acres of land and nearly 10,000,000 of inland water. All this, an area more than twice the size of Texas and nearly four times the size of California, was purchased from Imperial Russia in 1867 for $7 million. Even at that price, the deal was called "Seward's Folly" by its critics, after Secretary of State William Henry Seward, who negotiated the treaty. The Senate ratified it by a margin of only one vote.

Russians also looked askance at the transfer of sovereignty in a region closer to their country than to ours. It was defended on practical grounds, however, by the Russian minister to the United States, Baron Edouard Stoeckl. His letter from Washington to the chancellor at St. Petersburg, Prince Gorchakov, called attention to the fact that the pushing Americans had been too much for the British and French to handle. Russia, he said, could not hope to protect Alaska from "the greed of the freebooters."

"Although the fish, the furs, and some other comparatively insignificant products of our [Alaskan] possessions certainly did not measure up to the rich valleys of the Mississippi and Rio Grande, nor to the gold-bearing plain of California," the baron wrote home from the American capital in justifying the sale, "they did not escape the covetousness of the Americans."[24]

The westward-foraging Yankee was indeed a brash and formidable antagonist. He correctly assumed that his flag would follow him. He was often ill-mannered, ignorant, and a sharp dealer to boot—witness the unflattering testimony of such British visitors as Mrs. Frances Trollope, Charles Dickens, who was skinned in a land-promotion scheme, and later the young Rudyard Kipling. The French observers, St. Jean de Crèvecoeur and Alexis de Tocqueville, were more kindly and understanding. Whether they liked it or lumped it, the Yankee prevailed. His pluck and luck held up well, and the straws cast in his way were brushed aside. As for the aboriginal inhabitants, solemn agreements the Indians entered into with the white man's leaders in Washington availed them nothing.

The great westward trek of the Mormons from Nauvoo in Illinois to Utah took place before 1850. White-topped wagons of other settlers crawled out of Missouri and across the plains and mountains to Oregon and California in a mighty stream. The railroads began their drive to the Pacific, assisted by federal land grants of staggering generosity. In 1869, two years after the Alaska Purchase, the Central Pacific met the Union Pacific at Promontory Point, Utah. The gold and silver spikes driven there symbolized that the nation had been trussed up, east-west, by a slender steel band.

Nearly 2.5 million European immigrants arrived in the United States in the decade between 1850 and 1860. Another 15 million had flocked in by 1900 as the nation recovered from the agony of its Civil War.[25] Many of the newcomers joined the westward migration, while others swelled the towns or took up farming in places left unsettled or vacated by earlier settlers who had pressed on. Luring them was the promise of land, land at $2.50 an acre or for nothing, a farm, a homestead, wealth in a new country. There was plenty for all, it seemed, in the regions opening up beyond the rivers and mountains.

Some of the people were religious and God-fearing, others not. Some sought their fortunes to a banjo's tune, ready for fight or frolic, drinking what they could get. Some were as drab as the towns and communities they set up.

Farmers, artisans, promoters, speculators, criminals, bull-

25

whackers, gunfighters, soldiers, preachers, respectable women, prostitutes, mountain men, laborers, bankers, and always the lawyers—never had such a company been turned loose on a virgin continent. For many the promise was realized, and for many it was not. Few of the innocent and pure in heart managed to reach a new area ahead of the speculators and promoters.

From the flowering and wilting of Robert Morris to the present, the management and disposal of federal lands, including the laying out of new states, have been intertwined with politics and conflicting pressures. The Constitution provided for growth of the Union by declaring that Congress could admit new states, guaranteeing a republican form of government and protection against invasion. It became the practice to admit states after they reached a population level of 60,000 or so, and as it suited the national convenience.

The federal government held onto little or nothing in the arable East and Midwest. In the mountainous, scenic, and arid West, huge areas were retained because so much of that country was not fit for the plow. The western "public lands" states were simply carved from the federal domain, typically receiving less than 10 percent of the area within their borders. Alaska was granted the largest proportion—28.7 percent—but was slow in selecting it. Thus in 1976 the United States still held title to about 97 percent of Alaska, 86 percent of Nevada, 66 percent of Utah, 63 percent of Idaho, more than half of Oregon, and nearly half of Arizona, California, and Wyoming.[26]

Despite the fact that so much of these new states remained in federal ownership, they came in on an equal footing—legally and politically—with states admitted earlier, regardless of disparities in size and population. This welded the nation together, under terms of the Northwest Ordinances, and one would not have had it otherwise. The system fostered self-government and avoided colonialism at the political, if not at the economic, level. But it also fostered a chaotic, pell-mell kind of development, often marred by a contempt for planning, an excessive tolerance

26

for and manipulation by rampant private enterprise, and an emphasis on short-term exploitation at the expense of the long-term public welfare. There were absurdities. In the case of Alaska, the Statehood Act of 1958 gave to fewer than 200,000 Americans then residing in that territory special rights to a prodigious empire theretofore owned by all the nation's citizens.

We have seen how the United States made its major acquisitions of land as the border crept westward. Over the national history, the federal government has held title at one time or another to four-fifths of the gross area. It still had at the end of the 1970s about one-third, approximately 762 million acres. The Interior Department's Bureau of Land Management had about 60 percent of the total. The Agriculture Department's Forest Service, the next largest federal land manager, had nearly 25 percent. Most of this grazing and timber country, the standard scenery of the West, is public domain that has never left federal control. Only about 57 million acres have been deliberately acquired by purchase or other methods.[27]

Although Uncle Sam still has a domain the size of India, chiefly in the western states and Alaska, the federal land stewards acting under the authority of Congress and the president dispensed with a generous hand in the great disposals of the nineteenth and early twentieth centuries. In the period from 1781 to 1976, they got rid of a grand total of 1.144 billion acres of public lands. Some 287.5 million acres were taken up under the landmark Homestead Act of 1862, and other millions were sold or granted under various other settlement laws. Grants to states accounted for 328.3 million acres, and grants to railroads, another 94.3 million. Veterans received 61 million as military bounties. It is worth noting that the railroads, whose penetration of the West Congress was trying to encourage, got nearly a third as much free land as did the homesteaders.

It has been fully documented—the fact, indeed, was notorious—that the laws and regulations governing disposal of the public lands were savagely abused by speculators, mining com-

27

panies, timber operators, cattlemen, and the settlers themselves. Complaints about malpractices were loud and frequent, but Congress had difficulty finding effective remedies. Federal administration was often lax or corrupt. Powerful interests have been all too successful in weakening the federal land-managing agencies, which were given insufficient authority, personnel, and funds for the proper carrying out of their tasks.

Not only were the laws and regulations abused, but the land itself was mistreated. Timber was overcut. The pastoral lands were overgrazed. The land was being needlessly torn and ravaged under the aegis of the old 1872 Mining Law, which was still clinging tenaciously to life in the early 1980s despite well-nigh universal condemnation.

Congress's intent in the Homestead Act and other settlement legislation, including the reclamation of the arid West, was to benefit the sturdy yeoman, the family farmer. In carrying out this objective, still much venerated, there has been many a slip twixt cup and lip. The American farm economy is gloriously productive in terms of yield per acre, but in human terms the countryside is not the quiet repository of national strength it was meant to be. It has come to be, in many places, a repository of poverty, ignorance, and neglect. "Half the poverty in the United States is in the rural communities," Agriculture Secretary Bob Bergland said in 1977.[28] Land ownership was increasingly concentrated in the hands of large farmers and agribusiness conglomerates. Small farms were disappearing. When President Carter sought to enforce the original terms of the Reclamation Act, cutting out wasteful boondoggles and holding benefits to small holders as Congress itself had stipulated, there was a political fire storm.

To dwell upon the imperfections of the past is not to ignore the promising and favorable side of the record. Theodore Roosevelt's was not the only voice raised against the skinning of the land. There have been many, both before and since. The conservationist tide that was running in the 1970s had its origins deep in the national history and could be traced in both of the major political parties. After all, Yellowstone Park was set aside more than a century ago.

The national philosophy concerning the public lands changed as time went by. So did the perception of their value. Throughout most of United States history, it was assumed that except for parklands, forests and mineral areas, or other tracts reserved for special purposes, the federal government would eventually rid itself of the public domain. The assumption was that these lands would be disposed of in some fashion and that the federal authority was only its temporary custodian.

In 1970, one of the important recommendations of the Public Land Law Review Commission, which had been set up early in the Johnson administration, was that most of the land be retained.[29] Death thus came quietly, if death it was, to the notion that the federal land heritage would be flung away. What was left—once thought of as too high, too dry, too wet, or too remote to be of much use—had become valuable, and everybody knew it.

President Nixon, in his first message to Congress on energy a year later, pointed to the great energy potential in the public lands—oil and gas, coal, oil shale, geothermal sources. He might also have mentioned that these lands have 60 percent of the nation's softwood saw timber, which could do duty as fuel as well as construction material, if worst came to worst.

We have thus come to a time in which the federal government's third of the land is recognized to be more or less permanently in Uncle Sam's possession and is coming to be much treasured. Unfortunately, the fact that it has a higher value than formerly does not guarantee that it will be safeguarded. The pressures on it are increasing rather than slackening. This is demonstrated by the acrimonious debate over the wilderness system, in which stubborn resistance has been made to setting aside remote federal wild lands—in Alaska and elsewhere—and leaving them alone, for a while.

Without question, there has been a heartening increase in conservationist sentiment. Farsighted members of Congress have produced a harvest of good environmental laws in recent years. But it remains to be demonstrated that public support for these laws will hold firm in difficult times.

We shall examine in the chapters to come the development of public land policies affecting the major extractive industries— mining, the fossil fuels, timber, grazing. We shall also look at the giant publicly subsidized irrigation and water projects of the West, particularly those nurturing the Colorado River drainage system. We shall find ourselves winding up our inquiry in Alaska, where the lessons and mistakes of the past have a present application.

Through all of this fabric, much of it discouraging in its oft-repeated pattern of conflicting forces, the bright thread often will be the role of the conservationists, who, for all their faults, manage to keep before the public a shining vision of what the nation might become.

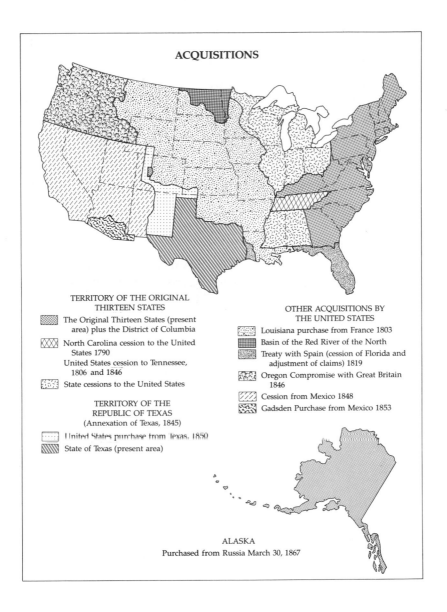

ACQUISITIONS

TERRITORY OF THE ORIGINAL
THIRTEEN STATES

The Original Thirteen States (present area) plus the District of Columbia

North Carolina cession to the United States 1790
United States cession to Tennessee, 1806 and 1846

State cessions to the United States

TERRITORY OF THE
REPUBLIC OF TEXAS
(Annexation of Texas, 1845)

United States purchase from Texas, 1850

State of Texas (present area)

OTHER ACQUISITIONS BY
THE UNITED STATES

Louisiana purchase from France 1803

Basin of the Red River of the North

Treaty with Spain (cession of Florida and adjustment of claims) 1819

Oregon Compromise with Great Britain 1846

Cession from Mexico 1848

Gadsden Purchase from Mexico 1853

ALASKA
Purchased from Russia March 30, 1867

Courtesy Bureau of Land Management.

CHAPTER 2

LAND GRABBERS, THE LAW, AND THE PROPHETS

What is the chief end of Man?—To get rich. . . . In what way?—Dishonestly if we can, honestly if we must. . . . Who is God, the one only and true?—Money is God.

> —MARK TWAIN, "The Revised Catechism," *New York Tribune,* September 1871

At the outset of my administration I was confronted with overwhelming evidence that the public domain was made the prey of unscrupulous speculation and worst forms of land monopoly.

> —Report of Commissioner WILLIAM A. J. SPARKS, General Land Office, for October 1885

Americans are accustomed to being told by their politicians that they, the people, are the wisest and most honest and upright citizenry on earth. The same litany is chanted by the popular press. If the electorate has had a choice between two candidates and has chosen the worse of the two, the fault is never the public's. The better candidate did not work hard enough, it will be said, or the issues were not properly presented to voters. It is a daring politician indeed who will venture to suggest, in a moment of truth, that Americans are by and large no better and no worse than other peoples and that they have been, above all things, fortunate.

The spirit of past times often is better reflected in fiction and in the chronicles of travelers than it is in the annals of officialdom or footnoted histories. For the Mississippi River and the opening up of the country beyond it, Mark Twain is the Homer from whom we can learn. There were other troubadours, of course. For the West, a little after Mark Twain, the most revealing account may well be that to be found in the short stories of North Carolina's sojourner in Texas, William Sidney Porter, the underrated and kindly minstrel who wrote under the name O. Henry.

At the higher levels, Porter is not to be mentioned in the same breath with Clemens, but he managed to capture well, in such books as *Heart of the West* and *The Gentle Grafter*, the captivating mixture of personal rectitude, nobility of spirit, and easy tolerance of civic dishonesty which came to typify the American frontiersman of the later period. O. Henry's less well-known "Bexar Scrip No. 2692," a story drawn from his years as a draftsman in the old Texas Land Office building at Austin, gives the darker side.[1]

Mark Twain had a clear eye for what he saw going on around him, and he also had, of all writers, an ear for the soaring hyperbole of the American frontiersman's discourse. He was discouraged about the prospects for democracy as he saw it practiced. In their novel *The Gilded Age*, he and his friend Charles D.

33

Warner gave the postbellum nineteenth century its epithet and described its flamboyant style. The novel's Beriah Sellers, a cheerful and gloriously fraudulent southerner down on his luck, epitomizes the blue-sky promoter and land developer of the day. Sen. Abner Dilworthy, a northern man of business, does well enough as the unscrupulous political windbag handling the Washington end of a deal to put a railroad through to the mythical prairie town of Napoleon by way of Slouchburg, Doodleville, Brimstone, Belshazzar, Catfish, Babylon, and Bloody Run.

In fact as well as fancy, there is a robust, engaging quality about the chicanery of President Ulysses S. Grant's administration and its aftermath. The public lands were there for the grabbing, the immigrants were pouring into New York, horizons were expanding. Public men did their own boodling, logrolling, and speech writing, to a greater extent than was true a century later. The time of the public-relations specialist had not yet come. Mark Twain had a gift for embroidering the truth when he told a tale, but he did not have to strain his talents for exaggeration and caricature when he and Warner wrote *The Gilded Age*. It was not necessary to depart from reality—not by much, anyway.

Before Samuel Langhorne Clemens rose to fame, he did a stint in Washington as private secretary to the ebullient Sen. William Morris Stewart of Nevada, a bearded Seneca of the West. They had been acquainted in Virginia City, where the senator made a fortune looking after the Comstock Lode, an immensely rich vein of silver ore. It was said of Stewart by an admirer that "his pleasure is not gold, but the getting of it."[2] He was born in a log cabin in Wayne County in upstate New York in 1825. From his boyhood, when he owned a good coon dog named Rover and parlayed Rover's skill into cash, Stewart displayed a sharp, unabashed, and thoroughly American interest in the dollar. He wandered to California in 1849 after attending Yale College and later became one of Nevada's first senators. In his western adventures he helped hang an Indian, survived threats of being

34

strung up himself, gave a good account of himself in brawls, and made a reputation as a tall, blue-eyed, fearless man of the frontier and a good lawyer to boot.[3]

Stewart wrote a book called *Reminiscences,* published in 1908, when he was in his eighties and had served twenty-nine years in the United States Senate. The senator recalled his past in a mellow, easy, blunt, anecdotal style that has something of the Twain flavor. His account of Clemens's brief stewardship as his secretary and fellow boarder at the nation's capital, published two years before Clemens died, was a humorous put-down of the famous author and lecturer. Stewart depicted Clemens as a vagrant newsman, notorious for lies and practical jokes, who needed a sinecure while writing *Innocents Abroad.*[4]

Mark Twain had remarked, for his part, that Senator Stewart was a man with more brass than the Colossus of Rhodes. Like other less colorful figures in Congress during his terms in office, the senator looked out for his own interests and for, as he saw them, those of his country. He championed the cause of the miners. He put his hand to the shaping of the 1872 Mining Law, which invited mineral seekers to make free with the public domain. He had the strength that comes from absolute confidence in the rectitude of one's own side of a cause. He was a leader among the powerful westerners who encouraged and then blocked Maj. John Wesley Powell's efforts to improve management of the arid lands in the late nineteenth century. He assisted the railroads and was duly rewarded. He had the frontier leader's sense of humor and way with people.

Senator Stewart, a Republican, is in retrospect more appealing than another towering figure of the same period, Sen. William Andrews Clark, the Montana and Arizona vote buyer and copper baron. A Democrat, Clark seemed cold and taciturn where Stewart was warm, rough tongued, and outgoing. Clark was born on a farm in Pennsylvania in 1839, moved with his parents to an Iowa homestead when he was seventeen, drifted west in 1862 after brief service in the Confederate army, peddled goods to miners, and staked a claim in the Jeff Davis Gulch in Montana. He got into banking, timbering, and ranching as well as copper mining. He came to own the rich United Verde mine at Jerome, Arizona, and five other mines yielding many millions. By the 1870s he was a rustic magnifico, taking his family to Europe every year.

Such was Clark's wealth that in 1899 he could afford to spend large sums in a notorious and successful effort to persuade the Montana legislature to elect him to the United States Senate.[5] Investigating the scandal, the Senate Committee on Privileges and Elections developed testimony that fifteen members of the Montana legislature had been paid by Clark's agents and nine more had been offered bribes. The committee recommended that Clark's title to his senate seat be declared void.

Clark was not a man to retire in shame and embarrassment. He defended himself stubbornly. He told the Senate he would resign. "I propose to leave my children a legacy worth more than gold," said he, "that of an unblemished name."[6] He duly sent in his resignation, but at a time when the governor of Montana, who was hostile to him, was out of the state. The lieutenant governor, who was friendly, took advantage of the governor's absence to appoint Clark to the Senate vacancy Clark's own resignation had created. This maneuver gave Clark a symbolic victory, and in 1901, none the worse for what had occurred, he was again elected to a full term. When he died in 1925 at his Fifth Avenue mansion in New York, leaving an estate valued at more than $200 million, he was accounted one of the richest men in the world. The Corcoran Gallery in Washington fell heir to the senator's art collection and displayed it with pride. His mansion, famed for its Circassian walnut, its pipe organ, and its Louis XIV salon, fell to the wreckers.

In the Senate Clark made no great show. He opposed repeal of the Timber and Stone Act by means of which he and many others had gathered to themselves large publicly owned timber tracts in the West. He also opposed early moves toward forest conservation, declaring in a speech that "those who succeed us

36

can well take care of themselves."[7] Few of Clark's successors have done as well as he, although many have tried.

Stewart and Clark, contrasting heroes of the Gilded Age, had qualities that enabled them to win large fortunes from the opening of western lands. They found the cornucopia abundant and flowing where hundreds of thousands of others got nothing but hard labor and an early grave. Both were self-made men who had gone out and sweated for new wealth in keeping with Herbert Spencer's Darwinian survival-of-the-fittest social ethic that was standard doctrine among well-placed Americans in that time.[8]

A more prominent place in the encyclopedias was reserved for a less acquisitive western contemporary of the two senators, Henry George, who advocated that the gap between wealth and poverty be closed by means of a single tax imposed on land. George was a Philadelphian who had sailed before the mast to Calcutta and wound up in San Francisco, where he eked out a living as a printer and newspaper reporter in the 1850s and thereafter. He was a witness to the gobbling up of California's riches by speculators. He never piled up a fortune of his own, and his single-tax idea did not take hold, but his writings on the inequities of the social system were the product of a first-rate, rational mind. They made a deep and lasting impression.

The distribution of American land and wealth went on apace. In the later part of the nineteenth century and earlier, the federal authority disposed of most of its good agricultural land. It gave away a treasure of precious metals and sold or granted millions of acres of valuable timber and mineral land to speculators and corporations that either took advantage of or got around the land settlement laws aimed at promoting agriculture. Among the speculators, of course, were often the small farmers themselves who sought to take up more land than the law allowed.

Eastern and foreign capitalists tried to buy up choice parcels before the settlers got to them. Local people, jealous of outsiders, conspired openly to keep the government from getting fair market value for land sold at auction. Sometimes they organized "claims clubs" with which they shook down or terrorized outsiders who came in to compete with men already on the scene. At a land sale in the Iowa town of Burlington in the 1840s, a steamboat captain named Aaron Harlan warned local residents that speculators might come in and buy tracts to be put up for sale. The captain urged adoption of a resolution that said, in effect, "The American government was instituted of, by, and for the people, and we are the people." Settlers showed up at the sale with their rifles. The land went for $1.25 an acre, with no competitors daring to bid up the price.[9] There were many such instances of intimidation.

Against these forces large and small, the central authority was weak. Federal officers not infrequently gave up and joined in the plunder.

The nineteenth century brought a boom in "town jobbing," a colorful type of speculation in which promoters tried to select favorable locations for new communities, with a view to attracting investors as well as settlers. Some were good sites that became cities. Others were like the metropolis of Napoleon envisioned by Mark Twain's Colonel Sellers, never more than a dream of the enterprisers seeking to stimulate interest in them, never more than rich and elegant paper cities.[10]

"Gain! Gain! Gain!" wrote the British newcomer to America Morris Birkbeck in 1817. "Gain is the beginning, the middle, and the end, the alpha and omega of the founders of American towns, who, after all, are bad calculators when they omit the important element of salubrity in their choice of situations."[11]

Birkbeck inveighed against the land jobbers whom he found infesting the country "like a pestilent blight."[12] He was enthusiastic, on the whole, about what he saw in Ohio, Illinois, and Indiana. His writings helped attract English settlers. Another Briton, William Cobbett, accused Birkbeck of painting too rosy a picture. Still another, William Faux, reported that a young woman had been bitten by a giant spider in Birkbeck's settlement in Illinois and had expired in a few hours. There was lively controversy about the charms of the new country, topped by the caustically unfavorable comments of the great English novelist Charles Dickens.

In his *American Notes,* published in 1842, Dickens inflicted painful wounds with his observations on manners and morality and on the gap that yawned between American pretentions and the reality. He compounded those insults in the American chapters of his novel *Martin Chuzzlewit,* which came out two years later.[13] Martin crosses the Atlantic to make his fortune as an architect in the splendid and shining municipality of Eden, which he eventually finds to be a clump of rude cabins in a fever swamp, somewhere past New Thermopylae, along a river in the western wilds. The experience strengthens Martin's soul, and he eventually escapes from a country that, as described by Dickens, was populated from one end to the other by tobacco-chewing knaves and fools, poseurs, murderers, scoundrels, insufferable braggarts, and bullies.

When Dickens returned to the United States in 1868, shortly before his death, he made a dinner speech in New York at which he paid generous tribute to the country for the changes that had taken place over the previous twenty-five years. He was able to note improvements in morals, manners, and the graces and amenities of life. He caused his remarks to be appended to future editions of the two books in which he had dealt unkindly with America.

Something similar happened in the case of the Irish poet Thomas Moore, who visited the United States early in the nineteenth century, found the country too raw for his taste, and delivered himself of some critical lines and observations that he later professed to regret. Possibly Moore was simply homesick. His poem "To the Honorable W. R. Spencer, from Buffalo, upon Lake Erie" is often quoted in American history texts, particularly the part about the young Republic being "rank without ripeness, quickened without sun, crude at the surface, rotten at the core" —and, perhaps, doomed to perish in the springtime of youth.

Moore found the United States "one dull chaos" hovering between the half polished and the half barbarous,

> Where every ill the ancient world could brew
> Is mixed with every grossness of the new;
> Where all corrupts, though little can entice,
> And naught is known of luxury but its vice!

By the time of Dickens's second visit, the Civil War had been fought, and the emerging nation had spilled rivers of blood to rid itself of one of the things Dickens had found repugnant—human slavery. Another, the chewing of tobacco and the copious expectorations that went with the habit, survived to the cigarette age. The fact that the Union had been preserved despite a frightfully savage war—a war that was impressive even by European standards and had advanced military science a notch or two—generated a grudging international respect.

The young Rudyard Kipling, traveling across the Pacific aboard the American steamer *City of Peking* in 1889, found the weather stormy and the conversation bracing en route to San Francisco. The Americans, he learned in the ship's salon, are given to running down their own country.

"Politics in America?" one said to Kipling. " —There aren't any. The whole question of the day is spoils. That's all. We fight our souls out over tram-contracts, gas-contracts, road-contracts, and any darned thing that will turn a dishonest dollar, and we call that politics. No one but a low-down man will run for Congress and the Senate—the Senate of the freest people on earth are bound slaves to some blessed monopoly."[14]

At San Francisco Kipling found himself among men who spat habitually, as a matter of principle. He found beautiful but ignorant women, high-and-mighty hotel clerks, flourishing free-lunch counters, and a hilly city in which the art of buying and selling votes flourished.

The visitors from overseas who tweaked the beard of Uncle Sam did not always get away unscathed, however. One American not entirely mollified by Dickens's latter-day change of heart was President Theodore Roosevelt. The vigorous, cocksure Teddy was fond of reading Dickens but dismissed him in a letter to his son Kermit as "an ill-natured, selfish cad and boor, who had no understanding of what the word gentleman meant, and no appreciation of hospitality or good treatment."[15]

"He was utterly incapable," Roosevelt told Kermit of Dickens, "of seeing the high purpose and the real greatness which (in spite of the presence also of much that was bad or vile) could have been visible all around him here in America to any man whose vision was both keen and lofty. He could not see the qualities of the young men growing up here, though it was these qualities that enabled these men to conquer the West and to fight to a finish the great Civil War, and though they were to produce leadership like that of Lincoln, Lee, and Grant. . . . Naturally he would condemn all America because he had not the soul to see what America was really doing."

The federal agency that handled and doled out the publicly owned domain through which Kipling and other bemused foreigners passed in the western reaches was the General Land Office, set up in 1812. It was a bureau in the Treasury Department until 1849, when it became the most important part of the new Interior Department. The General Land Office, a nebulous and diffused instrumentality, supervised the transfer of a billion acres or more of federal lands to states, companies, railroads, and individuals. It never had enough money or personnel to carry out its tasks properly. The land grabbers, western interests, and their spokesmen in Congress—sometimes one and the same— saw to that.

As new states were admitted to the Union, Congress gave them part, but by no means all, the federal lands within their borders. The states received lands for public schools, public buildings, roads, canals, and other purposes. More than seventy-

41

seven million acres were donated for common schools and twenty-one million for universities and related purposes. States also got a percentage of revenues from sale or lease of public lands that the federal authority retained. Some states were treated more generously than others. Louisiana's federal grant was 36 percent of its area; Florida's 64 percent; New Mexico's 16 percent; Arizona's 14 percent. Alaska, the largest and most recently admitted of the public domain states, got 28 percent and was allowed 90 percent of federal mineral revenues, while other states received 37.5 percent.[16] In all cases the federal government demanded the right of sovereignty over land it chose to keep in federal hands, a position the states had no choice but to accept.

In addition to the donations they received on admission to the Union, the states also were beneficiaries of general land grants authorized by Congress. For example, under the Swamp Land Acts of 1849, 1850, and 1860, Congress allowed states to choose swampy and overflowed federal lands, which were then given to them. The idea was that swamps unfit for man's use would be drained and made arable. The laws were poorly drawn, difficult to administer. There were myriad conflicts between federal and state claimants. The states asserted rights to valuable timberlands as swamp, some of which on investigation were found to be in high and dry areas "too mountainous and hilly for cultivation."[17] A tale often told is that in Mississippi a state agent was said to have chosen as swamp all tracts over which a boat could pass. He hitched a canoe to a work animal and dragged the canoe over good pine country. Uncle Sam was cheated in Oregon, Minnesota, Iowa, and elsewhere. Through 1905 nearly eighty-two million acres of federal lands had been chosen in the "swamp" benefaction, and more than sixty-five million had been approved.[18]

Another and more savory general federal grant to states was provided in the famous Land Grant College Act of 1862—signed by President Lincoln in the dark days of the Civil War and known as the Morrill Act after its sponsor, Justin Smith Morrill,

42

a member of Congress from Vermont.[19] Under that law each state not in rebellion was to receive 30,000 acres of federal land for each senator and representative in Congress as an endowment for colleges of agricultural and mechanical arts. States with no public lands were given scrip for land in public-land states, which could be sold to third parties. As southern states were reconstructed after the war, they too received an allotment. The western public-land states got 3.52 million acres under the Morrill Act, and the older states got 7.7 million acres in scrip. Among poorly educated settlers there was a stout initial resistance to what was contemptuously referred to as "book-farming"; but the land grant colleges became the backbone of public higher education in the United States.

In the first hundred years of the Republic, as in the second, state governments were worse land managers than was the federal, if that was possible. They were generally more vulnerable to pressure, a fact that goes far toward explaining enthusiasm for "states' rights." Louisiana's swamplands promptly fell into the hands of loggers and speculators who took them up in large chunks. California was notoriously corrupt.[20]

It was in the Homestead Act and its variations that the federal government came up against the individual American—leading him westward, providing him with great opportunities, exposing him to disappointment and despair, always leaving the way open for fraud. In this parceling out of virgin country was much of the romance and the heartbreak and the rollicking humor of the frontier as the nation moved toward the setting sun.

Congress approved the Homestead Act of 1862—the basic law—only after long agitation for free farms to all comers.[21] It was led by such reforming idealists as Horace Greeley, the New York newspaper editor. Andrew Johnson of Tennessee, later to be president, fought for the law. Southern states were against free land because they feared, in the period before the Civil War, that rapid settlement by northerners might weaken proslavery strength in the divided nation. There was xenophobia. A

43

Wisconsin land dealer, Cyrus Woodman, argued that free home-steads would "bring in upon us a vile horde of the most worth-less class of emigrants, men who will not pay taxes on land after it is given to them. . . . The poorhouses of the East and of all Europe will be emptied upon us. I have not much sympathy for these cattle."[22] President James Buchanan, the bachelor Pennsyl-vania Democrat, vetoed a homestead law in 1860. Free land, Buchanan said, was without constitutional authority. He consid-ered it favored latecomers over early settlers who had paid for their farms.

The West, however, wanted development, which meant set-tlers. With the South absent, the more liberal view won out in Congress. The law signed by President Lincoln was far more generous in spirit than the one Buchanan had rejected. Basically, it may be remembered, the law provided that a person could acquire 160 acres by living on them for five years. One could obtain still another quarter section—again, for emphasis, one-fourth of a square mile—by living on that land and paying the minimum government price, which was typically $1.25 to $2.50 an acre. And after passage of the Timber Culture Act of 1873, an enterprising spirit could gain a third quarter section by planting trees on 40 acres of it. In favorable terrain a good many trees were, in fact, planted where none had grown before.[23]

In countless instances the homesteading system proved to be what it was intended to be—an unparalleled opportunity for a hard-working settler to obtain a farm in a new land and bring his acreage to fruition. There was something glorious and high-hearted about it, something atavistic, primordial, and eminently satisfying. John Ise's *Sod and Stubble,* an account of a Wurttem-burg family homesteading in Kansas, would wring smiles and tears from the Mogul despot Aurungzebe himself.[24] But all too frequently the family moving west for a new home found much or most of the desirable land either barred to entry or already bought up. In many cases the enemy was the climate.

Land Grabbers, the Law, and the Prophets

Daniel Freeman's application for a homestead in Gage County in southern Nebraska, filed on January 1, 1863, was the nation's official "first." Later the Homestead National Monument was put up on the Freeman property. Freeman and his wife are buried there. Other early homesteaders did well in that country, but in a limited span of years Gage County's good free land was, of course, gone. By 1900 nearly half the farms in the county were tenant operated, and the population was in decline.[25]

Nearly always, despite rural indignation in Nebraska and elsewhere, men with money got their way. Not only did various land laws place millions of acres in the hands of private companies or investors holding it for lucrative resale, but in the decades before the Civil War and up to 1871 Congress made staggeringly large grants to railroads as a means of encouraging and financing westward penetration.

In the newly opened country a rail line meant commerce and a link with civilization. It meant nearly everything. Congress started authorizing rail rights-of-way through public lands in 1835, but not until 1850 did it begin providing grants of land as well. The first such grant was for a line from Chicago to Mobile, through Illinois, Mississippi, and Alabama. Sen. Stephen A. Douglas of Illinois, the Democratic advocate of popular sovereignty and "Little Giant" of the Lincoln debates, championed the rail project southward from Chicago. He also pushed for legislation authorizing federal help for railroads to the Pacific coast. Congress in 1862—a year of decision indeed for public lands—passed the Pacific Railroad Act and sweetened it for the recipients two years later. The law chartered the Union Pacific Railroad and sped it westward through Nebraska to meet the Central Pacific, chartered in California and given the mission of building eastward over the Sierras.

As a stimulus for their efforts, the Union and Central Pacific companies received twenty sections—that is, 20 square miles—of land for every mile constructed. They were allowed $65,000,000

45

in federal loans in addition to grants that absorbed 24,000,000 acres of public domain. The land reward was handsome, even princely. First of all, the railroads got a 400-foot right-of-way. Then they were authorized to have alternate square-mile sections—the odd-numbered sections on the survey grid—for 20 miles on each side of the track. The law provided that the companies, within three years after completing their road, had to sell or otherwise dispose of all land they had received. Any that might be left was to be subject to settlement at $1.25 an acre, or $200 for a 160-acre quarter section. The federal government retained mineral rights but permitted the railroads to take coal and iron lands and to help themselves to timber and stone along the way.

While the route for the Union Pacific was being chosen, it was necessary to forestall persons who might try to claim land ahead of the railroads. To do that, the law provided that the route be selected within two years and that the secretary of the interior, once informed of its location, would withdraw from future entry all lands on either side of the designated right-of-way for twenty-five miles. That meant closing to the homesteader and squatter a fifty-mile swath across the West, from Nebraska to California.[26]

Congress was even more generous in an 1864 law cheering the Northern Pacific Railroad Company toward its task of building a 2,128-mile line from Duluth, Minnesota, to Tacoma and Portland in the Pacific Northwest. The Northern Pacific received 45,000,000 acres, including nearly one-fourth of North Dakota and 15 percent of Montana. Since the road had to be rammed through what was mostly virgin wilderness, its backers were given 20 square miles, or sections, of land for each mile constructed in states, and 40 for each mile of track through territories, which began at what became the eastern boundary of Montana. Not only that, but the Northern Pacific, Congress later provided, could choose its lands from a strip that was 80 miles wide in states and 120 miles wide in the territories. Despite Congress' largess, the Northern Pacific ran into trouble. It plunged into bankruptcy in the panic of 1873 and did not complete its link to the Pacific coast until 1883.

The third transcontinental rail subsidy was conferred on the Atlantic and Pacific—subsequently, the Saint Louis and San Francisco and, farther west, the Santa Fe—in 1866. It called for a line via Albuquerque. The terms were the same as those given the Northern Pacific. A fourth grant came in 1871, providing for incorporation of the Texas Pacific Railroad and projecting a southern route linking up with the Southern Pacific Railroad at Fort Yuma.

There was a great scramble for federal rail subsidies in the decade of the Civil War. The speculation and political chicanery that accompanied it marred Grant's administration. Bribery was commonplace. In addition to the 100 to 110 million acres of public lands Congress lavished on the transcontinental railroads, grants were made or enlarged for other rail projects. States received federal grants for railroads and offered donations of their own. All of this challenged the talents of a colorful array of boosters and promoters. Through the efforts of United States Sen. Samuel C. Pomeroy—said to have been the model for the fictitious Senator Dilworthy of *The Gilded Age*—the Kansas town of Atchison drew the singing iron rails like a magnet when Pomeroy was in his prime.

In 1869, as the Union Pacific was rushing toward its rendezvous with the Central Pacific in Utah, Senator Stewart attended to the Central Pacific's needs in Congress. The giant Collis P. Huntington, who had emigrated from Poverty Hollow in central New York State to become a rail mogul in California, saw to it that Stewart was rewarded. A natural affinity seemed to bind these self-made, tough-minded titans of the West. As Huntington's *Collected Letters* reveal, he wrote to his associate E. B. Crocker as follows: "Stewart . . . has always stood by us. He is peculiar, but thoroughly honest and will bear no dictation, but I know he must live, and we must fix it so he can make one or two hundred thousand dollars. It is to our interest and I think his right." What the senator was to receive, by means of a masked conveyance, was fifty thousand acres of land in the San Joaquin Valley.[27]

This was the period of the scandal involving the milking of the Union Pacific by its construction company, Credit Mobilier of America, an affair to which Stewart helped call attention. The stockholders of the Union Pacific owned both the railroad and the construction outfit with the fancy French name. In this neat arrangement, Credit Mobilier made excess profits of some $20 million. Rep. Oakes Ames of Massachusetts, a wealthy shovel and tool dealer, promoted Credit Mobilier's objectives in Congress by selling stock in the company to twenty-two of his fellow legislators at prices well below what the stock was worth. The boodlers hoped to avoid an inquiry, but the affair came to public notice when Charles A. Dana of the *New York Sun* ventilated it during the 1872 presidential campaign.

Grant's first vice president, Schuyler Colfax of Indiana, was marred by the Credit Mobilier disclosures. So were the future president, Rep. James A. Garfield, House Speaker James G. Blaine, and the Republican candidate for vice president in Grant's second term, Henry Wilson of Massachusetts.[28] It took more than the Credit Mobilier exposure to cool the raw acquisitive passions of the Gilded Age, however, and Grant was reelected. The House in 1873 shrank from passing judgment on most of the great figures involved in the outrage but approved, after dramatic debate, a resolution of censure against Ames, declaring that it "absolutely condemns the conduct of Oakes Ames . . . in seeking to secure congressional attention to . . . a corporation in which he was interested." Ames, whose shovels were admired in the West and many other parts of the world, died in the year his colleagues smote him.[29]

The rationale for the federal rail subsidies of the mid-nineteenth century is obvious. Establishing a rail communications net was essential. The device of checkerboarding the land along the rights-of-way gave the rail companies land they could sell to finance their operations, while leaving in federal possession an equal acreage whose sale price was increased to $2.50 an acre. The government's sections would appreciate in value, theoretically at least, as the road was built. Meanwhile the country would be opened up to settlement and commerce, and the federal government, which intended to dispose of its holdings anyway, one way or another, stood to benefit.

Harsh conflicts arose, however, between the priviledged railroads and ordinary people trying to get land. The West wanted railroads but did not want huge tracts of desirable real estate sealed off from public entry indefinitely. The railroads became, next to the General Land Office, the largest dispensers of land for settlement. They did a herculean job of attracting settlers, advertising far and wide. They also found ways of holding onto large areas Congress had intended to be sold to citizens. There were no more railroad land grants after 1871. By that time the impression—the heel mark, so to speak—left by the open-handed, haphazard policy of earlier years could not be smoothed. It had been, and is, printed on the national map.

All in all, Congress gave to railroads an area nearly twice the size of Colorado and one-third as large as Alaska.[30] That does not include thirty-seven million acres once granted but forfeited after painful and tedious litigation because the railroads did not carry out their part of the bargain. Efforts to bring about forfeiture often took years, thanks in part to the fact that in 1875, in *Schulenberg* v. *Harriman,* the United States Supreme Court ruled that land grants could not be made forfeit except by action of Congress or the judiciary. In this case Congress had bestowed certain land on the state of Wisconsin for construction of a railroad that was never built. Frederick Schulenberg and his partners cut a quantity of pine logs from state land and floated them down the St. Croix River into Minnesota, where a Wisconsin state agent found and repossessed them. Schulenberg et al. challenged the seizure, and the Supreme Court found for the state,

49

holding that it still owned the land and the logs even though it had not complied with the terms of the federal grant.[31]

Long after the last of the direct federal grants, the railroads shared a princely dividend provided by Congress in the "forest lieu" section of the Forest Management Act of 1897.[32] This allowed settlers or owners of claims or patents within the newly created forest reserves to yield those tracts and choose, in lieu, an equivalent amount of vacant public land outside the reserves. It was contended, widely believed, and possibly true that pro-railroad members of Congress tailored the law in such a way as to permit rail barons to swap millions of acres of mountainous, desert, cutover, or otherwise worthless land for in lieu timber acreage of great value. The result was a great outcry. Finally, in 1905, the in lieu provision was repealed.[33]

Much of the western country the rail lines helped open to settlement was inclement and inhospitable, subject to terrible drought and to blizzards of great ferocity. To this the rusty windmills, ruined shacks, and deserted homesteads of the West bear witness. Disenchantment with policies that had transferred huge parcels of the best lands into the hands of railroads and speculators helped fuel the populist movement among farmers in the late part of the nineteenth and the first few decades of the present century.

Life on the Great Plains was very hard. The rigors suffered on the homestead farm of the northern prairies brought eloquent literary protest from sensitive men like Hamlin Garland, whose *Son of the Middle Border* tells what it was like to work on a farm in Wisconsin, Iowa, and the Dakotas when the fever of settlement was on the nation. He saw the beautiful but forbidding land and the lonely, boxlike habitations of the people—not clustered in villages as in Europe, but each one isolated and apart. He knew what life on the prairies had done to his mother and father. For him, an educated man, "no splendor of cloud, no grace of sunset could conceal the poverty of these people." To him, a follower of Henry George, the very prodigality of nature intensified a sense of social injustice.[34]

"This wasteful method of pioneering," he wrote, "this desolate business of lonely settlement took on a new and tragic significance as I studied it. Instructed by my new philosophy, I now perceived that these plowmen, these wives and daughters had been pushed out into these ugly shacks by the force of landlordism behind."[35]

There was a lot of that kind of thinking, nurtured by the cold and the relentless storms, the pitiless dry spells and grueling labor of the prairies and high plains. "Good God!" exclaims the sturdy Norwegian Per Hansa in happy exultation when he reaches his homestead in the Dakota Territory in the 1870s. "This kingdom is going to be mine!" As has often been observed, however, the principal figure in O. E. Rolvaag's novel *Giants in the Earth* is not Per Hansa but his homesick wife, Beret. For her the complaint is there are no shadows in the treeless expanses of blue-green grass, nothing to hide behind. Nothing but silence and emptiness. For her it is more desolate than the sea. The modern reader is haunted by the vision of the opening chapter, with the little caravan moving across the prairie under a bright sun and blue sky and the high grass extending as far as the eye can see in any direction, parting before the oxen and slapping against the wagon and then closing again behind it.[36]

Per Hansa eventually dies in a snowstorm and is found frozen with his back against a haystack, his face set toward the West. He has gotten what he came for—land of his own. It must, however, be wondered, as Henry George said, what happened when there was no more land toward which the landless might turn. The firstcomer, to be sure, had a right to own it; but there was only so much of it. What happened to the sacred concept of private property when the next person came, and the next, as generation followed generation?

"In the very nature of things," said George, "land cannot rightfully be made individual property. The principle is absolute. . . . No sovereign political power, no compact or agreement, even though consented to by the whole population of the globe, can give to an individual a valid title to the exclusive ownership

51

of a square inch of soil. The earth is an entailed estate—entailed upon all the generations of the children of man, by a deed written in the constitution of nature, a deed that no human proceedings can bar, and no prescription determine. Each succeeding generation has but a tenancy for life."[37]

That, of course, is what George Perkins Marsh, Lincoln's envoy to Italy, and subsequent conservationists have been trying to point out. Marsh said the human race received the earth for usufruct alone, not for consumption.[38] George called it "a tenancy for life." It is not necessary to go all the way with George's single-tax theory—as the United States certainly has not—to see that his notions had logic that the followers of Jefferson could not escape. If it was wrong to keep poor people off arable land that was vacant, as Jefferson believed, did not the same reasoning argue for a sharing of ownership when all the land had been taken up? What is the difference between Jefferson's view and George's, except that Jefferson saw the land as limitless while George, nearly a century later, could see clearly that the end was in sight?

Slowly and probably irrevocably—and certainly not for the worse—the golden age of private ownership in land was passing as the United States moved toward the future. The idea that a man could do as he pleased with his plot of ground—cut off the trees, pave it, build something on it, no matter what—had already been substantially altered. He was constrained to take his neighbors into account. He was subject to the demands of the state and to its concepts of the needs of the present and future. There was no longer an assumption that one person, living for an instant in time, had a right to destroy what had taken millions and millions of years to create and what, once destroyed, could not be replaced.

In Congress these perceptions were slow to take hold.

George Perkins Marsh of Vermont. An early conservationist. *Courtesy Library of Congress.*

CHAPTER 3

CONGRESS GUARDS THE LAND

Is it a fact of no significance that robbing the government is everywhere regarded as a crime of less magnitude than robbing an individual, or even a corporation?
—H. L. MENCKEN, 1925

What I wanted you to do is go to Washington and dig out this appointment for me. I haven't no ideas of cultivation and intrigue. I'm a plain citizen and I need the job. I've killed seven men . . . I've got nine children; I've been a good Republican ever since the first of May; I can't read nor write, and I see no reason why I ain't illegible for the office.
—BILL HUMBLE to Jeff Peters in O. Henry's *The Gentle Grafter*, 1904

Any fair analysis of the performance of Congress regarding the public lands—and lands generally—would have to give that many-tongued assemblage credit for much that is wise and good as well as blame for what is bad. Congress attempted an equitable distribution of the nation's vacant land estate. By initiative or acquiescence, Congress has acted to set aside and protect national forests and national parks, wildlife refuges and wildernesses. The sins of Congress have reflected, more often than not, the mood of the national electorate at a given time.

On the other hand, one gets nowhere by excusing the shortcomings of Congress—for all its faults, the world's most important deliberative body—as the inevitable shortcomings of democracy. The glories and imperfections of the democratic system of government were explored by the Greeks more than 2,000 years ago and were well understood by the founders of the American republic. In this country, it is expected to work.

Congress was the chief shaper of early settlement policies that spread Americans in a thin wash across the land. Subsequently, Congress was the architect of diverse and conflicting policies that drove people off the farms, disrupted the cities, exalted the suburbs, all but eliminated public mass transit by rail or roadway, irrigated new acreage to grow crops that were surplus elsewhere, and put the nation at the mercy of the automobile and airplane, not to mention the oil-rich sheikhdoms of the Middle East.

In recent years, Congress, federal officials, state governors, and others have been lamenting a departure from the countryside, a flight from harsh to kindlier climes, from farm to city. The note they sound is reminiscent of Oliver Goldsmith's "The Deserted Village" in eighteenth-century England—

> Even now, methinks, as pondering here I stand,
> I see the rural virtues leave the land

55

When Daniel Patrick Moynihan was a member of the American delegation to the United Nations in 1971, he called a visitor's attention, in his office in New York City, to a set of new maps he had just received from the Census Bureau in the Department of Commerce. The maps, reflecting the 1970 census, showed the population status of each American county in color and made it possible to see at a glance that people had been moving out of the great central regions and concentrating near the coasts. Large segments of the losing central basin of the United States had more people in 1900, 1920, or the 1930s than were living there in 1970. Lately, a trend back toward the countryside, toward the "Sunbelt" of the South and Southwest, has been noted.

"This country is spilling over at the edges," Moynihan remarked to his visitor as they looked at the maps spread out on his desk.[1] More than half the people live within 50 to 100 miles of the coasts, two-thirds in metropolitan areas. Moynihan, a Harvard professor who had been a White House aide and was to become President Nixon's ambassador to India, later envoy to the United Nations and then senator from New York, was the kind of American who worries occasionally about such matters.

The record of Congress in handling the federally owned lands is consistent with its record in dealing with national problems generally. A mixture of the sublime and the ridiculous. Clear vision clouded by myopia. Honesty tinctured liberally with fraud. A kind of schizophrenia, in which one hand built up what the other tore down.

When the Republic was young, the public lands were a matter of more immediate and direct concern than they were after the country had been settled. In the early days, land was the prime public business, a matter of keen interest to Congress and the citizenry. In recent decades, at least until the conservationist tide swelled during the 1960s, transactions involving what was left of the public domain did not occupy the center of the stage. They were the concern chiefly of westerners and western members of Congress who knew something of rocks and sand, saddles and sagebrush. Once the frontier had vanished—and along with it the ideal of giving every man who wanted one a 160-acre farm—the remaining lands in federal ownership were well-nigh forgotten for a time, except by those who wanted something from them.

Quite naturally, the committees of Congress dealing with what remained of the heritage came to be dominated by members from the West. More than 90 percent of the public lands outside Alaska, after all, are in the western states. Western politicians knew all about these lands and were familiar with the problems arising from them. The people and the interests forming the base of political support for western senators and representatives were in large part those seeking privileges and benefits in the public domain. There were advantages to this traditional tilt toward the setting sun. The people most directly concerned were the most effectively represented—or so it could be made to appear.

In the management of the federal lands, the legislative branch has been niggardly, greedy, provincial, and stupid over a long period of time. There have been occasional lightning flashes of vision and insight on Capitol Hill, but the background has been one of steady and eroding rain—gloomy, destructive torrents that have washed millions of acres down the drain. Sins of omission. Sins of commission. Negligence. Ignorance. Inept and unwise responses to petty pressures. Half-baked philosophical concepts, or none at all. Considering all this, it is amazing worse harm was not done.

A key sin of omission has been failure to give the land-managing agencies the moral support, men, and money they need for the proper discharge of a heavy responsibility. Far from being willing to provide the tools essential for good husbandry, Congress frequently has taken the attitude that federal officials trying to protect the common heritage are guilty of harassment.[2] They are "bureaucrats" seeking to frustrate honest citizens and business interests in the enjoyment of privileges deemed to be a

57

matter of natural right. Congress has passed laws so vague as to be impossible to enforce, has saddled federal land managers with local and national "advisory committees" oriented toward short-term gain, and, above all, has kept the federal land departments in an impoverished condition.[3] This has been quite deliberate.

Although Congress continued to strangle the federal land-managing agencies well into the eighth decade of the present century, the most blatant frauds and thieveries involving the public lands took place largely in the period between the Mexican War and the Spanish-American War. This was a space of more than half a century in which Congress either actively engineered or did nothing effective to halt the transfer of kingdoms, satrapies, and fiefs to private hands under circumstances other than honest. Historians Charles and Mary Beard, summing things up in 1944, described in forthright terms what had taken place:

> Millions of acres of valuable timber, minerals and grazing lands were literally stolen under the eyes of dishonest or negligent officials in the Federal Land Office, and other millions were wrested from the government by chicanery of one kind and another. In the history of political corruption, seldom, if ever, had there been transactions on a scale so prodigious or conducted with such brazen effrontery. Thousands of great fortunes in the East as well as the West were built out of resources wrung from the government for a pittance or for a bribe to its officials, if not actually stolen.[4]

In the nineteenth century Congress was more openly a handmaiden of private enterprise than later. Vernon L. Parrington's "Great Barbecue" —the bitter metaphor comes from his *Main Currents in American Thought*, published at the end of the 1920s—was on.[5] There was something in the land feast for everybody, rich and poor. Not until the meat began to run out did complaints arise that some had received the choice cuts while others got what was left. Parrington likened the politi-

58

cians of the period to table waiters who saw to it that favored guests dined richly, but also took care of the rabble, in a fashion.

Of those who drew the most from the common pot, Parrington said: "We may call them buccaneers if we choose, and speak of the great barbecue as a democratic debauch. But why single out a few, when all were drunk?"[6] To Parrington, much of the machine-made uniformity of American life in the twentieth century could be blamed on the triumph of private business interests—he called it the "new Whiggery" —in the Gilded Age. Whiggery is not a familiar term in the 1980s. Parrington thought of it as the kind of government that equates business interests with the public good.

The federal bureaucracy, sad to relate, has mirrored Congress in venality and responsiveness to pressure. Even in many instances where dedicated federal officials did seek to guard against destruction of the range and forests, it has been possible for frustrated spoilers to generate political forces through Congress which subdued the agencies and brought about the transfer or elimination of men considered too zealous. It has been as if Congress equated the public interest with the private interest, seeking its role not as the protector of what belonged to the people as a whole but as a hearty champion of the God-given right of a few individuals and corporate entities to rape and ruin the land.

"In no country in the world is the love of property more active and more anxious than in the United States," observed the Frenchman Alexis de Tocqueville after visiting the young nation in the 1830s.[7] De Tocqueville had private property, not public property, in mind. Another foreign observer, Thomas Babington Macaulay, foresaw trouble when the public lands ran out.

"Your national safeguard lies in your boundless public domain," said Macaulay in a passage quoted by Oklahoma's populist Sen. Fred R. Harris, Democrat, in 1971. " . . . But the time will come when this heritage will have been consumed, this safeguard will have vanished. You will have your crowded Birminghams and Manchesters, and then will come the test of your institutions."[8]

The great English historian was nothing if not opinionated, and he could be wrong on occasion, but it is true that the availability of free land in the West has been a safety valve and that the United States has had a singular hostility toward federal meddling.

When the Interior Department came into existence in 1849, senators opposing the creation of a "Home Department" saw in it a dangerous extension of executive power. The federal government, said Sen. James M. Mason, Virginia Democrat, was organized to manage foreign relations. Sen. John C. Calhoun of South Carolina, another Democrat, agreed with Mason. "Sir, it is time to stop," said Calhoun. "Ours is a federal government."[9] He meant that the powers of the central government are limited.

As has been noted, the Homestead Law was enacted the year the battle of Antietam was fought. In the period before the Civil War broke out, debate over free land was acrimonious. There was the famous exchange during February 1859 between Sen. Robert A. Toombs, the Georgia firebrand and future Confederate general, and Sen. Benjamin F. Wade of Ohio, a rough-tongued antislavery Republican and proponent of homesteading. Toombs voiced his contempt for demagoguery and spoke witheringly of "land for the landless." Georgia had been settled by General Oglethorpe with paupers from the poorhouses of Europe, Toombs said, but Georgians asked nothing of the federal government.

Senator Wade got up and denounced a proposal for purchase of Cuba by the United States, which the South favored. What southern Democrats wanted in Cuba, Wade taunted, was that island's Negroes.

"The question is, shall we give land to the landless or niggers to the niggerless," said Wade.

"Democrats," the Ohio Republican continued, as members laughed, "can no more run their party without niggers than you could run a steam engine without fuel. . . . That is all there is of Democracy, and when you cannot raise niggers enough for the market, then you must go abroad fishing for niggers through the whole world."[10]

Such was humor on Capitol Hill in antebellum days.

Once the homestead legislation pushed through with southerners absent, Congress declined to protect small settlers. Seldom did it temper the wind for the shorn lamb. Nor did it succeed in guarding the public interest generally from depredations by the small settlers themselves.

The flouting of the law was notorious. It could not have taken place without a good measure of public sympathy and support. The amiable Texas historian Walter Prescott Webb has pointed to a western feeling that statutes fashioned on the banks of the Potomac did not square with the realities of life beyond the Mississippi.[11]

The trouble, though, was not confined to the arid West. The Southern Homestead Act of 1866 reserved federal land in five states formerly in rebellion so that freed slaves could obtain 80 acres on which to farm. It was short-lived and conspicuously unsuccessful. To provide 80- and even 160-acre tracts for Negroes and poor whites in Alabama, Arkansas, Florida, Louisiana, and Mississippi, the law reserved 47,700,000 acres for homesteading. The desirable land in the South, however, was already gone. Southern leaders regarded the law as punitive. It was repealed in a decade, after various abuses. Like most Reconstruction measures, the Southern Homestead Act did not benefit the freed slaves and other landless persons of the agricultural class in the way and to the extent Congress said was intended. The black man, as a land claimant, was a minnow among barracuda.[12]

The land raids that took place under the nose of Congress by means of the Timber Culture Act, the Timber and Stone Act, and the Timber Cutting Act have been described. These laws of the 1870s eased the transfer of millions of acres to big interests that wanted them for logging or running cattle. In 1880, politicians even managed to get through a law that exonerated all against whom criminal suits had been brought for stealing federal timber, provided the culprits bought the land on which they had trespassed.[13]

Congress played an unheroic role in the prolonged and shameless rape of the American Indian. After the sporadic, one-sided military engagements following the Civil War, in which Sitting Bull and Crazy Horse, Cochise, Geronimo, and others were subdued or killed and their followers herded onto reservations, Congress passed the Indian Allotment Act in 1887. Under that law, called the Dawes Act because it was introduced by Republican Sen. Henry L. Dawes of Massachusetts, individual Indians and families were to be allotted 40 to 160 acres of tribal land.[14] After a quarter century the recipients, if judged "competent," were to become full owners of the land and also have full citizenship.

The Dawes Act, enacted three years before the final slaughter at Wounded Knee, was a way of hashing up the Indian reservations, some parts of which excited the cupidity of railroads and settlers. It looked toward gradual assimilation of the native people into the larger community. The objective seemed reasonable, but in practice what was achieved was another takeover of Indian lands. When the act was passed, the Indian reservations totaled about 138 million acres. In less than fifty years they dwindled to about 52 million. The smashing of the Indian culture and economy by the technologically more advanced white society proceeded as had been predicted in a minority report of the House Indian Affairs Committee in 1880. "The real aim of this bill," said the report, "is to get at the Indian lands and open them up to settlement.... If this were done in the name of greed, it would be bad enough; but to do it in the name of humanity, and under the cloak of an ardent desire to promote the Indian's welfare by making him like ourselves, whether he will or not, is infinitely worse."[15]

Two years after the Dawes Act was passed, Creeks and Seminoles who had been herded into Oklahoma from their ancestral haunts farther East were forced by the government to sell off their unsettled land, and Congress authorized the famous Oklahoma land rush of April 22, 1889. Settlers claimed nearly two million acres for homesteading in half a day. The town of Guthrie, built around a Santa Fe railway depot, had 15,000 people and a set of municipal officers by nightfall. Judging from the account by José Marti, the Cuban revolutionary poet, the pell-mell rush for what the Indians had owned was a fascinating but not a pretty sight.[16]

Congress made an attempt at reform in the Indian Reorganization Act of 1934, which ended the allotment system at a time of national economic distress. Nevertheless, the desire to "terminate" the Indians' status as wards of the United States and remove them once and for all from the federal teat persisted.

The lawmakers of the Gilded Age were slow and inept in adjusting the free-homesteading principle to the conditions that prevailed in the immense and partially intractable region west of the hundredth meridian—that is, the north-south line running from the mid-Dakotas to the Mexican border west of Laredo. In these lands, most of which have rainfall of less than twenty inches a year, the classic 160-acre farm often was not appropriate.

Congress did make a number of efforts to modify homesteading to the facts of life in the West. The first Desert Land Act became law in 1877.[17] It provided that for $1.25 an acre a settler could buy an entire section of land—1 square mile, or 640 acres—if he would irrigate the tract within three years after filing claim to it. The terms were 25 cents an acre down and the remaining dollar at the time the claimant could prove he had complied with the government's terms for bringing in water. It was a poorly drawn law, applicable to eleven states and territories. It was put to hilarious abuse. A man might sprinkle a can of water on his square mile and scratch a line or two with his plow, simulating an irrigation ditch. Cattle interests took advantage of the law to enlarge their spreads. In California, where huge Spanish land grants set an early pattern of large holdings, Senator George Hearst's San Francisco mining associates, James Ben Ali Haggin and Lloyd Tevis, made use of the Desert Land Act to grab 150 square miles overnight by advance planning, early knowledge, and aggressive use of dummy entrymen. They were able to snap up what they wanted before others knew what was afoot. Later these properties were incorporated as the Kern County Land Company, acquired by Tenneco in 1967.[18]

Such abuses of the congressional land laws did not go unreported at the time and have subsequently been called to public attention so often that they have become part of the nation's folklore. Congress itself has documented them. The Senate Subcommittee on Migratory Labor, in its 1971–1972 hearings on "Farmworkers in Rural America," produced volumes of testimony under the chairmanship of Sen. Adlai E. Stevenson III, Illinois Democrat.[19] The hearings gave a forum to those concerned about the extent to which the American dream of the sturdy family farmer, living on the land, had failed to come to pass. The witnesses included Paul S. Taylor of the University of California, Paul W. Gates of Cornell, Peter Barnes of *New Republic* magazine, Ralph Nader's associates, and other informed critics of the existing order.

Politics being the art of the possible, dependent upon and seldom soaring far beyond the views of an informed and educated electorate, Congress is sometimes at its best when it uses its immense prestige, power, and resources to gather and publish opinion on subjects of public concern. The green and buff volumes pour forth. Who reads them? One does not know, but the printed word, given time, has great penetrating power.

The old frauds and depredations of the nineteenth century are now thrice-told tales. They have more than nostalgic interest, however, because Congress and the nation still are dealing with

the consequences and sequelae and because the ancient she-
nanigans have modern counterparts that are quite as outrageous,
in their way. Maldistribution of the public lands has a profound,
persistent social and economic impact. California's massive private land holdings in federally irrigated areas were part of the
problem encountered when the Carter administration undertook reform of the Reclamation Act in the late 1970s.[20]

In the Desert Land Act of a century ago, Congress intended to
give the settler a square mile of land if he would undertake to
irrigate it. Later, out of humble beginnings and the urgings of
irrigation enthusiasts who banded together, came the great
federal reclamation movement, which recognized that the settler
needed federal assistance in getting water to his land. From the
standpoint of pork-barrel politics, the West received thereby
something to match the federal rivers and harbors outlays of the
watery East. Congress meant, once again, to subsidize the small
farmers and rule out the chiselers, speculators, and big-money
interests, but as in the past there was a wide gap between what
was intended and what was achieved.

For a time, in the dawn of the movement to bring in water on
a large scale, it had looked as if Congress might heed the warnings of Maj. John Wesley Powell, the Colorado River explorer,
who dreamed of applying intelligence and planning to the intrusion of humanity on the American desert.[21] The major, who
had lost an arm at Shiloh while serving on General Grant's staff,
helped root out the persistent "Myth of the Garden" —the idea
that the West could be divided neatly into family-sized holdings
like the less arid country—and the attractive though absurd idea
that "rain follows the plow," as if somehow the Almighty would
water the soil if man but scratched the surface.[22]

The major's enthusiasm for development and private ownership suited Congress, but his zeal for orderly planning did not.
In 1879, the year after Powell's report on the arid lands, Congress put a legislative rider on an appropriation bill and thereby
established the Interior Department's Geological Survey. Powell,

its second director, succeeding Clarence King, contrived to persuade Congress to give his agency the task of going ahead with the preparation of "a geological map of the United States." This broadened his mission and permitted him to build an empire. His prestige was enhanced by the report of the first Public Land Commission, which reflected his views and revealed how poorly the land laws had been working. A cycle of ruinously dry years began searing the Middle Border in 1886. Towns and farms were abandoned. In this setting, western members of Congress backed a resolution in 1888, demanding to know from the secretary of the interior whether the Geological Survey could analyze prospects for irrigation.

Major Powell was equal to the challenge. At his suggestion, Congress provided $100,000 in an appropriation bill rider. The move had the backing of Nevada's Senator Stewart and Sen. Henry M. Teller of Colorado. Teller had been secretary of the interior under Republican President Chester A. Arthur. He had been active, along with Stewart, in opposing land-law reforms. Later he was to resist the growth of federal forest reserves. Both senators supported the Powell move for irrigation planning only as long as they, and others of similar kidney, saw it as a step toward quick development in the West. What they did not foresee was that the irrigation surveys would be thorough and slow and that while the major bent to his task, "all lands made susceptible of irrigation" would be withdrawn from settlement.[23] The reason for the withdrawal, of course, was to prevent speculation in lands that might receive water.

A Maine senator asked Powell whether he had any doubt about the wisdom of the government's assumption of planning and control of the great rivers. Did he not think it better to leave such matters to nature "and the common incidents of human life?"

"You ask me the question, and I will answer," replied Powell. "I think it would be almost a criminal act to go on as we are

66

doing now, and allow thousands and hundreds of thousands of people to establish homes where they cannot maintain themselves."[24]

When it was seen that the much-criticized Desert Land Act and other settlement laws had been virtually halted pending completion of Powell's work, the major's base of support weakened. Congress would not tolerate the delays. Planning and conservation of resources had gotten in the way of the West's development. In 1890 the lawmakers swept away the framework for the irrigation study. Only the sites of reservoirs suggested by the Geological Survey, it was ordained, were to be reserved from entry by claimants. Moreover, any entries that had been made "in good faith" between 1888 and 1890 were to be safeguarded, leaving claimants in possession of their rights. Powell not only lost the fight but found himself the victim of a punitive effort. There was ridicule. An Alabama representative observed that the Geological Survey had been spending the taxpayers' money on research concerning Odontornithes, a group of toothed Cretaceous birds of which fossil remnants had been found. In 1892 the agency's funds were cut back, and Powell quit.

Nevertheless, support for the irrigation projects themselves was mounting in the West. People favored federal outlays for building such works, even though federal planning and red tape might be abhorrent. Railroads and real estate men took up the cudgels. The Congress and the nation heard wildly optimistic estimates as to the acreage in the arid region that could be "reclaimed" by irrigation. Richard J. Hinton, a geological engineer assigned to the Agriculture Department, forecast in the 1880s that 245 million acres could be made arable "provided that water can be obtained for that purpose" —an important proviso, as it turned out. He later cut his estimate to 121 million acres. By the turn of the century, the estimates of land that could be reclaimed had been scaled down to somewhere between 35 and 70 million acres—figures still much larger than the amount irrigated by all the heroic federal damming and ditching of the next seventy years, which came to only about 11 million.[25]

What the rain-hungry West needed, as Major Powell said, was water. Wry jokes have been told. When Arizonans were lobbying for territorial status during the Civil War, Senator Wade of Ohio, buttonholed by a zealot, said he had heard of the country, and "it is just like hell—all it lacks is water and good society."[26] Various changes and experiments were tried, but private efforts at irrigation, however determined, were a child's watering can moistening the Sahara. It came to be realized that the western deserts would not become gardens without the kind of massive intervention with nature that only federal authority could bring about.

President Theodore Roosevelt's first message to Congress, on December 3, 1901, favored reclamation by the government. He put the case this way: "The pioneer settlers on the arid public domain chose their homes along streams from which they could themselves divert the water to reclaim their holdings. Such opportunities are practically gone. There remain, however, vast areas of public land which can be made available for homestead settlement, but only by reservoirs and main line canals unpracticable for private enterprise. These irrigation works should be built by the national government."[27] Westerners in Congress fought Teddy Roosevelt savagely during his drive to conserve resources, but their enthusiasm for bringing water to the arid country matched his own.

Rep. Francis G. Newlands, Nevada Democrat, later a senator, had already proposed comprehensive federal action on irrigation at the time President William McKinley's assassination put Roosevelt in the White House. Congress, which had been worrying the subject for a decade, gave overwhelming approval to the Newlands Reclamation Act of 1902.[28] The new law was as important to the West's development as the Homestead Act. It provided that all money from sale of public lands in sixteen western states was to go into a "reclamation fund" for planning and construction of dams and other irrigation projects. Water users were to pay fees sufficient to meet the cost, but no mention was made of interest. No water rights were to be sold for land in private ownership, to any one landowner, for a tract larger than 160 acres. This was put in to answer critics who said that, without such a restriction, the benefits of irrigation at public expense would go mainly to speculators and railroads owning huge, advantageously situated tracts. The reclamation work was made the responsibility of the Interior Department, where its first director was Frederick H. Newell, the chief hydrographer for the Geological Survey.

Not surprisingly, sharp operators got ahead of the irrigation planners, just as had been the case in federal land enterprises of the past. Areas thought likely to be irrigated were bought up, with the result that the government paid high prices for lands to be inundated. The Interior Department initially failed to withdraw lands in project areas, leaving them exposed to entry. Settlers flocked in to wait for water when water was years away. The consequences of bad planning were misery and waste of money.[29]

Regardless of who benefited and who wound up owning the land, the Reclamation Act was a conservation measure of the first magnitude, in the sense that it created arable tracts in what had been desert. In another sense, though, it was destructive. It brought changes whose eventual outcome none could foretell, and it attracted population to areas that were fragile and might be unable, in the long run, to support intensive use. In the short view, water in the desert was gold.

The Bureau of Reclamation was formed in the Interior Department in 1923. Elwood Mead, formerly the state engineer of Wyoming, became the first commissioner. The bureau succeeded the old Reclamation Service, which had been set up in the Geological Survey under the 1902 legislation and had been separated from the survey in 1907. Mead undertook to correct deficiencies that had cropped up in the first two decades of federally planned irrigation. One of the troubles, a repetition of the old story, was that major benefits had gone to private property owners getting supplemental water rather than to people who settled on government land. The limitation on the amount of private land to be irrigated was not enforced. As we have seen, 160 acres of arid desert land was not enough for a family farm. Irrigated desert land was another matter.

A multipurpose expansion took place in 1928 when Congress approved the Boulder Canyon project on the Colorado River, a titanic enterprise intended to control the river and provide water for Arizona and southern California. The generation of electricity was an essential element in carrying out the multiple purposes of the dam, a concrete stopper designed to plug the river at the canyon in the name of irrigation, flood control, power production, river regulation, water supply, and navigation. Hoover was the first of a series of giant dams built to bring water and cheap power to a rapidly growing West, particularly southern California.

Under congressional mandates, moving toward annual outlays that ran into the hundreds of millions, the bureau proceeded to marshal battalions of cement and steel structures embracing entire regions and tying one river basin to another. As the years went by, the government found itself in the position of paying heavily to open up arid lands for agriculture while at the same time curtailing farm production, through a different type of subsidy, in fertile areas back East where water was plentiful.

The Bureau of Reclamation, nursed along by legislators, became vital to the economy of many parts of the West. Time brought changes in its mission. In the first ten years of the reclamation program, more than 97 percent of the activity was for irrigation. By 1966 only one-third was for irrigation, while the remaining two-thirds were for generation of hydroelectric power, flood control, municipal and industrial water supply, and other purposes. The bureau was supplying enough water for eleven cities the size of Denver.

Congress had little difficulty reconciling itself to the fact that reclamation in the West did not pay for itself in hard cash, as the law said it should. The money was not coming back into the federal treasury, but it was a welcome, golden rain in the dry country. Under the law, direct beneficiaries were to repay the government, and 85 percent of federal capital costs were to be recoverable. Through fiscal 1977, however, the total sum repaid came to $1.7 billion, or about one-fourth of the completed plant in service, of $6.6 billion.[30]

The arithmetic of the great western reclamation effort has been radiant, persuasive, and not entirely meretricious. The Reclamation Bureau was claiming in the early 1970s that it furnished water service to sixteen million people—about 30 percent of the population of the seventeen contiguous western states—and was irrigating nearly nine million acres of farmland with gross crop value running at $2.1 billion for the year.[31] Flood-control benefits of nearly $33 billion were spread on the ledger. If this were taken at face value, it was reasonable to ask why so small a portion of the government's capital costs had come back in. Congress failed to ask that question with any force. It showed little enthusiasm for seeing to it that large private landholders did not get undue advantage from federal water and for giving thought to the ultimate consequences of gargantuan works that did violence to nature.

When the Carter administration proposed the abandonment of marginal Bureau of Reclamation and Army Corps of Engineers water projects in 1977, there was a cry of anguish from Capitol Hill. Another furor came when Carter's interior secretary, Cecil D. Andrus, under pressure of court orders, attempted to enforce the 160-acre limitation as required by law. In fairness, it should be recorded that the economy-minded Democratic senator from Wisconsin, William Proxmire, publicly cited Andrus, early in 1978, for his "valiant effort" to carry out the seventy-five-year-old reclamation statute and defend the family farm. In water projects as in other areas, the legislative branch's sectionalism may well have done more harm over the years than has been done by naked venality and dishonesty. Mephistophelian wickedness has been rare. Without question, those members of Congress who have danced attendance on the mining, oil, timber, or ranching interests, to the neglect of the public business, typically have done so out of personal conviction and with no sense of wrongdoing. The true villains have been ignorance, stupidity, a certain butt-headedness, an attitude of mind. To those critical of the performance, it is appropriate to recall the remark of Shakespeare's Bassanio on opening the leaden casket: "What damned error, but some sober brow will bless it, and approve it with a text . . .?"

Congress's disapproval of common barnyard corruption among its membership has stiffened since the early twentieth century, when publisher William Randolph Hearst, the senator's son, revealed that leading politicians were on the payroll of Standard Oil Company.[32] Also somewhat attenuated is the old, joyous spirit of free enterprise and devil-take-the-hindmost exemplified by the battle of Sen. Ralph J. Cameron of Arizona to make good his mining claims in the newly established Grand Canyon National Park.[33]

Cameron, a fighter, had ventured West in the 1880s from Boston, where he was employed in a department store. He began locating claims in the canyon in 1902, at about the time the Santa Fe Railroad constructed a spur to the South Rim and built the El Tovar Hotel. The Cameron claims involved the site where the Santa Fe wanted to put up its hotel and also gave Cameron a foothold halfway down Bright Angel Trail, where he operated a down-at-heel tourist place called Indian Gardens and imposed a one-dollar toll on sightseers riding down the scenic route. The canyon area had been a national forest reserve since 1893. President Theodore Roosevelt, visiting the canyon in 1903, said, "Do nothing to mar its grandeur." The Forest Service and the railway struggled with Cameron, who had become a powerful Arizona politician and a leader of elements that wanted to exploit the canyon for mining, power, and commercial purposes.

The claims of Cameron and his associates still were clinging like an incubus to one of the world's great natural wonderlands when Congress approved establishment of Grand Canyon National Park in 1919. Cameron, a Republican, won election to the Senate when Harding ascended to the presidency in 1920. In the Senate, Cameron warred unsuccessfully against National Park Director Stephen T. Mather, the "Twenty-Mule-Team" borax king, but was able, in 1922, to have all the money for the park stricken from the appropriation bill for the Interior Department. The senator kept up his vendetta against the federal establishment, even though the United States Supreme Court rejected his canyon claims in the same year he was elected to the Senate. Finally the park rangers closed in on the senator's unsightly tourist spot at Indian Gardens, Arizonans wearied of his obstructive tactics, and he was defeated by Carl Hayden, a Democrat, in 1926.

To Americans hearing of the Cameron episode a half century or more later, it might seem puzzling that this ambitious and indomitable man was not driven from the Grand Canyon by the righteous indignation of his fellow citizens. In fact, he enjoyed a great deal of local support and sympathy until he overplayed his hand. Cameron expressed the spirit of the times. He was a citizen against the government. He had a right, and he asserted it. He fought for it. He stood for private enterprise and private development.

"I have always said that I would make more money out of the Grand Canyon than any other man," Cameron said at one point in the battle.[34] He spoke in a spirit well understood by his contemporaries and one that had not gone out of fashion in the 1980s.

As will be discussed in subsequent chapters, the efforts of Congress to treat the public lands as the province of the nation

73

as a whole have often been frustrated in the twentieth century by the same factors that contributed to Parrington's Great Barbecue of the nineteenth. Western domination of the relevant committees of Senate and House has been a major factor but by no means the only one. Much more important, in the battles over the public's minerals, oil, timber, and pasture, has been a general disinclination to put the national interest ahead of more strident claimants.

It is on Capitol Hill that the waves of conservationist rhetoric and reform wash against the rocks of political power. The old, traditional, cozy relationships—a set of politicians, a set of bureaucrats, a lobbying constituency—tend to persist.

There are times when an adverse lobbying effort can be overwhelming, even when congressional leaders are determined to take an initiative they are convinced is essential and long overdue. An example is the defeat of a federal land-use planning bill in the twilight of the Nixon administration. The United States Chamber of Commerce opposed it as a threat to private property. Right-wingers damned it. An abrupt volte-face by President Nixon helped drag it down.

What happened was fascinating to watch, albeit depressing and frustrating for Americans who understood that the nation had no land-use policy and desperately needed one. There were numerous federal programs that had an impact on local land use, but nothing in the nature of a federally led plan for coordinating federal, state, and local efforts. Yet the United States faced a task of rebuilding itself by the year 2000, with anticipated urban growth that would absorb an area the size of New Jersey each decade. In the early 1970s, the time seemed ripe for a successful assault on traditional concepts—a "quiet revolution," some called it.

After decades of discussion had come a bipartisan campaign by high-minded people in and out of Congress to move toward a national land-use plan, preferably one with teeth in it. The legislation had a promising start. It was embraced by President

74

Nixon, prior to Watergate, and then abandoned. It ran into difficulties from which its proponents could not, for the time being at least, extricate it. Not often in national history has a good cause suffered a more irrational, shabby comeuppance.

The remarkable thing was that trouble blew up like a storm in the Rockies, after an idyllic beginning in which environmental leaders in Congress and kindred spirits in the Nixon entourage worked in harmony to dispel the Yahooism that had frustrated land planning in the past. In Congress the leaders were Sen. Henry M. Jackson of Washington and Rep. Morris K. ("Mo") Udall of Arizona, both Democratic presidential aspirants. Downtown, the leaders were Russell E. Train, the first chairman of Nixon's Council on Environmental Quality, and Secretary of the Interior Rogers C. B. Morton.

Jackson, chairman of what was then the Senate Interior Committee, and Udall, heading the House Interior Subcommittee on the Environment, shaped modest bills aimed chiefly at providing federal grants to states while recognizing the traditional primary role of state and local governments in land planning. Participation was voluntary, but the bills provided for a degree of federal surveillance over state plans. Property rights were safeguarded in specific language. The Senate passed legislation by handsome margins in 1972 and again in 1973. Despite Udall's spur, the House version had a muddier track but seemed on the point of final action early in 1974.

Because of the Republican administration's unflagging support since 1970, there seemed no doubt that Congress would enact a law and the president would approve it. Train and the CEQ had taken the lead from the outset in calling for a national policy. Train, who had been head of the Conservation Foundation and later Nixon's under secretary of the interior, said improved land use "is the number one environmental priority in the United States today."[35] The president himself was an early advocate. On August 10, 1970, transmitting to Congress the CEQ's first annual report, he signed a message in which he said: "The

75

time has come when we must accept the idea that none of us has the right to abuse the land, and that on the contrary society as a whole has a legitimate interest in effective land use planning all across the nation."[36]

Not content with that, President Nixon proposed legislation to establish a national land-use policy the following year, and he pressed for it again in his environmental messages in 1972 and 1973. Writing to Senator Jackson in the spring of 1972, Nixon said unequivocally: "As a nation we have taken our land resources for granted too long. We have allowed ill-planned or unwise development practices to destroy the beauty and productivity of our American earth. Priceless and irreplaceable natural resources have been squandered. . . . The country needs this [legislation] urgently."[37]

In his 1973 environmental message, the president stated: "Our greatest need is for comprehensive new legislation to stimulate State land use controls. We especially need a National Land Use Policy Act authorizing Federal assistance to encourage the States, in cooperation with local governments, to protect lands of critical environmental concern and to regulate the siting of key facilities such as airports, highways and major private developments. Appropriate Federal funds should be withheld from States that fail to act."[38]

Nixon also praised the Senate in his special message to the Congress on National Legislative Goals in September 1973, for passing land-use legislation "incorporating many of the policies I have proposed" and for properly delineating "the respective roles of the Federal, state and local governments in land use regulation."[39] A few months later, when the House Interior Committee voted a comparable version late in January 1974, Secretary Morton applauded the action and urged prompt final passage.

Behind the scenes, though, all was not well. Long delays in the House had given hostile forces time to regroup. The United States Chamber of Commerce had become alarmed about the bill, which, it warned, might bring "sweeping federal intervention into a traditionally state and local matter—the use of private property." The chamber was not happy with material emanating from the CEQ, which challenged the landowner's traditionally presumed right to develop his property and suggested that the right to develop could be restricted without compensation.[40]

The chamber, along with mining and forest industry groups, the Farm Bureau, and the right-wing Liberty Lobby, put on an intense struggle to stem the tide and get behind Udall's nemesis on the Interior Committee, conservative Republican Sam Steiger of Arizona, who had been fighting hard but getting the worst of it. Steiger, born in New York City, had won the Silver Star for gallantry as an army lieutenant in Korea and gone on to become a rancher and horse breeder. He acknowledged that land planning was essential but maintained that the federal government should have nothing to do with it.

Thus encouraged, the cowboy-booted Steiger and like-minded colleagues marched to the White House early in February, after the House panel had approved the bill, and Steiger explained his objections to the president, by then feeling the chill blast of the Watergate disclosures. Secretary Morton was there. Steiger later attended a Chamber of Commerce meeting at which other opponents of the bill were present. A strategy evolved. An attempt would be made to block the bill in the House Rules Committee, which channels legislation to the House floor.

The upshot was that on February 26, 1974, the powerful Rules Committee voted nine to four against allowing Udall's bill to reach the floor. This was after the then minority leader, John J. Rhodes, another Arizonan, had formally announced that Nixon no longer supported it. Jackson and Udall reacted vigorously, indignantly. Udall told the House it was a "classic example of the kind of immoral White House double-dealing we have come to expect on environmental issues." Jackson wrote a tart letter to Nixon, expressing his "astonishment" and asking the president to make a clear statement of his position.[41]

77

As Senator Jackson noted, news reports were speculating that Nixon, expecting grievous trouble over Watergate and needing friends, was trying to curry favor with conservative House members. The Rules Committee reconsidered and sent the bill to the House floor, where, on a hot day in June, after weeks of lobbying by both sides, the House killed the bill by rejecting the rule 211 to 204. A majority thus surrendered its opportunity to debate the issue on its merits and choose or turn down either the Udall plan or a much weaker Steiger-Rhodes substitute, which Nixon was said to support. Secretary Morton also switched to the substitute, of course, but following the vote he put out a press release in which he deplored the House's "highly unusual action denying a full debate."[42]

In this bizarre situation, Jackson and Udall held a joint press conference. They bitterly lamented the finale. Jackson said he blamed the president "personally" and charged that land use, of vital public concern, "became an expendable pawn in the White House trading game of impeachment politics." He added that "pressure was put on Nixon by people he looks to for undying support in the impeachment process." Udall suggested that the president was "mortgaging the country's land for conservative votes on impeachment."[43]

No doubt Nixon's change of attitude was crucial to the legislation's fate, but Congress often has overridden presidential disapproval in matters close to its heart. A more persuasive reason for the eventual failure of the Ninety-third Congress to go forward with a national policy on land planning is to be found in what opposing members said in the debate preceding the House decision not to debate. Typical was the statement made by Rep. William J. Randall, Missouri Democrat, who said farmers of his area would have to accept Washington's decision as to "where every feed lot would be located" if the Udall bill became law.

"This bill is dangerous, it affects the rights of every land owner in America," Randall told the House. "Rather than providing for land use, it could be said it provides for non–land

78

use. No longer would any individual have full and complete control over their own property."[44]

Or mark the warning of Rep. Steven D. Symms, Idaho Republican: "I think that the best time to kill a rattlesnake is when you have a hoe in your hand, and that is right now."[45] Symms defeated Sen. Frank Church in 1980.

Needless to say, the forces that wanted to stave off federal intervention in land planning had a right to do so if they could, and they were undoubtedly correct in assuming that a stronger federal hand would tend to interfere with property owners' freedom to do as they liked. One must conclude, however, without contending that the Jackson and Udall proposals were perfect or would have worked miracles, that Congress as a whole in this instance preferred the status quo over the pain of facing up to a pressing national issue.

"Land planning is the businessman's gun control," remarked a Capitol Hill staffer in sardonic comment on the collapse. He meant that land-use planning, like gun control, triggers deep emotions in some people. These are subjects politicians like to leave alone.

The problem was put in much the same terms by Vermont's Gov. Thomas P. Salmon when he testified before the Udall subcommittee in 1975 about Vermont's venture into land planning at the state level.

"You know," Salmon said in an exchange with Steiger of Arizona, "the man's-home-is-his-castle syndrome and take your cottonpicking hands off me in terms of what I do in my land is not a frontier philosophy indigenous to the West. It is a philosophy that transcends this great land of ours."[46]

Former CEQ Chairman Train, discussing the matter in a 1980 interview, long after he had left the government, said that the land-use policy bill as it finally evolved was a tough one, containing sanctions that had been approved personally by presidential aide John Ehrlichmann. Train said the proposed law was drafted by William K. Reilly and Boyd Gibbons of the CEQ staff.

"Let me give credit to John Ehrlichmann," Train said. "The land-use policy bill was an odd animal to come out of the Nixon administration. If we hadn't been sort of in the heyday of the environmental movement, it might not have happened. And had it not been for some interest on the part of John Ehrlichmann in the problem, nothing would have happened."

Train, who personally wrote the land-policy statements signed by the president, said President Nixon was "a politician to the core. I know he had no personal interest in or even understanding of environmental matters, but he and certain of his staff in the White House saw this as an important issue to ride."

Stephen T. Mather at Glacier National Park. Mather was the first director of the National Park Service (May 16, 1917 to January 8, 1929). *Courtesy U.S. Department of the Interior.*

CHAPTER 4

THE FALL OF ALBERT B. FALL

Collectively as a government in business matters we are and always have been and always will be a failure.

> —Sen. ALBERT B. FALL during Senate debate in 1919, before he became secretary of the interior

I kept wondering whether the ghost of Albert Fall carrying a little black satchel might not emerge from one of the gloomy corners of this office.

> —Secretary of the Interior HAROLD L. ICKES, diary entry, 1933

Now Governor, we Montanans are especially sensitive since Tom Walsh explored Teapot Dome about the transfer of oil reserves from the Navy.

> —Sen. LEE METCALF at confirmation hearings on nomination of Gov. Walter J. Hickel to be secretary of the interior, January 1969

I n the Teapot Dome scandal that shocked a victorious and prosperous United States in the 1920s, public attention focused on a small black bag containing money. President Harding's luckless secretary of the interior, Albert B. Fall of New Mexico, went to jail for bribery. The wealthy oilman from whom Fall was charged with taking the bribe, Edward L. Doheny, was acquitted. Secretary Fall's misfortune impressed the nation's office holders and politicians deeply. The black bag lingered in memory, a nightmare for officials concerned with the public lands, particularly the naval petroleum reserves, and a beguiling dream for newspaper reporters.[1] But nothing quite like it happened again. The future brought pillage on a much more splendid scale, but generally it was all perfectly legal— nothing so simple and primitive as a wad of cash changing hands in a black bag, although the "laundering" of Nixon campaign funds in 1972 came close.

The tragedy of Secretary Fall is remembered today as a vivid example of a high federal official betraying the public trust for personal gain, but the details have grown dim. In a discussion of the public lands, it is necessary once again to recall the background and circumstances: how it came about that the United States set aside an oil reserve for the navy in Wyoming and how Fall managed to smear himself with oil and plunge to disgrace.

Part of the backdrop was that in the early 1920s there were grounds for fear that the nation might be running out of petroleum. Not until 1930 did the great East Texas oil strike give new reassurance of immense resources yet to be discovered.

As oil became more important as a source of fuel and wealth, oil prospectors came into conflict with nonmineral claimants on the public lands. The federal government in the early 1900s barred some lands from agricultural entry, chiefly to protect seekers for oil. Then in 1909 the cautious and conservative President Taft, moving to ensure a supply of petroleum for federal use, withdrew three million acres of oil land in California and Wyoming. Although he did so, he shared the doubts then widespread about the constitutionality of that kind of action by the executive branch. Therefore he asked Congress to provide validation by new law.

In accordance with Taft's request, the Pickett Act—taking its name from Rep. Charles E. Pickett, a Republican lawyer and banker of Iowa—was placed on the statute books in 1910.[2] It recognized the withdrawal power of the president but left the withdrawn lands open to invasion under the Mining Laws except for coal, oil, gas, and phosphates. That is, they remained open to hard-rock mining. The Pickett Act did not confirm previous withdrawals by the executive branch. In 1915 a decision of the Supreme Court in *United States* v. *Midwest Oil Company* upheld the constitutionality of the Pickett Act itself and suggested that inasmuch as Congress had gone along with some 252 earlier executive orders carving reservations from public lands, it had given its implied consent to the practice. It was debatable whether the Pickett Act put a restriction on powers the president already enjoyed, and to which Congress through acquiescence in the past had given its implied consent, or whether it added to the president's implied power. There was great confusion in the decade between 1910 and 1920 over the standing on public lands of oil companies, some of which expected that Taft's withdrawal would be overturned on constitutional grounds.

In the same period of time, while the navy was converting its ships from coal to oil and after much of the oil-bearing federal domain had gone into private ownership, the government moved to set aside naval petroleum reserves. In 1912 President Taft established Reserve Number 1 at Elk Hills in Kern County, California, and shortly thereafter Reserve Number 2 at Buena Vista Hills, adjacent. President Wilson established Reserve Number 3 at Teapot Dome in Wyoming in 1914, at the outset of World War I. After the war, in 1923, President Harding issued an executive order reserving a huge area in northern Alaska—about thirty-seven thousand square miles—as Reserve Number 4. In addition to the four petroleum reserves for the navy, three oil-shale reserves were set up in 1916, two in Colorado and one in Utah. At the time the petroleum reserves were created, about one-third of the Elk Hills tract and about two-thirds of the Buena Vista Hills reserve were already in private hands. The navy in the years that followed was to have a difficult time holding onto its oil and eventually lost it.

On the eve of the Teapot Dome episode, Congress had made a major change in the old Mining Law by approving the Mineral Leasing Act of 1920.[3] This action allowed access to oil, gas, coal, and certain other minerals on the public lands but provided for payment of a royalty. It put the fossil fuels in a category distinct from the hard-rock minerals that could be taken free. Ever since Taft's withdrawals, there had been pressure from the industry and from the western bloc in Congress to open up the federal oil lands. There was much debate in the decade of World War I over the fate of the government's holdings. Some wanted them turned over to the states; some wanted them sold; some wanted them leased; some proposed, without serious hope of success, federal development of the public's oil. Many westerners were reluctant to accept leasing, with its implications of continued federal surveillance, but a conviction grew that the federal oil could be gotten at in no other way. Utah's Sen. Reed Smoot, Republican chairman of the Committee on Public Lands, produced a bill that was reshaped by the House and finally, after many changes, became law.[4]

A frantic rush for oil leases started before President Wilson signed the leasing act. The zeal of oilmen to penetrate the federal oil reserves may be judged by what gradually came to light as the Teapot Dome scandal clouded President Harding's final months in office and blazed in headlines during the more sedate administration of President Coolidge. Shortly after the leasing act became law, Harding appointed former Senator Fall of New Mexico to be secretary of the interior. Fall, who opposed federal meddling in business, talked Navy Secretary Edwin Denby into giving administrative control of the navy's reserves to the Interior Department. The reserves had been jealously guarded by the previous navy secretary, Josephus Daniels, under President Wilson; but Denby, an unwary former marine officer, turned them over to Fall without giving the matter much thought. President Harding sealed the transfer with a secret executive order dated May 31, 1921. Secretary Fall, who had played poker with Harding in their Senate days, lost no time. He leased Teapot Dome in its entirety to the maverick oil magnate Harry F. Sinclair on April 7, 1922. This was done secretly, without bids. Eighteen days later, on April 25, Fall leased a large part of the Elk Hills reserve in California to Edward L. Doheny of Pan-American Petroleum and Transport Company, the man who in 1892 had drilled the first successful oil well in Los Angeles. Again there were no bids. Part of the Elk Hills agreement was that Doheny would retain the royalty oil due to the government for his lease and would, in exchange, build storage tanks for the navy at Pearl Harbor in Hawaii. In December Doheny's contract was extended to include all the navy's holdings at Elk Hills.[5]

These were highly questionable transactions at best, of doubtful legality, but Secretary Fall might have gotten away with them had he not benefited personally. Fall was a Kentuckian of distinguished manner. He had a keen blue eye, a drawling way of speaking, an erect carriage, a flowing moustache, and a firm chin. He was sociable. He had been a prospector in his early days, but had not prospered. It is said that when he became Harding's secretary of the interior, he owed eight years in back taxes on his ranch at Three Rivers, New Mexico. He was also a victim of personal tragedy, having lost two of his children in the 1918 influenza epidemic. He was in poor financial straits. Sinclair and Doheny, on the other hand, were rich.

The secret leases soon came to light. In mid-April of 1922 Sen. John B. Kendrick, a Wyoming Democrat, obtained passage by the Senate of a resolution asking the Interior Department about reports then current in his state that the leasing of Teapot Dome to private persons was in prospect. Kendrick had already written to Secretary Fall after hearing from a Wyoming oilman that something strange was afoot. The senator's inquiry was made on the very day Fall and Denby signed the lease to Sinclair.[6] About a week after the Senate passed Kendrick's resolution without debate, Acting Interior Secretary Edward C. Finney made a public statement in the absence of Fall, who was on a western inspection trip. It was revealed officially not only that Teapot Dome had been leased to Sinclair's Mammoth Oil Company but that the department was getting ready to lease Elk Hills to Doheny's Pan-American. The explanation was that the navy's oil was being drained away by neighbors, so the government had to arrange for its development or suffer its loss. Secretary Fall replied to Kendrick April 21, admitting what had been done and pleading in justification that naval preparedness and the nation's security were involved. There was a color of legitimacy to Fall's explanation, since relations with Japan at that time were poor and American leaders were worried about the Japanese navy.

What had come out was sufficient to cause Sen. Robert M. LaFollette, the Wisconsin Progressive, to offer a resolution April 21 which the Senate passed eight days later. The resolution provided for a full inquiry by the Committee on Public Lands on the leasing of naval reserves to private interests. The Interior and Navy departments were called on to submit all pertinent records. Late in June Secretary Fall submitted a heavy mass of material to the Senate and also wrote a report to President Harding.[7] The president sent the report to the Senate along with an approving letter in which Harding said "the policy decided upon and the subsequent acts have at all times had my approval."

For many months nothing much happened. The press lost interest. The Harding administration was hostile to the inquiry, and the Republicans controlled the Senate and, of course, the Public Lands Committee. Early in 1923 Sen. Thomas J. Walsh of Montana, a Democrat born at Two Rivers, Wisconsin, was appointed to head the investigating subcommittee. It was an unlucky choice, from Fall's standpoint. Walsh was an Irish-American Catholic of monumental integrity. He prepared himself with great thoroughness and pursued Fall, his fellow westerner and former Senate colleague, with quiet, deadly tenacity. Meanwhile, Fall resigned from the cabinet in good order at about the time—January 1923—that Walsh was designated to chair the inquiry. Fall left the government in March and found work with the Sinclair interests. In the spring of 1923 Fall joined Sinclair himself on a trip to Russia, the objective being the negotiation of oil concessions on Sakhalin Island.

All of this occurred before the damning facts about Fall's personal involvement with Sinclair and Doheny came out. Senator Walsh spent months looking through the evidence. The Republicans sought delay of the inquiry. President Harding, exhausted by the labors of the White House, set out in June aboard the presidential railway car *Superb* and boarded the transport *Henderson* at Tacoma for Alaska. On his return he was tired and ailing, thought to have eaten tainted crab. The president's death August 2 at the Palace Hotel in San Francisco caused sincere grief and national mourning, for he was an amiable, handsome man and much beloved. It was not until October 25, 1923, well after Harding had been laid to rest at Marion, Ohio, that Walsh opened public hearings, with Fall as his first witness.

Former Secretary Fall demonstrated himself to be an accomplished liar, despite his clear blue gunfighter's eyes and direct manner. He had received nothing, he said, from either Sinclair or Doheny. He had gotten only expense money for accompanying Sinclair on the Russian trip. There was sympathy for him in the Senate and in the country at large. The Washington press gave him kindly treatment. He was widely believed when he said the leases had been issued in the interest of national security. A parade of other witnesses followed him—naval officers, federal officials, and Doheny and Sinclair. Doheny said he expected to make $100 million from Elk Hills, and he insisted the lease was in the government's interest. Sinclair estimated Teapot

Dome at more than $100 million. He was asked whether Fall had profited in any way. Not at all, he replied, unless Fall could be said to have gained from a shipment of cattle Sinclair sent from his New Jersey farm to Fall's New Mexico ranch early in 1922— six registered holsteins and some prize hogs. This gift was made after Sinclair had gone to Three Rivers to talk with Fall about the Teapot Dome lease.

New Mexico was not such a crowded state that the appearance of blooded stock on Fall's ranch went unnoticed by his neighbors, but more direct and persuasive evidence was needed if Walsh was to bring him down. Fall was widely admired as a true-blue westerner. He had been praised by former President Theodore Roosevelt in 1918 as a person who, to a peculiar degree, "embodies the best American spirit."[8] Walsh also was respected, but as Fall's pursuer he found himself for a time blackguarded by leading newspapers as a "mudgunner," character assassin, and "scandalmonger. Nevertheless, the patient and tireless Walsh, an honest politician from a state that had been a wellspring of western-style corruption, kept stalking his man.

Bits of evidence began to come in which encouraged the chase. Former Senator Fall was learned to have shown signs of an affluence to which he had not been accustomed. Editor Carl C. McGee of the *New Mexico State Tribune*, no friend of Fall's, testified on November 30 that Fall had been "dead broke" as lately as 1920 and had been trying to raise cash; yet it appeared that in December 1921 Fall had bought the Harris ranch adjoining his own property at Three Rivers for $91,500. In addition, he had paid ten years' back taxes in 1922 and had built a hydroelectric plant and reservoir costing about $40,000. It had been in December 1921—four months before the Teapot Dome lease— that Sinclair had paid his call at Three Rivers in his private railway car.

As the newspapers began to prick up their ears, former Secretary Fall was asked for an explanation of his expenditures, which seemed to total about $175,000. He pleaded ill health as a bar to his appearance but wrote a letter reaffirming that he had received nothing from Sinclair or Doheny and informing Walsh that he had borrowed $100,000 from Edward B. ("Ned") McLean, the wealthy owner of the *Washington Post*. McLean was a member of Harding's inner circle and had often, like Fall, been in attendance at White House poker and bridge parties. He was sojourning at Palm Beach when Fall, on the day after Christmas 1923, identified him as the source of the money. McLean desperately sought to forestall a subpoena, begging to be excused on grounds of "severe sinus trouble" and other ailments. He confirmed that he had indeed lent Fall $100,000. Walsh came under heavy pressure, generated from many quarters, to spare McLean the ordeal of cross-examination.

Instead of ordering the nervous and frightened McLean to Washington, Walsh took the train to Palm Beach as a committee of one. There Walsh went to McLean's cottage and found out that McLean had in fact given Fall $100,000 in checks late in December 1921, but that Fall had returned the checks without cashing them, explaining that he was getting the money elsewhere. From whom? McLean had no idea. Walsh then tried to seek out the elusive Fall, who was staying in a Palm Beach hotel as McLean's unregistered guest. Fall would not see Walsh, but through McLean and McLean's attorney he sent Walsh a letter saying he had gotten the $100,000 from another donor—not McLean.

The McLean episode provided comic relief for a drama that quickly drew to a climax as the presidential campaign year began in January and February of 1924. Two sons of former President Roosevelt—Archibald, who had just resigned as vice president of a Sinclair subsidiary, and Theodore, Jr., assistant secretary of the navy—went to see Walsh on a Sunday afternoon and appeared before the investigating committee the following day, January 21. Both had become worried lest something discreditable might be going on. Archie had thrown up his job for that reason. Archie said Sinclair's private secretary, A. D. Walberg, had confided to him that he, Walberg, was in possession of $68,000 in canceled checks Sinclair had given to the foreman of Fall's ranch. In his turn Walberg, already under subpoena, told the senators about a check for $80,000 he thought might have gone to Fall and another $25,000 in Liberty Bonds given to Fall much later. As for Archie's narrative about the $68,000 in canceled checks, Walberg said Roosevelt had misunderstood him. "I might have said six or eight cows, and Mr. Roosevelt probably thought I said sixty-eight thous," Walberg conjectured.[9] The reek of oil was becoming stronger. The first substantial evidence of fraud had been presented.

Fall had been caught in a lie, Sinclair had gone to Europe with extraordinary haste, and it remained for Doheny, the Los Angeles petroleum baron, to clear up the mystery of the $100,000 loan McLean had disavowed at Palm Beach. It appears that Doheny, feeling the heat of the headlines about a matter concerning which he knew a great deal, had been driven to consult his lawyer, Gavin McNab. Doheny was advised by McNab to lose no time in going to Washington. The two of them traveled first to New Orleans, where they found the wandering and hapless Fall and urged him to return to the Senate panel and disclose the true source of the money. Fall vacillated, whereupon Doheny and his lawyer continued to Washington and McNab asked permission for Doheny, a small man with spectacles and a gray moustache, to appear as a voluntary witness.

Thus it was that a scant three days after the Roosevelt-Walberg revelations concerning Fall's business with Sinclair, the sixty-eight-year-old Doheny fascinated Washington and the nation with a narrative of how it came about that he had lent Fall $100,000 on an unsecured note dated November 30, 1921, when Doheny was seeking the Elk Hill leases. Kipling or O. Henry could not have improved on the story, the essential elements of which were that two young men knocking about the West had met in a mining camp and then met again, years later, when one was a multimillionaire and the other an impecunious cabinet officer of the United States.

"It was a personal loan to a lifelong friend," Doheny told the senators. He said he regretted not having mentioned the loan in his earlier testimony, but he would continue to insist that Fall had not profited from the contract. He had lent Fall the money to enable him to buy a ranch in New Mexico. He lent the money personally, out of his own funds, and the gesture was unrelated to any oil contract. The $100,000 was delivered to Fall's office in the Interior Department by Doheny's son E. L. Doheny, Jr., who took it from New York to Washington in a satchel—the famous "little black bag." Doheny explained that $100,000 was "a bagatelle to me" —meaning no more than a loan of $25 or $50 might mean to a person in ordinary financial circumstances. In response to a question Doheny said he saw no impropriety in lending money to an officer of the government with whom he was transacting business.

This was, of course, pay dirt. On the day that Doheny testified, former Secretary Fall arrived back in Washington, obviously in a sorry plight. He told reporters he was a sick man. The committee put him under subpoena. He contended he was not well enough to appear, but a commission of doctors said he could testify. He finally confronted his former peers on February 2, 1924, in a scene vividly described by the contemporary historian Mark Sullivan. It was, Sullivan said, one of the most tragic spectacles Washington had seen. Fall entered the crowded chamber leaning on a cane. He was bent in stature. His clothes were baggy. He declined to answer questions on the ground that his responses might tend to incriminate him. He left on the arm of his lawyer, his eyes cast downward. The room was so silent, it was reported, that the tapping of Fall's cane could be heard as he moved down the corridor and made his escape.

It is a commonplace that people in public life, like other people, are not always what they seem to be. Sullivan, who wrote for the *New York Tribune* and left a remarkably readable and perceptive account of the twenties, commented that Fall offered a facade that to an extraordinary extent did not square with the reality behind it. "He was," said Sullivan, "ostensibly a rich man, but actually not; he was ostensibly courageous but actually a coward; ostensibly he seemed a man with an exceptional code of pride, including what is commonly called honor, but actually he was a liar."[10]

Angered by the inquisition and affronts to which he was subjected by Democrats, the short-tempered Doheny went on the offensive in further testimony before the Walsh committee. He asserted that he had employed a number of prominent Democrats, including William Gibbs McAdoo, who was President Wilson's son-in-law, had been Wilson's secretary of the treasury, and was a candidate for the Democratic nomination for the presidency in 1924. "I paid them for their influence," the oil magnate said.[11] Many were spattered with Doheny's oil brush, but none came out looking so black as Albert B. Fall. When Sinclair got back from Europe, he returned to the committee chamber in March but added nothing. He declined to answer questions, saying he was reserving his evidence for the courts. Sinclair, unlike Fall, scorned to seek the protection of the Fifth Amendment. The Senate voted him in contempt, and he was immediately indicted on that charge.

As was true a half century later, when President Nixon's position in the Watergate affair gradually eroded until it became indefensible, Republicans defended Fall initially but finally abandoned him when the full dimensions of the scandal became clear. The turning point came when President Coolidge, a few days after Doheny disclosed the $100,000 loan to Fall, announced under prodding by Walsh that he would name special counsel for prosecution of the naval reserve cases. This took the matter out of the hands of Attorney General Harry M. Daugherty, who had guided Harding to the White House and was roundly distrusted. Coolidge named Owen J. Roberts of Philadelphia, a Republican lawyer and future Supreme Court justice, and Atlee W.

Pomerene of Ohio, a Democrat who had served in the Senate. Roberts and Pomerene had Coolidge's firm support. Among other things, they discovered that some $200,000 in Liberty Bonds had been made over by Sinclair to the credit of Fall or his son-in-law.

The immediate political consequences of the Teapot Dome case were not great, although the long-term effects, in terms of a sour and lingering aftertaste, were substantial. Denby and Daugherty resigned. Walsh was touted for the presidency. He received hearty applause when he presided as permanent chairman over the Madison Square Garden convention that nominated John W. Davis, a New York corporation lawyer, to oppose Coolidge. The Democrats did their best to capitalize on the Fall exposures and other scandals. Their *Campaign Book* for 1924 contained a searing polemic by Walsh. The voters, however, chose to remain with Coolidge of Massachusetts, who revered Big Business and exemplified honesty, frugality, and respectability. He was for business and against federal meddling. Coolidge and the secretary of the treasury he inherited from Harding, Andrew W. Mellon, conferred immense largess upon the nation's wealthy in the Revenue Act of 1926, which, among other things, put in place the 27½ percent depletion allowance for oil.

It was some time after Coolidge became president in his own right that the courts dealt with the Teapot Dome defendants and the issues that had been raised. Coolidge had kept quiet, saying only that the guilty would be punished and the interests of the government protected. Walsh's final report in June cast blame only on Fall, Sinclair, and Doheny, a conclusion some found disappointing. In the same month indictments were returned against Fall, Sinclair, and the Dohenys—father and son—in what was then called the District of Columbia Supreme Court. The indictments charged Fall and Sinclair with conspiracy, Fall and the senior Doheny with conspiracy, and Fall and both the Dohenys with bribery. A technicality caused dismissal of the indictments, whereupon fresh ones were returned. Doheny and Fall were acquitted late in 1926 on the conspiracy charge. When Sinclair and Fall were tried nearly a year later, late in 1927, the judge declared a mistrial because Roberts, as prosecutor, demonstrated that Sinclair had hired detectives to shadow the jury. On a retrial in April 1928, Sinclair and Fall were acquitted. The judge held Sinclair in contempt of court and gave him six months in jail.

Sinclair, as *St. Louis Post-Dispatch* reporter Paul Y. Anderson remarked at the time, never lost the iron nerve that took him from a Kansas drugstore to one of the world's great oil fortunes. When a jury declined to convict Sinclair of conspiring with Fall in 1928, Roberts was quoted as having made the following grim statement to a newsman after the jury came in and the happy Sinclair was returned to his backslapping friends, his blonde and sobbing wife, and his aged, tearful mother: "It is simply impossible to convince a Washington jury that it is wrong to defraud the government."[12]

Not until October 1929 did Fall stand trial for accepting a bribe—the $100,000—from Doheny, and fate did not treat him kindly.[13] He sat in a courtroom in a wheelchair and saw a jury, some of its members unaccountably smiling, bring in a verdict of guilty. There was an emotional scene during which Fall's womenfolk wept and one of them fell ill. Doheny, who was still to be tried, railed at the bench. Fall was sentenced to pay a fine of $100,000 and spend one year in prison. Eventually he was confined from July 1931 until May 1932, the first officer of cabinet rank to go to jail in the annals of the United States, if not the last.

In March 1930 Doheny was acquitted of the charge of bribing Fall, even though Fall had been convicted of receiving the money. The lawyer who represented Doheny and Fall, Frank J. Hogan, was widely reported to have gotten a fee of $1 million for his efforts. There was grousing about the wealthy defendants

95

being let off, notwithstanding that both Doheny and Fall did suffer great inconvenience, and Sinclair saw the inside of a jail. Doheny's son met a violent end.

The Teapot Dome and the Elk Hills naval reserves were returned to the Navy Department, which kept them for another half century. The government filed suit to annul the leases to Sinclair and Doheny, bringing both actions in March 1924. Federal courts found that Teapot Dome had been obtained through "collusion and conspiracy" between Secretary Fall and Sinclair. In the California case the United States Supreme Court declared that "fraud and corruption" were involved.

Partly to rid the Republican party of the onus of scandal, President Herbert Hoover took action shortly after he assumed office in 1929 to forbid any leases or disposal of government oil lands, except such as Congress might make mandatory. There would, Hoover announced, be "complete conservation of government oil in this Administration." The commissioner of the Land Office received instructions to slam down the window on applications and to turn down some 20,000 then pending. A drive was instituted to wipe inactive permits off the books. The public domain was reopened to oil leasing late in Hoover's term, in 1932, by which time the great East Texas field had come in and the fears of an oil shortage—very real in the 1920s—had given way to worries about a glut.

It is remarkable that the Teapot Dome episode, involving only a few hundred thousand dollars at most, was vividly recalled after more than four decades during which the public had been fleeced of tremendous sums—not by dishonesty, but on a point of law, perhaps, or a shift in the political climate.

Look, for example, at the rich oil reserves on Alaska's North Slope. These were the property of the federal government and all the people of the United States prior to 1959, when the state of Alaska was admitted to the Union. The United States, knowing oil was there, had set aside Naval Petroleum Reserve Number 4 in the western North Slope in the twenties. The new state claimed tracts to the east and leased them to oil interests for a few million dollars before the state obtained full title. In 1968 the Atlantic Richfield Company announced that its Prudhoe Bay field was estimated to contain five to ten billion barrels. Later the experts said the field contained upwards of thirty billion barrels, possibly a great deal more. It was the largest oil find in the history of North America, and whatever oil was present doubled or tripled in value while still in the ground. Thus was transferred from the federal domain, in a brief time, mineral wealth of immense value. Congress and federal officials blessed the transaction.

The energy squeeze that helped bring Alaska's North Slope into production also bore heavily on the Navy's reserves as the nation looked for more domestic oil in the 1970s. Republican Presidents Nixon and Gerald R. Ford advocated tapping of the remaining naval oil in the lower forty-eight states and development of the immense federal holding in Alaska. In the Naval Petroleum Reserves Production Act of March 1976, Congress, despite some resistance from its military committees, authorized production from the oil reserves in California and Wyoming and transferred the Alaskan reserve—Pet 4—from the Defense Department to the Interior Department.[14] Then in August 1977, in the first year of the Carter administration, the three oil and three shale reserves still under the navy were transferred to the new Department of Energy.[15]

There was a tendency as time passed to minimize the misdeeds of Fall, who survived his ordeal and went to his ultimate reward at El Paso in 1944; but the circumstances of Teapot Dome as a classic example of malfeasance in high public office were not forgotten.

For many years Secretary Fall's oil portrait lay stored in an obscure corner at the Interior Department, subject to damage by bats and birds. It had been slashed and was in deplorable condition. In 1966 and 1967, Secretary Stewart Udall had the painting resurrected and placed alongside those of other former cabinet officers in the long corridor outside the secretary's office.

"He was the secretary—a part of history," Udall said. "My reading of history is that he was the kind of secretary we would say today is very industry oriented."

Albert B. Fall, secretary of the interior 1921–1923. *Courtesy U.S. Department of the Interior.*

CHAPTER 5

THE FEDERAL SENTINELS

I find that I have omitted to notice the passage by Congress, after night of this day's proceedings, of a bill to establish the Department of the Interior, or Home Department. It was presented to me for my approval late at night and I was much occupied with other duties. It was a long bill containing many sections and I had but little time to examine it.

> —Diary entry by President JAMES K. POLK after signing measure establishing Interior Department, March 3, 1849

I believe that conservation is no longer a pious ideal. It is an element of our survival. Many resources are limited and precious. My efforts will be focused on curbing old habits of overconsumption and misuse, seeking instead to use less and to use better.

> —CECIL D. ANDRUS at his Senate confirmation hearing January 17, 1977

---

lbert B. Fall had been a senator, but he was a member of the president's cabinet when he got into trouble. As Teapot Dome illustrates, there is difficulty in trying to deal separately with the triumphs and failures of one branch of government, as if they stand distinct from those of the others. It is like separating the strands of a braided buggy whip. In nearly every noteworthy event, what finally occurs is the result of complicated interactions among the executive branch, the elected representatives on Capitol Hill, interested citizens and lobbyists, and, not infrequently, the courts.

Nevertheless, having looked briefly at the record of the Congress in matters affecting the public lands, we should glance at the federal agencies that do the bidding of the president and the Congress. Later on, at the expense of some repetition, we shall consider in more detail how well these various forces have worked together in the management of the public's hard-rock minerals, its fossil fuels, its timber, its pasturage, and the land itself.

The central government's landlords, of course, have had little or nothing to say directly about what happened to state-owned or private holdings. They have had charge of federal holdings only, and even where the land was federal—that is, owned by all the people—their authority has been anything but full and complete. It has been limited by Congress, as of course was desirable and in any event unavoidable, and by countless pressures brought to bear on the executive as well as the legislative branches of government. The agencies have been very much exposed to the winds of politics.

Largest of the federal guardians of land is the Interior Department, a big, easygoing bureaucracy, more than 75,000 strong, symbolized by the familiar seal with the bison on a western prairie, mountains and a sunburst in the background. The department sometimes has resembled the wounded buffalo described in Francis Parkman's *The Oregon Trail*—huge, not very bright, doomed by the arrows shot into its hide, about to roll

roll over and die. The old beast has charged his tormentors savagely now and then. He has shown flashes of spirit and made some forward strides admirable to behold. But often he has just stood there—as he did in the energy "crisis" of the 1970s—too big to ignore, taking his punishment, uncertain of his direction.

There has always been a conflict in the missions assigned to the great federal land-managing agencies. It is the conflict, no doubt also unavoidable, between the task of conserving for the future and the task of exploiting for present use. At the same moment one agency may play the defending angel while another, in the same building, perfumes the sheets for the ravager. This ambivalence causes tensions in the Interior Department and within its land-managing handmaidens—the Bureau of Land Management, the Fish and Wildlife Service, the National Park Service, the Bureau of Reclamation, the Bureau of Indian Affairs—which in sum are responsible for nearly three-quarters of the federal government's holdings. The same conflict tears at the Agriculture Department's Forest Service, which has another 24 percent. To some degree, the conflict is irreconcilable. If what has been pristine wilderness is mined or logged or crisscrossed with roads, for example, it is gone from the wilderness ledger forever. For the most part, lands thus traversed by man can be put to multiple use without their being ruined. Even so, where a type of use is tantamount to destruction, as in mining, the struggle between environmentalists and developers is for keeps.

Obviously, all the remaining wilderness cannot be preserved. Obviously, some land must be mined. In other ways, the needs of mankind must be served. It is a matter of degree. All that can be hoped for, really, is that where decisions are irrevocable, they will be made intelligently.

The venerable Interior Department, redolent with American history and inseparably bound up with the growth of the West, was created by Congress in 1849, at the very end of the admin-

102

istration of President Polk and following a majestic expansion of the national borders by the Mexican War. Interior began life as the Home Department, into which were gathered the General Land Office, from the Treasury Department, and the Office of Indian Affairs (later the Bureau of Indian Affairs), from the War Department. The new agency also enfolded the Patent Office, the Pension Office, and the Census Office, along with some embryonic agricultural activities that eventually developed into the Department of Agriculture. Interior was the government's housekeeper. One of its duties was looking after the public buildings.

At the outset, there had been only three federal departments—state, treasury, and war. Many domestic functions were simply parceled out. From Washington's time, it had been suggested that a home department be created. The innovation was formally proposed in 1817, but no action was taken. In 1848, Secretary of the Treasury Robert J. Walker brought forward plans for a new interior department. Walker, burdened by the minutiae of land sales, did not relish having his Treasury Department saddled with disposal of the empire newly wrung from Mexico. In pleading for relief, he recalled that he personally, as secretary of the treasury, had been asked to adjudicate more than 5,000 land-title cases in the period from 1845 to 1848.

On the wintry, snowy night of March 3, 1849, Congress was in the final hours of its session, and President Polk, a Democrat, was on the Hill to see the session out and wind up his administration.[1] His successor, Zachary Taylor, was a Whig. On that night the Senate completed action on the Interior Department bill, and Polk signed it dubiously, as he said, without having time to give it careful consideration. The Senate approved the measure thirty-one to twenty-five after prolonged debate during which John C. Calhoun and others warned that the power of the executive was becoming too great and that too many offices were being created. "Well," said Daniel Webster, who supported the bill, "the government is increasing; the business of the government is increasing. There is a great deal more work to be done."

Thomas Ewing was the first secretary of the interior. He was a former senator from Ohio, a keen lawyer and orator, and something of a land speculator in his own right. It is said that he had read the entire Bible before he reached the age of eight. As a youth he labored in a salt works. With his earnings he freed his father's farm from debt and entered college. He stood more than six feet tall and was of powerful physique. He had already served as President William Henry Harrison's secretary of the treasury.

There were only about twenty-three million people in the United States when Ewing assumed his new duties. A stingy, grudging Congress was in no rush to provide money and personnel. Ewing noted in his first report, in December 1849, that the establishing act had authorized the appointment of a secretary—that is, himself—and one chief clerk, but no other clerks. The law had said the president was to transfer from the Treasury Department to the Interior Department such clerks as were needed. But it had turned out, Ewing complained, that no treasury clerk could be transferred. He had therefore borrowed two clerks from the General Land Office, one each from the Indian Office and the Pension Office, and had gone out on his own hook to hire five more. He reported that his department would need a permanent force of ten, at a total annual compensation estimated at $14,200.[2]

Comparisons bridging so much time may be meaningless, but it is interesting to reflect that from these humble origins came a mighty structure that in modern times had in the office of the secretary alone—only the capstone of the whole edifice—permanent positions for 1,114 persons at an outlay of nearly $16 million for salaries and expenses.

Secretary Ewing made his first report two years after the war against Mexico and a little more than a decade before the bombardment of Fort Sumter in Charleston Harbor. "Old Rough and Ready" Taylor, the slaveholder who had beaten Santa Anna at Buena Vista, was serving his brief period in the White House. A new party that favored a free homestead law and whose motto was "Free Soil, Free Speech, Free Labor and Free Men" had made a good showing in the elections. It was the year of the California gold rush and a time of rancorous debate over the question of whether slavery would be extended into the newly acquired lands. Buffalo roamed the prairies in countless thousands. The Indians who depended on them for food and shelter were still, as the Harvard youth Parkman had seen in 1846, not yet corralled, beaten, and contaminated by the white man.

"The wild tribes of Indians, who have their hunting grounds in the great prairie, through which our emigrants to California pass, have, during the present year, been more than usually pacific," Ewing told Congress.

"They have suffered our people to pass through their country with little interruption, though they traveled in great numbers, and consumed, on their route, much grass and game. For these the Indians expect compensation, and their claim is just. The prairie is their pasture field; the buffalo their herds, and if used by us, they ought to be paid for."

Secretary Ewing agreed with the commissioner of Indian affairs, he said, that treaties ought to be negotiated with the Indian tribes in which they would yield a right-of-way through their country for settlers and permit the use of grass and game, in return for payment consisting of "small annuities in useful articles of merchandise, and agricultural implements and instruction." Ewing argued that this would gain the goodwill of the Indians and provide a guarantee for their good conduct, inasmuch as dependence upon the United States would become habitual and they would be fearful of losing the federal largess if they misbehaved.

"And by these means, and with the aid of religious and benevolent societies," stated Ewing, "they may be, perhaps turned

105

from their roving habits, their thirst for war and bloodshed allayed, and they may gradually be won over to agriculture, and ultimately to civilization.

"This is the more important as the time is at hand when the herds of buffalo, which are now rapidly disappearing, will be insufficient to supply them with subsistence."[3]

The first secretary did not know much about Indians or the ruthlessly predatory forces that were closing in on them. His assumption that the aborigines would be better off farming reflected the nineteenth century's implacable, superficially benign paternalism toward primitive peoples. In that regard, at least, the Interior Department improved in the next 130 years. It remained willing to sweep the Indians aside where they threatened serious interference with national or local objectives, but some of the old condescension vanished.

In 1971, during the thrust to settle the Alaska native claims issue so that the oil companies and the state's developers could go into action, Secretary Rogers C. B. Morton reflected the change when he remarked to the House Interior Subcommittee on Indian Affairs: "We want to make sure that the life style of these Alaska natives is determined by them. We are not advocating the superimposition of an urban or industrial culture on these folks."[4]

One of Secretary Ewing's problems, as he organized his department, was the multiplicity of legal entanglements arising from bounty lands given to soldiers of the Mexican War as well as from private land claims and from clashes with Indian tenure. These, as he said, were sure to increase as the nation absorbed what became Oregon and California and New Mexico. The General Land Office had no solicitor when Ewing assumed his duties, that post having been abolished in 1842. The secretary could not be expected to handle all these troublesome and tedious legal matters himself.

At the close of the 1970s, there had been forty-one secretaries of the interior since Ewing, including President Carter's nominee, former Democratic Gov. Cecil D. Andrus of Idaho. The worst in terms of public record was Albert B. Fall in Harding's administration. A list of the best would include a handful of strong, farsighted, and able men—among them certainly Carl Schurz under President Hayes, Lucius Q. C. Lamar in Grover Cleveland's first administration, Ethan A. Hitchcock under Theodore Roosevelt, the formidable Harold L. Ickes under the second Roosevelt, and Stewart L. Udall under John F. Kennedy and Lyndon B. Johnson. Andrus seemed destined to be ranked in this group. Remarkable progress toward conservationist goals was made under Johnson and during Nixon's first term. The degree to which this was due to secretarial performance and leadership was difficult to assess immediately. Outside pressures for more careful husbandry gained terrific momentum in the late 1960s.

Stewart L. Udall, an Arizona attorney and member of Congress who had backed Kennedy for the presidency, was an excellent choice. He had imagination, vigor, and intelligence. Initially, the press treated him as a foot-in-mouth bumbler. He decided to stay out of sight for a while and learn his job thoroughly. At the suggestion of the distinguished western writer Wallace Stegner, Udall got a grip on things by researching and writing a book.

This was *The Quiet Crisis,* published in 1963. It was built around a procession of major figures—Jefferson, Thoreau, George Perkins Marsh, Carl Schurz, John Wesley Powell, Gifford Pinchot, John Muir, the two Roosevelts, and the urban planner Frederick Law Olmsted. The book had a favorable impact. It was obviously the work of a conservationist, a person who cared deeply about the land.

The 1960s were a time of environmental ferment and unrest. Udall as the titular master of the federal dominions was in the center of the arena. Under him, the department made its annual illustrated *Conservation Yearbook* a plea for change. The effect, as with *The Quiet Crisis,* was to call the public's attention to the wonders of the natural world while warning against abuse. The message of Rachel Carson's *Silent Spring,* an eloquent 1962 polemic against chemical pollution, was not lost on Udall. Carson had done much of her work while a biologist in the Fish and Wildlife Service.

Secretary Udall's Interior Department remained a friendly haven for environmentalists and ecologists. At the end of his time in office, which was extraordinarily long, Udall could take personal credit for the Wild and Scenic Rivers Act of 1968, which he proposed, and a great deal else. Although from a mining state famed for copper production, he wound up his tenure as secretary with a harsh, forceful attack on the antiquated Mining Laws.

This is not to say that Udall's record was perfect or that he had no credible detractors. During the Johnson administration, when Udall was in charge of the Interior Department, extensive leasing of federal and Indian coal lands, later to be criticized as excessive, took place. Udall encouraged certain water and power developments in the Southwest which needed more study and reflection than they got. His rhetoric, one veteran bureaucrat said, was sometimes better than his performance. Nevertheless, Udall was a sensitive secretary who understood what was meant by the term *quality of life*—much discussed at the time—and perceived the gravity of the threats to it.

Udall, in short, was the kind of person who ought to be appointed to head the Interior Department but seldom is, given the politics of the western lands. His successor had a much less favorable background as he entered office but demonstrated an independence of spirit that must have been as surprising to Nixon, who appointed him, as it was to the environmentalists.

Walter J. Hickel, Republican governor of Alaska and Nixon's first secretary, is difficult to place in the gallery. A small-time booster and developer who went to Alaska penniless and estimated his net worth at $5 million or more in 1969, he was looked on as an abysmal choice.[5] People thought he was anticonservationist and tainted by oil. He owned a 2 percent interest in Alaska Interstate Company, a Texas concern involved in the transmission and distribution of natural gas in Alaska. He had remarked at a Washington press conference shortly after his nomination: "I think we have had a policy of conservation for conservation's sake."[6]

This impolitic utterance, matched by others, did nothing to allay misgivings about the bumptious, pugnacious Wally Hickel, a onetime Golden Gloves welterweight in Kansas. He had an exceedingly rough time at his Senate confirmation hearings, by far the roughest encountered by any in Nixon's cabinet. That ordeal past, he turned out to be a tough and shrewd, if erratic and poorly educated, director of the Interior Department. He was a quick learner in the conservationist game. He showed ambition, vigor, and independence. He was very much his own man—anything but a lickspittle for the oil industry, and not subservient to the iron-visaged White House myrmidons captained by H. R. ("Bob") Haldeman or to anybody else.

Official Washington never figured Hickel out. Among the skeptical and the sophisticated, it was widely assumed he wanted to be vice president in the second Nixon term and was seeking to dislodge the ill-starred but then still popular Spiro T. Agnew, who had been baiting young people. When the presidential axe fell upon Hickel's neck late in 1970, for reasons not fully clear but apparently triggered by his public championing of Vietnam-alienated youth, he had come to be regarded as a rough diamond of some quality. He departed the government at the president's invitation on the day before Thanksgiving in 1970 following a television interview in which he remarked: "If I go away, I'm going away with an arrow in my heart, not a bullet in my back."[7] In the jungle around Nixon, this was more easily said than done.

After the cat-and-mouse game was over, the White House added a characteristically Byzantine touch. Frederic V. Malek, West Pointer and Harvard Business School graduate who was then the inner cabal's personnel hatchet man, descended on the Interior Department the day after Thanksgiving, set himself up in the undersecretary's office, and personally saw to the firing of six of Hickel's subordinates, including several brought down from Alaska. Later, Malek said he had acted on orders from Nixon and Haldeman. One of the non-Alaskans dismissed was Leslie L. Glasgow of Louisiana, assistant secretary for fish and wildlife. Glasgow had been on the outs with Under Secretary Fred J. Russell, a southern California real estate developer, and had rubbed the White House the wrong way by criticizing Nixon land-disposal plans.

The handling of the Hickel dismissals was viewed as unnecessarily harsh and graceless. No doubt the abrupt defenestration of these men was a reflection, in part at least, of the frustration the Nixon administration felt in its efforts to shape a huge bureaucracy to its liking.[8]

Hickel's replacement, Secretary Morton, went in as a known quantity, the scion of a Kentucky flour-milling family and an amiable Squire Allworthy of the Chesapeake Bay gentry with all the right instincts about good husbandry of the land. Where Hickel had suffered through days of senatorial interrogation before he was confirmed, Morton had no difficulty except that Philip S. Berry, president of the Sierra Club at the time, entered a lonely dissent. Berry termed Morton a spokesman for the oil industry, saying he was "not a distinguished nor a committed conservationist." The dissent, which got nowhere, earned Berry a scolding.[9]

Morton had been a respected member of the House for ten years and had been chairman of the Republican National Committee as Nixon took office. A warm, immensely likable Yale graduate, Morton knew the great world of politics and had the merits and defects of a team player. It was said he had trouble making a decision. He liked to agree with people. When he was chivied on Capitol Hill about things that needed to be done, he had a habit of responding with the disarming assertion "I couldn't agree with you more." The reassured questioner, however, might find himself disappointed in any expectations the genial secretary might have led him to have, for Secretary Morton, like his predecessors and those who followed him, headed a department in which woefully small amounts were being made available for restoring pasturelands, buying and improving major parks, and managing the giant segment of the United States for which he was responsible. His explanation for nonfeasance was lack of funds, the rigors of the national budget. Nevertheless, the fact was that the oil-rich Interior Department was operating at a profit.

For fiscal year 1973, for example, when the federal budget was squeezed by the Vietnam War, Morton was able to report that the Interior Department's revenues from public-lands sales and leasing—mostly oil and gas—would be about $1 billion more than Congress was being asked to appropriate for the department.[10] The budget request was for $2.5 billion. Meanwhile, the books looked good, but the federal lands did not. Their needs were well known but continued to be put off for another day.

This was an unusual year because the Interior Department's revenues were swelled by release of more than $1 billion in escrow funds from a court case involving Louisiana. Even so, it is a lamentable fact that throughout most of the 1970s the receipts of the department substantially offset its budget results without generating much of an increase in outlays for looking after the land that produces the wealth. "We're extracting, and putting nothing back," was the way one federal official summed it up in 1972."

Most of the Interior Department's revenues were coming from federal leasing of oil and gas rights on the Outer Continental Shelf, an activity that was bringing in billions from private industry as the prospective energy shortage worsened. Substantial sums were being realized by the government from sale of minerals, timber, and other commodities extracted from public lands onshore, which are our principal concern, but the big

111

money came from submerged lands. In these circumstances, the essential task of restoring the national pasturelands and forests was put off when the budget was tight. The job was neglected.

The Interior Department came close to being gutted of its senior subcabinet-level officials when President Nixon began his second term in office. New and largely untried men were put in their places. After his reelection the president made a clean sweep of the operational assistant secretaries, with the exception of the wealthy and dynamic Florida conservationist Nathaniel P. Reed, who continued as assistant secretary for fish and wildlife and parks. Interior Department functions were realigned, and greater emphasis was placed on the national search for domestic energy supplies. Such was the thoroughness with which the president changed the guard at upper levels that it was almost as if Nixon felt he had won the game in his first term and, in the manner of an Ivy League football coach, was sending in a second team of players so that they could win their varsity letters.

The Nixon administration's late 1972 and early 1973 penetration of the Interior Department might have gone further, it was said by officials there, had not Secretary Morton intervened to halt the bloodletting. As it was, gore ran in the corridors for some days. There was no clear pattern inasmuch as some of the men who departed were as staunch friends of the extractive industries as those who replaced them. But the consequence of the decapitations was to downgrade the assistant secretaries, undermine the Civil Service system, and concentrate more power in the Office of Management and Budget, directly under the White House.

Morton, his subordinates, and their predecessors had long trumpeted warnings of a national energy shortage. Even so, the rapidity with which the shortage materialized had not been clearly foreseen, so that the widening apprehension of crisis that followed the 1973 Yom Kippur War in the Middle East hit Morton's department with hurricane force, rattling the windows. Intensified by the Arab oil embargo, the storm exalted energy considerations over those of conservation and threatened to wreck such progress as had been made in caring for the land and improving the environment.

In the aftermath of President Nixon's resignation over Watergate, and while the energy storm was still raging, President Gerald R. Ford shifted Secretary Morton to the Commerce Department and named Stanley K. Hathaway, former Republican governor of Wyoming, to be secretary of the interior. The Senate confirmed Hathaway in June 1975 despite conservationist objections. After being in office only about one month, Hathaway entered Bethesda Naval Hospital for what doctors called "depression brought about by physical exhaustion." He resigned late in July. There followed an interregnum before President Ford came up with a successor, Thomas S. Kleppe, former Republican representative from North Dakota. Kleppe's qualifications were not readily apparent. He encountered little enthusiasm and little opposition. He was sworn in October 17, 1975, the first native of his state to serve in the cabinet.

Kleppe was competent, straightforward, and skilled in the ways of Capitol Hill. He seemed unlikely, however, to have much stomach for tucking away large tracts of federal land for future generations. He made that fairly clear at his first press conference.

"Every time we take an additional piece of land and for one reason or another congressionally mandate it for whatever purpose," Kleppe said, "and lock it up forever from the standpoint of whatever minerals that particular piece of land may possess, that's a rather morbid thought."[12]

As had been the case with Hickel of Alaska in the first Nixon administration, neither Hathaway nor Kleppe was regarded by environmentalists as a good choice for secretary of the interior in terms of background and sympathy with the nation's new attitudes toward its lands. President Ford, it was believed, wanted to make a political concession to the West and might have chosen worse. "Where do they find these guys?" asked a Senate

113

Interior Committee staff member at the time Kleppe was approved.[13] The remark was made privately, of course, in a tone more weary than disapproving. Where indeed?

A choice that sat better with critics of recent secretaries was Carter's selection of Andrus, a plainspoken westerner who as governor had insisted on trying to preserve the quality of life in Idaho while also building a reputation for encouraging a practical, selective development of his state's resources. He had been in the lumber business himself. An enthusiastic trout fisherman, a chain smoker of cigarettes, an unassuming man who stood in line with the rank and file for "a bowl of soup" in the Interior Department's cafeteria, Andrus was not easily daunted. He was not afraid of industry pressures, nor was he overawed by the mounting resentment in the West over Carter's initiatives in curbing water projects and in melting some of the fat from the irrigation pork barrel.[14]

As former Secretary Udall remarked in his law office overlooking Pennsylvania Avenue in an interview ten years after leaving the Interior Department, there are many ways of judging a cabinet officer.[15] Did they produce new ideas or concepts? Were they good defenders of the public interest? On the educational side of the job, were they good teachers or public advocates? In researching and writing his book, trying to educate himself for the immense responsibilities he faced, Udall came up with only one nineteenth-century secretary of the interior he thought worthy of a chapter. That was the German immigrant Carl Schurz, who served under President Rutherford B. Hayes from 1877 to 1881 and gave strong support to John Wesley Powell.

"I once looked up the terms of the secretaries," Udall said. "The average term was about twenty-seven months, which was just long enough to learn the job."

You might expect that Teddy Roosevelt's Secretary Hitchcock would be a large figure, Udall said. Hitchcock, a cold and implacable foe of wrongdoers, was inherited from McKinley and served nearly as long as Udall did, in a time of change and aggressive presidential leadership. The reason Hitchcock did not take a major role in the conservation movement, Udall suggested, was that Roosevelt's favorite adviser, Pinchot, set up the Forest Service in the Agriculture rather than in the Interior Department, which Pinchot regarded as a "giveaway" agency.

Udall then noted that Richard A. Ballinger, under President Taft, had been a disaster and that the Ballinger-Pinchot controversy over Alaskan coal could be thought of as the only time the Interior Department had cost a president an election. Taft's schism with Roosevelt elected Wilson in 1912.

"The only cabinet officer who had gone to jail in this country was Albert Fall," Udall pointed out. " —Of course, Nixon changed that."

Talking about the so-called revolving-door aspect of federal service then and now, with people who have held high government posts going to the private side and vice versa, Udall mentioned that oilman Doheny in the Teapot Dome hearings had boasted that four members of the Wilson cabinet, including Interior Secretary Franklin K. Lane, worked for him after leaving office.[16]

Udall never thought much of Lane, he said, and felt Harold Ickes's conservation achievements were modest. Ickes was, of course, colorful and a fighter. Udall spoke with respect of Benjamin Harrison's secretary, John W. Noble, for forest policies developing late in the last century, and he had a good word to say for twentieth-century Republicans Fred A. Seaton under Eisenhower, and Morton under Nixon and Ford. Hickel, he remarked, was "about as much of an environmentalist as the President of Exxon."

"To tell you the truth," Udall said over the coffee table in his office, " [Hickel was] a developer. He had 'the Alaska attitude,' as we always called it. After he was out of the government and back in Alaska, he again showed his true colors."

On Secretary Andrus, the self-assured Idaho Democrat brought in by Carter, the book looked very good at the close of the 1970s. With Carter's defeat, Andrus made a graceful exit. He had made many compromises with the West's desire for development, as had Carter, for that matter, and as former governor of Idaho he knew the problems of the state-federal relationship, but he was a very different man indeed from James G. Watt, the Denver lawyer President Reagan nominated to be his successor. Watt, a former Interior Department official, was president of the Mountain States Legal Foundation, a nonprofit organization backed by business and commercial interests. In the courts, Watt had often challenged the environmentalist position. It was clear from the outset that he planned to lead the Interior Department along new paths—toward the Slough of Despond from the viewpoint of the environmentalists, but upward toward Beulah-land as many in industry and the West looked at the world.

Andrus had presided over the department at a time when it was asserting its authority with more firmness and seemed more certain of its ground. He inherited from Secretary Kleppe a sprawling, ill-knit empire that had grown prodigiously since Ewing's time. It was in process of reorganization and was losing some of its eighteen or so agencies to the new Energy Department, which was formed in mid-1977. In November of his first year in office Andrus's payroll was running $101 million a month, and he was directing 77,025 employees, of whom 68,376 were full-time. The department had undergone a reshuffling in the early 1970s and was confidently believed to have further growth ahead as the core of the proposed and long-discussed Department of Natural Resources, a development Andrus hoped would include transfer of the Forest Service from the Agriculture Department. The concept of putting all the land-managing agencies in the same tent was logical but not easy to bring to pass.

Carter's appointments of subcabinet officials to serve with Andrus were generally well received and consistent with his environmentally oriented campaign. The president named James A. Joseph, head of the Cummins Engine Foundation at Columbus, Indiana, to the department's second highest post. Joseph

116

was the first black to become under secretary of the interior. To the four assistant secretary posts with line responsibility over federal lands, Carter appointed Guy R. Martin of Alaska for land and water resources, Robert L. Herbst of Minnesota for fish and wildlife and parks, Forest J. Gerard of Montana, a Blackfoot Indian, for Indian affairs, and Joan Davenport for energy and minerals. A career federal employee, Davenport was the first woman to rise to the assistant secretary level in the Interior Department.

The heaviest direct burden of suzerainty over the federal heritage fell on Martin, who had been Alaska's commissioner of natural resources, and on Herbst, who had been Minnesota's. Martin succeeded Jack O. Horton, a well-to-do Wyoming rancher, Princeton graduate, and Rhodes scholar, as the official in charge of the ugly duckling Bureau of Land Management as well as the Bureau of Reclamation and the Office of Water Research and Technology.

Something was said about the Bureau of Reclamation and its colossus role in western development when the activities of Congress were under discussion. More will be said later. After the bureau had been cut down to size by Carter, it was shorn of some of its glamour by receiving a new and totally unglamorous name—the Water and Power Resources Service. Here it will be called, for clarity, simply the Bureau of Reclamation.

As for the Bureau of Land Management, or BLM, as it has long been known, this agency is of tremendous importance, and its history and future are basic to the thrust of this book. Feeble until recently but now taking on more vigor, the BLM was guardian as the 1970s ended of nearly nine-tenths of the land managed by the Interior Department and about six-tenths of all federally owned lands. Most of the western federal pasturelands are under the BLM, as is a huge segment of Alaska. The BLM is also the money conduit or collection agent for monies flowing into the Department of the Treasury—billions of dollars a year— from the federal lands. Unfortunately, it has not been allowed to plow much of the money into the land.

117

The Bureau of Land Management was formed in 1946 through marriage of the old General Land Office and the Grazing Service. "BLM land" is what is left of the old unappropriated public domain after the great disposals of the nineteenth and early twentieth centuries. It is the kind of land the traveler sees while driving through Arizona, Nevada, or New Mexico. To most Americans, the BLM is not a household name. One might call it the infantry of the land-managing agencies—underprivileged and up against the nitty-gritty. We shall see it at closer range in what is to come.

On Herbst, as assistant secretary for fish and wildlife and parks, descended the mantle of another able and well-to-do Republican, the aforementioned Nat Reed of Florida's exclusive Hobe Sound. Herbst took charge of the United States Fish and Wildlife Service and the National Park Service along with the Bureau of Outdoor Recreation, later known as the Heritage Conservation and Recreation Service.

The Fish and Wildlife Service, next largest to the BLM in terms of acreage it is responsible for, was established in its present form in 1956 by act of Congress. Its Wildlife Refuge System began in 1903, when Teddy Roosevelt set aside Pelican Island on Florida's east coast as a sanctuary for the brown pelican. In 1905 Congress established a refuge for buffalo in the Wichita Mountains of Oklahoma. Three years later came the Klamath Lake Reservation to protect waterfowl along the Pacific flyway. The concept of federal intervention was strengthened by the Migratory Bird Treaty of 1918 with Britain. Amateur scientists and sportsmen pressed for arrangements with Canada and Mexico. In the 1930s depression, when many Americans were hungry, edible wildfowl might have been doomed had not special efforts been made to save them. Jay N. ("Ding") Darling, a newspaper cartoonist and outdoorsman, figured in these efforts and became the first head of the United States Bureau of Biological Survey, the forerunner of the Fish and Wildlife Service.

In the Fish and Wildlife Act of 1956, Congress authorized refuges for the safeguarding and protection of all kinds of wildlife. In 1966, the growing accumulation of land set-asides was officially designated the National Wildlife Refuge System, and in the same year the Endangered Species Conservation Act provided the first authority specifically to shelter vanishing wildlife. The thrust of the refuge system is to protect wildlife by ensuring that a suitable, protected habitat is available. There is the usual ambivalence, however, in the mission of the Fish and Wildlife Service. It is charged with protecting wildlife but is also saddled with the responsibility for helping destroy animals and birds that are thought to be endangering health, crops, or property. The federally assisted program for poisoning, shooting, or otherwise getting rid of coyotes in the West has been particularly controversial.

Toward the end of the 1970s, the Fish and Wildlife Service had an empire about one-twentieth the size of BLM's, encompassing a total area of nearly thirty-one million acres—an area approximating Louisiana, or Pennsylvania, or Tennessee. The service stood to take over another thirty million acres or so from federal holdings in Alaska. Already it had close to 390 national wildlife refuges extending across the nation and from the Arctic Ocean to the South Pacific and from the state of Maine to the Caribbean. Many of the refuges were too wet or marshy or faraway—in the Aleutians, for example—to attract the avaricious eye. Some, like the Kenai Moose Range and the Arctic National Wildlife Range in Alaska, either had been successfully invaded or were actively coveted by searchers for oil and other minerals. The director of the service from autumn of 1973, continuing under Andrus, was Lynn A. Greenwalt, a career man and son of a career man in the service. He was hard put at times to fight off raids on his far-reaching and thinly policed domain.

Next was the National Park Service, established by Congress in 1916, with 24,412,105 acres, a select collection of scenic and historic areas approaching in aggregate the size of Virginia and deemed to merit a special level of protection. All but about one-fifth of the national park area had been part of the original public domain. The major parks and most of the spectacular scenery were in the western states and Alaska. By the beginning of 1965, though, when the National Park Service was preparing to observe its golden anniversary, it owned some land in virtually every state. It was operating thirty-two national parks, including the world's first—Yellowstone, dating from 1872—and a plethora of other properties set aside as historical parks, monuments, military parks, battlefields, seashores, memorials, parkways, recreation areas, and even the White House itself. It looked forward to a great expansion in Alaska.

Even during the Grant administration, when despoilers were running wild, sensitive Americans managed to safeguard some of the West's incomparable scenery. Congress in 1872 set aside two million acres on the Upper Yellowstone River in what was then Wyoming Territory. Thus was rescued from settlement, occupancy, or sale a natural wonderland of a quality nowhere else to be found. It was to be, Congress said, "a public park or pleasuring-ground for the benefit and enjoyment of the people." Nearly a century later John Ise, tracing national park policies, termed the Yellowstone Act "so dramatic a departure from the general public land policy of Congress, it seems almost a miracle." Not only was an area three times the size of Rhode Island saved from private encroachment, but the area's timber, minerals, and oddities of nature were to be kept "in their natural condition."

The establishment of Yellowstone, an event of prime importance, was preceded by federal action in setting aside four land sections of the Arkansas Hot Springs in 1832 and by President Lincoln's signing in 1864 of an act that transferred the lovely Yosemite Valley to the state of California for public use and recreation. Federal protection was extended to the mountain country around Yosemite in 1890, an action urged by the naturalist

John Muir. The state enclave, which had been neglected and badly abused, was ceded back to the United States in 1905 and became part of Yosemite National Park. Before 1900 six national parks had been reserved or created. Poaching and vandalism were a grievous problem in the early days. It took federal troops to guard both Yellowstone and Yosemite.[17] Congress was incredibly stingy about providing money. Not until six years after Yellowstone became a federal reserve did the legislators appropriate $20,000 to protect, preserve, and improve it. First of a proud line of National Park Service directors, when the agency was formally set up in 1916, was the aforementioned Stephen Mather, an energetic Republican borax tycoon and outdoors enthusiast whose wealth enabled him to take a strong, independent stance.

What the uncurbed human animal will do is sometimes outrageous and amazing. An acting superintendent of Yellowstone in the 1890s, plagued by vandalism and lacking personnel to check it, referred to Muir's words: "The smallest reserve, and the first ever heard of, was in the Garden of Eden, and though its boundaries were drawn by the Lord, and embraced only one tree, yet the rules were violated by the only two settlers that were permitted . . . to live on it."[18]

Initially the parks were protected somewhat by their very remoteness, even though some of the worst depredations took place when people could reach them only by train or by horse or mule. The first gasoline-engine vehicle to enter Yellowstone National Park under official permit was a Model-T Ford in 1915. In 1971 more than half a million automobiles entered the park, bringing most of the annual visitation of more than two million people.

Among the well-known Interior Department officials who got their walking papers after the 1972 election was the powerful and popular George Hartzog, director of the National Park Service. Hartzog, who was reared on a South Carolina farm, read Blackstone in a country lawyer's office. He grew up to become a

121

shrewd political tactician in the capital's bureaucratic jungle. He was hard driving and able, but some conservationists disliked him. Some thought he was doing too much to "develop" the parks to accommodate more people, too little to "protect" the parks from being overrun by motorized millions. He had been appointed director late in the Kennedy administration and thus was an overripe melon, from the Nixon standpoint.

Despite urgings that a career professional be appointed to replace Hartzog, the White House named Ronald H. Walker, who had been President Nixon's special assistant in charge of travel, including trips to the Soviet Union and China. The Sierra Club termed the appointment "profoundly disturbing."

"I have selected Ron Walker," Secretary Morton said, "because he is a dedicated person of unusual talent and ability."

Walker was thrown into a difficult job for which he lacked experience. He served until 1975, when he was succeeded by Gary E. Everhardt, a career National Park Service official with seventeen years in the field. Everhardt was followed in mid-1977 by another career officer, William J. Whalen. In the spring of 1980, Whalen was succeeded by yet another insider, Russell E. Dickenson.

The other two important land-managing agencies in the Interior Department are the Reclamation Bureau and the Bureau of Indian Affairs, each having much smaller holdings than the National Park Service. The Reclamation Bureau had about 7,551,500 acres and the BIA nearly 5,000,000, in addition to more than half a million held in trust for Indians. The troubled BIA, which had its beginnings in 1824 under President James Monroe, suffered the public embarrassment of having its Washington headquarters building seized and sacked by Indian militants shortly before Nixon's reelection.

During the intense struggles of the 1970s over the fate of federal holdings, the only important agency outside the Interior Department was Agriculture's Forest Service, second only to the Interior Department's BLM as an administrator of federal land.

122

The Forest Service, dating from 1905, supervises more than 187 million acres of land in forty-four states, Puerto Rico, and the Virgin Islands. All but about 17 percent is original public domain. Here again, as with the BLM, the National Park Service, and the Fish and Wildlife Service, the acreage is mostly in the West and Alaska. It includes, however, tracts of cutover land in the eastern states, largely along the Appalachians, acquired under the Weeks Law of 1911. In total, the Forest Service has about one-fourth of all federally owned land, compared to BLM's 60 percent. The National Forest System has 155 national forests, 19 national grasslands, and 16 land-use projects of various kinds.[20]

At a time of controversy, the veteran chief of the Forest Service, Edward P. Cliff, was succeeded in April 1972 by another career professional, John R. McGuire. Cliff, a Mormon born in Utah, rose from the ranks and was every inch a forester but was stiff-necked and inflexible in dealing with conservationist objections to overcutting in the national forests. McGuire, a Wisconsin man with a master's degree in forestry from Yale, took the research route to the top. He was more diplomatic and approachable than Cliff. In July 1979, McGuire was succeeded by another career man, R. Max Peterson, a Missourian.

A painful barrier to professionalism in the Forest Service was that President Nixon himself, responsive to soaring lumber prices, was calling for an ever-greater timber output. The White House and the Office of Management and Budget were making decisions that should have been made by people who knew something about trees and cared about them. Nor were conservationists reassured by Nixon's announcement, early in 1973, that the presidential counselor for natural resources—a new post—would be the secretary of agriculture.[21] The man holding that position was the vinegar-tongued Earl L. Butz, a Purdue University farm economist and champion of agribusiness.

We shall look further into the background and prospects of the Forest Service and the Bureau of Land Management, which, although in separate departments of the federal government, have been sister agencies in their management of the grazing lands of the West. Each also has been involved in timber production, the Forest Service for obvious reasons and the BLM because it has charge of the magnificent "O & C" revested timberlands in Oregon as well as sizable tracts of commercial forest elsewhere.

Keep in mind that the Forest Service and the BLM lands not only constitute the largest by far of the federal holdings but also are the most vulnerable. By and large, they have the least protection against various types of use—logging, mining, entry for recreation and hunting, and so on. Until 1976 the BLM was the neglected and maltreated sister, the Cinderella, but in that year Congress finally passed an act giving it a mission and a *raison d'etre* beyond tomorrow.[22]

As will be seen in the next chapter, the threshing out and simplification of the nation's public-land laws have been a goal not easily achieved.

Carl Schurz, secretary of the interior, 1877–1881. *Courtesy U.S. Department of the Interior.*

Cecil D. Andrus, secretary of the interior. *Courtesy U.S. Department of the Interior.*

CHAPTER 6

WINNOWING THE LAWS

The law locks up both man and woman
Who steals the goose from off the common,
But lets the greater felon loose
Who steals the common from the goose.
> —ANONYMOUS; quoted by Edward
> Potts Cheyney in *Social and Industrial*
> *History of England,* 1901

If you put a lawyer, a banker, and an industrialist in a barrel and roll
it down hill, there will always be a son-of-a-bitch on top.
> —Saying attributed to A. C. TOWNLEY,
> founder of the Non-Partisan League
> of North Dakota

E very now and again, in a fit of tidiness and atonement, Congress has reared back and tried to take a look at the complex tangle of laws relating to the public lands which it and other bodies have passed. There are many thousands of such laws. The thicket of statutes is a boon to the western lawyer and a pain to the federal administrator. Just as hard cases make bad law, so bad law makes fat fees. It is a fact sad to contemplate, but there is a point beyond which clarity is not in the interest of the legal profession. Only the most cynical would contend that the lawyers who make the laws write them in a deliberately ambiguous way, with pens dipped in mud, to confuse the lay public and enrich those who follow the legal trade, but sometimes it looks that way.

Not infrequently it happens that the worst laws—the execrable and rapacious 1872 Mining Law, for example—are the hardest to expunge from the books. They develop a life of their own. They have to be burned out or charmed away with stump water like warts, or have stakes driven through their hearts. The late John P. Saylor, Republican representative from Pennsylvania and a member of the most recent public lands study commission, once confided to a newspaper reporter that he suspected a chief reason for the old Mining Law's durability was the gold it showers on law offices throughout the West.

Of the four studies of laws and public land policies that have been made since the late 1870s, by far the most comprehensive and in many respects the most intelligent and useful was the last—the massive survey completed in June 1970 by the Public Land Law Review Commission under chairmanship of Rep. Wayne Aspinall of Colorado. The Aspinall survey took about five years and cost more than $7 million. It published its findings in a bland and somewhat unctuous document called *One Third of the Nation's Land,* a staff product of the late twentieth century. The commission was weighted heavily on the side of mining, timber, and other commercial users. It reached conclusions that, while excellent in some respects, were wrongheaded

127

and shortsighted or overly cautious in others. On the one big, burning, controversial issue that meant more than anything else, the commission came up with the right answer.

What was the issue? It was the question, long a stumbling block to serious planned management of the BLM's unappropriated lands, of whether the federal government really intended to dispose of—get rid of—the public domain, as was suggested by the burden of past laws. On this point the Aspinall commission was reasonably clear. It made a negative answer. It recommended, on page 1 of its report, that "the policy of large-scale disposal of public lands reflected by the majority of statutes in force today be revised and that future disposal should be of only those lands that will achieve maximum benefit for the general public in non-federal ownership, while retaining in federal ownership those whose values must be preserved so that they may be used and enjoyed by all Americans."[1]

Reading this, one might shrug and protest that in 1970 federal retention of the public domain—with its mighty rivers and majestic mountains and sweeping vistas—surely was a foregone conclusion. No federal commission, one might say, would have dared recommend otherwise. Had not President John F. Kennedy in February 1961 termed the BLM's lands a "national resource" that ought to be kept in public ownership and managed for the benefit of future generations? Had not Kennedy's new secretary of the interior, Stewart L. Udall, announced policies at about the same time that ended the disposal of public lands at low cost? Did not these actions reflect a change in the attitude of the American people toward the real estate they own in common? The answer to all these questions is the affirmative; yet the recommendation of the Aspinall commission was useful, extremely useful, as a final nail thumped into the coffin of outmoded doctrine.

It will be remembered that the first of the great public lands studies, conducted nearly a century earlier, in 1879, grew out of a widespread dissatisfaction with the way the laws had been working out—confusions, ambiguities, frauds, blatant wrongs. John Wesley Powell favored reform. So did the National Academy of Sciences. The criticism was not that the federal lands were being disposed of, but that the disposal was not being managed honestly and efficiently. Congress passed an act creating a commission of five members. These were Commissioners James A. Williamson of the General Land Office and Clarence King of the Geological Survey, both ex officio, and three persons to be named by President Hayes. The president appointed Powell, soon to succeed King as head of the Geological Survey, Alexander T. Britton, a highly successful land lawyer and investor, and Thomas Donaldson of Ohio, who had been a General Land Office official in Idaho. The commission assembled a great store of firsthand information in its travels, which included several months of wanderings by train and stagecoach.[2] It focused its attention on the Far West, particularly California, rather than on midwestern states, where most of the homesteading activity was then going on. It pointed to blatant wrongdoing and recommended changes, some of them in line with what Powell had been saying about the nonarable nature of much of the western land.

The policy of the United States, the first commission reported, had been to devote the public lands "to settlement by industrious citizens." The nation accepted as fundamental that "he who tills the soil should own the soil." As was made manifest, the settlement laws needed correction, buttoning up, better supervision. In California, Harry C. Hill, a San Francisco witness, denounced "the shameless frauds of various kinds that are continuously practiced in mining cases." The venality of judges in Utah and Nevada was proverbial. Men had gotten rich by buying and selling juries. In all the mining camps, it was said, there could be found "affidavit men" willing to swear to anything, for a price.

Joseph Russ of Humboldt County in California, in the redwoods country, told the commission that existing land laws "made men perjure themselves." However well intentioned the law might be, he said, "it certainly operates as a reward for crime."

At Salt Lake City, L. S. Burnham of Bountiful, Utah, identifying himself as a Mormon but not a polygamist, gave it as his opinion that getting land in Utah depended on a man's standing with the leaders of the Mormon church.

The commission pointed to the puny size of the General Land Office, which had only 223 people nationwide. The commissioner himself was receiving $4,000 a year—a substantial income at the time—but nobody under him received more than $2,000, and the total outlay for personnel was only $273,220. The panel recommended salaries of $6,000 for the commissioner, and $3,000 for his major assistant, as well as an increase in personnel to 229, at an annual salary cost, all told, of $321,040.

These would have been significant increases had they been granted. Members of Congress themselves during that period, and up until 1905, had salaries of only $5,000 a year, compared with more than $60,000 in 1981. Nevertheless, even when allowance is made for the dollar's rocklike solidity—then compared to now—and for the fact that the national population was only about sixty-three million, the General Land Office was wretchedly small and poorly paid. It could not and did not protect the government or the public generally from the scandalous conditions documented by the commission.

The first commission's five-volume report, concluded by Donaldson's fretful but solid *The Public Domain*, was a voice crying in the wilderness, but few were willing to hear or heed the lamentation. Donaldson, a friend of Walt Whitman's, was a copious writer with a taste for drudgery. His work is indispensable but is marred by inaccuracies and hot language. Among other things, he objected to the transfer of public land to immigrants from southern Europe. Why give land bounties to Italians? he asked. He favored a citizens-only policy for the public lands—by which he meant citizens from north European countries.

Congress paid little attention to the 1879 commission.[3] Closer to the legislative mood, at that time, was the disastrous Timber and Stone Act of 1878, which, along with other laws purporting to help the small settler obtain timber, turned out to be a boon to loggers and speculators.[4] Under the law, unappropriated and unreserved public lands in California, Oregon, Nevada, and Washington Territory could be purchased at $2.50 an acre if valuable chiefly for timber or stone and unfit for farming. This was an open invitation to abuse and apparently was intended to be just that. Dummy entrymen were brought up, and hundreds of thousands of acres of the world's most valuable timberlands, including much of California's redwood forest, went out the federal door.

The commissioner of the General Land Office was an important official in the nineteenth century. He presided over a lively activity of great public consequence, one in which nearly everybody was interested. Abraham Lincoln once tried to become land commissioner but did not get the job. The GLO was patronage ridden and understaffed for its prodigious work load, but such commissioners as S. S. Burdett and James A. Williamson in the 1870s and Noah C. McFarland and William A. J. Sparks in the 1880s submitted annual reports in which they spoke out frankly against fraud and other abuses.

William Andrew Jackson Sparks, the commissioner under Cleveland from 1885 to 1887, was a lionhearted public servant. He did not hesitate to talk about "unblushing frauds" in his annual report. He was born in Indiana and got his early schooling in a log house. He read law. In his early twenties he spent three years as a receiver in a federal land office in Illinois. It is said that when he relinquished his receivership, an apparent error of three dollars was reported in his accounts. Young Sparks traveled to the national capital by stage, confronted Washington officials, demanded and got a reexamination, and established that his books had been absolutely correct. As commissioner, he assailed timber operators who had been pillaging federal lands. He

131

exposed raids on the California redwood country. He dared to single out big lumber companies and railroads by name. He got permission to use cavalry to tear down illegal fences in Wyoming.

The boldness and zeal Sparks showed in protecting public property stirred up powerful enemies. He was attacked in the press and in Congress. Interior Secretary Lamar supported him up to a point, but then the pressure became too great. Sparks was not a comfortable man to have around. The two men fell out over an action Sparks took against a railroad in Wisconsin. Trumpeting to the last about "gross piracy of public lands," Sparks had to resign.[5]

It is seldom that a public official has spoken with the candor that invigorated Sparks's 1885 report. He quoted one of his inspectors, A. R. Greene, as follows:

> The idea prevails to an almost universal extent that, because the government in its generosity has provided for the donation of the public domain to its citizens, a strict compliance with the conditions imposed is not essential. Men who would scorn to commit a dishonest act toward an individual, though he were a total stranger, eagerly listen to every scheme for evading the letter and spirit of the settlement laws, and in a majority of instances I believe avail themselves of them.
>
> Our land officers partake of this feeling in many instances, and if they do not corruptly connive at fraudulent entries, modify their instructions and exceed their discretionary powers.[6]

The first commission called attention to the looting of a federal timber trove that was fast disappearing. It was revealed by the Interior Department in 1888 that American and Scottish interests had acquired 57,000 acres of redwoods in Humboldt County, valued at $11 million, under the Timber and Stone Act. In some instances men from a sailors' boardinghouse had been paid $50 each to make the entries. These outrages were widely known; yet Congress answered the pleas for repeal of the Timber and Stone Act by extending its provisions in 1892 to all of the so-called public lands states. The law remained on the books until 1955.

It was a time in which the West was filling out at a rapid rate. Few wanted to slow down the pace of the expansion or obstruct the federal cornucopia when there seemed to be plenty for all. Despite this, a mood of reform was strong as the nineteenth century ended. Times were hard. There were soup kitchens in the cities and tramps in the country. The Populist party railed against corruption and Wall Street. Conservationists worried about a sickening waste of public timber and minerals.

The second public lands commission was created, not by Congress, but by President Theodore Roosevelt, who in 1902 suggested to Congress that another study was needed and then went ahead with it when he saw no action from Capitol Hill.[7] Roosevelt appointed a panel of three men: General Land Office Commissioner W. A. Richards, the former governor of Wyoming; Frederick H. Newell, a Geological Survey hydraulic engineer later with the Reclamation Service; and Gifford Pinchot, the future head of the Forest Service. Many people were outraged, even in the West, by the rate at which railroads and loggers were accumulating large timber holdings. Commissioner Richards had succeeded Binger Hermann, who got involved with corrupt elements in the Northwest and was fired late in 1902 by Interior Secretary Hitchcock. Hermann's fellow Oregonians promptly elected him to the House of Representatives. The Oregon land scandals, which were notorious, led to the trial and conviction in 1905 of United States Sen. John Mitchell, a Republican.[8]

The Roosevelt commission urged repeal of the Timber and Stone Act, as had the 1879 panel. It also inveighed against the notorious "forest lieu" provision of the Forest Management Act of 1897.[9] As has been noted, forest lieu provided that settlers or owners of land within the newly established forest reserves could give up that land and select, in lieu of it, an equal amount of vacant land elsewhere. Among the chief beneficiaries were the Santa Fe, Northern Pacific, and Southern Pacific railways, which were able to swap worthless mountain or desert tracts for valuable property outside the reserves. Forest lieu was unpopular in the West because it gave outsiders—the railroads, for example—an advantage over local claimants. Congress repealed it in 1905 but provided that exchanges the secretary of the interior had already agreed to could go forward.

The sorry history of the forest reserves under the Interior Department's General Land Office was one reason for the eventual transfer in 1905 of more than eighty-five million acres of federal timberlands to the Agriculture Department, where they became the province of Pinchot's Forest Service. Interior Secretary Hitchcock and his land commissioner, former Governor Richards, favored rather than opposed the transfer to another bureaucracy.

The Roosevelt commission's report to the president in 1904 found little favor in the West. It was substantially ignored by Congress, as the 1879 study had been. It recommended better management and a fee system for federal grazing lands, but another thirty years were to pass before action was taken.

President Herbert Hoover in 1930 brought about the third study of the public lands. The Great Depression had begun to lay waste the country. The Interior Department and the Republicans were still reeking with the brimstone of Teapot Dome. Across the Mall, in the Agriculture Department, the Forest Service was unpopular with ranchers because of its efforts to cut down on the number of animals permitted to graze in forest reserves. President Hoover and his interior secretary, Ray Lyman Wilbur, a friend of the national parks but not of federally managed pasturelands, proposed in 1929 that the unappropriated public domain be ceded to the states. Hoover told Congress that the states were more competent to manage the public lands than the federal government was. "Moreover," said he, "we must seek every opportunity to retard the expansion of

134

federal bureaucracy and to place our communities in control of their own destinies."[10] This was the classic Republican viewpoint, later to be revived during the Carter administration as the Sagebrush Rebellion. As has been observed by historian Paul W. Gates, Hoover's attitude was not very different from that taken a century earlier by John C. Calhoun of South Carolina.[11]

Congress authorized at President Hoover's request the establishment of the Committee on the Conservation and Administration of the Public Domain. The president had been talking about conveying surface rights to the states, not mineral rights. His proposal involved some 190 million acres of unappropriated public domain, along with 10 million withdrawn in 1909 for use as "stock driveways" and 35 million that had been set aside for federal coal and oil shale reserves. Let the lands be managed, it was argued, by those who ran cattle on them. The federal government was incapable. Or, in the words of Hoover, "for the best interest of the people as a whole, and people of the western states and the small farmers and stockmen by whom they are primarily used, they should be managed and the policies for their use determined by state governments."[12]

President Hoover appointed a twenty-two-member commission of which the chairman was James R. Garfield, the son of a president and for two years secretary of the interior during the administration of the first Roosevelt. Secretary Wilbur and Secretary of Agriculture Arthur M. Hyde were members ex officio. Others of note included Commissioner of Reclamation Elwood Mead, former Chief Forester William B. Greeley, former Sen. H. O. Bursum of New Mexico, and several well-known editors and writers—Gardner Cowles of the *Des Moines Register*, George Horace Lorimer of the *Saturday Evening Post*, and Mary Roberts Rinehart, novelist.

In its report of 1931 the Garfield commission took a position in many respects consistent with the conservationist viewpoint.[13] All lands should be properly and responsibly managed and regulated. The federal government should keep portions valuable for national parks, national forests, wildlife refuges, military purposes, reclamation projects, and the like. Federal agricultural and grazing lands, however, eventually should wind up in private ownership. Meanwhile, that part of the public domain suitable for grazing should be granted to states, with mineral rights remaining in the federal government until states had a mineral program matching the federal one. State boards were to look over the federal forest lands to decide what might be added to the national forests and what should be sliced away and added to the vulnerable public domain.

It turned out that the western states did not particularly covet the unappropriated public lands—presumably the least desirable, inasmuch as nobody had claimed or reserved them—without the minerals. This was "getting the lid without the bucket," one governor said. There was objection from Pinchot and others to the proposition of reopening for state-level review the forest lands already set aside. Strong sentiment was expressed for federal retention and management of the grazing lands. Hoover's confidence in state control was not always shared by those familiar with it.

The Garfield commission recommendations got a bad press. The magazines denounced them as a giveaway, a retreat.[14] The prices for livestock dropped by one-half in the early 1930s. Over the great plains a withering drought was about to set in with devastating effect. Dust Bowl days were just ahead. In retrospect, it was not a time for cutting the federal umbilical cord, but the commission's report served to call attention to the need for a national decision. In the depression years Congress passed the Taylor Act of 1934, thereby organizing 147 million acres of publicly owned grazing lands into grazing districts under management of the Interior Department's Grazing Service.[15]

At the end of World War II, the Grazing Service was at a low ebb, its appropriations cut to the bone, and the old General Land Office was overwhelmed with paper work and tenanted by political hacks. President Truman issued a reorganization plan in

1946 consolidating the two weaklings to form the Bureau of Land Management. It was widely depicted as a shotgun wedding carried out at the insistence of triumphant cattle and sheep lobbies. These in turn were being eviscerated in public debate by a Harvard historian and western conservationist who knew them well, Bernard DeVoto of *Harper's Magazine*.[16]

Secretary of the Interior Julius A. Krug estimated at the time of the consolidation that forty-six million acres of the public range were in critically bad shape, all but destroyed by erosion and overgrazing. After passage of another quarter century, BLM directors were still reporting to Congress that forty-nine million acres were in poor to bad condition. And the BLM was still being starved for money with which to care for the lands and restore the range, just as in the past.

Before taking up the fourth and last of the great public lands studies, which was instituted under President Johnson and produced its report in President Nixon's first term, let us digress a moment to discuss the Bureau of Land Management as it developed after the Truman merger. The BLM, be it remembered, has responsibility for 60 percent of federal holdings. Its directors, little known to the public though they may be, are lords of a tremendous domain.

Marion Clawson, who served as BLM director in the period from 1948 to 1953, observed in his 1971 book *The Bureau of Land Management* that the old General Land Office had gone stagnant by the turn of the century. He recalled that the dashing Pinchot had worked a short time for the GLO but had found it hopelessly riddled, in Pinchot's view, with politics, ineptitude, and corruption. Subsequently Pinchot went to the Agriculture Department, and so did the forest reserves, previously under the GLO. Clawson wondered, somewhat wistfully, how things might have turned out if Pinchot had elected to stick with the Land Office and try to reform it.[17]

"It now seems obvious," Clawson wrote, "that the General Land Office simply missed the boat, that it was unable to understand the nature of the social, economic and political changes taking place in the country as the frontier disappeared and industrialization took hold."[18]

Thus the GLO went through several sleepy, moribund decades before Truman merged it with the Grazing Service in 1946. Although it had lost more than 150 million acres to the Forest Service, it brought to the wedding a timber dowry in the form of the "O & C" lands in Oregon—2.6 million acres of rich, productive logging country. This was what remained of a grant made to the Oregon and California Railroad in 1866, taken over subsequently by the Southern Pacific and then much later, after a long court battle, recovered by the federal government. In 1916, when the Forest Service had fallen into disfavor, Congress gave jurisdiction over the revested lands to the Interior Department.

At the time of the merger, the General Land Office and Grazing Service had 695 employees, 330 of whom were in Washington, D.C., and the others in field offices. In the next quarter century the total work force grew more than fivefold, while the Washington staff was reduced to 286. Although clearly not able to lift the tremendous burdens heaped upon it, the BLM has shown steady improvement as a professional organization. Clawson said in his book that when he came aboard in 1948, after working elsewhere in the Interior Department and in the Department of Agriculture, the fledgling BLM had only one person holding a doctoral degree. "Today it has several," he wrote in 1971. The BLM was not politicized to any great extent—not, at least, until the second Nixon administration—and that fact had both advantages and disadvantages in the highly political Washington environment.

BLM directors, named without fanfare by the secretary of the interior, have tended to be good, honest, substantial men, career officers who cut little ice in the big city on the Potomac. Fred W. Johnson, last of a long line of general commissioners, was the first director. Johnson was ailing and getting along in years. He was soon succeeded by Clawson, whom Secretary Krug brought in from BLM's regional directorship in California despite opposition by Sen. Sheridan Downey of that state. Clawson, a Nevadan, held a Harvard Ph.D. in economics.

Worth a note, in passing, is that Clawson himself was summarily ousted in 1953 by President Eisenhower's secretary of the interior, former Gov. Douglas McKay of Oregon, a prosperous automobile dealer. "He called me in one afternoon and said he wanted to have his own man in," Clawson recalled many years later, without regret.[19] Clawson, a Democrat but not an active one, said he inquired at the time whether McKay had a substantive reason for the dismissal, but "he didn't have any policy—no convictions." There was a job outside the federal bureaucracy waiting for Clawson, who wound up in Resources for the Future, but he nevertheless kicked up a row about politics in government. He was told that the protest he had made might have saved the necks of others, since Sherman Adams, Eisenhower's assistant, had passed word down to let up on political appointments.

There was at the time an unfortunate attitude toward career personnel, Clawson indicated in an interview, not only in the Interior Department under McKay but also in the Agriculture Department, under Secretary Ezra Taft Benson, who leaned toward the philosophy of the ultraconservative John Birch Society. Benson, Clawson recalled, had gone so far as to call agriculture personnel together and tell them, as Clawson recalled it, "From now on, you're going to have to do an honest day's work for your wages." Benson was "a damned fool to say that," in Clawson's opinion. As for Secretary McKay, to whom Clawson said he was grateful in retrospect for propelling him toward a fine career, the ousted BLM director stated, "I always felt McKay was small caliber, but not vicious at all."[20]

Clawson was followed in the federal post by a noncareer man, Edward Woozley, who headed the BLM during the Eisenhower administration, from 1953 to 1961. It was under

139

Woozley, a former land commissioner for the state of Idaho, that the agency was given the task of handling oil and natural gas leases on the Outer Continental Shelf. In the year he assumed office, Congress made good on Eisenhower's campaign promise to turn the so-called tidelands over to coastal states and asserted federal jurisdiction over submerged lands farther seaward. Offshore oil became a rich and splendid federal province, developing rapidly after 1947, but none of the glitter rubbed off on the BLM. Like an underpaid bank teller with a patch on his pants, that agency raked in the billions and passed them along, going home to a crying wife, a bare cupboard, and a bowl of soup.

BLM Director Woozley, at times forced to run his bureau without much guidance from or contact with the interior secretary's office, yielded to Karl S. Landstrom, a career public servant who headed the BLM during most of the Kennedy administration. A professional forester, Charles H. Stoddard, was director from June 1963 to June 1966. Stoddard, outspoken by BLM standards, ran afoul of lumber barons and politicians during a controversy over a land swap involving BLM acreage in Oregon. Dynamic and brilliant but impatient, he showed a flash of the spirit that had animated Land Commissioner Sparks in the nineteenth century and was, like Sparks, eased out. He was succeeded by Boyd L. Rasmussen, Udall's choice and the first United States Forest Service veteran ever to become BLM director. Rasmussen served for five years, three under President Johnson and two under President Nixon. He resisted political intrusion, named key men to major posts, and fought despoiling of the public lands by mining and other user interests. He was willing to battle, but he chose his ground carefully.

Leaving Director Rasmussen precariously *in situ* under Nixon, we must return to the fourth of the land-law reviews. This had its origins, performed its considerable labors, and made its report during the tenures of Stoddard and Rasmussen. In large part, it was the fate of the BLM land that was at stake.

Great changes in public attitudes had taken place. Decisions that had been put off had to be made. Congress realized this. Under the Taylor Grazing Act of 1934, the future Bureau of Land Management had received limited authority for classification of land for various purposes. Congress in 1960 approved a landmark law called the Multiple Use and Sustained Yield Act, ordaining that the national forests were to be administered "for outdoor recreation, range, timber, watershed, and wildlife and fish purposes."[21] Four years later, during the Johnson administration, the Classification and Multiple Use Act of 1964 greatly extended the BLM's authority.[22] Basically, the intent was for the bureau to look over its holdings and either classify them as suitable for retention in federal hands under the multiple-use concept, like the national forests, or else dispose of them. The law's thrust was to recognize the BLM's right to manage lands for recreation and other uses for which the past gave no clear mandate.

In September 1964, with President Johnson in office, Congress passed an act establishing the Public Land Law Review Commission—a body destined to be called "Plerk" for short.[23] Wayne Aspinall demanded the review as his price for withdrawing his opposition to the wilderness bill, also approved that year.

The act declared it to be Congress's policy that public lands of the nation "shall be (*a*) retained and managed or (*b*) disposed of, all in a manner to provide the maximum benefit for the general public." By "public lands" was meant all the federally owned lands except Indian reservations.

"Because the public land laws of the United States," said the commission's organic act, "have developed over a long period of years through a series of Acts of Congress which are not fully correlated with each other and because these laws, or some of them, may be inadequate to meet the current and future needs of the American people and because administration of the public lands and the laws relating thereto has been divided among several agencies of the Federal Government, it is necessary to have a comprehensive review."

141

This was a broad assignment. To carry it out, Congress established a nineteen-member commission of bipartisan character. It was to consist of three Democrats and three Republicans from both the Senate and House interior committees—a total of twelve from the legislative branch—and another six to be appointed by the president. The nineteenth member was to be the chairman, elected by a majority of the other eighteen.

Aspinall, a Democrat from western Colorado, in Congress since 1948 and long chairman of the House Interior Committee, was elected to head the commission at its organization meeting in July 1965. He had a reputation for being honest, hardworking, and intelligent, but biased toward exploiters of the public lands. Conservationists regarded him as hostile to their objectives. For vice chairman, the commission picked H. Byron Mock, one of the six members appointed by President Johnson. Mock, a Salt Lake City lawyer well versed in the mining, timber, and range-management fields, had been chief counsel of the Grazing Service and later a regional director of the BLM.

The other presidential appointees were Robert Emmet Clark, professor of law at the University of Arizona, Tucson; Maurice K. Goddard, secretary of Forests and Waters, Harrisburg, Pennsylvania; former Gov. Philip H. Hoff of Vermont; Laurance S. Rockefeller, chairman of the Rockefeller Brothers Fund, New York; and Nancy E. Smith, a supervisor of San Bernardino County in California, replacing Mrs. John Glessner Lee of Connecticut, who resigned.

Of the thirteen members of Congress on the commission, including Chairman Aspinall, all six senators and four of the seven House delegates were from the western public-lands states. This gave the body a tilt toward the setting sun which persisted throughout its deliberations.

The authorizing act provided for an "advisory council" composed of federal liaison members from nine departments and agencies and twenty-five nonfederal members appointed by the commission itself. In addition, the chairman was to invite the governor of each state to designate a representative to work in shaping the project.

In the federal government, advisory councils are as numerous as Cadwallader's goats in ancient Britain. The concept is pervasive. The first such council, it is said, was appointed by President Washington to help him deal with the Whiskey Rebellion. There is much to be said for advisory councils as a means of enlarging public participation in government, but the device can be abused in ways that advance the cause of special pleaders and frustrate the public interest. In the 1970s, Sen. Lee Metcalf, Montana Democrat, was successful in a battle aimed at bringing about reforms.[24]

The Aspinall commission's nonfederal advisors, twenty-five in all, formed a body in which the industrial and agricultural user groups—mining, livestock, timber, agriculture, oil—had a good deal more than a majority. Most members were from the West. They included such stalwarts as W. Howard Gray of Reno, Nevada, a specialist in public land law and chairman of the Public Lands Committee, American Mining Congress; H. A. True, Jr., of Casper, Wyoming, chief executive officer of True Oil Company and chairman of the Interior Department's National Petroleum Council; Bernard L. Orell, vice president of Weyerhaeuser Company, Tacoma, Washington; and others of similar backgrounds. Conservationists could take comfort from the fact that C. R. ("Pink") Gutermuth, vice president of the Wildlife Management Institute at Washington, D.C., was on the council.

As Aspinall noted, his commission's activities represented the first time Congress and persons appointed by the president had sat down together in a common effort to "study, deliberate and decide" what the land laws should be. He himself had introduced the authorizing legislation, modeling it after a bill setting up an earlier study group called the Outdoor Recreation Resources Review Commission.

Aspinall firmly believed that Congress, not the executive branch, should make policy. The thrust of land laws enacted

143

through the early 1960s, he said, "was aimed at placing the land and its resources in the hands of the individual citizen, or in any case divesting the federal title.

"Now the geographic frontier is gone. . . . We are a different nation and a different people. The era during our economic, social and political maturation when most of our public land laws were enacted is gone, as are the primary purposes for which they were enacted."

The commission held a planning meeting at Camp Hoover in the Shenandoah National Park in the spring of 1966, established offices on K Street, and hired a staff that totaled no more than forty-eight at any given time. The staff director was the late Milton A. Pearl, who had been assistant to Aspinall on the House Interior Committee. Under the law as originally written, the commission was to have submitted its report by the end of 1968, but the work was slow in getting started, and many difficult problems had to be talked over, many an old ghost laid to rest.

Congress extended the deadline to June 30, 1970, and increased the commission's funds from $4 million to $7.39 million. In a way, the six-year period of the Aspinall study served as a stall, a device for putting off action. Nothing important relating to the public lands should be done, some argued, until the commission had made its report. Much of the impetus for the study had been generated by efforts of conservationists in the 1950s and early 1960s to set aside large tracts of wild, remote, and unspoiled country—already in federal ownership in national parks, forests, wildlife refuges, and the public domain itself—to be designated as "wilderness" and left alone.

Aspinall was for years the rock on which the wilderness movement broke its lance. He did not favor locking up the lands, particularly their mineral resources. To do so, he argued, was exalting one use of the land above others. The Wilderness Act of 1964 finally was approved, but only after its sponsors had agreed to leave areas classified as wilderness subject to federal mining and leasing laws through 1983.[25]

The reputation of Aspinall as an earnest, sharp, hard-minded westerner, who thought that what God had put into the earth should be taken out by man, was well known to conservationists, who had been fighting him for years. This and the obvious dominance on the commission of western "user" interests led to a widespread and not altogether well-founded assumption that the group might advocate a blatant giveaway of the lands. The press left the commission to its labors, most of which were too complicated to explain in brief space. The commission did some traveling in the West and in various ways got the views of more than 900 witnesses. It asked Paul Wallace Gates of Cornell University to write his *History of Public Land Law Development*, an immensely valuable 828-page book that contains a chapter on mineral law development by Robert W. Swenson of the University of Utah. Other studies that were commissioned covered thirty-three subjects. As might be expected, some of the research material was excellent, some of small merit.

It was Aspinall's show from first to last. His martinet approach, keen interest, and familiarity with the subject matter kept the commission moving. Aspinall's opposite number in the Senate, Chairman Henry M. Jackson of what was then the Interior Committee, was a commissioner but did not like to tangle with Aspinall. Jackson attended few meetings. Other congressional members often failed to show up.

At long last, the neat, 342-page green and yellow report, rich with charts and maps and illustrations, was made public on June 23, 1970. Aspinall introduced it at a news conference held, very appropriately, in the main hearing room of the historic old Cannon House Office Building on Capitol Hill.

All in all, *One Third of the Nation's Land* is an intelligent, well-organized document that deserved more attention than it received. It recognized at the outset that the nation was not going to get rid of its remaining land heritage—that is, any substantial part of it. This amounted to adoption of a new, more positive approach in which uncertainty was removed, and the government could move more confidently to take care of what re-

145

mained. The commission also recommended, as a guide for future policy, that the United States ought to get full value for the use of the public lands and their resources, except that full "market value" need not be charged where there was no consumptive use. The commission recommended fair market value as the basis for grazing fees.

The Aspinall commission departed from righteousness, however, in some of the report's fine print. It failed to take a firm stand against the rampant abuses permitted by the 1872 Mining Law, a statute that had allowed miners to rip and strip the public domain for a century and take away what they found. It recommended wholesale "review" of the unappropriated public domain, and of lands withdrawn by executive action rather than by Congress, to determine what their fate should be. It urged further hog-tying of federal land managers. It held that the oilman, the miner, the logger, and even the rancher should pay for benefits, but urged steps to smooth the way for these entrepreneurs and rid them of pesky bureaucrats. Although the industry lobbyists and land lawyers had not carried all before them, it was clear they had gotten in their licks.

Chairman Aspinall did not want his report cluttered up with minority views. He avoided them by striving for a broad general agreement, making concessions to the progressives, knocking heads together among the Neanderthals a time or two, and calling the findings a "consensus report."[26] As Aspinall said in his cover letter to President Nixon, "the absence of a member's separate views does not necessarily indicate that there is unanimity on the details." Nevertheless, in a few instances separate views were appended to the report as footnotes. Commissioner Clark, a western legal scholar of broad gauge and liberal bent, marred the smooth flow of Aspinall's text with three caveats. In one of them he was joined by Commissioners Goddard, Hoff, and Morris K. Udall.

Firstly, right at the beginning, Clark could not swallow in its entirety a commission generality to the effect that areas set aside by executive action for national forests, national monuments, and other purposes had been run through without adequate study and consultation, whereas those anointed by Congress were the product of careful consideration and wisdom. The fact is that little would remain today of the more valuable federal reservations had not various presidents, at various times, intervened to save them. Clark demurred mildly, suggesting that "this report must be read against nearly 200 years of history and no doubt a nongovernment report would contain similar inferences that would emphasize perhaps disproportionately the past inaction, delays, and piecemeal approach of Congress."[27]

The second Clark dissent, with which Goddard, Hoff, and Udall were associated, came when the commission recommended what the four described as "only minor surgery" on the frequently denounced but durable old Mining Law. The dissenters recommended that the distinction between "locatable" hardrock minerals, like gold or silver or copper, and "leaseable" minerals, like oil, be wiped out. It would be preferable, they said, to have a general leasing system for all minerals except those designated by law for outright sale. Clark, Goddard, and Hoff also advocated the abolition of all noncompetitive leasing, whereas the report hedged a bit by recommending competitive sale "whenever competitive interest can reasonably be expected."

Finally, Clark disagreed with the commission's finding that there is no reason why land bought up by the federal government because of its run-down and eroded condition should not be restored to farming. Modern soil conservation programs, the commission said, will be insurance against a repeat of the 1930s Dust Bowl. Clark favored letting marginal lands alone, for the same reasons that caused the government to acquire them. Following the 1970 report, under pressure of a world grain shortage, millions of acres of American farmland that had been set aside were put back under the plow.

The minority view that Clark considered most important was the one on the old Mining Law. On April 8, 1970, a few weeks

147

before the report was wrapped up, Clark circulated among most commission members his proposed dissenting statement, urging a leasing system for all minerals.[28] Under leasing, it should be pointed out, the United States does not surrender ownership and is able to insist on decent care for the land. In contrast, as we have seen, the old Mining Law does involve transfer of ownership and fosters a situation in which the government has little if any leverage.

Clark felt so strongly about the 1872 law and its shortcomings that he went to the offices of several members of Congress who were commission members. Rep. Morris K. Udall, Arizona Democrat and brother of the former secretary of the interior, was the only one who joined forces with Clark. In his missionary work on Capitol Hill, Clark learned for the first time that there was to be no disagreement with Chairman Aspinall. He was keenly disappointed that Rep. Saylor of Pennsylvania, an ardent conservationist and the ranking Republican on the House Interior Committee, turned him down, as did another easterner, Rep. Roy A. Taylor, a Democrat from North Carolina. A third disappointment was presidential appointee Laurance Rockefeller, who was not in politics and had nothing much to lose.

Aspinall, although he came from a mining constituency and reflected the traditional miner's viewpoint, had become convinced that the hard-rock miners were going to have to pay the government a royalty on minerals extracted. He told them so, flatly and bluntly, as was his custom. The largess allowed by the old law, under which an immense treasure of valuable metals like copper and silver had been carted away from the public domain without payment, could not go on forever. In this respect at least, Aspinall's consensus report did turn its back on the American Mining Congress. It recommended that a royalty be paid on mineral production from the public lands.

Clark, a close friend of Stewart L. Udall and of the Democratic Sen. Clinton P. Anderson of New Mexico, another commissioner, got along very well with Aspinall, whom he respected as

148

an honest, able man whose attitude might have been different had he not represented a mining district. "There's nothing wrong with his head," Clark once said. Clark made no secret, however, of his chagrin that members of Congress who had no problem of ties to the West "did not have the courtesy or the guts" to tell him to his face that they would not support his statement on leasing until it was too late for him to do much about it.[29]

In addition to its reluctance to scrap the old Mining Law, another thing that got the commission into trouble with conservationists was its fiddling with the multiple-use concept. It will be remembered that this concept had come to the fore when Congress, in 1960 and 1964, provided authority for multiple-use management of lands set aside or classified for retention in federal hands. As a practical matter, the land was to be open to various compatible uses. In a forest, for example, campers and bird–watchers were to be accommodated as well as loggers.

Aspinall's report paid homage to the multiple-use philosophy, discussing it in a thoughtful and perceptive way, but recommended that the "highest and best" use of particular areas should be recognized as "dominant" over others in the management of public lands. The commission proposed a general preference for mineral exploration and development, a dominant role for grazing on federal pasturelands, and, with particular and ominous emphasis, a dominant role for logging on public lands that are large producers of timber. Highly productive areas in the national forests and on BLM lands, said the commission, should be classified for timber production and put under a separate management.

These recommendations reflected an exploitative, cash-register attitude toward the public lands. They came at a time when environmentalists were up in arms over mining in scenic areas and oil spills offshore, and at a time when the Forest Service was under heavy fire for clear-cutting and overly zealous logging. They overshadowed, as Aspinall might well have feared, a number of constructive and forward-looking proposals in the report which were more to the liking of conservationists.

Another deeply troubling aspect of the report was its insistence that Congress ought to undertake a new and careful review of all executive branch withdrawals and reservations of public lands made in the past and, furthermore, all of the BLM retention and disposal classifications under the Classification and Multiple Use Act of 1964. The purpose was to "free" the public lands of encumbrances that might bar effective planning in the future. The commission suggested that the review could be accomplished in ten years. It therefore proposed that all existing withdrawals terminate after that period of time.

"Recent criticism of withdrawal policies has come primarily from economic user groups, such as the timber and mining industries," the commission noted, "since many withdrawals curtail economic uses of the public lands to favor recreation or noneconomic values."[30]

To the conservationist, the proposal for congressional review meant that many an ancient battle of the dim past might have to be refought. The thrust of the conservationist movement as it relates to the public lands, be it understood, has been to try to erect safeguards around them, fending off private interests that want to exploit. The thrust of commercial and economic pressures is to tear down the safeguards so that the lands will be accessible.

One Third of the Nation's Land and other major works of the commission received a searching and critical, sometimes caustic, analysis in a volume published the same year—1970—by the Natural Resources Council of America, a private, nonprofit group of national and regional organizations having to do with conservation of natural resources and the environment.[31] The book was dedicated to Gutermuth.

Hamilton K. Pyles, former deputy chief of the Forest Service, coordinated the Council's project. He said many of the report's recommendations were excellent but lamented an "obsession with economic factors." The judgment of Lynton K. Caldwell of

150

Indiana University, an architect of environmental laws, was that the report was on the whole better than its critics might have realistically expected.

As had been the case with the three earlier reviews, the Aspinall commission's work had no immediate cataclysmic effects. Congress was in no hurry to do the commission's bidding. For the BLM, however, the report was followed by a steady progression toward permanent status.

Rasmussen's departure after surviving two years of a new Republican administration made way for the seventh BLM director, Burton W. Silcock, who had been the agency's Alaska state director since 1965. Silcock, like Rasmussen, originally came from Idaho. He had been with the BLM since 1948. In Alaska, where he had responsibility for two-thirds of that immense state's land area, he had been cited for a fire-fighting plan—fighting fires in wild, remote forest areas was a major BLM function—and for preparing the Interior Department's "stipulations" to be imposed on the oil industry combine that wanted to construct the trans-Alaska pipeline. The ill-fated Secretary Hickel had wanted to bring Silcock to Washington, but Hickel was out of the cabinet before Silcock got the appointment.

It was predictable that Silcock would not be entirely happy or at home in the high-octane political environment of the national capital. Sincere, quiet, slow of speech, he took his assignment very seriously and showed marked compassion for and kindness to people. He lacked force as an administrator. One could not imagine Silcock, an outdoorsman who liked bird-watching and canoeing on the Yukon, and a person to whom his church—the Mormon church—was very important, stooping to any kind of petty backbiting or unseemly maneuvering. On the other hand, as a good BLM soldier, he was unlikely to embarrass his superiors by trying to lead charges toward goals they did not support. He made no splash in Washington.

When Silcock was sworn in as BLM director in the Interior Department auditorium on a hot summer day in 1971, Secretary Morton commiserated gracefully with him and his family at the

151

climatic adjustment they would have to make, being newcomers
from Alaska. Morton hailed the professional tradition of the bureau and saw a new day at hand for the public lands, which he
thought should be managed properly. "There is a demand—and
rightfully so—that these lands in a true sense of the word be
public lands," Morton said.

The reality was that the BLM would need, if it were to do a
good job, about three times as much money as was likely to be
made available. In the absence of a significant escalation in financial support, rhetoric was not much help. It is true that the
bureau's annual appropriation for management of lands and resources had doubled from 1962 to the time Silcock assumed the
directorship, moving from $33,350,000 for fiscal 1962 to $66,235,-
000 a decade later. Even so, what Congress was allowing Silcock
for looking after his immense fief was not much more than it
provided for running the Smithsonian Institution.

The ante for the BLM continued moving up in the 1970s, but
the emphasis was on energy—getting out the oil, getting out the
minerals. There was intense and growing recreational pressure
on BLM lands, but not until 1965 was the bureau able, with the
help of sympathetic members of Congress, to get an initial appropriation of $750,000 to build "sanitary and protection" facili-
ties. Until then the bureau had no means of dealing with tourists or cleaning up after them. It invented a symbolic evangelist
in jeans and broad-brimmed hat, called Johnny Horizon, who
dispensed litter bags and admonished people sternly: "This is
your land, keep it clean." With the public use of BLM lands
climbing past fifty million visitor days a year, however, the bureau needed more than a symbol and a slogan.

By the turn of the decade of the 1970s, the BLM's budget request for fiscal 1980 had climbed to a more respectable figure—
close to $500,000,000 exclusive of permanent appropriations—
but it is relevant to recall that when Director Silcock appeared
before the House Appropriations Subcommittee in March 1973,
he was allowed to request a total of less than $123,000,000, an

increase of $13,379,000 over the previous year.[32] He asked for an additional 254 permanent jobs, moving from 3,916 to 4,170. These were picayune increases, considering the backlog of work and the encouraging eloquence of Secretary Morton. More than half the additional money—$7,400,000—was to be spent for surveillance and monitoring of the trans-Alaska pipeline, an industry project. Most of the rest was for Alaska native claims, the Outer Continental Shelf leasing chore, and other energy-related functions. Only $363,000 of the increase was for range management, bringing the total sought for that purpose to $7,226,000— an item so small that it could be lost in the defense budget. Silcock asked an increase of $300,000 for protection of wild horses and burros on the public lands and an equal amount for dealing with the problem of off-road vehicles, estimated at some four million motorcycles, dune buggies, snowmobiles, and the like. His total request for "resource management, conservation, and protection" came to $74,662,000, including the energy-related increases mentioned.

The subcommittee, chaired by Julia Butler Hansen of Washington State, needled Silcock about the small size of his budget and the amount of unfinished work that was piling up. It came out that BLM faced the need for completing cadastral surveys— that is, surveys to impose rectangular grids marking off land boundaries and subdivisions on most of the 40 million acres in Alaska involved in native claims and on 160 million acres in the lower forty-eight states. Under questioning, Silcock said the native-claim surveys would be done by 1986 and the rest of Alaska by 1992. Finishing cadastral surveys in the lower forty-eight states would take 350 years, at the prevailing rate. Most of the BLM's recreational lands were not being cared for. Half the grazing range was in only "fair" or worse condition, and half the BLM watersheds and 40 percent of the bureau's wildlife habitat were in less than satisfactory shape.

Rep. Hansen prodded Silcock about the inadequacy of his budget requests. At one point, the director noted that revenue

153

from the sale and lease of resources—oil, forage, timber, and the land itself—had totaled more than $4 billion for 1973. The chairwoman interrupted him, and this exchange occurred:

HANSEN: This is $4 billion off your lands?

SILCOCK: That is off the public lands and OCS [Outer Continental Shelf] in fiscal year 1973.

HANSEN: Your total budget for the management of these leases, and so on, is $122,000,000.

SILCOCK: That is correct, for 1974.

HANSEN: It tells the story right there.[33]

In response, Silcock explained that the budget "has been developed within the context of tight fiscal restraints." That was true, beyond doubt. It was true also that BLM's receipts were swollen during 1973 by court release of $1.1 billion that had been held in escrow pending settlement of a dispute over jurisdictional boundaries with Louisiana. Even so, the estimated receipts for 1974 were more than $2.3 billion, and Hansen's point held good. The contrast between what the BLM was taking in and what was being spent—at a time when the bureau did not have enough personnel to deal with vandalism and litter nor enough money to repair its pastures—was shameful.

When Jack O. Horton was named by Nixon to be assistant secretary of the interior, Silcock was appointed to succeed him as cochairman of the Joint Federal-State Land-Use Planning Commission for Alaska, an agency charged with helping carve that immense state into federal, state, and private parcels. Silcock was happy to return to the north. His confirmation by the Senate in July 1973 triggered an event conservationists had foreseen with considerable dread for some months and had tried to prevent. That was the pending appointment by Secretary Morton of the new BLM director to succeed Silcock, a forty-three-year-old former Idaho lumberman and rancher, Curtis J. Berklund.

Berklund did not qualify, in the conservationist view, as a professional career man experienced in natural resources management. They did not like the look of him. As far back as Feb-

154

ruary, a group of nineteen environmental organizations had sent a telegram to Secretaries Butz and Morton, urging that a careerist from the BLM or the Forest Service be chosen to follow Silcock. Notwithstanding that, Berklund was duly appointed, and Morton said his qualifications were unique. The new director had been a successful logger and stockman in Idaho, where he was a Republican activist, campaign contributor, and protege of conservative Republican Sen. Len B. Jordan of that state.

The appointment of Berklund was termed "tragic, terrible" by Stewart M. Brandborg, then executive director of the Wilderness Society, who saw it as a lapse into the "dinosaur type of thinking" about the public lands, a yielding to pressure from the extractive industries. Nobody could tell for sure, of course, how Berklund would do. Born in Wisconsin, he was graduated from North Park College in Chicago. In his early twenties he suffered a logging accident in Michigan. An open freight car was being loaded, and the collapsible metal side fell inward, crushing his legs. He recovered and went on to manage various interests in Idaho, selling out in 1967. He then visited twenty-two countries, making studies of forestry and range management. With the aid of presidential assistant Peter M. Flanagan, he joined the Interior Department in April 1970 and was assigned to the BLM. He was cited for superior performance as chairman of an Interior Department committee that developed legislative proposals in response to the 1970 report of the Public Land Law Review Commission.

In the BLM directorship, Berklund was quickly caught up in the "energy crisis" that President Nixon proclaimed in the fall of 1973. He teamed up well with Assistant Secretary Horton, the Rhodes scholar from Saddlestring, Wyoming, and other members of the department's Republican elite. He had a dynamic, shrewd, down-to-earth quality that reminded one of former Parks Director George Hartzog. A conservationist who objected to both but liked them, nonetheless, remarked that it was because both were "gutsy guys." Berklund plunged into the expansion of oil leasing offshore, glowed when bids for federal timber and oil shale went up, and undertook, at Morton's bidding, to straighten out and plan the mining of federal coal that awaited the power shovel in the West. He pushed for more money, more people, and the long-awaited BLM organic act from Congress. Privately, he groused about the straitjacket imposed by the all-powerful Office of Management and Budget.

It was time, Berklund said, for the politicians to give the BLM a clear and unequivocal mandate for managing the land, and time for the bureau to receive the money and strength to do it. He proclaimed that the old days when men took what they wanted from the western public domain were gone forever. Conservationists, aware of Berklund's background and the business-oriented configuration of the Nixon Interior Department, remained skeptical.

"Historically," former BLM Director Stoddard wrote of his own stewardship in the 1960s, "BLM had a reputation of being an agency which merely processed requests for use of public land resources with a custodial—not managerial—viewpoint. This was the result of a history of political and economic pressures on decision-making. Strength of administration by BLM directors was usually rewarded by transfers elsewhere or firing. A showing of strength meant controversy and in the Department of the Interior controversy has always been shunned whenever powerful interest groups brought on political pressure."[34]

In the old days of thievery and more or less open fraud, the men in charge of the General Land Office made annual reports in which—if they were brave and independent spirits, as sometimes they were—they pointed to the worst of the abuses. The old-fashioned bureaucrats sat down with pen in hand and wrote their own reports. Some of those reports are worth reading a century after the ink dried. With the decline in the federal land manager's prestige and the assumed decrease in the importance of the leftover lands, the annual report dropped out of use. The

BLM in the 1970s was putting out each year a dry compendium called *Public Land Statistics,* which consisted largely of tabular information innocent of conclusions or philosophy. On those rare occasions when a salvo was fired about a crying evil, it came from the secretary of the interior himself, as when Udall, shortly before leaving office in 1969, damned the 1872 Mining Law as a giveaway.

The BLM directorship pattern came to be that of an honest broker, doggedly professional, doing the best he could and running his loosely held and well-nigh limitless fief with what he had. He was at the north end of the Interior Building, distant from the real seats of power, which are at the south. When he got off the elevator, he passed two handsome murals by John Steuart Curry—one of the 1889 Oklahoma land rush, the other a quiet, somber depiction of a homesteader in a Union army–style military kepi building a fence while his wife sits demurely in front of their sod prairie hut, peeling vegetables. The director thus had history and tradition behind him, but he had no real constituency. He was not known to the public. It was easy to go over him or around him.

The BLM finally got its organic act, though, late in 1976, when Congress approved a landmark piece of legislation called the Federal Land Policy and Management Act.[35] There had been some narrow escapes, but in general conservationists were able to beat back the efforts of promining and prograzing lobbyists to shape the bill. The new law gave the BLM a mission and poured some concrete around the Aspinall commission's conclusion that the United States would hold onto its public lands. It enhanced the BLM's status a bit by providing that the director would henceforth be appointed by the president, with the advice and consent of the Senate.

Not until January 1978, more than a year after the law was passed, did President Carter appoint a successor to Berklund. The nominee, quickly confirmed, was Frank Gregg, a Coloradoan and former Izaak Walton League official who had served for ten years as chairman of the New England Basins Commission. Gregg, a former combat infantryman and a fishing and skiing enthusiast, also had been vice president of the Conservation Foundation. His credentials as a conservationist were excellent. He impressed people as pleasant, serious, intelligent.

A pragmatist, Gregg quickly embraced the efforts in Congress to provide more money for care of the western range. He also encouraged a tendency for stockmen to get together with conservationists and sportsmen and other users to improve range conditions. He had little patience with the so-called Sagebrush Rebellion against federal ownership.

"Most of these lands remained in federal ownership for a damned good reason," he pointed out in a 1979 interview. "They remained in federal ownership because they were not economically attractive for homesteading. . . . The notion they would be a bonanza in state or private ownership is simply not true."

As a boy in Colorado, Gregg said, he shared the view out there that the West had been raped by the East, and he had been bitter about it. "There is a feeling that the West was left with little but ghost towns and abandoned mines, while people elsewhere made the money," he explained. Later, he came to feel strongly that good management of federal lands in federal ownership offers the best chance of preserving the special character of the American West.[36]

Gregg did not say so, but one of the things that assisted in the rape of the West was the Mining Law of 1872. Unfortunately, the new BLM organic act specifically left this law in place, although it eliminated some glaring abuses. We shall look now at the Mining Law and its consequences.

American Flats Country, west of Lake City, Colorado, contains mountains rising up to 14,000 feet. On the border between public lands and Uncompadre National Forest, BLM is developing a vast recreation complex. *Courtesy Bureau of Land Management.*

CHAPTER 7

THE BOWELS OF THE EARTH

The Nation benefits by discovery of previously unknown mineral resources which will supply its expanding economy. A royalty-free title to these buried deposits is small enough reward to those who spend huge amounts of capital in discovering and developing them.

— Statement on behalf of the American Mining Congress, 1968

Finally, the mining law is a blatant give-away of resources that should be managed in the long-term national interest.

— Interior Secretary STEWART L. UDALL, January 15, 1969

Let's not deprive the little man of his right to come in and reap the fruit of something he has discovered. It is not right or equitable for the little man to be so severely penalized.

— EDWARD H. PEPLOW, executive secretary, Arizona Mining Association, 1971

A gainst the general background already sketched in, we should now be ready to look in some detail at the major economic uses to which the public lands have been put—mining, the extraction of various fuels for energy, timber production, and grazing. As we deal with these subjects individually in the next series of chapters, we shall see that each major use has a colorful history of its own.

We shall also see, at the expense of considerable repetition, that these histories have strong similarities. Almost invariably, the forces at work are the same. There is always the tension between development and conservation, between the private interest and the public interest, between the local viewpoint and the national viewpoint, and between present and future needs. Let us begin by taking a longer glance at mining.

For more than a century, the hard-rock miner in his individual and corporate manifestations has enjoyed special privileges on the public lands. In early times, in the day of the pick-and-shovel prospector, those privileges made more sense than they do now. The modern mining industry and its allies on Capitol Hill and in the government guard those privileges jealously. So effectively was the status quo defended that at the end of the 1970s, after ten years of public outcry, the special status accorded to mining was essentially unchanged. It still created a vulnerability that hampered the national effort to preserve wilderness and parkland values in what remained of the public lands in Alaska and elsewhere.

Those who dig the hard rock for gold and silver and copper and molybdenum have traveled a different road from those who extract oil, coal, and natural gas. They are the beneficiaries of the General Mining Law of 1872, a congeries of makeshift statutes that reached fruition in the same year that Congress established Yellowstone National Park.[1]

That body of law, which we have already mentioned disapprovingly, invited citizens and those who had applied for citizenship, in the words of former Interior Department Solicitor

161

Frank J. Barry, Jr., "to go upon the lands of the United States and help themselves to any valuable minerals they find thereon."[2] The invitation blessed the wanderings of the grizzled prospector with his burro a century ago, just as in the 1970s it smiled upon the activities of giant corporations like Anaconda, Kennecott, Phelps Dodge, and AMAX, as well as the treasure hunting of other entrepreneurs, large and small. There has been little substantial change, although some erosion has taken place.

Solicitor Barry became mightily vexed with the Mining Law while serving under the Democrats with Interior Secretary Stewart L. Udall, who had been his law partner in Tucson. Udall, although he came from a state where copper was king, also grieved under the law's burdens, so much so that he fired a memorable Parthian shot at it as the Republicans assumed office early in 1969. He called it a blatant giveaway.

"This outmoded law," Secretary Udall wrote to Aspinall's Public Land Law Review Commission, "has become the major obstacle to the wise conservation and effective management of the natural resources of our public lands."[3]

As we know, the Aspinall commission viewed the old law in a more friendly light. The miner was not to be deprived of his ancient dispensation easily. He was unlikely to give up without a struggle a preferred status that was comparable, let us say, to that of an elite patron who has the right to enter a restaurant, go around the waiting line, pick his own table, demand service, and leave without paying the check.

This was in contrast to the situation of another prime customer on the public lands, the oil industry, which had been placed under a degree of constraint by the Mineral Leasing Act of 1920. Oil became a "leasable" mineral, as distinct from "locatable" minerals, like gold or copper. Thenceforth oil, coal, phosphate, sodium, oil shale, gas, and certain other substances could be taken off the public lands only by lease from the federal government, with payment of rent or royalty. Not so in the case of the "locatable" minerals. The hard-rock miner remained pos-

162

sessed of the right to enter and search, stake his claim, and take his findings for nothing. If he could prove a valuable discovery, one that would reward the efforts of a "prudent man"—to quote the legalese—he might apply for and obtain a patent, thus acquiring full ownership of the land at nominal cost.

Keep in mind that we are talking here mainly about the "unappropriated" public lands, such as those administered by the Bureau of Land Management. The miner's entry to federal lands "reserved" for various purposes may be barred or limited, in varying degrees.

There is an engaging, nostalgic, primitive American quality to the mining industry's response to the attacks lately made upon it and upon its law. Perhaps because of the star boarder's privileges they long enjoyed, or the tough world in which they lived, the mining captains lagged behind their oil colleagues in getting into the twentieth century. Their public relations are not as smooth, sophisticated, and dainty as oil's, and they are still inclined to roar and complain when prodded. They can be self-righteous.

J. Allen Overton, Jr., president of the American Mining Congress, put moral overtones into his industry's struggle. A West Virginian formerly with the Commerce Department, he has an evangelical style of speaking. It led him to soaring heights in a July 1971 address to the Idaho Mining Association at Coeur d'Alene, at a time when his industry was vexed by the environmentalists. He fretted about the attack in Congress on surface mining. The mining industry, as he saw it, was fighting for its life against twin dragons of the 1970s—"Their names are EVIL and MISREPRESENTATION."

Overton objected, he said, not to Americans who had sincere and honest differences with the mining industry, but to those who were "radicalizing the environmental movement." These he saw as a different breed. He pointed to a satanic, adroitly managed attempt to cause the American pattern of life to "degenerate into the purposeless pottage that Karl Marx and Frederick Engels declared it to be." National interest must be put above selfish interest, he said, and principles above popularity.

"Above all," he told the miners of Idaho, "we need God as the directing force of our society and our politics, our schools, our mining operations and in our factories. I can assure you that the top officers of the mining industry hold a common abiding principle purpose for their companies: To be good stewards of the riches of creation and to endeavor to neither selfishly waste nor wantonly destroy the handiwork of our Creator."[4]

At its convention in Las Vegas that fall—doubtless an uncomfortable locale for such stalwart defenders of the faith—the American Mining Congress heard as usual from a broad assortment of members of Congress and from the flower of the Interior Department's officialdom. The meeting resoundingly endorsed a bill called the Mineral Development Act of 1971, introduced by Aspinall in the House and by Alan Bible, Nevada Democrat, in the Senate. It was put forward as an updating of the old Mining Law, and the miners accepted it because their own lawyers had drafted it. After all, hostile outsiders wanted to expunge the old law altogether, to rip it out and substitute a leasing system. The AMC "with great reluctance" went so far as to support payment of a 2 percent royalty, a point on which Aspinall had told them they must yield.

From the standpoint of the critics urging a thorough cleansing and a bright new start, the AMC's bill was inadequate. Congress took no conclusive action that year or in subsequent years through 1980. The industry's tactics achieved delay, if nothing else. A crucial period was the fall of 1977, when the House Interior Subcommittee on Mines and Mining held three days of hearings on two contrasting proposals.[5] One bill, supported by President Carter, Interior Secretary Andrus, and the conservationists, called for the repeal of the 1872 law and the institution of a leasing system. Carter had laid down the guidelines in an environmental message in May. The other bill, drafted by the American Mining Congress and introduced by Rep. Philip E.

Ruppe, Michigan Republican, retained the framework of the old law while seeking to clean it up and improve it.

Industry witnesses and their supporters at the hearings contended the administration bill, which had been introduced by Rep. Phillip Burton, the conservation-oriented California Democrat, gave the secretary too much discretion. Andrus objected to the Ruppe bill on grounds that it would give him no discretion to favor other uses besides mining in land areas with known mineral content. The industry pleaded hardship. With copper prices down and much unemployment in the mining states, spokesmen said, further burdens and uncertainties should not be imposed.

The outcome was that neither the administration's bill nor the AMC's, which was damned by conservationists as worse than nothing, prevailed. Congress turned to more pressing matters, and the hoary old 1872 law sailed into the 1980s, warts and all. This was a sweet victory for the miners and their western advocates. It was foreshadowed on the first day of the 1977 hearings, when Representative Udall of Arizona, brother of the former secretary and by now the chairman of the full House Interior Committee, made it clear he had abandoned the effort to jettison the old law and was switching to the Ruppe approach.

"It seems you can make a pretty good argument for junking the old law entirely," Udall told Andrus in explaining his new position. "I have made that argument for the last ten years. I introduced a bill to do that very thing, but I think you could also make a good argument that we can do what needs to be done at this time without bringing a troubled industry to its knees."[6]

Representative Udall might also have noted that a good argument could be made for a western politician's need to behave like one occasionally, if he expected to be reelected. In fairness to him, he had been very busy. He had been an early contender for the 1976 Democratic nomination for the presidency, and after that he had been engrossed in shaping the Surface Mining Control and Reclamation Act of 1977—which covered coal but not other minerals—and with the endless labors involved in trying to achieve an intelligent, equitable land settlement in Alaska.[7]

While in a charitable mood, one can also understand the mining industry's stubborn devotion to the old law that had for so long given the miner his *laissez-passer* to the public lands, guarding his status and enabling him to thumb his nose at the federal bureaucracy.

What the miners, large and small, want above all else from the federal government is unhampered access to the public lands—that is, the right to enter them without hindrance and explore, and the right to exploit what they find. They do not want to see these rights become dependent on official whim or cluttered with red tape. Their vehemence on the point seems at times to approach the paranoid.

What the environmentalists want, on the other hand, is a curbing of an easy access from which multiple abuses have flowed. They challenge the sanctimonious assumption that development of a mineral deposit is ordinarily "the highest economic use of land." Inasmuch as modern mining often forecloses other uses for hundreds, perhaps thousands, of years, they would like to see cost analyses done before land is surrendered for that purpose. A change to leasing is the logical answer. It would not be a panacea, as witness the serious and costly damages that have resulted from the leasing of oil, coal, and other minerals covered by the 1920 act; but leasing would mean at least that the government would get something for its minerals, instead of giving them away, and would own the land after the mining was over. It would also, as the miners correctly perceive, give public officials more say-so over what happens to public property.

At stake in this battle over the public lands is a trove of minerals as rich as King Solomon's mines. Inasmuch as the federal government has neither charged for nor kept a record of hardrock minerals taken from the public lands, there is no way of telling precisely what proportion of the nation's minerals these lands produce. Look at the BLM's statistics for 1976 as an example. They show that federal onshore lands yielded 167,134,792 barrels of oil, close to a trillion cubic feet of natural gas, and more than 46,000,000 short tons of coal, potash, and other minerals that are "leasable."[8] This was in addition to production from the Outer Continental Shelf. There are no figures for gold, silver, copper, uranium, molybdenum, and other such minerals because, under the old Mining Law, the federal government gets nothing for them. Nobody knows how many billions of dollars have been carted away, over the years, without any accounting whatever.

The Public Land Law Review Commission took note of that fact in 1970 but seemed undisturbed by it. The commissioners observed that nine-tenths of the public lands are in the western states and that these states produced more than nine-tenths of the nation's domestic copper. These states also were yielding 95 percent of the mercury and silver, all of the nickel, molybdenum, and potash, and half the lead. "In fact," said the Aspinall commission, "most of the known domestic resources of metallic minerals other than iron are situated in the West."[9]

There is no point in crying over spilt milk, or over copper and gold and silver from which the federal authority derived no direct compensation. The United States as a whole has benefited from the harvesting of minerals, and there is something to be said for a system in which the entrepreneur is king and the winners are taxed after a fashion.

Be that as it may, we are engaged in an educational exercise that involves glancing backward in order that we may look to the future with more confidence, and in this spirit it is worthwhile to recall the origins and consequences of the hard-rock mining law. Long before the Civil War, the nation developed the tolerant, indulgent attitude toward mining which has prevailed since. First it was gold and silver, then copper and the lesser metals. Lead—essential for military purposes—had always been important.

167

For Americans rushing westward, the mining fever may be said to have begun in 1848 with the discovery of gold at Sutter's Mill on the American River in California. President Polk, the Scotch-Irish Tennessean who had enlarged the nation by half a continent, said in a message to Congress in December of that year: "The accounts of the abundance of gold in that territory are of such an extraordinary character as would scarcely command belief."[10] This was loose gold, placer gold, gold broken out of primary deposits and washed down into stream beds and gravel banks, where it could be winnowed out with such primitive tools as spade and pan. Men rushed to California in eager hordes.

The siren song lured adventurers from all over the world: Cornishmen, Australians, Missourians, New Englanders, Mexicans, Chinese. The forty-niners—100,000 or more—traveled to the Mother Lode country in northern California overland, by the sea route around the Horn, or by a combination of sea and land via the Isthmus of Panama. They streamed into San Francisco and fanned out into the mining camps, places with such names as Poker Flat and Slumgullion. Wherever they came from, the early miners originally were trespassers on the federally owned public domain. They had no legal standing. Local regulations were worked out in the goldfields as a matter of necessity. The main purpose was not to protect the miner against federal intervention but to safeguard the firstcomer against claim jumpers.

For two decades that included the bloody upheaval of the Civil War, Congress wrestled with the task of putting the western mines under federal law. Some consideration, but not much, was given to proposals for setting up a permit system and obtaining revenue from the gold that was being taken from land that, technically, was the property of all citizens. In its first year, the California strike yielded about $10 million. The zenith year's take of 1852, about $80 million, was even more impressive by the standards of the time. And soon the lightning of discovered gold was flickering over other western hills.[11]

Thousands of California argonauts, many of them disappointed at their luck on the golden shore, threw down their shovels and pushed east and northeast in the 1850s to investigate reports of easy pickings in other places. When the Mother Lode's placer gold thinned out and the search came to involve heavy machinery, it was time for the miner without capital to move on. Some Californians turned back to the great basin between the Rockies and the Sierra Nevada, well-nigh uninhabited then except for wandering Indians. They joined newcomers from the East who had crossed the plains. Late in the decade, gold was found in the Colorado Rockies near Pike's Peak as well as on the eastern slope of the Sierras in Nevada Territory, where the fabulous Comstock Lode came to light.

There were other booms during the Civil War. In the Montana camps clustered in the Rockies near the Continental Divide, the fever ran high. A stream ten miles long was overrun and staked along its full length in a few hours. Some distance north along the arc of the mountains, wandering miners found gold in 1864. Two years later, just to the northeast, the town of Butte was laid out. Butte was to prove "the richest hill on earth" because of a less regal metal, copper, but the heyday of copper and the wars of the copper kings came later, well after the North and South had settled their differences.

As mentioned earlier, the miner's tenure on the public lands in the pre–Civil War and immediate postwar periods was weak and uncertain. He had no real right there. Although no federal official was disturbing him, voices were being raised in Congress to the effect that the western mineral lands, being so rich, should be sold or otherwise managed in such a way as to produce revenue. Before the passage of the Homestead Act, at least, the farmer had been made to pay for what he got. Why not the miner?

There had been an illuminating debate concerning this subject on the eve of Fort Sumter, when in 1860 Sen. William McKendree Gwin of California urged a mining amendment to a proposed homestead law. Gwin wanted to give miners in his state and Oregon legal status on the public domain.[12] Congress had already shown a disinclination to allow Mexicans to share in California's abundance. Now Gwin explained that one of his purposes in offering the amendment was to exclude some 50,000 to 60,000 Chinese then working in the mines. These men he likened to "grasshoppers or locusts"—no better than slaves. Blacks, it goes without saying, were not even mentioned.

Gwin's proposal was defeated despite such xenophobic appeal as it may have had. The charming and level-headed Sen. Albert G. Brown, who was soon to lead a company of Mississippi Volunteers in the war, picked idly at the logic of Gwin's case. He could not see, he said, why a gold producer should have rights in federal land any more than a cotton producer.

"I protest against the idea," Brown said, "that the man who first occupies it [the land] because he digs gold out of it, is entitled to it any more than the man who first occupies a piece of ground, and digs cotton out of it, is entitled to that."[13]

There are differences between the mining of gold and the cultivation of cotton, but the principle that federal mineral lands have value and should fetch a price had its champions. In 1865, about two months before General Lee surrendered at Appomattox, Rep. George W. Julian of Indiana was recommending that the United States reduce its war debt by subdividing and selling its mineral lands. Westerners had no use for Julian's public-sales idea, and Julian, a Republican advocate of homesteading and a tireless exposer of land frauds, turned out to be no match for the brassy and ebullient mining cabal led by Senator Stewart of Nevada, Mark Twain's friend.

Not only was Julian's threat parried, but the miners counterattacked and won. Stewart and his associates played an audacious trick. A bill had been shaped by Stewart to legalize the miners' occupation of federal mineral lands. The Senate seemed favorably disposed, but the House allowed the miners' bill to languish in Julian's public-lands committee. Stewart's forces found a Trojan horse. They seized upon an entirely different, unrelated bill that had been passed by the House after going through the Committee on Mines and Mining rather than through Julian's panel. It was a bill authorizing right-of-way over public lands to ditch and canal owners in California.

Tearing out the approved bill's substance, the Stewart group inserted Stewart's mining bill in the shell. Then, when the bill as amended in the Senate went back to the House, the indignant Julian could not muster the votes to kill it. He damned the changeling eloquently in House debate, complaining that certain senators, "eager and impatient of delay," were lurking about the House chamber urging passage.

What the miners' advocates proposed, Julian said, was nothing less than "revolutionizing the whole land policy of the government, abdicating in the name of the nation its authority and jurisdiction over the richest mineral possessions on the face of God's earth, found imbedded here and there over a million square miles of our national territory."[14]

At another point, Julian waxed sarcastic when proponents argued that the Stewart bill was "acceptable" to Nevada, California, and other mining regions.

"Why, undoubtedly it is acceptable to them," he exclaimed. "I should deem it marvelous if they did not accept a free gift of the gold and silver to be found interspersed over a million square miles of the richest mineral land on the globe."[15]

The House voted overwhelmingly against the representative from Indiana. Whatever the imperfections of Julian's land-sales bill, he was right in seeing that the plan he opposed so unsuccessfully was a stupendous giveaway. In that first General Mining Law of 1866, the legislators addressed themselves to the lode type of claim—that is, veins of quartz or other rock in place. Congress said that "the mineral lands of the public domain . . .

are hereby declared to be free and open to exploration and occupation." The 1866 act also provided that water on public lands could be "appropriated" under state law. This made it possible for water to be diverted to private lands, reducing the value of those in public ownership.

Having dealt with lode claims, Congress in 1870 added a supplement covering placer deposits, of which the obvious example is loose gold occurring in gravel along a stream. The final embellishment came in 1872, when the basic law relating to both lode and placer claims went on the books without much ado. In that year, Congress approved language stating that "all valuable mineral deposits in lands belonging to the United States, both surveyed and unsurveyed, are hereby declared to be free and open to exploration and purchase, and the lands in which they are found to occupation and purchase, by citizens of the United States and those who have declared their intention to become such."

Twenty acres was the size established for mining claims. In the case of placer claims, an association was authorized to locate up to 160 acres, the same area as a conventional homestead. The taking of an additional 5 acres for a mill site was allowed. As for the locator or claimant, the law required him to do $100 worth of "assessment work" each year in order to maintain possession against adverse claimants. If the locator wished to own his claim in fee simple, he could obtain a federal patent by proving he had made a valuable discovery, showing that he had spent $500 improving his property, and having the claim surveyed. The fee was $5 an acre for lode and $2.50 for placer claims.

Thus were established within a six-year period the miner's freedom to explore and to occupy and, by implication, his right to free removal of what he found. In setting what might seem today to be very low fees for outright ownership of mineral land, Congress was not so improvident as might appear. After all, there was plenty of free land available for farming under the Homestead Act, and a claimant willing to pay $5 an acre for

172

mineral land was not likely to have his motives scrutinized. Another, less obvious, advantage to the miner in the way things were set up was that the miner could make use of a piece of land, legally secure in his tenure, without owning it and therefore without paying taxes to the state. This was a boon in California, where miners had no wish to share the cost of government then borne by the holders of large Spanish land grants.

Without question, Congress had made life easier for the miner and prospector. He could stake out his own claim or buy a claim from another. Having done that, he could use the property indefinitely, as long as he did the work required by law, which in later years sometimes was little more than a symbolic bulldozing that scarred the land. He could occupy the unpatented claim, use its timber for mining purposes, and take away minerals. In fact, until he might decide to apply for a patent and take ownership, he had no obligation to inform federal officials that he had filed a claim at all. Until the 1976 Federal Land Policy and Management Act was passed, he had only to file at the nearest country courthouse. Into modern times, there was no way for federal land managers to know, without making expensive and tedious inquiry, how many mining claims encumbered federal property, or who owned them. And a claim adjudged to be invalid might be erased one day, only to be replaced by a new claim filed the next.

None of these quirks mattered a great deal at first. Getting the gold and silver and copper out of the rocks was in the national interest. In 1872, nobody but the miner wanted twenty acres in the mountains. The shortcomings of the Mining Law, in terms of the national interest, became apparent later when the country began to fill up and land was less abundant and relatively expensive. From the first, however, one of the safeguards the original legislation did have was the requirement that a mining claim must contain a "valuable" mineral deposit, later interpreted as one justifying "a prudent man in the expenditure of labor and

173

capital" to develop it.[16] Since the courts early construed this language to mean that a deposit had to be valuable currently, rather than prospectively in the future, the Interior Department and other agencies were able to prevent mining companies from tying up great blocks of public land for speculative reasons.

The "prudent man" doctrine also has been the basis for federal challenge of people who made use of the old law to get land for nonmining purposes—a vacation cabin in the mountains, for example. An Interior Department lawyer once remarked wryly that half the privately owned recreation cabins in the Rockies are on old mining claims that have gone to patent. Another, former Solicitor Barry, said many present and past mining company executives have mountain retreats on patented mining claims—claims that "were never intended to be mined and never will be mined."

"In the fatness of the years following the Second World War," Barry recalled, "city dwellers went into remote areas and located thousands of claims along mountain streams, setting up rod and gun clubs and excluding the public. To stop this practice, the Common Varieties Act was enacted in 1955. It provides that common varieties of certain minerals like sand, gravel, stone, pumice, et cetera and the lands in which they occur are no longer subject to location under the 1872 Act. The secretary of the interior and the secretary of agriculture were authorized to sell such minerals. The mining industry protested, but not too much. After all, it still gets its lead, zinc, copper, iron, silver and gold free of charge."[17]

Such subversions of congressional intent were typical of the federal land laws and are a standing joke in the West. There was no lack of legitimate mineral development, some of it very successful and productive indeed. In the 1870s, camps here and there grew into mining towns that looked as if they would be more than transitory. Canvas was good enough for the placer miner with his pan and sluice and shovel, but the big lodes called for streets, sidewalks, stores, banks, and housing for work-

174

ers. Underground mining meant capital, most of which had to come from the East. There had to be mules and wagons, teamsters to drive the loads, and men who labored in tunnels far below the surface, in mines owned by other men.

Much has been written about the free and easy, riotous early days of the bonanza towns—Butte, Jerome, Tombstone, Deadwood. The careers of the giants who struck it rich have been set down, often uncritically, but not always. We must be content here with a brief sketching in of the scene.[18] The towns are scattered over the West, having different scenic backdrops and climates but histories that are strikingly similar. Each had its frontier captains of industry, its politicians, its itinerant scoundrels, its saloons and desperados and vigilantes, its red-light districts and boot hills, often its homegrown entrepreneurs who challenged the ruthless financial brigands of the moneyed East. Each produced a flow of mineral wealth for the nation, along with a crop of new millionaires. Each caused an environmental mess that it was nobody's business to clean up. And when and if the ore played out, the town went into quiet collapse, and it was almost as if the brawling, sweating, hopeful thousands had never been there at all.

Butte came to stay. The future copper metropolis in western Montana had its origins in a minor gold strike along Silver Bow Creek in the 1860s and then had a brief fling in silver before devoting itself to the metal for which it is best known. The aforementioned William Andrews Clark, aggressive young merchant and bankroller who three decades later was to buy his way into the United States Senate, arrived at Butte in 1872, the year of the Mining Law.

Clark, who could take care of himself in any company, cut a wide swath in Butte but did not have the town to himself. There were two other grand panjandrums of the copper wars raging there late in the nineteenth century. One was Clark's enemy, Marcus Daly, an Irishman who made his appearance at Butte in 1876 and bought control of the Alice silver mine for $30,000. As a boy, he had sold newspapers in New York City, later emigrating to California and the Comstock Lode in Nevada. Third in the triumvirate, a much younger man than the first two, Frederick Augustus ("Fritz") Heinze, was born in Brooklyn of German Lutheran parents and showed up in Butte when he was only twenty, about 1889. He was noted for his audacious, unscrupulous, and amazingly brash fight against the Standard Oil Trust and Amalgamated Copper Company, later Anaconda.

Long before Anaconda—"the company"—threw its coils around the state of Montana, the Clark-Daly feud was ablaze. The annals are not clear as to how and why it began. Clark and Daly had a brief truce when the territory, seeking to become a state, held its constitutional convention with Clark as chairman. The mines had been bringing in $25 to $40 million annually without paying any taxes to speak of. The two antagonists made common cause in holding mine taxes to the minimum as Montana entered the Union, which it did in 1889. Over the protest of cattlemen, the miners drilled into the bedrock of the new state constitution a provision that mines and mining claims would be taxed "at the price paid the United States therefor," meaning $2.50 or $5 an acre, a most lenient amount. The ranchers bucked and bawled at having to shoulder more than their proper share of the cost of government, but copper spoke decisively. Clark told the convention that protection must be given "those brave pioneers who have come out here and made the wilderness blossom as the rose, and opened up these great mountains and brought their hidden wealth to light—

"Yea, I say, it is the duty of the members of their convention to throw such safeguards around this great industry as are proper and just; this great industry that is the foundation of almost all the prosperity of this country, and has made all the valleys and mountains of Montana productive."

In the 1890s, Butte was a roaring copper town, part of the great world. Its Silver Bow Club was a place of some elegance and style, but the ugliness of Butte was legendary, and her copper fumes and smoke made night of day. It was said that the very cattle slaughtered around there had coppery teeth, much in demand as curiosities. Montana's cumulative mineral production rose to nearly $3 billion by the 1950s, two-thirds of it copper, but there had been hard times along the way. In the panic and depression of 1893, both Clark and Daly ordered gold coin shipped in—Clark, $400,000, and Daly, $700,000—to keep Butte going. At the turn of the century, Clark's persistent courtship of a Senate seat finally paid off, as has been told. A remark attributed to Clark—"I never bought a man who wasn't for sale"—has become a classic.

As Clark went to the Senate in 1900, his old enemy, Marcus Daly, died in New York of Bright's disease. Daly had just sold his copper holdings in the Anaconda mine to Amalgamated Copper—Henry H. Rogers and the Standard Oil Trust. Rogers paid about $39 million. It was in this period that the third giant of the Montana copper wars, Fritz Heinze, waged his fiery, devil-may-care battle against the titans of Boston and New York. Heinze used corrupt Montana courts and the intricacies of the 1872 Mining Law to plunder rich ore in eastern-owned mines adjacent to his own. Standard Trust bought out the Bostonians. Heinze prevailed in the courts in 1903, after which Amalgamated shut down its operations, throwing thousands out of work. Victory for Heinze was sweet but brief. In another three years, Butte's fighting Hotspur had been skinned by the Trust, and "the company" lived on to rule the state and finally, early in 1977, to be devoured by an oil giant, Atlantic Richfield.[19]

Gustavus Myers's muckraking *History of the Great American Fortunes*, brought out in 1909, documented that not a few of the massive accumulations of private wealth in this country had their origins in the mineral riches of the western domain.[20] Boston's affinity with western copper enriched the Hub of the Universe, if not the mining towns. The Shaw, Agassiz, and Livermore families in Boston were chief owners of the lucrative Calumet and Hecla Copper Company in Michigan, a venerable

177

organization said to have yielded $155 million to its stockholders in the period between 1871 and 1923.[21] Thus it was that young Harvard boys such as Robert Livermore were roaming the West around the turn of the century. Livermore's journal, published as *Bostonians and Bullion,* provided a revealing account of life on the far slope of the Colorado Rockies around Telluride and the rough treatment given to striking miners.[22] Professional toughs were called in from the outside and deputized. A new Colorado governor "friendly to capital," as Livermore phrased it, declared martial law and sent in troops. After bloodshed and violence, union sympathizers were put on freight cars and shipped out.

Some of the titans of the early mining days operated in several states. Like Senator Clark, they got themselves elected to Congress by fair means or foul and helped shape the law to the miner's liking. One example was George Hearst, the rough-hewn Missourian who piled up enough money from the western mines to grubstake his flamboyant son, William Randolph Hearst, in a fabulous newspaper-publishing venture. Born in 1820, George Hearst started as a pick-and-shovel miner in California and, with the financial backing of San Francisco promoters Lloyd Tevis and James Ben Ali Haggin, did well in Utah, Nevada, Montana, New Mexico, and South Dakota, where in the later 1870s the three entrepreneurs bought the original Homestake mine properties in the Black Hills at a reported price of about $70,000.[23] The Homestake got into minor trouble with the federal government for denuding its environs of timber, but it was a success story with which no one could quarrel, a veritable Ophir that by the 1930s had produced $233 million in gold and nearly $58 million in dividends.

Flush with the gold rolling in from the Homestake and other holdings, including Anaconda's copper and silver revenue in Montana, George Hearst embraced California's Democratic party. He failed in a race for the governorship, but the winner, Gov. George Stoneman, appointed him to the United States Senate in 1886 to fill an unexpired term. The following year the

California legislature elected Hearst to a full six-year term. The seat was said to have cost him "a cool half million."[24] Senator Hearst died in Washington, D.C., early in 1891, much lamented by his friends and leaving an estate very conservatively appraised at $18 million.

More than a decade later, in 1906, following bloody war at Cripple Creek and the defeat of the Western Federation of Miners, the United States Senate received into membership Simon Guggenheim of Colorado. Simon was the western representative of a famous brotherhood—the seven sons of Meyer Guggenheim, who emigrated from Switzerland to Philadelphia in 1847 and went to work as a peddler in the anthracite coal towns, trudging about with a pack on his back, selling shoelaces, ribbons, and safety pins. Father Meyer, prospering as a merchant, bought an interest in silver mines at Leadville around 1880. The mines proved rich. The Guggenheims got into the smelting business in Colorado in the 1880s. Later they built smelters in Mexico. After Rogers of Standard Oil had formed the Amalgamated Copper Trust at Butte, in 1899 he took the lead in organizing a western smelters' trust, incorporated as the American Smelting and Refining Company. At first the Guggenheims refused to join; they battled and defied it. In 1901, though, when the smoke of a complex financial struggle had cleared, they were in control of ASARCO. It was a glorious coup.[25]

Simon Guggenheim, the next to youngest of the sons, was anything but a flamboyant, western-style politician, but he knew how to spend money freely in behalf of Colorado's Silver Republicans. At the time the Guggenheims were bucking the smelter trust, he was popular in the state. After the Guggenheims took over the trust, he was lampooned as a moneybags. He donated turkey dinners and suits of clothing to poor boys in Denver, gave a building to the Colorado School of Mines, distributed largess, entertained handsomely, and was duly elected by the Colorado legislature. It was said that Guggenheim had contributed $50,000 to help elect to the state Senate

179

men who would support his candidacy. There appears to be no doubt that he purchased his election, after the fashion of the times.

"You have bargained off this senatorship for so many dollars," said Colorado Republican Sen. Merle Vincent, addressing his colleagues. Late in January of 1907 Simon hooked his private railway car to a Rock Island train, and he and his wife headed for Washington, D.C.[26]

It was not until 1913 that the Constitution was amended to provide for election of United States senators by popular vote rather than by choice of the legislatures of the states. In fairness to Senators Hearst and Guggenheim and to Senator Clark of Montana it should be said that they gained their seats at a time when candidates for the exclusive club on Capitol Hill were expected to be men of substance, openhanded and generous.

Clark first got rich in Montana, but the pride of his later years was the opulent United Verde copper property at Jerome, a bleak town perched high in the Black Mountains of central Arizona.[27] He saw a specimen of United Verde ore in 1885 at the New Orleans World Exposition. The basic claims had been purchased for $15,000 in 1880 by Dr. James Douglas, acting in behalf of Philadelphia clients. Three years later those and added claims brought $90,000, and the United Verde, incorporated in New York and using smelter coke shipped from Wales and brought overland from California, got into production. A financial panic caused a shutdown, and in 1888 the future Senator Clark bought United Verde by getting in ahead of the Phelps Dodge interests, which also wanted it. By the time the mine was worked out in 1953 it had produced more than $500,000,000 worth of copper, silver, gold, and zinc.

Chroniclers of the picturesque but somehow melancholy history of Jerome recount with satisfaction how the shrewd, tight-fisted Clark derived no benefit from an immensely rich strike made in 1914 on a "fractional claim" called the Little Daisy, just down the hill and to the east of the United Verde. This was a snippet of unclaimed land in the mosaic surrounding Clark's mine. It was acquired and developed by a triumvirate that included James S. ("Rawhide Jimmie") Douglas, son of the Dr. Douglas who had bird-dogged the United Verde some years back, before Clark bought it. The new mine, called the United Verde Extension, or UVX, electrified the mining world and revived the copper boom at Jerome. It produced $125 million in metal and $42 million in dividends before being shut down in 1938. James S. Douglas and his associates held onto their stock. Douglas's son, Lewis Williams Douglas, worked for his father at the UVX after serving as an artillery officer in World War I. His father built a copper-roofed home at Jerome for him and his bride. The son represented Arizona for nearly four terms in Congress, became President Franklin D. Roosevelt's director of the budget, and served after World War II as ambassador to the Court of St. James. This final British connection was curiously appropriate, inasmuch as the Arizona town had been founded and named after Eugene Murray Jerome, a New York financier who was first cousin to Jennie Jerome, Winston Churchill's mother.

Jerome, now a ghost town with a magnificent view of the Verde Valley and the Mogollon Rim, is only one of the Arizona copper legends. There are Ajo, Bisbee, Tombstone, Douglas, the Silver Bell mine, the Inspiration, the Bagdad, and a host of others. In 1917 alone, Arizona produced 712 million pounds of copper, worth more than $194 million, to meet the demands of World War I. In the same year the much-detested Industrial Workers of the World—the "Wobblies"—caused strikes in the mines, and two men were killed near the Mexican border at Bisbee, where the big producer was the Phelps Dodge Copper Queen.

In the wake of the IWW violence, in the summer of 1917 a group of Bisbee citizens and deputies rounded up more than 1,200 strikers, put them in freight cars, and sent them across the state line into New Mexico. For a time a man had to have a passport to get into Bisbee, which in its zeal had corralled "loyal" workers and men of substance as well as Wobblies. In fact, Maurice Denn, who owned the Denn mine, was caged up with the strikers until somebody recognized him and got him out. Bisbee's forceful handling of its labor problems outraged some people. The sheriff and stalwart citizens, including Phelps Dodge President Walter Douglas, were indicted in federal court at Tucson. Nothing came of it.

The fabled copper kingdom of Arizona is a good vantage point from which to ponder the mineral riches that have been taken from federal lands in the West under the old mining statutes with no payments made and no records kept. By 1970 the state's copper output was valued at $1.07 billion for the year, and Arizona had been the nation's leading copper producer for more than sixty years, through lean times and fat. The state's total copper production through 1969 was more than $11 billion. Consider the United Verde mine at Jerome. Under Senator Clark and his heirs, its yield was more than $350 million in copper, gold, and silver. Phelps Dodge bought the property for $20 million in 1935 and extracted another $120 million in ore before shutting down in 1953. To the south at Bisbee, Jim Daley's twenty-acre claim, the Irish Mag, turned out to be worth $15 million in dividends before its day was over. Where did the money go? Not to Jerome and Bisbee, to be sure. Not to the miners, who drew $2 or $2.50 a day. The state and earlier the territory of Arizona saw some of it, but not much. There was no federal income tax before ratification of the Constitution's Sixteenth Amendment in 1913. Those who made money in the halcyon days were allowed to keep it.

Now everything has changed except the old Mining Law with its standing invitation to the miner to go upon the public domain, find what he can, and take what he wants. The prospector and his burro have gone into the flaming sunset to be seen no more, gone the way of the high-grade ores worth taking out by mule train.

The Bowels of the Earth

In the 1900s Daniel C. Jackling in Utah showed the way to the modern open-pit mine, with its low-grade ore, its yawning cavity, its $600,000 electric power shovels, and its 125-ton trucks crawling like bugs in the depths. Such mining outclassed the small entrepreneur and was clearly work for huge corporations with complex machinery and immense amounts of capital.

As the 1970s arrived, when Arizona was producing about 12 percent of the world's copper, nearly three-quarters of Arizona's production came from eleven mines owned by five companies, with Phelps Dodge accounting for one-third of the total output. Kennecott and Asarco each had 9 percent. One of the industry's showplaces was the Twin Buttes area south of Tucson. Back in the 1920s, this barren moon landscape had been considered non-mineral in character by the General Land Office. A half century later, however, Anaconda was getting into production with its $250 million open-pit mine at Twin Buttes, where in 1950 low-grade ore had been found resting beneath hundreds of feet of overburden. The soil around Anaconda's property had already been pockmarked by the adjacent pits of the Pima mine, ASARCO's Mission mine, the Esperanza of Duval Corporation, and most recently by Duval's new Sierrita mine. These companies were prepared to process ore yielding only about fifteen pounds of copper to the ton, compared with an average of forty-eight pounds or more to the ton in Arizona before 1920.

At Twin Buttes there were immense moraines of waste rock and soil from the mining operations, a hundred or more feet deep and piled high on some of the world's most beautiful desert country. When the wind blows, these send up clouds of dust into the clear sky. Efforts were being made to stabilize them and improve their appearance with vegetation.[28]

The wholesale giveaway of the public's minerals in the past is water over the dam, but as a philosophical exercise it is interesting to ponder how differently things might have turned out in the western mining states, from the standpoint of the local and national public interest, if the federal government had retained mineral rights and imposed royalties on metals taken off and if down-at-heel state governments in western areas, notoriously sensitive to the mining interests, had demanded more of the yield in taxes. The reality during many decades was otherwise.

Hard-rock miners, like their brethren in the oil industry, have been permitted to charge depletion for federal tax purposes on minerals that belonged to all citizens until the day before yesterday. It was to this curious practice that former Solicitor Barry, who went on to teach law in Oregon and became a council member of the Wilderness Society, was alluding in a half-humorous way when asked in the mid-1970s whether he thought the copper companies could afford to pay a royalty.

"They get a 15 percent depletion allowance on *our* copper," Barry remarked at Washington's Cosmos Club. "I don't see why they shouldn't."

When the Nixon administration came to power, the American mining industry was prospering but was suffering, nevertheless, from a feeling of insecurity. Conservationists were on the rampage. Traditional attitudes were under challenge. Like the oil-men, the miners found high ground for a counterattack in the unquestionable fact that the nation was entering a period of relative scarcity. Rich domestic ores were either gone or going. The minerals cornucopia was not what it had been. The United States until just before the onset of World War II had been a net exporter of minerals, but by 1970 imports totalled $4 billion above and beyond exports. With American demand spiraling upward and with the oil crunch ahead, the deficit was destined to become much worse.

Surely this was no time, the mining industry argued, to throw roadblocks in the path of those seeking the raw stuffs on which America's progress and prosperity depended. Rather, it was a time for encouraging words and a hearty three cheers. The Congress in these circumstances took its time about tightening up the old Mining Law. It bestirred itself instead, under the urging of Colorado's Republican Sen. Gordon Allott, to approve in 1970 an admirably brief piece of legislation called the Mining and Minerals Policy Act.[29] This affirmed that the federal government, in the national interest, would foster and encourage private enterprise in the development of "sound and stable" domestic mining ventures.

One thing the federal authority could certainly do for mining, the industry made clear during testimony on the Allott bill, was to leave open the gate to the public domain where most of the remaining discoveries were likely to be made. Charles F. Barber, president of ASARCO, said no regime of law could be effective unless the mining industry had the right of access.

"Valuable mineral deposits are rare indeed and no one can know with certainty where they may lie hidden," Barber told a Senate subcommittee. "A national minerals policy, therefore, should assure that the public lands, with very limited exceptions, remain open to exploration for minerals and to mining. It is important to the nation that no area be closed to exploration and to mining in the absence of a compelling national interest."[30]

The cry of the miner that he must have access to the places where minerals may be found, and enjoy security of tenure so that the investment will not be lost, is understandable enough. Minerals, he says, are where you find them. The AMC's Overton is fond of recalling that the late Sen. Robert Kennedy of New York once suggested that mines should be placed where they will reduce pockets of high unemployment. Overton uses the story to make the point that a mine cannot be elsewhere than where the ore body exists. In many instances, not because of the villainy of the industry, but because rich mineral deposits often concentrate where there have been giant upheavals and a wearing down over geologic time, this may be in a scenic place where mining is an aesthetic intrusion.

It may be copper in the Glacier Peak Wilderness in Washington State, where Kennecott has a claim amid surroundings of staggering beauty. It may be molybdenite at Little Boulder Creek in the White Cloud Peaks of Idaho's Sawtooth Range, where ASARCO has ventured. It may be copper, gold, silver, or something else in southwestern Colorado's lovely Uncompahgre country, where hundreds of claimants have filed. It may be far north in Alaska, where Anaconda is looking for billions in copper, silver, and other metals on the fringes of the proposed Gates of the Arctic National Park.

"Where you find minerals is where the mountains are," said James Boyd, who served as executive director of the National Commission on Materials Policy, authorized by Congress in 1970.[31] It would have been difficult for President Nixon to have found a more capable and knowledgeable man than Boyd to direct the commission's labors. An Australian who got his education at the California Institute of Technology and the Colorado School of Mines, he served on Eisenhower's staff in World War II, later heading the Interior Department's Bureau of Mines before joining Kennecott as exploration manager and finally in 1960 becoming president of the Copper Range Company.

Boyd's viewpoint was, of course, industry oriented. On the environmental side, his commission was balanced by the presence of Lynton K. Caldwell of the University of Indiana. When the group made its final report in June 1973, it harked back to the Paley commission established by Truman in the early 1950s and looked forward to striking a balance between the nation's appetite for materials and the need for protecting the quality of life. It proposed federal curbs on strip-mining and sensible changes in the mining statutes. It said the federal government should "facilitate access to public and private lands" to promote the search for scarce minerals.

As to scarcity, Boyd's attitude was cheerful, optimistic, pragmatic. Raw materials are well-nigh infinite, he said, but as time goes by they will cost more and be more difficult to extract. It was a matter of paying the price. The commission gave no houseroom to the direful forebodings expressed in 1972 by the Club of Rome, an international body of scholars and others who warned that world population and economic growth rates simply could not continue.

"Those unaware of the vast potential of our earth's finite crust," said Boyd and his colleagues, "fear increased consumption levels will deplete the earth's resources. Faulty comparisons of currently known mineral reserves with future demand, predicated upon exponential projections, serve to accentuate these fears."[32]

While acknowledging the abuses that had occurred under the antiquated Mining Law, the Boyd commission could not bring itself to damn the law outright. As in the case of the Aspinall report three years earlier, the impression was left that capital punishment was not necessarily appropriate. A shave and a haircut and a clean pair of overalls would do.

The mining industry's aversion to proposals that would encumber federal lands with a greater degree of protection had much support in the Interior Department itself, particularly in the Nixon and Ford administrations. In 1975, for example, the AMC published an article—"Is Our Account Overdrawn?"— written by two interior officials in the minerals field, Gary Bennethum and L. Courtland Lee. Bennethum and Lee pointed with alarm to the cumulative effect of recent public-land withdrawals. From 1968 to 1974, they reported, the proportion of public lands barred from exploration and development under the Mining Laws had risen from 17 percent to about 67 percent, or more than two-thirds. They found a comparable escalation in lands closed to mineral leasing. Noting the prospect that within twenty-five years the United States would be totally dependent on imports for twelve essential mineral commodities, the Interior Department men found the implications "staggering" and asked whether the nation had already withdrawn so much land that the American long-term mineral position would be jeopardized.

Although Bennethum and Lee professed to reach no conclusions, their article amounted to credible and respectable backing

187

for the posture taken by mining executives and business-oriented federal managers. The AMC reprinted the article as a circular and gave it wide distribution. Interior Secretary Kleppe, under President Ford, lent a sympathetic ear and mentioned the withdrawal question in his address to the AMC early in 1976. He established a task force on mining withdrawals to satisfy, as Bennethum expressed it, "a growing concern that the availability of federal land for mineral extraction is being restricted without central awareness and direction."[33] Within a few months, the Republicans were out and the Democrats were in, but the concern remained.

To the uncritical eye, the Bennethum-Lee case seemed compelling, but conservationists were quick to give the other side. As the facts set forth in the AMC article indicated, much of the 1968 to 1974 ballooning of withdrawals was due to the requirements and pressures generated by the Alaska Native Claims Act of 1971. Massive set-asides were necessary to keep federal lands in Alaska from being overrun while planning, selection, and distribution were taking place. The conservationists, determined to preserve millions of acres of the best for parks and wildlife refuges, argued that areas closed to mining now could always be thrown open in the future, if necessary. Moreover, they said, withdrawal was the only weapon effective against the abuses of the old Mining Law.

It was not until late in President Ford's administration that Congress agreed to move against the long-standing evils caused by the stale and unpatented mining claims that encumber federally owned mountains, deserts, pastures, marshes, and forests. These are estimated to number between six and ten million, and they have imposed a burden of helplessness on federal managers. The claims were filed at various times at local courthouses all over the West. Under the ancient practice, there was no way of cleansing the land of these obstacles in broad strokes. In the BLM's so-called organic act, however—formally known as the Federal Land Policy and Management Act of 1976—Congress ordained that all past unpatented claims had to be registered with the appropriate federal office within three years and that all claims must henceforth be documented annually. Failure to file would be considered abandonment. This should have been done long ago, of course.

There can be few more ridiculous things in federal annals, surely, than the spectacle of battalions of Interior Department and Forest Service lawyers trying to detach mining claimants, prior to the change. Ordinarily it was not the big companies that caused trouble, but small, jackleg outfits or individuals trying to get a piece of land for nothing. Comic relief and perhaps a public service in exposing the absurdities of the old Mining Law were afforded in the early 1970s by the warfare being waged between federal and western state officials and Merle Zweifel of Shawnee, Oklahoma, a mining claimant extraordinaire.

Zweifel, who had served time in Texas in the 1950s on a mail-fraud charge, turned out to be the Appleseed John, Paul Bunyan, and Robin Hood of the western range. His Zweifel International, an organization describing itself as the "world's largest claim location service," had the proud slogan We Fly Farther and Stake Faster. Through his enterprise, Zweifel International assembled what he described as "more than 20,000,000 acres of lode and placer mining claims located in the states of Arkansas, New Mexico, Colorado, Wyoming, Utah, Arizona, Nevada, and offshore the east and west coast of North America." He once estimated that his holdings might be worth a trillion dollars.[34]

In the latter part of the 1960s, Zweifel and his treasure hunters swooped down on the shale-rich Piceance Creek basin of western Colorado. The federal government's shale is leasable—not subject to location under the 1872 law—but Zweifel claimed other minerals, notably aluminum. He and his associates staked a blizzard of 2,910 claims covering 465,000 acres. The Interior Department, which was tidying up choice federal tracts for lease to big outfits, challenged him. The department's lawyers at the Federal Center in Denver were put to tremendous labor.

When the attorney general of Nevada accused Zweifel of failing to do the legally required assessment work on his claims, Zweifel made a virtue of it. He said he did not want to inflict unnecessary damage to the environment by rooting around with a bulldozer. His dauntless effrontery and his running of the 1872 statutes into the ground helped make it embarrassingly difficult to defend the law as Holy Writ, even though sober brows continued to bless it. In any event, Zweifel was not a comfortable companion for the likes of Anaconda, Kennecott, or Phelps Dodge.

The BLM's organic act of 1976 went far toward dealing with the problem of nuisance mining claims, but it did not touch the more basic problem involving the miner's priority status on the public lands. As we have seen, the mining industry continued to resist the thoroughgoing reforms sought by the Carter administration and in 1977 managed to beat back the assault. The reform effort lost its steam. House Interior Committee Chairman Udall, who earlier had championed the environmental forces, abandoned reform for the decade.

Reform's swan song could be heard clearly at the 1977 House subcommittee hearings presided over by Rep. Abraham Kazen, Jr., Texas Democrat—for the decade of the 1970s, at least. Interior Secretary Andrus led off with a plea for repealing the 1872 Mining Law and replacing it with a leasing arrangement.

"Mining is a principal industry in many of our western states," Andrus said, "and when that industry sneezes, too often an entire state runs a fever. But mining cannot be preeminent because it is important. There are other land values, there are other natural resource values, and all must be taken into consideration when assessing a mining development."[35]

As for the withdrawals about which the industry had complained, the secretary said one reason for the withdrawals was the outdated law, which made it impossible for federal land managers to control mining activity any other way. Andrus was well aware, he said, of the deep emotions aroused in the West when the old dispensation was threatened, but he was hopeful that the need for a new law could be discussed without passion, in the context of the here and now. Andrus's and the administration's position had strong support from witnesses representing three conservationist groups, the National Wildlife Federation, the Environmental Policy Center, and the Wilderness Society. A fourth witness, from the Society of American Foresters, called attention to mining damage in forests but took no position on the legislative proposals.

Otherwise the mining industry had a clear field and dominated the testimony. The leading industry spokesman, followed by Gov. Scott M. Matheson of Utah and nine other witnesses, was Howard L. Edwards, associate general counsel of the Anaconda Company and chairman of the public lands committee, American Mining Congress.[36] Edwards did not oppose all change. He agreed to payment of a royalty and to having reasonable environmental controls set forth in the modernized law. He insisted, however, that a switch to leasing for hard-rock minerals would be tantamount to a moratorium on new exploration. He expressed the industry's fear of giving the secretary discretion as to what lands should be leased. Another mining spokesman said the administration wanted to give the secretary "absolute, tyrannical authority."[37]

At the hearings many a tear was shed about the hard times through which the mining industry was then going, but in 1979 copper made a vigorous comeback. What the 1977 hearings boiled down to was a controversy over whether miners or federal officials should decide the fate of a piece of federal land. The miners won. Faced with pressure for thoroughgoing reform, they had come forward with an alternative proposal of their own fashioning, a proposal that in important respects left them better off than before. The miners' bill was not acceptable to the conservationists, and the outcome was a stalemate.

To gain a comprehension of how these things are done, it is not necessary to pry behind the scenes. One need only read

191

through the printed 1977 hearings—called *Mining Law Reform*—
to sniff the prevailing winds. The industry's witnesses were welcomed with hearty camaraderie and sympathy, as if an apology
were in order for bothering them. While symbolically dusting
off the chair for these sturdy patriots, with a servility that verged
at times on the comic, western congressmen listened politely but
without enthusiasm to Andrus and his thinly ranked
supporters.

We shall see in the chapters to come—on the fossil fuels, timber, and grazing—that this is an old story. When great public-
lands issues are at stake, the general public interest all too often
is poorly represented.

Copper open pit mine at Ajo, Arizona. *Courtesy Bureau of Land Management.*

CHAPTER 8

PENNSYLVANIA, TEXAS, AND BIG OIL

Although Texas had this almost boundless public domain, it was given away, dissipated, and squandered with a reckless abandon. . . . It was as carelessly disposed of as was the family fortune in the traditional proverb of the profligate son.

—RALPH W. YARBOROUGH in a foreword to Thomas Lloyd Miller's *The Public Lands of Texas, 1519–1970*

This discovery set off the wildest, most irresponsible, and wasteful binge the oil industry has ever seen.

—Chairman JIM C. LANGDON of the Texas Railroad Commission in testimony before the Senate antitrust and monopoly subcommittee May 21, 1969, referring to the East Texas strike of 1930

I t is likely that most of the oil and natural gas remaining to be discovered in the United States will be found on federally owned lands, either onshore or below the shallow seas, but the first strike was in Pennsylvania—not a public-lands state—and two immensely significant later ones were in Texas, which retained its public lands when it came into the Union and proceeded to dissipate them, Texas style.

When the so-called energy crisis began to seize the attention of the nation and the world in 1973, the oil age in the United States was only a little more than 100 years old, even though oil, along with natural gas and coal, had been folded in the earth for millions of years. Until the late 1880s, wood was the principal fuel used in the United States. The Mississippi River steamboats in their day of glory picked up wood at stations along the riverbank. Coal overtook wood and was itself overtaken in the 1940s by oil and gas. At the time the energy shortage became an issue of consequence, domestic supplies of oil and gas seemed to be faltering as the search for them became more difficult, while coal—an abundant resource in the United States—was fated to climb ahead despite the pollution, danger, and toil that went with it.

In the United States, the intensified search for the oil, gas, and coal that remained in the ground raised the pressure for exploitation of the public lands in the West, in Alaska, and on the Outer Continental Shelf.

On November 7, 1973, President Nixon delivered to the nation an energy statement in which he launched Project Independence, an ill-starred campaign to make the United States self-sufficient by 1980.[1] At that time, American dependency on oil imports had increased from 20 percent in the 1960s to about 36 percent. The imported supply came mostly from Venezuela and Canada, only about 10 percent from Arab nations. In 1973 the Organization of Petroleum Exporting Countries, or OPEC, dominated by Persian Gulf and North African states with two-thirds

195

of the world's proven oil reserves, imposed a 400 percent increase in prices. That autumn, the Arab oil producers clapped an embargo on shipments to the United States and other nations they felt were supporting Israel in the brief but savage Yom Kippur War. These events demonstrated in a dramatic way the vulnerability as well as the staggering cost of the overseas oil-supply line.

It was doubted from the outset that President Nixon's objective of self-sufficiency could be achieved even if all possible measures were taken to exploit domestic energy resources, regardless of cost or damage to the environment. To most Americans, though, the effort made sense, from the national security standpoint, as a way of avoiding foreign exchange outlays that threatened to become prohibitive and minimizing dependence on foreign sources. The nation, exuberantly consuming one-third of the world's energy resources, could not afford to have its motors, factories, heaters, and air conditioners halted at the whim of Middle Eastern sheikhs or anyone else. It did not want to be blackmailed on foreign policy. It could not tolerate uncertainty about petroleum supplies for military aircraft, tanks, and naval ships.

Both the national security argument and the fear of fantastic imbalances in the nation's balance of trade weighed heavily against conservationist efforts to protect the American environment from further ravages. The energy crisis put conservationists on the defensive, while at the same time it sanctified and advanced a long wish list of aims which the energy industry— the oil and gas people, the coal producers, the utilities—had been seeking for years. At the top of that list was the deregulation of natural gas. The industry insisted, not without logic, that federal regulation of gas prices had kept this clean and convenient fuel artificially cheap. In consequence, it was contended, gas supplies had been wasted and depleted by widespread use as boiler fuel, replacing dirty coal. The shortage of gas had caused conversion to oil, also in short supply. Industry argued that if

196

Pennsylvania, Texas, and Big Oil

gas were allowed to rise to its true, unfettered market price, along with oil, then development of new sources would be encouraged. Coal would be cleaned up, somehow or another, and take its rightful place under the boilers.

In addition to the deregulation of natural gas, which President Nixon had advocated in his energy message to Congress on April 18, 1973, the captains of energy sought easier access to the public lands and the Continental Shelf, tax benefits, speedy approval of the mammoth Alaska pipeline project, a tempering of federal environmental laws to permit increased use of coal.[2] These actions, they argued, would speed the production of fossil fuels from domestic sources. The Nixon administration echoed industry's demands in its administrative actions and its proposals to Congress.

Nevertheless, although the immense and politically powerful oil interests of the nation tried to gain what they could from the energy shortage, it was not all cakes and ale for them. When Americans could not get gasoline for their automobiles and heating oil for their homes in the crisis winter of 1973–74, public wrath ran high. It was obvious, as Senator Jackson of Washington said, that the close and friendly partnership between oilmen and the federal government had not been working well. The industry was accused of manufacturing the shortage in order to raise prices and line its pockets. Its leaders were haled before congressional committees, lectured like schoolboys, and made to answer embarrassing questions. For a time, when public indignation was hot and members of Congress were hearing from their constituents, oil found itself hard put to fight off restrictive legislation. Congress published mountains of hearings, studies, and reports that peered into the complexities of the industry, national and international. In due course the queues at the gasoline service stations disappeared, the interest of press and citizenry turned elsewhere, and very little was done.

Illustrative of the difficulty of bringing out the facts about the oil industry in a definitive, readily comprehensible way was the

197

most dramatic and well-publicized set of hearings at the time. They were held in January 1974 by Senator Jackson's Permanent Subcommittee on Investigations.[3] Jackson summoned spokesmen for the seven largest American oil companies—Exxon, Mobil, Texaco, Gulf, Standard of California, Standard of Indiana, and Shell—and sat them in a row before live television cameras. Senators questioned the oilmen on successive days about their profits, their service stations, how much they made on a gallon of gasoline, their taxes, their drilling operations, their operations overseas, and their relations with the sheikhs. Comparing the first nine months of 1973 with the first nine months of the previous year, the committee's chief counsel reported that total net earnings for the seven had gone up by 46 percent, ranging from 32 percent for Standard of Indiana to 60 percent for Gulf worldwide.[4]

It is fair to say that Jackson and the other senators seemed to be trying to get to the bottom of the oil problem and the oil witnesses were trying to respond. A great deal of information was sought, provided, and duly printed. The trouble was, it was all too vast and detailed and complex. Like so many congressional hearings, it was a fox hunt in which the pack bayed and yapped and covered a lot of ground without catching a fox—if there was a fox. As befitted the nation's most powerful financial, industrial, and political force, the oil industry pushed its cause with vigor in Congress and in the public prints and through the electronic media. It took its lumps for having contributed largely to President Nixon's campaign for reelection in 1972, an offense no sophisticated observer found unusual, and it benefited from steadily rising energy prices. It managed to survive.

Yet the titans did suffer damage. Even though the ramifications of the oil industry at home and abroad were perceived only murkily, the exposures of the early 1970s brought a loss of status and prestige. The industry and its associates in the government had failed to keep gasoline in the pumps. The industry, despite its tax incentives, had allowed domestic oil production to slump and had ventured overseas where recent misfortunes had shown them to be the errand boys rather than the masters and exploiters of the Middle Eastern oil-producing states. The system, for the moment at least, had broken down. In 1976 the major companies found themselves fighting a move in Congress to break them up.[5]

Sweating under the television lights in the old Senate Caucus Room, responding politely to the questions of Senator Jackson's panel, the representatives of the seven American majors spoke for an industry born in 1859 near Titusville, Pennsylvania. "Rock oil," they called it back then—an evil-smelling substance valued for medicinal purposes.

The first commercial oil well in the world was drilled on Oil Creek in the Titusville area, a good distance north of Pittsburgh and west of the Appalachians, by a one-time New York & New Haven railway conductor, Edwin L. Drake. He was a cordial and clever but not very provident man. Quitting his railway job for health reasons, he bought stock in the Pennsylvania Rock Oil Company and was engaged by that firm to go to Titusville. He studied and applied the techniques of salt-well drilling, drove a protective metal pipe to bedrock, and struck oil at sixty-nine and one-half feet. It was not a gusher, but oil—1,000 barrels a day—oozed up in sufficient quantity to be barreled and sold. Unfortunately for Colonel Drake, as he was called, he did not patent his drilling process. Titusville boomed, pipelines were laid to rail shipping points despite the rancor and sabotage of teamsters, and the first oil fever brought in a motley horde. Drake himself got little besides a place in history. After the Civil War he was found to be living in poverty in New York. The grateful citizens of Titusville chipped in to help his family, and the state of Pennsylvania granted a $1,500 annual pension. He died in 1880 at Bethlehem. His body was brought to Titusville, and a monument was set up to him and his wife. "He shook the boughs for others to gather the fruit," said Dr. F. B. Brewer, a physician of Titusville.[6]

199

The same comment could not be made of John Davidson Rockefeller, the first and greatest of the oil giants, who was twenty years younger than the sickly and neuralgic Drake, outlived him by a good half century, and was the world's richest man when he died in 1937. Born in upstate New York, the son of an itinerant peddler of quack remedies, Rockefeller was blessed with the Baptist faith, sobriety, and a sound instinct for bookkeeping. In his youth he moved to Cleveland, where he saved his money and made himself a competence. The Titusville strike attracted him. Its chaotic, feast-or-famine economics did not. He applied his organizational genius to an infant industry. Getting into the refining end of the business, he made rebate deals with railways to squeeze out competition. Kerosene for lighting was his product, and he sold it far and wide. Out of his Standard Oil Company of Ohio, organized in 1870 with $1 million capital, came the fabulous and puissant Standard Oil Trust. The trust aroused the nation to anger and finally was split asunder in 1911 by the United States Supreme Court, victim of the Sherman Anti-trust Act.

Out of the splintering of the Standard Trust emerged four of the seven major American companies that figured in Senator Jackson's hearings of early 1974. These were the mammoth Exxon, formerly Standard of New Jersey; Mobil, formerly Standard of New York; Standard of California; and Standard of Indiana. The original Rockefeller company, Standard of Ohio, which became an independent following the 1911 court order, ranked about fifteenth among the nation's oil companies in the early 1970s. Standard of New Jersey had been the central holding company for the Standard Trust from 1899 until the breakup.

The Pennsylvania oil boom that gave the Standard Trust its start involved lands that never had been part of the federal domain. Drake's strike stimulated a search that spread gradually, extending into New York, the Midwest, and eventually across the Mississippi into the mid-continental basin, the Gulf Coast, Texas, and California. There was a flurry of oil exploration in

200

remote California shortly after the Civil War. California yielded oil in the 1870s and Colorado in the 1880s. Long before Doheny figured in the Teapot Dome case, he brought in the first successful well in the Los Angeles area, in 1892. The burning thirst for minerals in the nineteenth century centered on hard-rock ores and, to a much lesser extent, coal, as far as the federal lands were concerned. That changed with the development of a mass market for oil and its products. Interest in the offshore oil preserves, and in who owned them, became keen when the Creole field one mile off the coast of Louisiana began producing in 1938.

Texas is not a federal public lands state, but the great petroleum discoveries there must be touched upon briefly because they are essential to an understanding of the oil industry's development. As has been noted, Texas retained its own unappropriated public domain—about 150 million acres—on entering the Union in 1845. This was in contrast to the practice with western public-lands states and explains why, in the 1970s, the United States owned more than 86 percent of Nevada but less than 2 percent of Texas, mostly "acquired" for defense, park, or reclamation purposes. The record of Texas for squandering that state's patrimony is even worse than that for the federal government for the public lands owned nationally.[7]

It was the promise of land in generous amounts that drew Americans to Texas in the first place. Under Mexican law, a settler and family head could get more than 4,400 acres for $117. The Texas Constitution of 1836 provided generally that all Texans who were heads of families, excepting Negroes and Indians, were entitled to one league and one labor of land—roughly 4,600 acres. Fraud was rampant in the handling of these and other dispensations. In Texas, it has been said, the words *land* and *fraud* were very nearly synonymous.[8]

As one contemplates the oil riches uncovered by the Spindletop gusher near Beaumont in 1901 and the East Texas strike along the Sabine River in 1930, there is point in recalling that when Spain and Mexico ruled Texas, all minerals were reserved to the sovereign. In the early days of statehood, Texas kept all mineral rights. During the Civil War, the state sought to reclaim from its private owner a salt lake in Hidalgo County called El Sal del Rey. This matter being in dispute, the state's constitutional convention of 1866 formed a committee to study it, and that committee recommended release of all mines and minerals to owners of the soil. The Texas Constitution of 1876 enshrined the mineral-release doctrine. In 1912 the Texas Supreme Court held that the state had no claim to minerals on land granted prior to adoption of the 1876 constitution. "Thus an argument over this salt lake caused Texas to lose billions of dollars in oil, gas, sulphur and other minerals," wrote Thomas Lloyd Miller in his book, *The Public Lands of Texas, 1519–1970.*[9]

One way or another, Miller wrote, Texas managed to sell or give away 91 percent of its lands without reserving the minerals. In a foreword to the book, former United States Sen. Ralph W. Yarborough, a Democrat, said Texas had squandered an almost boundless public domain with reckless abandon. He pointed out that although 42.4 million acres had been put aside in the nineteenth century for the state's public schools, even the minerals in lands reserved for education had been disposed of without compensation, except for about 8 million acres. An idea of the sums at stake can be obtained from the fact that in the 1960s, despite all the whittling away and bad management, the landed estate of the Texas public permanent school fund was yielding about $50 million a year.[10]

In 1840, a few years before joining the Union, Texas was estimated to have a population of about 60,000, not counting Negroes and Indians. In its early decades the state was land-poor and strapped for funds with which to fight Indians, throw in with the South in the Civil War, and beat off Mexican incursions. There was no oil of commercial significance until 1894, and it was not until just after the turn of the century, when the state had more than 3,000,000 people, that the Goddess of Petroleum smiled on Texas, particularly on a plot called Big Hill, or Spindletop, which was part of an old Mexican land grant.

The Standard Oil Trust's grip on the budding oil industry loosened somewhat on that morning on January 10, 1901, when Capt. Anthony F. Lucas's Spindletop well came in with a roar heard around the world.[11] This was a gusher, the first to be seen outside Russia. Out of the 1,020-foot-deep hole drilled into a low mound south of town, tremendous subterranean pressures ejected pipe, mud, rocks, gas, and greenish black oil. The sound of it stampeded cattle. The oil came up in a steady stream, six inches wide and pluming 100 feet above the derrick. It formed a lake of oil below the Lucas well, collecting there for weeks until finally, on March 3, the lake was ignited by a spark from a train and was consumed in a blaze of glory.

Captain Lucas, born in the Austrian province of Dalmatia and educated at the Polytechnic Institute of Gratz, had been an Austrian naval officer before moving to the United States, where he found his way into salt mining in Louisiana. Lucas had a theory that oil occurred in association with salt domes. He took over an oil-drilling project on Big Hill—later Spindletop—in swampy prairie country between Beaumont and the Gulf of Mexico. The work had been started by a visionary one-armed Texan, Patillo Higgins, but Higgins ran out of money.

So did Lucas, but the captain, a tall, impressive man with a moustache, managed to obtain outside capital. It was not easy. He approached Standard in New York, and Standard sent to Beaumont an experienced oil executive, Calvin Payne, who looked at the property and told Lucas he would never find oil. Experts from the United States Geological Survey also were discouraging. A favorable reaction, however, came from a University of Texas field geologist, William Battle Phillips, who was sympathetic to Lucas's salt-dome theory. At Phillips's suggestion, Lucas got in touch with John H. Galey and Col. James McClurg Guffey, partners in a Pittsburgh oil-prospecting firm. Guffey and Galey were renowned as wildcatters. They put up $300,000 and gave Lucas a one-eighth interest of which one-tenth went to Higgins, the original entrepreneur. The money was lent by Andrew W. Mellon of the T. Mellon and Sons Bank.

Galey, who had a nose for oil, went to Big Hill at Beaumont and thrust a stick into a hog wallow. Lucas drilled there, and within a few months Spindletop gushed oil. It was a hill that had been in private ownership since 1834, when it formed part of a land grant by Mexico to a man named John A. Veatch.

The Standard Oil Trust, at the time the Spindletop well brought thousands of boomers to the sleepy town of Beaumont, directly controlled 58,000,000 barrels of the oil then produced annually in the United States and had much to say about what happened to the other 10,000,000. By 1902 the Spindletop field, which Standard did not control, was producing 17,421,000 barrels. The Standard people disliked Texas in that period because one of their subsidiaries had been barred from the state for anti-trust violations in marketing kerosene. As has been noted, a Standard scout misjudged the Beaumont area's potential. The Mellons put up $3 million for development of the field, weathered a drop in oil prices to three cents a barrel, eventually took over J. M. Guffey Petroleum Company, and in 1907 formed Gulf Oil Corporation, one of the three non-Rockefeller majors represented at the 1974 Jackson hearings.

Also entwined with Spindletop were the two other companies not sired by Standard: Texaco and, to a lesser extent, Shell Oil Company. The Texas Company was formed in 1902 from the one-year-old Texas Fuel Oil Company, with Buckskin Joe Cullinan as president and such colorful figures as John W. ("Bet-a-Million") Gates, Texas Gov. Jim Hogg, and state Sen. Jim Swayne in the background. Three-quarters of a century later, the company, which changed its name to Texaco in 1959, was second in size to Exxon among the American oil giants and was operating in eighty-five countries. Shell's fortunes were influenced by Spindletop when Jim Guffey, allied with the Mellons, contracted in 1901 with Shell Trade and Transport Company to supply 4.5 million barrels of oil. It turned out that the terms—twenty-five cents a barrel over a twenty-year period—were ruinously low. According to the account of James A. Clark and

Michel T. Halbouty, Andrew Mellon himself went to England and negotiated a workable arrangement.[12] The oil was piped to Port Arthur on the gulf and found its way into world commerce in Shell's tankers. Royal Dutch Shell formed Shell Oil, an American corporation, by consolidating its American companies in 1949.

In the early excitement around Beaumont, there was an assumption that the Standard Trust would enter the field in one guise or another. As expected, a large refinery erected outside Beaumont turned out to have Standard connections. Ultimately Standard absorbed the Texas-based Humble Oil and Refining Company as its domestic subsidiary. Spindletop, however, broke the monopoly, Spindletop with its terrible waste and disorder, its colorful tales of hard-fisted plungers, and its onion patch of derricks.

Less than a decade after the Spindletop strike, the Standard Oil Trust's political machinations were revealed in a diverting way. This was during the 1908 presidential campaign, when William Howard Taft, Roosevelt's handpicked successor, was the Republican candidate. Bit by bit, newspaper magnate William Randolph Hearst made public juicy extracts from a mass of correspondence that had been purloined from the files of John D. Archbold, a vice president of Standard Oil and valued lieutenant of John D. Rockefeller himself.[13] Hearst, campaigning for a third-party candidate, spiced his speeches in various towns with letters from Archbold to Sen. Joseph B. Foraker of Ohio and to Mark Hanna, the Grand Old Party's chieftain in that state. The letters showed that Archbold had been giving Foraker and Hanna instructions as to what legislation he wanted them to support and what he wanted them to oppose. Archbold mentioned money sent to Foraker. The sensational Hearst disclosures tarred several leading politicians of both parties, exposing them as Standard hirelings and ending their public careers. The scandal was shrugged off. Archbold went on to become president of Standard of New Jersey, and Taft, endorsed by Rockefeller, won the election. It was a documented case of industry control over government which might have blown the dome off the capitol in 1972 when money still was flowing into political channels in a mighty torrent but was managed with more finesse—at least until the Watergate disclosures following the election revealed what had been going on in high places.

We have already seen, in the discussion of the Teapot Dome scandal in chapter 4 how President Taft withdrew three million acres of federal lands in 1909 and was supported in that action by Congress's enactment of the Pickett Act.

As if Spindletop were not enough, the prodigal geologic formations below Texas soil produced an even bigger strike in 1930 at the outset of the Great Depression. This was the great East Texas field, the find of Dad Joiner, a wandering oilman who struck it rich when he was well along into the wintry years.[14]

Alabama-born, the son of a noncommissioned officer in the Confederate army, Columbus Marion Joiner was said to have learned his letters by copying from the Book of Genesis in the family Bible. He was a great quoter of Scripture, and he knew poetry. At the age of sixty he drifted from the Oklahoma oil fields to Rusk County in east Texas, where after quixotic misadventures he brought in the Daisy Bradford Three well on a farm near Overton on October 5, 1930, a Sunday. The drill found the oil-producing Woodbine sand at about 3,500 feet. Beneath the bleak rural countryside was the "ocean of oil" for which wildcatter Joiner had been searching. The East Texas field, with a capacity of about six billion barrels, was the largest found on the North American continent until the Prudhoe Bay discovery on the Alaskan North Slope was announced by Atlantic Richfield in 1968. The estimate for Prudhoe Bay was ten billion barrels, very conservatively.

Out of East Texas, which was inundated almost overnight by oilmen, boomers, crooks, and laborers seeking jobs in hard times, came a glut of new petroleum which quickly halved the price to fifty cents a barrel. In the town of Kilgore, buildings

206

were torn down to make way for derricks. The countryside bristled with them, crowded so close in some places that the legs of adjacent derricks touched. There were tent cities, vice dens, honky-tonks. Sgt. Manuel T. Gonzaullas of the Texas Rangers cleaned out some of the riffraff by chaining them up in an abandoned Baptist church until they agreed to leave town. Gonzaullas was known in Texas as the Lone Wolf. They called his chain of miscreants Lone Wolf's Trotline. He and his rough justice became part of the legend.

The East Texas field had more than 3,600 wells within fifteen months after Dad Joiner's Daisy Bradford Five began to flow, and the wells had produced more than 109 million barrels. Joiner sold his interest in the well to Haralson L. Hunt of Dallas, an Illinois farm boy who had become a skilled poker player and was on his way to becoming one of the wealthiest men in the world. The wildcatter who made the strike, much beloved by his fellows and sometimes harassed by money troubles, went on to search for more oil until he died. Hunt never joined the big spenders among the oil rich of Texas. He got a reputation for being tightfisted and eccentric, using some of his funds to advocate a curiously bucolic type of economic and political conservatism.

The East Texas field was immense—220 square miles. Exploiting it, once found, took capital, technology, and organization. Humble was in early. So were Sun, Amerada, Shell, and others. The number of lawyers in the area increased greatly, and they found much work to do straightening out titles and leases.

In East Texas, as elsewhere, there was dreadful waste. Many more wells were drilled than were needed to extract the oil that was required and could be sold at a profit. Multiple drillings reduced the subterranean gas pressures that forced the oil to the surface. Until well after World War I the gas was flared—burned off—or otherwise dissipated. The reason so many wells were drilled was the first-come, first-served "rule of capture" that had prevailed in the oil fields since a decision of the Pennsylvania

Supreme Court in 1889.[15] Just as under the old common law of England, a wild animal belonged to whoever captured it, so the oil under the ground was the property of the person who brought it to the surface. If a man owning oil property did not drill, his neighbors might get his share. He could no more afford to wait than could a child sharing a soft drink with several others, each with his own straw.

When the East Texas field was discovered in 1930, there had already been determined efforts to bring oil production under control and thereby keep prices from plunging. As early as 1919 the Texas legislature acted to conserve oil and gas and prevent waste. The task of carrying out the new statute was given to the Texas Railroad Commission.[16] The commission promptly issued Rule 37, which prescribed that no well could be drilled within 300 feet of another or closer than 150 feet to a property line. In the 1920s the commission launched itself on a career of limiting and prorating oil production in an effort to equate supply with market demand. By the time Joiner's drill was reaching for the Woodbine sand, the commission was trying to hold Texas wells to a daily output of 750,000 barrels.

There had already been clamor for federal action, growing in part out of the Teapot Dome scandal and arising also from fears that the nation might quickly exhaust its oil reserves. Henry L. Doherty, an oil executive of vision and talent, had waged war on excessive drilling in the hectic times following rich discoveries in California, Oklahoma, Kansas, and elsewhere. Doherty favored federal intervention, a concept detested by most of his colleagues. President Calvin Coolidge set up the Federal Oil Conservation Board in 1924, calling for industry's help in moving toward "practical conservation." The industry, through its American Petroleum Institute, made a study and came up with the patently false conclusion that waste was negligible.[17]

With East Texas came the deluge. Naturally enough, the sentiment in that area was to cash in on nature's bonanza and produce as much oil as possible. The Texas Railroad Commission was slow in trying to curb output in the new field. Its Rule 37 on the spacing of wells was honored more in the breach than the observance. The commission granted exceptions freely. In one case at Kilgore, as Clark and Halbouty noted in their book *The Last Boom,* a dozen wells were permitted on a lot measuring 60 by 150 feet. The governor of Texas was Ross Sterling, former president of Humble Oil, who bided his time. Oil prices dropped below fifteen cents a barrel. There was a bitter struggle between forces wanting prorationing and those opposed.

The Texas Railroad Commission in May 1931 put a 160,000-barrel-a-day limit on the field. But the proration order was not obeyed and late in July a federal court declared it invalid. In this tense and confused situation, on August 4, 1931, Gov. William ("Alfalfa Bill") Murray of Oklahoma ordered out troops and shut down the Oklahoma oil fields "until we get dollar oil." Some of the East Texas operators wired congratulations to Murray, expressing regret that the same kind of courage and leadership had not been manifest in Texas. In mid-August Governor Sterling declared martial law in a proclamation that denounced certain producers as being "in a state of insurrection against the conservation laws of the state." Governor Sterling spoke of "open rebellion" in the East Texas field. Brig. Gen. Jacob F. Wolters of the Texas National Guard, in private life general counsel for what later became Texaco, was put in command of troops.

In the months that followed, not even General Wolters's horse cavalrymen in their floppy campaign hats could enforce the mandate of the Texas Railroad Commission. The term *hot oil—* meaning oil over and above the prorated amount—entered the vocabulary. Many operators felt it was nobody else's business how much oil they produced. Things got so bad that the North Texas Oil and Gas Association asked President Franklin D. Roosevelt to step in. Other oilmen feared Roosevelt and the ambitions of his interior secretary, Ickes. Federal agents arrived in East Texas but, like state officials, could not curb the flow of hot oil. It was slowing down, however, when a Texas lawyer, F. W.

Fischer, successfully attacked the National Industrial Recovery Act in the United States Supreme Court.

Fischer, who had gotten his start behind mules in the Oklahoma Territory, argued that Congress had not given the president the right to regulate oil. The Supreme Court agreed in January 1935. Chief Justice Charles Evans Hughes said that constitutional authority was lacking for what had been done. Even though transporting hot oil might have damaging consequences, Congress had not prohibited it. This was a victory for Fischer and his clients, but the majority in the industry wanted a stop to the bleeding and the chaos. Gen. Hugh Johnson, the administrator of the National Recovery Act, asked Congress to cure the defect bared in the Supreme Court ruling. Sen. Tom Connally, Texas Democrat, joined with Sen. Thomas P. Gore, Oklahoma Democrat, in pushing through Congress the Connally Hot Oil Act, which became law in February, a few weeks after the Supreme Court had acted.[18] The effect was to give federal backing to state efforts to regulate oil production and support prices.

It has been estimated that fully 100 million barrels of East Texas oil had illegally escaped into the marts of trade before the Connally plug was put into place. Thus was order established, of a sort. The period of egregious waste drew toward an end. Demand rose mightily over the next four decades. It was stimulated by World War II, by the burgeoning of the automobile, by the expansion of an advanced industrial economy based largely on petroleum and its products. The oil industry waxed fat and powerful, protected since 1913 by generous federal tax concessions, bulwarked against ruinous overproduction by state compacts, and guarded from the competition of cheap overseas oil by order of President Eisenhower, who established the Mandatory Oil Import Program in 1959. Despite these encouragements of domestic production, drilling in this country went into decline after 1957. By the oil-short winter of 1973, the United States needed more foreign oil than it could get.

Pennsylvania, Texas, and Big Oil

Titusville, Spindletop, East Texas: these were three major chapters in the fascinating history of the American petroleum business. They form a background against which the renewed assault on the federal lands, launched when the energy shortage began to bite deeply, can be better understood. East Texas has been described as the last oil boom of the classic type—rugged individuals rushing to make their fortunes. After East Texas, by and large, the struggle to find more oil became a battle of the mastodons. The last strike, Prudhoe Bay in 1968, was not for the likes of Dad Joiner. Digging a well on the North Slope required the financial and technical resources of an Atlantic Richfield. In East Texas a well could be drilled for less than $26,000. On the North Slope or somewhere on the Outer Continental Shelf, logistical problems are savage, drilling may cost multiple millions of dollars, and the bonus to be paid on an attractive federal lease can reach into the stratosphere.

Another element of the oil business which grew too large for small operators was transportation by pipeline. During World War II the federal government spent $150 million to build the Big Inch and Little Inch oil pipelines from Texas to the industrial East. The Big Inch, twenty-four inches in diameter, was run from near Longview at the northern edge of the East Texas field a distance of 1,400 miles to the eastern seaboard in the New York–Philadelphia complex. The Little Inch, twenty inches in diameter, started farther south, near Beaumont, and paralleled the Big Inch most of the way. They delivered huge quantities of crude and refined oil products. The oil industry had pushed for the project, which was authorized after the Japanese attacked Pearl Harbor and after the vulnerability of tankers had been demonstrated. Secretary Ickes, who headed the Petroleum Administration for War, gave the task of getting the job done to J. R. Parten, an oil executive who had operated in East Texas. The government wanted industry to build and operate the Big Inch. Oilmen thought the government should build and operate it.

211

What happened, of course, was that industry built the line with the government supplying the political clout and the money. After the war the lines were shut down, sold to Tennessee Eastern Transmission Corporation, and converted to gas, by then emerging as a fuel second only to oil.[19]

More staggering by far than the Big Inch and the Little Inch was the mammoth trans-Alaska pipeline project for which the oil companies on the North Slope of Alaska sought federal approval after the Atlantic Richfield strike on Prudhoe Bay. With private capital, at a cost estimated at billions of dollars, an industry combine successfully proposed building a line forty-eight inches in diameter, running about 800 miles across high mountains and permafrost bogs from the frozen Beaufort Sea north-south through Alaska to the warm-water port of Valdez on the Pacific. It was designed to drain the North Slope field at the rate of two million barrels a day.

Thinking back to Colonel Drake's makeshift well at Titusville just before the Civil War, oozing oil by the bucketful, one must be impressed by the gargantuan growth of an industry that by the 1970s had produced more than 100 billion barrels of oil and in 1971, by estimate of the Chase Manhattan Bank, boasted a worldwide gross investment in fixed assets of $223 billion, of which $101 billion was in the United States and the rest flung from the Persian Gulf to the ends of the earth. In this country were 218,000 miles of pipelines representing a gross investment of $7 billion, owned chiefly by the major oil companies. Not wanting to be caught with nothing but oil, the companies had leased or bought 30 percent of proven domestic coal reserves, including large holdings on the public lands. They owned a greal deal of uranium capacity, and they were the chief bidders for federal leases of oil-shale and geothermal properties. The after tax profits for twenty-one majors rose by 58 percent to $9.3 billion in 1973 and were continuing to climb at a fantastic rate as a result, in great part, of their overseas operations, from which some in Congress wanted to divest them.

Pennsylvania, Texas, and Big Oil

When Senator Jackson railed at the big oil companies in 1974 and told them the vaunted "partnership" between industry and the federal government was not working, the implication was that the oil industry had failed to keep its part of the bargain. The industry had received billions in tax advantages and other benefits to encourage the production of oil. It had failed to keep the nation supplied, as witness the shortages of fuel oil and the queues at the gasoline pumps.

Whereas the United States was importing 28 percent of its oil in 1921, the nation became a major exporter in the 1930s and in 1938, with World War II on the horizon, was shipping 530,000 barrels a day and supplying 30 percent of the world's petroleum demand. This country took and held the lead among oil producing nations, but its own rate of consumption rose so prodigiously that in 1948—a decade after the export peak—it slipped back into the debit column and stayed there. Initially the import requirement was only about 146,000 barrels a day. Two years earlier, in 1946, the United States began getting more of its energy from the petroleum hydrocarbons than from coal, and about 1960 coal lost its dominance in the world energy market. There was a vigorous expansion of drilling activity and new discoveries in this country during the decade after World War II, but after 1956, despite all the oil tax benefits and subsidies, a decline in drilling set in. New oil was becoming harder to find.

Inevitably the apparent thinning down of the flow from the oil cornucopia that had provided cheap gasoline for the automobile age called into question the industry's long-standing economic perquisites, particularly those that had always been defended in the name of national security and energy independence.

Oil's tax benefits have been bountifully productive of millionaires. When the graduated income tax came on the scene in 1913, Congress allowed oil and some other extractive industries to deduct as much as 5 percent of gross income when computing taxable income. This was rationalized as a way of recouping ex-

213

pended capital. It was comparable to the depreciation allowed other industries. The special tax treatment for oil was expanded to encourage production in World War I, and in 1926 the industry emerged with Congress' blessing on a right to deduct an arbitrary 27½ percent of gross income. This percentage depletion allowance, as it was called, was defended on the theory that the taxpayer's oil or gas, an irreplaceable capital asset, was being depleted. Since estimating the amount underground and its value was too complex and difficult, the law allowed an arbitrary depletion percentage. It amounted to a unique bonanza because, in contrast with the depreciation allowance familiar to most industry, which is charged against capital investment and eventually used up, it went on and on, year after year, regardless of the original investment. Thus an oil property might yield in tax benefits during its life many times what had been put into that property. The percentage depletion allowance was a splendid gift in 1926, when corporations were taxed only 13½ percent and the maximum individual income rate was only 25 percent. It became more splendidly generous as those rates rose. When the allowance was reduced to 22 percent in the Tax Reform Act of 1969, the industry estimated that its "tax burden" had been increased by half a billion dollars a year.[20]

Further losses were ahead, however. Even at the lower rate, percentage depletion's cost to the government—that is, to taxpayers generally—was estimated for oil and gas alone at $2.6 billion in fiscal 1975. On March 26, 1975, Congress approved a $22.8 billion tax cut containing a compromise provision that repealed the oil and gas percentage depletion allowance for major oil companies.[21] Sen. Russell Long of Louisiana, a Democrat, always resourceful, held out for a permanent exemption for independent small producers whose first 2,000 barrels a day were to be treated in the old way. Nevertheless, it was estimated the oil industry's taxes were raised about $2 billion a year.

A particularly interesting aspect of percentage depletion, applying not only to oil and gas but in lesser degree to coal and

214

many other minerals, is that it holds not only in the case of private lands but even when the asset being depleted is extracted from federal lands under lease. It applies also to copper and various nonleasable minerals taken from the public's land under the 1872 Mining Law. In either case, private individuals and organizations could claim a substantial tax benefit for the diminution of an eons-old mineral reserve that either was still or had recently been publicly owned.

By way of sketching in the background for the energy wars of the 1970s and early 1980s, the emphasis in this chapter has been on the origins of the petroleum age and on the immediate aftermath of the Arab oil embargo as exemplified by the Jackson hearings of early 1974. A detailed account of the subsequent pageantry, as Presidents Nixon, Ford, Carter, and eventually Reagan addressed themselves to solutions, would be out of place in a book about the federally owned lands.

Fortunately, there has been no lack of serious and intelligent efforts to inform the public about the threatened energy shortage and its implications for the nation and the world. Presidents, federal agencies, and the Congress have issued a steady flow of exhortations and reports. The Ford Foundation's Energy Policy Project, directed by S. David Freeman, came out with its final report in 1974.[22] The National Energy Strategies Project of Resources for the Future, a nonprofit research organization, issued a fat report in 1979. Harvard Business School's Energy Project came out with a book the same year. There were many others.

President Carter shared the view of his immediate predecessors that American dependence on imported oil must be reduced, and that the way to bring this about was to curb domestic consumption by letting prices rise to higher levels while intensifying a search for domestic energy sources. The decisions ahead were politically difficult, not only for the president but for Congress. Accepting the assumption that the demand for energy was increasing while supplies of oil and natural gas were diminishing, Carter promoted conservation of energy and the cutting

215

of oil imports and gasoline consumption. He urged a dramatic increase in coal production. He sought to breathe leadership into the struggle by calling it the moral equivalent of war.

Congress offered no rose-strewn path for Carter's energy proposals. He suffered defeats as well as victories. It was a time of uncertainty and low national morale. Citizens were upset by an inflation that seemed intractable, by the revolution in Iran and the Soviet invasion of Afghanistan. The price of gasoline topped $1 a gallon in August 1979, and the annual cost of imports— some $8 billion in 1973—soared to $48 billion in 1978, to $60 billion in 1979, and toward $90 billion in 1980.[23]

Nevertheless, President Carter in seeking reelection could claim credit for having done much to safeguard the American environment while biting the bullet on energy conservation and the decontrol of energy prices. The Democratic party's 1980 platform said its highest legislative priority had been "the development of our nation's first comprehensive energy policy." It said the Republicans had fostered dependence on foreign oil, a policy that led to "America's petroleum paralysis."[24]

The Carter administration's legislative achievements came in three segments following the establishment of the new Department of Energy in October 1977. The first was the National Energy Act, on which the House took action shortly before adjournment in October 1978.[25] It consisted of five separate laws, aimed at promoting conservation, decontrolling the price of new natural gas by 1985, increasing the use of coal, encouraging development of solar energy, and other purposes.

Carter's second legislative achievement was the Crude Oil Windfall Profit Tax Act, passed in March 1980 and intended to collect a total of $227 billion.[26] Such a tax had been advocated by the president in his April 1979 energy message, when he took action to decontrol the price of oil gradually over a time period ending September 30, 1981. He warned the oil industry that he would fight to tax away much of the profit that would result from decontrol.

216

Thirdly, on June 30, 1980, shortly after the windfall profit tax was enacted and less than six months before his defeat, Carter put his signature on the Energy Security Act.[27] This established the independent, government-sponsored Synthetic Fuels Corporation with the mission of stimulating, by 1992, the production of two million barrels a day of synthetic fuels—such as shale oil, crude oil from liquefaction of coal, and the like. The immediate authorization was $20 billion.

President Reagan went ahead with immediate decontrol of oil prices shortly after he took office in 1981.[28] It was anticipated that he also would proceed right away with decontrol of natural gas prices. In his campaign, Reagan had exalted production of energy above conservation of energy, arguing that the nation is in fact energy rich. He blamed the government and government restrictions and regulations for the difficulties, which he suggested would disappear if the private enterprise system were allowed to work.

In the Reagan-Carter debate at Cleveland on October 28, 1980, the former governor of California spoke of vast supplies of energy yet to be found on the Outer Continental Shelf. He also touched critically on the withdrawal in recent years of millions of acres of federal lands no longer subject to mineral exploration.

"It is believed," Reagan said, "that probably 70 percent of the potential oil in the United States is probably hidden in those lands, and no one is allowed to even go in and explore to find out if it is there. This is particularly true of the recent efforts to shut down part of Alaska."[29]

Those Americans who found Reagan's views on energy simplistic, if not downright wrong, could not deny his skill at telling a harassed electorate what it wanted to hear.

CHAPTER 9

TIDELANDS AND THE OUTER SHELF

Talk about corruption! Talk about stealing from the people! This would be robbery in broad daylight—and on a colossal scale.

> —President HARRY S. TRUMAN, *New York Times,* May 18, 1952, before vetoing tidelands oil bill.

The attack on the tidelands is only part of the effort of the Administration to amass more power and money. . . . The policy of the Washington power mongers is a policy of grab.

> —Republican candidate DWIGHT D. EISENHOWER in Louisiana, *New York Times,* October 4, 1952.

n the struggles of the 1970s over publicly owned fuel reserves—oil, natural gas, coal, uranium, oil shale, geothermal steam—the issue of what constituted a federal giveaway of the American people's resources was an underlying factor. Even more important was the issue of how much control the central government should be allowed to assert over such matters as how, where, and at what pace the fuels belonging to the public were to be exploited.

There was also the battle over the relative merits of federal, state, local, and private suzerainty. Adlai E. Stevenson said in 1952 it was not wise policy for the Congress "to institute a practice of giving away" such national assets as the submerged lands to individual states, but Stevenson lost the election. Some of the great public questions that arose in the energy crisis of the 1970s had been debated in the 1940s, 1950s, and 1960s in the fight over the so-called tidelands, the regulation of natural gas, and the leasing of coal.

Although coal is far and away the most plentiful mineral resource in the United States and has the greatest potential value, federal coal has not played a great role in major overall coal production until the last few years. We may put coal aside for the moment and deal with the titanic legal and political head-knocking that took place over tidelands oil and the regulation of natural gas. Finally, coal—the public's western coal—will make a new entrance in shining habiliments.

The struggle over the tidelands in the 1940s and 1950s taxed the capabilities of some of the most able lawyers in the land. It was finally settled, not by the closely reasoned briefs filed on both sides of the issue, but by political action. The oil-rich coastal states—notably California, Texas, and Louisiana—lost the battle in the courts and then prevailed upon President Eisenhower and Congress to grant them victory.

Naturally enough, there was no burning interest in who owned the offshore lands before it was learned that great quantities of oil, gas, and other minerals were to be found there and

219

before the technology for capturing them had been developed. As early as 1896 oil was produced in shallow water off California, by means of a wooden platform built out from shore. The great Lagunillas field in Lake Maracaibo in Venezuela was penetrated by Venezuelan Gulf in 1926. In 1938 the Creole field was discovered a mile and a half off the Louisiana coast. The initial find off southern Louisiana, which was to become one of the richest oil- and gas-producing areas in the world, was made in about twenty-five feet of water. Only nine wells were drilled in the Gulf of Mexico through 1946, including four off Texas, but in 1947 Kerr-McGee Oil Industries Incorporated made history by completing the first subsea well from a mobile platform. The company, using surplus World War II naval craft, found oil in Ship Shoal Block 32, a distance of twelve miles from the Louisiana coast. From these events great consequences flowed. It was obvious that a tremendous wealth of resources was at stake. By 1947, the year of the Kerr-McGee strike, the state of Louisiana had already leased 675,385 offshore acres for exploration.

But who owned the close-in offshore lands? Was it the federal government, representing all the people, or was it the coastal states? The issue was debated in the 1930s as tidelands oil became attractive, was decided by the courts in the federal government's favor beginning in the late 1940s, and finally was politically resolved in favor of the states in the early 1950s. It has been fashionable to assume that the law was all on the federal side and was subverted by politics and the machinations of the oil industry, favoring state control as weaker and more easily manipulated. Actually, law and custom were to some extent on the side of the states.

In England by the eighteenth century the principle was well established that the crown owned the coastal seas and what lay beneath them, at least as far out as the three-mile limit—roughly a cannon shot from shore. With the winning of independence from England, was it not to be argued that the several states acquired all the rights that the crown had enjoyed, up to and including the crown's rights in the marginal seas? And was it not further to be argued that states subsequently admitted into the Union came into the same rights as the original thirteen, inasmuch as they came in on an equal footing? And did not the Constitution reserve to the states all powers not delegated to the central government? When had the states given up their rights to the tidelands? From these elements good lawyers could and did make a respectable case. Buttressing their position was a long history of federal acquiescence in state control of close-in waters.

For example, Interior Secretary Ickes, who certainly was not a creature of the oil colossus or a doctrinaire foe of strong federal authority, followed a state's right policy on submerged lands from the time he assumed office in 1933 until 1937. There is no doubt about this. As pointed out by Ernest R. Bartley in *The Tidelands Oil Controversy*, Ickes wrote a letter in December 1933 to one Olin S. Proctor of Long Beach, refusing Proctor's application for a federal mineral-prospecting permit in waters off the California coast.[1] Ickes told Proctor that the state of California had title to soil under the ocean within the three-mile limit. Under the public land laws he could grant Proctor no rights, he said, either within or outside the three-mile limit. Ickes was following a line of action which had been established in the Interior Department since 1926. Years later, when Ickes changed his mind about ownership of the tidelands, the Proctor letter came back to haunt him, for it was a clear, unequivocal statement.

In 1937 Secretary Ickes was lunching at the White House when President Franklin D. Roosevelt raised a question about ownership of oil offshore within the three-mile limit.

"I told him that I would get an opinion from my Solicitor on these questions," Ickes recounted in his secret diary. In March 1938 Ickes noted that he and the secretary of the navy were about to join in a request that the attorney general initiate court action to find out whether the federal government had title to the oil lands just off California. If so, he proposed creating another reserve for the navy. Ickes confided that his solicitor—that is, the Interior Department solicitor—was very doubtful of the federal title. On the other hand, House Judiciary Committee Chairman Hatton W. Summers of Texas thought the United States already had title but suggested bringing suit to put it beyond question.

As World War II approached, there was concern about reserving more oil for the navy. At the request of Secretary Ickes, Sen. Gerald P. Nye of North Dakota, whose state had no direct interest in such mineral treasures as might lie below salt water, introduced a bill in 1937 declaring that the land below marginal seas was public domain and belonged to the federal government. This was later withdrawn, to be replaced by a Senate joint resolution instructing the attorney general to "assert, maintain and establish" federal title and possession. The Senate passed the resolution in August 1937. Early the next year the House Judiciary Committee under Chairman Summers approved a different resolution, which said oil conservation in the submerged lands was necessary for national defense, for the navy's maintenance, and for proper federal management of interstate commerce. The House version died without coming to a vote.

In the Seventy-sixth Congress, which convened in 1939, there was a jumble of proposals, but no action was taken. Debate gave evidence of confusion and widely diverse viewpoints. President Roosevelt's Natural Resources Committee, reporting in January 1939, said that since there was doubt about the ownership of oil and gas in offshore lands, it would be wise and timely to make a bold assertion of the national interest. "It is one of the unfortunate errors of our national development that early in our history the public ownership of all subsurface mineral wealth was not declared," said the president's committee.[2] By "public ownership" the committee obviously meant federal ownership.

During World War II the nation's oil reservoirs were bled to fuel the Allied military effort, and by the war's end the winds in Congress had shifted toward the states and the petroleum indus-

222

try. Chairman Summers of the House Judiciary Committee held hearings in the summer of 1945 on various "quitclaim" measures in which federal rights in the submerged lands would be renounced and title established in the states. The House passed the quitclaim bill in September 1945. In the Senate, Sen. Pat McCarran of Nevada rushed a similar measure through in April of 1946. There was surprisingly little opposition. Among federal executive officers, only Ickes testified against the Senate bill. Forty-six of forty-eight state attorneys general backed the quitclaim bill, which was passed. President Truman vetoed it in August 1946.[3] Congress did not override him.

President Truman rejected the quitclaim bill of 1946 for the reason that the issue was by that time before the United States Supreme Court. The Justice Department in the previous year, a little more than a month after Roosevelt's death, had filed an action to enjoin an oil company—Pacific Western—from taking additional oil from an offshore area near Santa Barbara which the company had leased from the state of California. Attorney General Robert Kenny of that state entered the fray, saying state sovereignty was under attack. Secretary Ickes was unhappy with the suit as originally filed under United States Attorney General Francis Biddle, who apparently revived the idea of testing the matter in court at the suggestion of Washington lawyer Thomas Corcoran. Ickes wanted the action brought, not against a private company, but against California. Biddle's successor, Tom Clark of Texas, was reluctant to alter what Biddle had done, and Ickes went to President Truman, who told Clark to do what Ickes wanted. Accordingly, in October 1945 Clark brought an original action against California in the United States Supreme Court.

Before President Truman vetoed the quitclaim bill of 1946, he had issued a proclamation in September of the previous year—only a few weeks after victory over Japan was celebrated—asserting for the first time the federal government's sovereignty over "natural resources of the subsoil and sea bed of the continental shelf beneath the high seas but contiguous to the coasts of

223

the United States." The Truman proclamation, signed also by Acting Secretary of State Dean Acheson, noted that the government was aware of the long-range worldwide need for new sources of oil and other minerals and that such resources were to be found under parts of the Continental Shelf. The seaward limits were not defined, nor was mention made of the issue of state's rights within the three-mile limit. A White House press release said the Continental Shelf was considered to be that area of submerged land contiguous to the continent and covered by no more than 100 fathoms—600 feet—of water. It gave witness to the heightened interest in offshore oil, and in who owned it, that this step was taken at a time when the new president and the nation were frantically busy with global postwar problems.

Another indication of heightened interest was the clash between Truman and Ickes over Truman's nomination of Edwin W. Pauley of California to be undersecretary of the navy, culminating in Ickes's resignation from the cabinet. Pauley was a well-to-do oil operator and Democrat on the west coast. Truman named him early in 1946. Pauley had been treasurer of the Democratic National Committee. He had gathered oil money for the party and had actively supported Truman for vice president in 1944. As an oil man, Pauley had interests in offshore production and had labored for state control of the tidelands. Ickes blamed Pauley for seeking to hold up the federal suit against California, finally filed in 1945. He waged a vigorous public battle against Truman's nominee and went so far as to testify to Pauley's alleged unfitness before the Senate Naval Affairs Committee. He said that in September 1944 he and Pauley had a meeting at which Pauley pledged he would raise $300,000 for the Democrats if Ickes would call off the federal effort to lay claim to the submerged lands. Pauley denied any such pledge had been made. There was an acrimonious struggle, well covered by the press. So hot had Pauley been about state control of the tidelands, Ickes said, that he lobbied for it on the train after President Roosevelt's burial at Hyde Park.

The Ickes-Pauley controversy was never definitively resolved one way or the other. Ickes warned the Democratic party of what had happened to the Republicans in the Teapot Dome episode and sent in his letter of resignation, suggesting he leave March 31. Truman moved the effective date to February 15. The nomination of Pauley finally was withdrawn.

The pleadings in the California case were voluminous. The state contended, among other things, that California's boundaries extended three English miles out into the marginal sea under the 1849 state constitution, adopted before admission to the Union, and that the state was admitted to the Union on an equal footing with the original states, which had comparable rights acquired from the English crown. The Supreme Court brushed these arguments aside in a decision on June 23, 1947, when it ruled for the federal government. The majority opinion was delivered by Associate Justice Hugo Black, who said the question of who owned the bed of the sea became of great potential importance only when oil was discovered there at the beginning of the century.

"Those who settled this country," Justice Black wrote, "were interested in lands upon which to live and waters with which to fish and sail. There is no substantial support in history for the idea that they wanted or claimed a right to block off the ocean's bottom for private ownership or use in the extraction of its wealth.[4]

There was no reason for either the states or the federal authority to focus attention on ownership of the three-mile belt until the California oil issue came to the fore in the 1930s, Black pointed out, and it was not to be thought that the federal government, which represents all the people, could be deprived of its interests by ordinary court rules designed for private disputes over individually owned pieces of property.

"Now that the question is here," continued Justice Black, "we decide . . . that California is not the owner of the three-mile marginal belt along its coast, and that the Federal government rather than the state has paramount rights in and power over that belt, an incident to which is full dominion over the resources of the soil under that water area, including oil."[5]

As was pointed out by Associate Justice Felix Frankfurter in his dissent, the court denied to California proprietary rights in the tidelands but did not declare that the United States had title. There was a confused aftermath. The state attorneys general, led by the eloquent and ambitious Price Daniel of Texas, joined the cry for a rehearing and reversal. Truman's first veto of quitclaim legislation, in August 1946, came many months before the California case was argued. Less than a month after the decision was announced, the Governors' Conference at Salt Lake City, in midsummer of 1947, asked Congress to pass a law giving to the states what the Supreme Court had denied them. Many more quitclaim bills were filed, and it was at a hearing on one of them, in March 1948, that Attorney General Clark confirmed that suits would be filed against Texas and Louisiana. Meanwhile, offshore oil production lagged because of the uncertainty of ownership. Shortly before Christmas that year, the anticipated federal complaints against Texas and Louisiana were filed, and on June 5, 1950, the Supreme Court decided, as it had in the California case, that national rights must be paramount.[6]

Above the legal reefs of the tidelands controversy swam the politicians. President Truman, speaking at Austin as he sought to retain the nation's highest office in 1948, commented soothingly in a campaign speech that Texas was "in a class by itself; it entered the Union by treaty."[7] As is well known, there was a strong flavor of oil money and oil talent in the Dixiecrat movement that campaigned for tidelands and state's rights in the 1948 presidential election after holding a rump convention at Houston. Leander Perez, who argued Louisiana's case before the Supreme Court, was a Dixiecrat leader who got rich off oil revenues in Plaquemines Parish. He tried unsuccessfully to scrub Truman from the Democratic ticket in his state. As it turned out, the Democrats lost four southern states—Louisiana, Mississippi,

Alabama, and South Carolina—to the state's rights forces headed by Strom Thurmond and Fielding Wright. Truman did not, however, lose Texas.

The Democrats in their 1948 platform made no mention of the tidelands issue, nor did they in 1952. For the duly elected President Truman, however—triumphant despite polls showing he would lose—the proposition of a congressional surrender of federal rights had no appeal. There was no doubt that Congress favored a quitclaim bill. The issue came to a head in the spring of 1952, with another presidential election coming on. Sen. Blair Moody of Michigan, a Democrat, called quitclaim "a scheme that makes Teapot Dome look like a conservation project." Sen. Lister Hill of Alabama, a liberal southern Democrat, proposed that federal royalties from offshore oil be used for education. In May, action was completed on an outright quitclaim bill proposed by Sen. Spessard Holland of Florida, a conservative Democrat. Truman declined to go along. In a speech to the Americans for Democratic Action he was characteristically blunt. The oil lobbies, said he, wanted vast treasure turned over to a handful of states where "powerful private oil interests hope to exploit it to suit themselves." Truman talked about "robbery in broad daylight—and on a colossal scale."[8] He vetoed quitclaim for the second time on May 29, 1952.[9] Again, Congress did not override.

The man on the white horse, as far as the claim of coastal states to tidelands was concerned, turned out to be Dwight D. Eisenhower. The general's candidacy was espoused by Texas oilman Sid Richardson and by the industry generally. But Sen. Robert Taft of Ohio also had oil support. Before returning from his assignment as commander of the North Atlantic Treaty Organization in France, Eisenhower early in 1952 wrote in a letter to H. Jack Porter, a Texas Republican in the oil business, that he favored state ownership of the tidelands. He hedged a bit when he was back in the United States and learned that the Supreme Court had ruled on the question; but the Republican convention that named him as its standard-bearer put in its platform these

227

words: "We favor restoration to the states of their rights to all lands and resources beneath navigable inland and offshore waters within their historic boundaries." During the campaign Eisenhower championed the cause with enthusiasm, and there is no reason to believe his heart was not in it. Gov. Adlai Stevenson of Illinois, the losing Democratic nominee, took the opposite position.

Barnstorming through traditionally Democratic states along the Gulf Coast, General Eisenhower took his stand in Louisiana on October 13 and repeated it the next day in Texas. He said in New Orleans that he would, if elected, sign quitclaim legislation surrendering tidelands rights to the states. At Houston he appeared on the same platform with Texas Attorney General Daniel, an anti-Stevenson Democrat running for Tom Connally's seat in the Senate. Signs bore the legend "Ike Save Our Tidelands."

"The attack on the tidelands is only part of the effort of the Administration to amass more power," Eisenhower told the Texans. He asked what would happen to the Great Lakes and the inland lakes and rivers if Washington pushed on with its "policy of grab." He saw perils ahead for Oklahoma, Illinois, Iowa, Kansas. "What of Florida fisheries, of kelp in Maine, or real estate built on reclaimed soil in New York and Massachusetts?" he asked. Inasmuch as Stevenson had been saying boldly in Texas and elsewhere that he backed the ruling of the Supreme Court, Texas Democrats were in open revolt or in disarray. The Democratic governor of Texas, Allan Shivers, later a pipeline executive, announced he could not support Stevenson. General Eisenhower, in his turn, was charged by the Congress of Industrial Organizations with espousing the state's rights view of tidelands ownership in an effort to win Louisiana, Texas, and California.

When Eisenhower trounced Stevenson and gathered much of Dixie into the Republican camp, he and his administration and the Democrats who agreed with them quickly carried out the tidelands campaign pledge. One who did not agree was President Truman, who had called the proposed transfer a "hundred billion dollar steal" and managed early in 1953, in the final days of his presidency, to sign an executive order setting aside the submerged offshore lands as a naval oil reserve. He said: "It has been, and still is, my firm conviction that it would be the height of folly for the United States to give away the vast quantities of oil contained in the continental shelf and then buy back this same oil at stiff prices for use by the Army, the Navy and the Air Force in defense of the Nation."[10]

The year of congressional decision to reverse what the Supreme Court had said about the tidelands was 1953, and the months were April and May. President Eisenhower was in the first spring of his first term. It was testament to the strength of the oil interests in the nation, to their political and financial hold on both major parties, that they were able to put through a proposition that benefited a few states at the expense of the rest and was being denounced, loudly and publicly, as a brazen grab.

This is not to say that all proponents of state control were lackeys of the oil barons and all opponents heroes. To the minds of many, from oil states and elsewhere, the states had always owned the offshore oil as a matter of right and justice, and it was Washington that was attempting a grab, as candidate Eisenhower had said. To those of this persuasion, action by Congress to override the court would simply put right an egregious wrong and restore things to the way they had been. Texas Land Commissioner Bascom Giles's characterization of the Supreme Court's decision in the California case illustrates the attitude. He called it "claim jumping"—that is to say, seizing for the federal government lands to which the states had already laid claim in proper and legal fashion.

The Senate debate on quitclaim occupied the whole of April and continued into early May. It was hard fought, acrimonious, and educational. The vehicle for giving states their offshore lands to the three-mile limit or "historic boundaries" was a bill introduced by Senator Holland of Florida. Also under discussion were a proposal affirming federal ownership of the entire Conti-

229

nental Shelf, from low tide seaward, by Sen. Clinton P. Anderson of New Mexico, Democrat, and Senator Hill's amendment to the Anderson proposal, earmarking federal oil and gas revenues for schools. From the time the debate got under way on April 1, quitclaim had the green light. Defenders of the public domain staged something in the nature of a filibuster, to the annoyance of Republican Majority Leader Taft. Like the Irish patriot Robert Emmet in the British dock at Dublin, they were allowed a flight of oratory before execution was done.[11]

Those senators holding out against giving the tidelands to the states included Paul Douglas of Illinois, Wayne Morse of Oregon, Hubert Humphrey of Minnesota, James E. Murray of Montana, Herbert Lehman of New York, Estes Kefauver of Tennessee, Anderson, Hill, and others. They warned that if the bill passed there would be no end to the claims by states and other interests against the nation's common heritage. Morse, the independent maverick, spoke for twenty-two and a half hours at a stretch, setting a new record. The quitclaim legislation, said he, "is the grab bag into which they propose to stuff the rich natural resources of the nation for the benefit of a greedy few." Two freshman Democrats, Albert Gore of Tennessee and Henry M. Jackson of Washington, did their bit to keep the offshore lands in federal hands.

"Mark my word," Humphrey told the Senate, "the grazing lands and the timber lands will be next, and then the multiple purpose dams.

"Does anyone think this is fantastic? It is not. For if a few coastal states can come in here as they are and demand a part of the ocean, how much easier it will be in the future for other interests to come in and demand the rich natural resource prizes within the states themselves."

Senator Humphrey, future vice-president and unsuccessful candidate for the presidency, said millions of dollars had been spent in propagandizing the American people to prepare them for the giveaway.

Douglas of Illinois tried to convey an idea of the value of the Continental Shelf's resources, which he said had been estimated to be worth from $50 billion to $300 billion. One billion dollars, he said, would make a pile of $1,000 bills 660 feet high—higher than the Washington Monument. Thus it would take 50 to 300 such towering stacks of paper currency, he suggested, to make up the sum at stake. He said giving the tidelands away would lead to demands for the rest of the Continental Shelf.

"As members of the Congress of the United States," Murray of Montana said, "we must realize that we are serving in the nature of trustees of this vast underseas wealth, and in the years to come we will be called upon to account for our stewardship."

Senator Lehman predicted that yielding to Louisiana, California, and Texas today would mean yielding to Wyoming, Nevada, Montana, and Washington tomorrow. He said: "The forests will go. The parks will go. The water power will go. What will remain?"

Lister Hill of Alabama stood up and recalled how the great old Roman from Nebraska, George W. Norris, "stood singlehanded, alone, and fought the exploiters and the robber barons." Hill's estimate of the grand total at stake in the public domain was $1.732 trillion. With Taft upset, asking senators to be brief, and tempers at times getting short, Kefauver helped the discussion along.

"I can see little or no difference," said Kefauver, "in giving away the oil resources under the sea—because we say they are within a state's boundaries—and giving away any of the rest of the national wealth which happens to be located within a state's boundaries. . . .

"If we establish the principle that the national heritage can be given away today, there will be precious little of it left by the time our children have grown to responsible citizenship."

Kefauver's point was precisely that of Republican Sen. George W. Malone of Nevada. Malone held that coastal states had no right to the oil offshore, but if they were nevertheless going to have it, he would offer an amendment to the Holland bill giving states ownership of all minerals in all public lands.

"If old-established land policies are going to be broken," Malone explained to a newspaper reporter, "let us at least be consistent all down the line. I have been opposed to the Holland bill, but if we're going to let the coastal states have the minerals in the public lands along the seacoast, I see no reason to discriminate against the other states in this regard."[12]

Malone's viewpoint supported the Pandora's box theory that opponents of quitclaim had been talking about. Twenty-five Democrats in the Senate sent an appeal to President Eisenhower asserting that the tidelands surrender would be "highly detrimental to the interests of the United States." As the debate wore on, Majority Leader Taft ordered day and night sessions. Rows of cots were ordered set in place so that the Senate could remain at work around the clock. At length, agreement was reached for a vote on a certain day, the cots were sent away, and the Senate on May 5, 1953, passed the quitclaim bill by vote of fifty-six to thirty-five. Morse said it was a sad day for the American people. George D. Aiken of Vermont, a Republican against the bill, commented that for many years a determination had been building up in certain groups to "get at the natural resources of the nation."

"I pray to God that President Eisenhower will have the strength to turn these people back," Aiken said.

The House passed the Senate's bill eight days later, and the struggle was over.[13] The state of Texas quickly sought control over oil and gas leasing in the Outer Continental Shelf, seaward of the area now given to the coastal states. The Senate Interior Committee rejected that move.

Having yielded the tidelands, Congress moved quickly to tie up the rest of the Continental Shelf as federal property. This was done in August 1953 by passage of the Outer Continental Shelf Lands Act.[14] Under this law it was laid down that "the subsoil and seabed of the outer Continental Shelf appertain to the

232

United States and are subject to its jurisdiction, control, and power of disposition." To the coastal states, the submerged-lands law passed a few months earlier had granted rights seaward of mean high tide to their historic boundaries, not to extend farther than three miles along the Atlantic and Pacific coasts and three marine leagues (ten and one-half geographical miles) in the Gulf of Mexico. There was a period of confusion and squabbling about the seaward limits of the strip turned over to states; it was finally resolved in 1960 when the Supreme Court held that Texas and Florida extended three leagues into the Gulf but that Louisiana, Alabama, and Mississippi had a much shorter apron— three nautical miles. There were further court proceedings to establish the boundary between state and federal holdings, with states trying to assert claim to lands forty miles or so farther out and the federal government contesting such claims.

A great treasure was in the balance in the decisive decade of the 1950s. The coastal states, despite their struggling and the political drama of the tidelands surrender, got only about 15 percent or less of the wealth lying offshore. The federal government made good its title to the rest. Of the continental seabeds adjacent to the United States, about 48,000 square miles were or became state lands, while federal lands between the state limit and a depth of 200 meters (about 600 feet) totaled about 805,000 square miles, and federal lands to a 2,500-meter depth added another 478,700.

In the 1970s the nation's recoverable offshore resources were said to include 200 billion barrels of oil and natural gas liquids and 850 trillion cubic feet of natural gas. The Interior Department leased nearly eight million acres on the Outer Continental Shelf from the beginning in 1954 through 1973 and was making plans to triple the amount of lands annually put up for lease. It became commonplace for the high bids received in lease sales to exceed $1 billion. The first 1974 sale brought more than $2 billion. From 1954 through 1968, offshore oil and gas brought more than $4.5 billion into the federal coffers, mostly from the Gulf of

Mexico, particularly off Louisiana. The eleventh annual report of the Council on Environmental Quality, published in December 1980, carried an estimate, made by the U.S. Geological Survey, that the Outer Continental Shelf was supplying about 9 percent of the oil produced in the United States, along with 23 percent of the natural gas.[15]

Although unexplored Outer Continental Shelf areas and the northern reaches of Alaska hold promise of further discoveries that could be large, the Outer Continental Shelf's potential has been revised downward in recent years and is not spectacular. The Department of Energy in its 1979 report to Congress carried an estimate that the entire Outer Continental Shelf, including the Gulf of Mexico, was thought to have only 12.5 to 38 billion barrels of undiscovered recoverable oil and 61.5 to 139 trillion cubic feet of gas.[16] This is not much, considering that oil production in the United States peaked in 1970 at 3.5 billion barrels, while natural gas reached maximum production in 1973 at 21.7 trillion cubic feet. Both have been declining since.[17] Overall, United States reserves are thought to be about ten times annual production. And domestic oil production, as we know, is only about half what the nation consumes.

The Interior Department speeded its Outer Continental Shelf leasing program at the direction of President Carter in his energy message of April 1979. Secretary Andrus issued a final five-year leasing program in June 1980, making more undersea tracts available for exploration by private industry.[18] Difficult environmental and sometimes political problems were encountered when selected tracts were close to populated or scenic shore areas or where there was danger of spills or other hazards.

Chronologically and philosophically, the history of the offshore oil lands, close in and far out, has some parallels with the history of the nation's regulation of its dirty but plentiful coal and of natural gas, a clean and amazingly efficient fuel that came into its own following the defeat of Germany and Japan in World War II.

Plaskett Ridge Road looking down on Sand Dollar Beach on the Pacific Ocean, California. *Courtesy U.S. Forest Service.*

CHAPTER 10

THE PUBLIC'S COAL, NATURAL GAS, AND OIL SHALE

Kentucky produces expensive horses and expensive whiskey. It also produces expensive coal.

> —Interior Secretary ROGERS C. B. MORTON in his "Coal is the Answer" speech before the National Coal Association at Louisville, October 23, 1974

The Federal Government is not in the business of leasing coal for speculation.

> —Interior Secretary THOMAS S. KLEPPE, February 16, 1976

n May of 1975 the late Sen. Lee Metcalf held hearings on new federal coal-leasing policies. One of the witnesses before Metcalf's Interior Subcommittee on Minerals, Materials, and Fuels was Edwin R. Phelps of St. Louis, board chairman of the National Coal Association and president of Peabody Coal Company.[1] What occurred was a confrontation of sorts between Metcalf, a Montana Democrat and zealous defender of the public interest in the public lands, and Phelps, head of the nation's largest coal company and biggest holder of federal coal leases.

Phelps put forward the industry argument that any increases in the federal charge for a resource like coal are ultimately passed along to consumers and that a company's profits also go to the people, inasmuch as they are passed to stockholders. This is a line of reasoning frequently heard when the complaint is made that the private companies extracting resources from the public's lands should pay more for that privilege. Metcalf challenged it.

"The stockholders of the Peabody Coal Company are not the American people, and you know very well they are not," the senator told Phelps. "They are huge banks and insurance companies, and the American people are the general run who do not own stock in any corporation."[2]

Metcalf pursued the coal industry's representative with vigor. It is just not true, he said, that it makes no difference what the companies pay, because ultimately the people pay. "You know it is not true and the people of America know it is not true," he said.[3]

Senator Metcalf, along with Rep. Morris K. Udall of Arizona and others, labored for passage of an effective law for curbing the damage caused by surface mining of coal. Phelps and his industry fought to avoid the burden. After President Ford had twice vetoed bills passed by Congress in 1974 and 1975, fearing loss of jobs and coal production, President Carter on August 3, 1977, signed into law the Surface Mining Control and Reclama-

237

tion Act.[4] Carter remarked that he was not completely satisfied with the legislation. He thought it should have been tougher.

All was not confrontation and bitter words between the coal men and the environmentalists, however. There was an effort to get together and apply the "rule of reason" to coal-policy issues. Under auspices of the Georgetown University Center for Strategic and International Studies, a balanced group of industry and environmental people—Phelps included—came together in 1976 to try to outline areas of agreement. The leaders were Gerald L. Decker of the Dow Chemical Company and Laurence I. Moss, former president of the Sierra Club. Among the members were Michael McCloskey, executive director of the Sierra Club, environmental lawyer Bruce J. Terris, and a number of others who had won their combat infantryman badges in the life-quality wars. In February 1978 the National Coal Policy Project, as it came to be called, issued a report with the cheerful and encouraging title, *Where We Agree.*[5] It was released at a news conference at which young people tried to hand out a dissenting statement from the Environmental Policy Center. They were told they were not welcome.

The project's most interesting conclusion was one that tended to soft-pedal the controversy about a prospective ripping of coal from the West's scenic pasturelands. Despite all the talk about western coal, it was asserted, most of the anticipated increase in national coal production would occur by means of deep mining in Appalachia and the Illinois basin—that is, east of the Mississippi River. The report challenged federal estimates that only 46 percent of the nation's coal reserves are east of the river. The project's task force held that 65 percent, based on tonnage, was a closer to accurate figure.

There was no way to tell how much ice the unofficial report of the National Coal Policy Project would cut, but the attempt to achieve a rational consensus won wide acclaim as praiseworthy. The participants made no pretense of having reached agreement on all coal-related environmental issues, but the effort to get together outside the courtroom might, it was thought, have a promising future. The Rockefeller, Ford, Mellon, and Sarah Scaife private foundations helped finance the project, as did a long list of industrial concerns and several federal agencies. Nonindustry funds paid all expenses of the participating environmentalists.

Coal has a long history of usefulness and controversy. In the West's early days, gold and silver and copper on the public lands had great appeal not only because of their intrinsic value but because they could be packed or wagoned out of remote places. The uses of coal were known, of course, but as a bulk commodity it was valuable solely where there was a market and a means of getting it there. Only gradually did the presence and value of the oil beneath the surface come to be realized, particularly the oil underlying submerged offshore lands. It was the public's coal, among the fossil fuels, that first became a national concern.

Congress passed a law in 1873 governing the sale of federal coal lands at a minimum of $10 an acre, with limitations on the size of tracts that could be acquired by individuals or groups.[6] Railroads and coal companies made use of dummy entries to get more coal than the amounts to which they were entitled. In some cases they proceeded under the Homestead Laws. The first President Roosevelt took forceful action. In 1906 Roosevelt, telling Congress the existing coal law put a premium on fraud, withdrew from entry sixty-six million acres of known coal lands in seven western states and the territories of New Mexico and Alaska. Already some thirty million acres of public coal lands had gone into private hands. Roosevelt was willing to allow settlers to take up land underlain by coal deposits, but only if the United States retained rights to the minerals. He argued that mineral rights should be looked upon as "public utilities," enjoying a status comparable to that of forests and navigable streams.[7]

Teddy Roosevelt's coal withdrawals did not go unchallenged in what he described as the "lusty young commonwealths" of the West. Rep. Franklin W. Mondell, a Wyoming Republican and coal developer, protested. Mondell insisted that the Constitution in Article IV provides that "Congress shall have power to dispose of and make all needful rules and regulations respecting the territory or other property belonging to the United States."[8] That being the case, said he, the president does not have such power. It had been this same Mondell who, a decade earlier, had attacked the forest reservations—twenty-one million acres— made by President Cleveland. The actions of Cleveland, Mondell had said, were "as outrageous an act of arbitrary power as a czar or sultan ever conceived."

Mondell, a competent advocate, spoke for many others. He blasted the conservation policies of the Interior Department, calling them "state socialism." In the autobiography Roosevelt wrote some years later, Mondell was dismissed as a politician who "consistently fought for local and private interests as against the interests of the people as a whole."[9]

After Taft entered the White House as Roosevelt's handpicked successor, the citizenry was treated to a classic case of private against public interest, this time involving the Alaska coal lands. Taft did not share Roosevelt's commitment to the fields and forests. His choice for secretary of the interior, replacing James R. Garfield, was a Seattle lawyer, Richard A. Ballinger, a known foe of federal land ownership. Ballinger clashed with Pinchot who still was head of the Agriculture Department's Forest Service. Taft backed Ballinger.[10] A syndicate involving J. P. Morgan and the Guggenheim interests had become involved in coal claims in Alaska. A young agent of the General Land Office said the claims were fraudulent. Getting the impression that Ballinger intended to approve the claims nonetheless, the agent took his story to former Secretary Garfield and then to Pinchot, who made the information available to Taft. Inasmuch as Ballinger had been mixed up in the Alaska claims—called the Cunningham claims—as a private attorney, Pinchot expected that the president would dismiss him.

Instead, President Taft obtained a detailed reply from Secretary Ballinger and decided, on the strength of it, to uphold Ballinger. The offending land office agent was fired, and the gallant Pinchot himself was dismissed after he embarrassed and defied Taft. *Collier's* magazine printed a series of articles. The press championed Pinchot. Louis Brandeis defended him. After a congressional inquiry that made headlines for months, a committee majority found no fault with what Ballinger had done, suggesting that the charges grew out of a "strong feeling of animosity created by a supposed difference of policy respecting the conservation of national resources." Not long thereafter Roosevelt broke with Taft on the conservation issue, led the Bull Moose secession from the Republican party in 1912, and set the stage for the election of Woodrow Wilson.

Pinchot was not a hero in Alaska where local interests wanted to exploit the territory's coal and felt frustrated, as indeed they were, by Roosevelt's 1906 withdrawals and Taft's 1910 order confirming what Roosevelt had done. Pinchot was burned in effigy as a man who wanted to bottle up Alaska. At Cordova in 1911 a "coal party" led by the president of the Chamber of Commerce marched to a wharf with shovels and proceeded to throw hundreds of tons of expensive imported Canadian coal into the bay. The Cunningham claims were swallowed up in the Chugach National Forest, and there was no development of coal lands in Alaska until 1914.

Coal was to move toward a heroic role in the energy crisis of the 1970s, but in the period from 1900 to 1974 coal's share of the nation's total energy inputs dropped from more than 70 percent to less than 20. Coal was overtaken by oil in the 1940s and, in the 1950s by natural gas, the fuel that in times past had been thrown away.

The presence of gas as a natural phenomenon—"burning springs" and the like—had been noted in colonial days, and the first practical use apparently came about in the 1820s at Fredonia in New York State, about forty miles from Buffalo. At an inn there called the Abell House, visited by the Marquis de Lafayette in 1825, gas was used for lighting and cooking, to the amazement of stagecoach travelers. In 1872 workmen finished an iron pipeline two inches in diameter from Newton to Titusville, scene of the early Pennsylvania oil strike. The piped gas was used for household purposes. In the western boom, though, this magnificent resource that came hissing up out of the earth initially was treated as a dangerous and unwanted by-product of the search for oil with which it was usually associated. It was wasted or "flared"—that is, burned off—in tremendous quantities. There was, of course, no way of capturing and holding it. As late as 1970 gas was being flared in the offshore wells of Cook Inlet of Alaska, and in 1974 a person flying over the Persian Gulf at night could discern flares blazing like stars on the dark waters below.

Not surprisingly, the political history of the natural gas industry is as unsavory as that of the oil industry that controls nearly three-quarters of it. Natural gas is transported by pipeline. In the nature of things it was not likely that several competing pipelines would be built to serve the same community. Therefore natural gas has a built-in monopoly characteristic that was obvious and was early recognized. In evaluating the energy crisis of the 1970s, it is important to keep in mind that natural gas, in contrast to oil and coal, had been subject to federal regulation since Congress passed the Natural Gas Act of 1938.[11]

Industry's bitter struggle to remove the federal fetters from natural gas, such as they were, affords an interesting example of the influence that can be brought to bear on the executive branch and Congress. The 1938 law gave the Federal Power Commission jurisdiction over transportation and sale of gas in interstate commerce. Initially the FPC's authority was not thought to extend to the pricing of natural gas at the producing end—at the wellhead—but as time went on it became apparent to some that the FPC could not regulate the price of gas after it left the interstate pipeline without also having something to say about wholesale prices charged by producers. A leader in promulgating that point of view—anathema to the industry—was Leland Olds, chairman of the FPC under President Franklin D.

242

Roosevelt and later under Truman. Olds pressed the point hard and successfully. He was a veteran public servant, honest and oriented toward the public interest, skilled in cutting through the complexities of utility rates.

When President Truman reappointed Olds for a third FPC term in 1949, the chairman's enemies mauled him savagely and blocked his confirmation in the Senate. Two who figured in the assault were powerful western Democrats, Sen. Lyndon Johnson of Texas and Sen. Robert S. Kerr, an Oklahoma oil millionaire. Johnson was chairman of the Senate panel that inquired into Olds's fitness for the nomination. Radical writings that the nominee had published in labor papers in his youth were dredged up. A Texas congressman with an oil and gas constituency testified that Olds had attacked patriotism and the Fourth of July while praising Lenin and Lenin's works.[12] There was more of this, with the result that Olds was tarred as a Communist. He was not confirmed. It was a show that rivaled the mockeries of justice being staged in the Soviet Union at that time.

President Truman made an unsuccessful effort to save Olds. When the effort failed Truman appointed in Olds's stead former Sen. Mon C. Wallgren of Washington State, who had been a poker-playing companion of the president's and was not of comparable quality to Olds as a regulator of utilities. Truman vetoed the Kerr bill for deregulation of natural gas in 1950, but in a brief space the political and philosophical attitude of the FPC board shifted toward the industry position. In 1951 the commission voted four to one against asserting FPC authority to set rates of the Phillips Petroleum Company, the largest producer of natural gas moving into interstate pipelines.

The FPC then came under legal challenge by the Wisconsin Public Service Commission and consumer agencies in other states. On June 7, 1954, the Supreme Court decided by five to three vote that consumer advocates were right and the reluctant FPC and the oil industry were wrong. The court held that the commission had a duty to regulate wellhead prices.[13] For oil and gas entrepreneurs it was a black day that lived in infamy, a day to which the industry's ills of the future were to be traced with sorrow and indignation.

Twenty years after the direful ruling, the American Petroleum Institute put out a press release in which it said that the *Phillips* decision "quite probably did more to bring about the current energy shortage than any other one action by the courts, government, or industry." The decision, said API President Frank N. Ikard, who had been a representative from Texas before he became the industry's ambassador plenipotentiary in Washington, had brought upon the nation twenty years of confusion and chaos.

What the law as interpreted by the courts had done, the oil industry argued with a conviction shared by many outside the oil business, was to peg the price of natural gas at an artificially low level relative to nonregulated fuels, like oil and coal. That encouraged the rapid expansion of demand for natural gas while discouraging the search for new supplies. Then when natural gas went into short supply, users who could not obtain gas switched to oil. The switch to oil stepped up demand for that fuel, of which an increasing quantity had to be shipped from overseas at heavy cost. So the argument ran.

To a remarkable extent the controversy over natural gas regulation occupied the time of Congress and the FPC in the period from the early 1950s into the 1970s. Oilmen and their friends looked on deregulation as a philosopher's stone that would turn methane into gold and enrich the yield from methane's less cleanly sisters, oil and coal. The *Phillips* decision of 1954 forced wellhead price-fixing down the throats of the commission, which under President Eisenhower was chaired by Jerome K. Kuykendall, a utilities lawyer. Congress moved in hot haste in 1956 to whip through a deregulation bill bearing the names of Sen. J. William Fulbright and Rep. Oren Harris of Arkansas, but Eisenhower vetoed the bill after revelations that an attempt had been made to buy the vote of Sen. Francis Case of South Dakota.[14]

As had been predicted by Associate Justice William O. Douglas, a liberal dissenter in the case, the *Phillips* decision imposed a complex and difficult task on the Eisenhower FPC. Setting wholesale prices for individual producers turned out to be beyond the commission's capabilities. It resorted in perplexity to a system of fixing wellhead rates in geographic areas. Not until 1965 was the first pricing formula evolved, for the Permian Basin of west Texas and southeastern New Mexico. Out of that came a tangle of lawsuits and a great caterwauling from the industry. Rates for a second large producing area, southern Louisiana, were not laid down until 1971. It was intended that these rates cover all costs plus a fair rate of return. The producers remained dissatisfied.

Clamor for removal of the restrictions on natural gas reached a high pitch when President Nixon and his industry-oriented FPC under Chairman John N. Nassikas swelled the chorus in the early 1970s. By that time, natural gas was meeting fully a third of the United States' energy demand, compared to oil's 42 percent, and was powering 43 percent of American industry. In the period between 1950 and 1970, gas consumption increased at nearly twice the annual rate for oil. Gas was serving 150 million people through a network of pipes and mains estimated by the American Gas Association to represent a total investment of $46 billion.

Immense sums were involved. Spurred by the Nixon team and the captains of energy, the FPC under Nassikas permitted a substantial escalation of natural gas prices from 1969 to 1974, providing an overall increase estimated at $2.5 billion. Under the deregulation that was being sought, another $4.5 to $9 billion a year would be added to consumers' gas bills. Such was the estimate attributed to an FPC economist by the Democratic Study Group in 1974. The late Sen. Philip A. Hart, Michigan Democrat,

245

used a rule of thumb—a one-penny increase in the price of 1,000 cubic feet of gas cost consumers at least $200 million a year and caused the uncommitted gas reserves of the nation to rise in value by $10 billion. The industry insisted that an end to federal price-fixing would have little effect on consumer costs.

With so much at stake, it was not strange that the big oil companies took a passionate interest in breaking the federal yoke. They controlled about 72 percent of gas production and reserves, just as they had one-fifth of coal production and 30 percent of coal reserves, not to mention half the uranium. Even if one were persuaded by the logic of their case, it was difficult to work out a way to allow gas to rise to higher price levels, as many people thought it should, without creating windfall profits.

Another complexity was that the federal regulatory authority covered only the 70 percent of natural gas flowing into interstate commerce. The FPC did not fix prices for "intrastate" gas—the 30 percent produced and sold for use in the same state. This meant that gas that did not cross a state line could be sold in time of scarcity for a higher price than permitted by the FPC interstate-gas price limits. It put the long-distance consumer at a disadvantage and provided an inducement for certain industries to move to such gas-rich states as Texas, Louisiana, and Oklahoma, where they might find reliable supplies of gas—at a price. This privileged status was passionately guarded. Misgivings in the producing states were a cause of the prolonged delays in congressional action on President Carter's comprehensive energy bill, which finally was approved as the Ninety-fifth Congress adjourned in mid-October of 1978 and went home.[15]

It was considered a major victory for Carter that the approved legislation, although badly cut up in many ways, did wipe out the troublesome dual market in natural gas, placing both intrastate and interstate under federal regulation until 1985. Meanwhile, a phased-in deregulation of new gas prices was to take place, and the wholesale price of new gas was to be allowed to double by 1985. Such was the compromise.

The Public's Coal, Natural Gas, and Oil Shale

While the producers of oil and natural gas wrestled with Congress, coal as the nation's abundant energy resource—the ugly duckling of the fossil fuels—had trouble achieving the resurgence that had been predicted for it. Coal's difficulty was its dirtiness, its sulphur, its reputation as a notorious polluter. Coal needed a relaxation of the new environmental laws in order to regain its place under the boilers. It could offer abundance. It asked for acceptance.

Coal was mined in Virginia as early as 1787. National production in 1820 was 3,000 tons. As America grew, extending its roads and waterways and railroad net, coal fueled the boilers of steam engines and ships and factories. It warmed the houses and tenements, and it soiled the laundry flapping on the line. By 1900 bituminous production was more than 200 million tons, and by 1918 it had increased to 579 million. It dropped to 310 million tons in 1932 but rose to 631 million in 1947, sagging after World War II. Oil and gas cut into the markets for coal. The railroads began their conversion from coal to diesel fuel in 1944. Production did not pass the 600-million-ton mark again until 1970, when it went to 602,932 million. In the nation at large, the Geological Survey has estimated total coal resources of just under 4 trillion tons. Coal accounted for nearly 70 percent of the country's total estimated recoverable resources of fossil fuel, compared with only 7 percent for oil and natural gas combined and 23 percent for oil shale, a material rich in potential but not yet tapped.

Nevertheless, despite the superb American coal resource, coal early in the 1970s was providing only 18 percent of the more than nine-tenths of the nation's energy coming from fossil fuels, while oil and gas accounted for 76 percent.

Another striking imbalance was that, although roughly half the recoverable coal was thought to lay west of the Mississippi, chiefly in the six states of Montana, Wyoming, North Dakota, Colorado, New Mexico, and Utah, the western states produced less than 39 million tons, or 7 percent of the national total, while federal lands accounted for only about 9 million tons, or 23 percent of the western share. The poor federal showing reflects a long history of low activity on federal coal lands, but is remarkable when one considers that the United States owns about 40 percent of the nation's coal and 60 percent of the West's.

But great changes were afoot. The American coal industry in the 1970s had turned toward the setting sun. With the energy pinch coming to be felt, it was inevitable that the West, a vast area with half the coal but producing less than a tenth of the annual output, would become increasingly attractive to exploitation. The federal government was the largest owner, influencing as much as 80 percent of western coal lands because of ownership patterns, and the western railroads, because of their early land grants, were the second largest. Much of the West's coal lay in flat beds hundreds of feet thick, close enough to the surface for strip-mining. It cost less to mine, and it was relatively low in sulphur, a prime advantage in meeting air-pollution requirements.

V. E. McKelvey, director of the United States Geological Survey, told a Dallas meeting of the Geological Society of America at the time of the Arab oil embargo in November 1973 that the western states have 850 billion tons of coal within 3,000 feet of the surface. Although western production was less than 40 million tons in 1972, he said, the National Academy of Sciences was projecting that western coal output would rise to 220 million tons in the year 2000. Another speaker at the same meeting, President Carl E. Bagge of the National Coal Association, emphatically denied that surface mining would tear up the West and leave it in ruins. He said the Arab hand was on the American gullet, but future salvation might lie in coal—particularly western coal.

Bagge, a former member of the Federal Power Commission, sang coal's praises and expressed the industry's woes and fears as Congress and the Interior Department shaped coal policy. He was effective. As a poor boy in Chicago, it had been his custom to go down to the rail yards and pelt the engine firemen, who, if sympathetic to the fuel needs of the oppressed, might throw back a few chunks of coal. At Dallas, Bagge spoke lyrically of the nation's huge coal reserves, the waiting treasures in the West. He quoted the remark of Wyoming's Secretary of State Fenimore Chatterton in 1902: "Coal? Wyoming has enough to run the forges of Vulcan, weld every tie that binds, drive every wheel, change the North Pole into a tropical region, or smelt all hell."

The immense coal deposits of the northern Great Plains states often lay beneath good pastureland. Their targeting by industry and the Interior Department caused trepidation among ranchers in the Big Sky country. In October 1971 the Bureau of Reclamation printed the *North Central Power Study*, which had been launched by Assistant Secretary of the Interior James R. Smith and was done in cooperation with suppliers of electric power.[16] It outlined grandiose plans for the area's coal and water, causing an uproar as the citizenry got wind of it. In September 1974 the Interior Department issued a "draft interim report" on northern Great Plains coal development, and in August 1975, piling Pelion on Ossa, it published the final report.

There was much hoopla about expanding coal production to confound the Arabs. But despite Interior Secretary Morton's "Coal Is the Answer" speech to the National Coal Association in late 1974, despite Morton's prediction that production might go to 2 billion tons a year, despite President Ford's Project Independence goal of 1.2 billion tons by 1985 and Carter's plea for a similar effort, despite the industry's trumpetings of confidence, a spectacular increase was long in coming.

Accordingly, coal lobbyist Bagge took only modest pride in announcing early in the nation's Bicentennial Year that the bituminous coal industry had mined 638 million tons in 1975, for a new production record. He called it a national disgrace that the record broken in 1975 had stood for twenty-eight years. Blaming the slow progress on environmental curbs and "bureaucratic shilly-shallying," he urged the federal government to act resolutely to encourage a massive return to coal. And he encouraged Congress to water down the Clean Air Act and the National Environmental Policy Act.[17] He asked the lawmakers not to reenact the "punitive and restrictive" strip-mine bill vetoed by President Ford.

Bagge was quite right in saying that environmental considerations were blocking, or at least delaying, a prompt renaissance for coal. Interior Department officials had been making the same complaint. Uncertainty about clean-air requirements cast doubt on coal's acceptability for burning in utility plants and factories, and this uncertainty made it more difficult for coal operators to get capital for new mines, based on firm contracts with users. Environmentalists attacked the expansion of coal on grounds that it would foul the air and ravage the land. In June 1973 an equally divided United States Supreme Court affirmed a lower court decision that held, as contended by the Sierra Club and others, that the Clean Air Act imposed a standard of "no significant deterioration" where air quality was already high.[18] This meant that pristine areas, such as the rural Southwest, could not be permitted to "pollute down" to national ambient air quality standards, unless the law was changed.

The environmentalists, then, deserved a share of praise or blame, depending on the viewpoint, but other factors also had an important role in retarding the opening up of the federal coal lands in the West. One was federal mismanagement of coal leasing in the decade of the 1960s, a situation so disturbing that Secretary Morton imposed a freeze on further leasing in 1971 so that the Interior Department could regroup and find out what was going on. The leasing moratorium continued, despite industry's protests, until Secretary Kleppe lifted it in January 1976.

Secretary Morton put a stop to further coal leasing, and to issuance of "prospecting permits" by which permittees could obtain noncompetitive leases, following receipt of a revealing report issued by the Bureau of Land Management in November

1970. The report was drawn up by Gary Bennethum, a mineral economist in BLM's branch of upland minerals. It was the first bureau-wide assessment, and it left no possible doubt that valuable coal lands were slipping from the federal government's grasp at an accelerating rate, with very little to show for them.

With charts, graphs, and a brief text, Bennethum made the situation very clear. What had happened in the 1960s, largely, of course, under the Democrats, was that the BLM had leased hundreds of thousands of acres of choice federal coal on bargain-basement terms, to lessees who had gotten control of billions of tons at minimal cost and were producing not so much as a scuttleful. As of November 1970, the figures showed, the bureau had issued coal leases covering 773,000 acres of public and acquired land and prospecting permits for another 762,000 acres. The acreage under lease had tripled since 1960 and doubled since 1965. The acreage under prospecting permits had more than doubled since 1960 and had gone up by 50 percent from fiscal 1969 to 1970, reflecting great activity in the first year of the Nixon administration. Although the amount of recoverable federal coal under lease was at least 8.6 billion tons—enough to supply the nation's requirements for fourteen years—total 1970 production from federal lands was less than 7.5 million tons. That compared with a wartime peak production of 10 million tons in 1945, when only about 80,000 acres were under lease.

Bennethum showed that more than 91 percent of the total federal acreage under federal coal lease was not producing a single ton of coal. Six among the ten largest acreage holders were nonproducers. The top fifteen held about 60 percent of the acreage under lease. So-called lease brokers, rather than coal producers or users, held most of the coal prospecting permits.

"Development of federal coal leases is not taking place," the report concluded. ". . . Despite tremendous increases in the number of acres under coal lease and the large reserves contained in these leases, coal production from public lands is remaining constant and has actually decreased slightly in 1970. This is occurring at a time when demand for coal is increasing and coal prices are at their highest levels in decades."

To avoid further aimless alienation, Secretary Morton blew the whistle and instituted a moratorium of nearly five years during which the Interior Department shaped a new, more controlled leasing policy that came to be known as EMARS, an acronym for Energy Minerals Allocation Recommendation System. The thrust of the new policy, as finally announced by Kleppe in January 1976, was to give the Interior Department a firmer voice in where, when, and how the immense federal coal reserve was to be exploited by private industry. Coal spokesmen complained about the leasing freeze and insisted that they knew best, but the Interior Department was under intense pressure to get away from the old, passive, free-and-easy attitude that had permitted the coal landslide of the 1960s.

Conservationists made use of the National Environmental Policy Act to block what they knew could lead to a prodigious upheaval of the western landscape. Under the law, the Sierra Club, National Wildlife Federation, and other groups filed suit in 1973 to halt further federal action in coal development on the northern Great Plains until the development had received adequate study. They wanted regional, rather than local, impact statements. This was the noted *Sierra Club* v. *Morton* action, which the Supreme Court finally decided in the government's favor in June 1976.[19] A roadblock to resumption of federal leasing remained, however, in another action brought in 1975 by the National Resources Defense Council and three other plaintiffs against the department. This suit, called *NRDC* v. *Hughes*, successfully attacked the new EMARS program.[20] A September 1977 federal court ruling enjoined further leasing, and the Interior Department's hands were tied until February 1978, when Secretary Andrus announced that an agreement had been reached with the plaintiffs and was awaiting court approval.

The Interior Department pushed doggedly ahead despite a drumfire of criticism from conservationists, the industry, and Congress. Its May 1974 draft of a two-volume environmental-impact statement, weighing the pros and cons of digging the government's western coal, was denounced as "grossly inadequate" by the Sierra Club. The President's Council on Environmental Quality and the Environmental Protection Agency found grievous fault with it. The National Coal Association, from its vantage point, also expressed unhappiness. Pondering all these things in its heart, the department then recast and shortened the draft before issuing a one-volume, 420-page final "programmatic" statement in September 1975. When this one failed to stand up under court scrutiny, Secretary Andrus inherited the task of fashioning a better one.

Although a major thrust of the criticism was aimed at preventing a ripping up of the western coal states similar to what had already occurred in Appalachia, the concern was not all related to the environment. The General Accounting Office, Congress's "watchdog" agency, took the Interior Department to task in 1972 and again in 1975.[21] It pointed out that four of the fifteen largest acreage holders of federal coal leases were oil companies or were controlled by oil companies and that in calendar 1974 only two of the four had produced coal.[22] The amount of federal coal already under lease, which had been conservatively estimated by Bennethum at 8.6 billion tons, turned out to be closer to 16 or 17 billion tons, with another 12 billion tied up in applications for preference-right leases—the kind issued without competitive bidding because the seeker, theoretically at least, has explored for and found coal on federal lands.

A significant contribution to public awareness of what was wrong with the government's coal leasing was the workmanlike study published in May 1974 by Alice Tepper Marlin's Council on Economic Priorities, a nonprofit organization based in New York City. The study, called *Leased and Lost*, was a damning exposure relating not only to publicly owned but to Indian lands, where much of the recent coal activity had taken place. With admirable clarity, it explained how entrepreneurs had gotten hold of rich federal and Indian coal holdings, mainly in the 1960s, without paying very much, typically without competitive bidding and under circumstances that permitted them to hold the land indefinitely, for speculative purposes, without producing coal.[23] "No pretense may be made that the public has ever received fair market value for its coal," the council said. Peabody Coal Company President Phelps, speaking for the industry, stated the study was based on an oversimplified analysis. He said it "reflects complete ignorance of what is going on in the development of western coal, and, as a result, has done a great disservice to the public." According to Phelps, the only reason anybody sat on coal reserves prior to 1970 was that there was no market, particularly for western coal.

Congress sought to tighten the stable door with the Coal Leasing Act Amendments of 1975, which provided for a royalty of not less than 12½ percent of the value of coal mined. The new royalty rate, applicable to leases issued after mid-1976, was more realistic than the fixed per-ton royalty rate ranging from seventeen and a half to twenty cents a ton provided in leases issued before 1970. BLM testimony before the House Appropriations Subcommittee in March 1978 told the story.[24] In fiscal 1977, the testimony ran, federal leases produced 50.4 million tons of coal valued at $433.7 million, but the royalties to the federal treasury amounted to only $9.9 million, or about 2.3 percent of the value of the coal taken out. One reason for the disparity between the coal's value and what the treasury received, it was noted, was that in the past five years the value of coal from federal land had gone up by 90 percent.

Summing it all up, one could predict as the second half of the Carter administration got underway that the development of western coal was about to detonate with terrific force.

The Public's Coal, Natural Gas, and Oil Shale

An environmental threat comparable to that of western coal development was posed by oil shale, which amounted to 23 percent of the nation's recoverable reserves of fossil fuel. The future for oil shale, however, remained tantalizingly uncertain. The Interior Department labored in the early 1970s to encourage private development of the immense federal holdings of oil shale, but shale did not yield its riches easily. It was gold in the sea. It always seemed five years away from harvest, a harvest tantalizingly near but fringed around with economic and technological problems that made those of coal seem childishly easy.

Oil shale is a laminated marlstone rock that ranges in color from gray through brown to black, depending on its richness. It is of sedimentary origin, formed thirty to fifty million years ago in the mud of marine lakes, and it contains an organic substance called kerogen, which, if heated to between 700 and 900 degrees Fahrenheit, yields a raw shale oil that can be refined to various petroleum products. There is a long history of use by man. In the Middle Ages oil shale was used as a solid fuel in Europe. The familiar "ichthyol" medicinal ointment was made from rock mined in Austria and Switzerland from the fourteenth century onward. In North America and abroad in the nineteenth century, there was production of liquid fuel from shale. The French began commercial production in 1838. The Scots had a shale industry from 1850 to 1964. The Soviet Union and China are making oil from shale today in Estonia and Manchuria.

The United States, rich in this as in so much else, has a great store of oil shale, estimated at the equivalent of 2 trillion barrels of oil or more. That is about four times the entire crude oil reserves of the world—Persian Gulf, Middle East, and all—as known in May 1975. It dwarfs conventional reserves uncovered by the Spindletop, East Texas, and North Slope strikes. It towers over the nation's total recoverable nonshale petroleum resources, offshore and onshore, which the Interior Department in April 1975 put in a range between 273.3 and 493.3 billion barrels—that is, less than half a trillion at the outside.

Considering the magnitude of the treasure waiting to be unlocked by improved technology or rising oil prices, there is no wonder that the rich deposits of oil shale enfolded in the western mountains have fascinated Americans, even though they have not yet paid off. The most promising areas for production are in the Green River formation, where shale occurs in an arid, 25,000-square-mile domain of western Colorado, eastern Utah, and southwestern Wyoming. Here there are said to be high-grade shales—meaning at least ten feet thick and averaging twenty-five gallons or more to the ton—that represent about 600 billion barrels of oil, with an additional 12 million barrels in shales of lower grade.

The people of the United States own 72 percent of these western oil shale lands, just as they own most of the western coal. About three-quarters of the known deposits of the Green River formation are in the Piceance Creek basin of Colorado, between the White and Colorado rivers on the western slope of the Rockies. A total of some 84 percent are in Colorado. Twelve percent of the reserves are in Utah, the rest in Wyoming. The three-state shale region is sparsely populated, having less than 120,000 people, about 3 to the square mile. It receives rainfall that varies from seven to twenty-four inches a year. It is high, ranging from 5,000 to 10,000 feet. In the event of the development of its underlying reserve, the world's largest known deposit of oil shale, this stark and rugged land would be forever changed.

In the old days, before passage of the Mineral Leasing Act of 1920, oil shale was a locatable mineral like iron or copper and was subject to the staking of claims on the public lands under the 1872 Mining Law. After World War I there was a flurry of concern about future supplies of oil, with the consequence that many shale claims were filed in the years immediately preceding the Mineral Leasing Act. The Department of Justice challenged some of the claims that fell into the hands of major oil companies but lost in the Supreme Court in June 1980.[25]

Private commercial interest in the exploitation of shale oil, an expensive and tedious business at best, sagged with the East Texas strike of 1930 and the glut of cheap oil that followed. Not only was domestic oil plentiful, but the giant resources of the Middle East came on-stream at two or three dollars a barrel. Federal interest had manifested itself in the setting aside of two naval oil shale reserves by presidential order in 1916 in Colorado and Utah and a third such reserve in 1924 in Colorado. After long dormancy, interest revived during World War II. Congress authorized research on shale in 1944, and from that time until 1954 the Interior Department's Bureau of Mines developed a mining facility at Anvil Points near Rifle, Colorado, on the naval shale reserve. This provided a useful demonstration but caused nervousness and displeasure among some in the oil industry. The National Petroleum Council, an Interior Department advisory group composed of industry leaders, advised Eisenhower's Secretary McKay that further government effort was not needed and the facility should be shut down. Congress discontinued funds, which brought the work to an end. Sen. Estes Kefauver, Tennessee Democrat, called it a clear-cut case of domination of federal policy by the oil industry.

Meanwhile, private operators were not idle as the prospects for oil shale, always alluring although far-off, underwent a renaissance. Union Oil Company of California opened a mine and set up a retort on its own land in the Parachute Creek country in Colorado between 1956 and 1958. A Mobil Oil combine that included Exxon, Amoco, Phillips, Conoco, and Sinclair rented the Bureau of Mines facilities near Rifle between 1964 and 1967 and processed 300 to 400 tons of ore a day. Later the Paraho Development Corporation, with Standard of Ohio, Mobil, and a dozen or more other participants, leased the same property. In 1965 the Colony Development Company, a joint venture including Standard of Ohio and The Oil Shale Corporation (TOSCO), later joined by Atlantic Richfield as operator, got underway on Parachute Creek. These efforts involved the investment of many mil-

257

lions of dollars. By 1970 there were about twenty oil companies and a number of other concerns and persons owning oil shale land in Colorado, mainly on the southern edge of the Piceance Creek basin in the so-called Mahogany Zone.

President Nixon in his 1971 energy message asked the secretary of the interior to begin "a leasing program to develop our vast oil shale resources, provided that environmental questions can be satisfactorily resolved."[26] These questions had long been apparent. One was the problem of waste disposal—what to do with the great quantities of spent shale once the oil had been removed. Another was the problem of obtaining water for the recovery process in a country where water is scarce. There were many others.

At the president's direction, Secretary Morton in November asked industry to nominate tracts suitable for leasing. He noted that ten companies were drilling in Colorado and Utah at the time. Step by step, the Interior Department moved to go ahead with leasing and at the same time comply with the National Environmental Policy Act. Morton issued a three-volume draft environmental impact statement in 1972 and followed it up in mid-1973 with a final six-volume document analyzing the effect of a full-scale oil shale industry as well as the limited prototype leasing then being considered.[27] In January 1974, the department revealed it had accepted a bonus bid of $210,305,600 for one of two Colorado tracts. That bid, offered by Standard Oil of Indiana and Gulf, came to $41,319.84 an acre. It was the highest bid per acre ever made in a federal mineral lease sale. In all, six tracts were nominated, two each in Colorado, Utah, and Wyoming.

There are two approaches to the extraction of oil from shale. One entails the mining of the shale, which is broken out, taken to the surface, crushed, and put through a retort in which heat is applied and the oil captured for further processing. The other is the *in situ* method wherein the shale is heated in the ground and the need for waste disposal is largely avoided.

In the department's study, the changes in store for the three-state oil shale country were set forth in a dispassionate, matter-of-fact way. Tens of thousands of new people would come. Population could nearly double in less than fifteen years. Air and water would be degraded. Wildlife habitats would be disturbed. To produce a quarter billion barrels of oil a day meant the mining of 134.5 to 149.5 million tons of shale a year and the disposal of 3 to 3.5 billion cubic feet of spent shale. Producing a million barrels a day meant mining 538 to 598 million tons of rock and winding up with 12 to 14 billion cubic feet of waste a year.

"It is assumed that most spent shale will be initially disposed of in box canyons," the impact statement said.[28] Conservationists were quick to dramatize the terrible immensity of these problems. It was one thing to mine a few hundred tons of oil shale and build a pilot plant that produced a trickle of oil. It was quite another to chew up mountains of shale and spit out an ever-higher mountain of dust and rocks.

The Council on Environmental Quality cited impressive statistics in its sixth annual report. Pointing out that the Stanford Research Institute expected that oil shale would be adding about three million barrels a day to the American energy stream by the year 2000, the council published a table showing that an industry of that size would generate 3.25 million tons of solid waste a day. This enormous quantity, the council said, would be nearly nine times greater than the total volume of postconsumer solid waste left by the combined residential and commercial sectors in the entire United States in 1973. Moreover, the industry's daily water requirements—some 417 million gallons—would be enough to supply the household needs of all the people living in the Washington, D.C., metropolitan area.[29]

In the end, it seemed likely that the fate of western shale would be decided, as it always had been, by economics. High though oil prices soared in the energy crisis and into the late 1970s, the production of oil from shale remained too expensive to compete, or so it appeared. Atlantic Richfield put a damper on

259

optimism in October 1974, when it announced that Colony Development Corporation was suspending plans to start construction of a commercial plant on Parachute Creek in spring 1975.

"The decision by the four companies in this venture was mandated by the forces at play in today's economic and political climate," said Hollis M. Dole, general manager of Colony and a former assistant secretary of the interior. It was explained that inflation had increased the cost estimates for building the plant by 40 percent in six months. In 1973 the cost was estimated at $450 million for a 50,000-barrel-a-day plant. The new projected cost was more than $800 million.

Colony's backing away, described as a temporary suspension that would be reconsidered when the atmosphere cleared, was a widely publicized retreat on the oil shale front, but it did not alter the fact that the industry had shown a lively interest in the federal effort. The Geological Survey reported bonuses totaling $448,797,600 in fiscal 1974 from the leasing of four tracts in Colorado and Utah. This was a substantial investment, strongly suggesting confidence on the part of the companies involved that the razor-backed difficulties of their task would be overcome, with federal assistance. Kleppe nursed them along in 1976 by granting them more time to pay remaining installments on their bonus bids.

When President Ford spent two weeks at the Colorado Rockies resort town of Vail in August 1975, he had taken time to inspect the Paraho aboveground retort and mine at Anvil Forks on the naval reserve.

At the Paraho site President Ford was greeted by former Democratic Rep. Wayne Aspinall and company officials, who gave him a hair-raising ride up a steep and dusty mountain road to the mine and then took him down again to show him the retort and a garden plot where efforts were being made to grow grass on compacted shale waste. Ford seemed impressed.

"Until you can see something on the ground," he said, "I don't think you appreciate the actual potential."

260

Before the president departed in his helicopter, he stood on a knoll where a small crowd had gathered and expressed conviction that America's oil shale could be exploited without damage to the environment. He added that a breakthrough in technology would be welcome. A little earlier, at Vail, Federal Energy Administrator Frank G. Zarb had told reporters that oil shale technology was still about five dollars a barrel away from achieving a commercial, competitive product.[30]

Toward the end of the Carter administration, the Democrats could claim that oil imports had been cut by one million barrels a day from the previous year and that per capita energy consumption was decreasing. Because of rising oil prices, however, the bill for imports was escalating at a frightening rate. It was a heavy financial outflow to which many of the nation's ills, including inflation, were traced.

Coal production rose to a record level of 760 million tons in 1979, an 8 percent increase over 1977. The Department of Energy projected that by 1995, when total production might be above 1.5 billion tons, the West's share will have grown dramatically to 47 percent of all United States coal production.[31] In 1978 the West's share was 25 percent.

Aware of the environmental difficulties associated with coal, shale, and other possible oil substitutes, conservationists had more enthusiasm for conservation of energy and resort to renewable sources like solar energy than for a crash effort to develop synthetics.

On the other hand, there were suggestions, as the Department of Energy put it in November 1980, that "it appears that the economics of liquid fuel production from shale are about to become favorable."[32] Inevitably, in any event, broad support had developed for an all-out attempt to kill the energy dragon with the magic of American technology.

As part of the national effort to end dependence on foreign oil, Congress early in 1980 approved the Energy Security Act, establishing the Synthetic Fuels Corporation and giving it the mission of encouraging commercial production of oil and gas from coal, oil shale, tar sands, and "biomass"—crops or municipal wastes.[33]

President Carter also wanted Congress to set up an Energy Mobilization Board to push aside red tape and speed completion of nonnuclear energy projects. The House voted it down.[34] There had been conservationist opposition arising from fears that the board might bulldoze legitimate environmental concerns.

Rip-Off

Engelhardt in the St. Louis Post-Dispatch

CHAPTER 11

FALLEN TIMBERS

Outside the tropics, American forests were the richest and most productive on earth, and the best able to repay good management. But nobody had begun to manage any part of them with an eye to the future. On the contrary, the greatest, the swiftest, the most efficient, and the most appalling wave of forest destruction in human history was then swelling to its climax in the United States; and the American people were glad of it."

> —GIFFORD PINCHOT in his autobiographical *Breaking New Ground*, speaking of 1885

Pinchot . . . looked upon the nation's forests not as cathedrals but as woodlots, and the wilderness concept advanced by John Muir drove him bananas.

> —Under Secretary of the Interior JOHN C. WHITAKER at Oakland, California, October 29, 1974

Today, the once great forests of our nation have been depleted to the point that would shame Paul Bunyan. . . . It is time, in short, to cease measuring the value of our public forests on the scale of board-feet of timber.

> —Sen. GALE MCGEE in testimony April 1971

Frederick Weyerhaeuser was born in the village of Niedersaulheim, southwest of Mainz, less than twenty years after Napoleon's defeat at Waterloo. As a boy in Germany, he worked on his father's farm. He joined the stream of migrants to the United States, arrived at Rock Island in Illinois in 1856 at the age of twenty-one, and went into the timber business. He was a strong, intelligent man of upright character. He prospered and his tribe increased. He died in 1914, leaving four sons. Sixty years later a great-grandson, George H. Weyerhaeuser, was president of the Weyerhaeuser Company with headquarters at Tacoma in the Pacific Northwest. For 1973, an excellent year in the lumber trade, he reported net sales of $2,301,731,000 and net earnings of $348,811,000. The company's earnings were more than twice those of its nearest competitor.

"The Tree Growing Company," Weyerhaeuser called itself, and not without some justification. It owned the world's largest private inventory of timber, with cutting rights as far away as Indonesia and Borneo. In its 1973 report the company said its land and timber division had planted 322 million trees on 497,100 acres since 1969. "Within the next three years alone," the company said, "we will plant more than half a billion trees and fertilize 1.5 million acres, managing forests at a level of intensity which will, in a fifty-year time span, at least double the growth which otherwise could have been anticipated in unmanaged stands. We will also invest in new nursery and seed orchard facilities that will double our internal seedling production capability."

It was at the turn of the century, at about the time the long-suffering pineries of the Great Lakes states were playing out, that Frederick Weyerhaeuser, by then a renowned and prosperous entrepreneur of sixty-five, pulled up stakes in the Midwest and set up offices in the Pacific Northwest, where most of the nation's remaining virgin sawtimber was to be found. Here were the immense stands of Douglas fir in western Washington and Oregon—55,000 square miles of magnificent trees awaiting the saw and axe. Some of them towered 250 to 280 feet, clean and straight, and some of their trunks were 8 to 10 feet wide at the base. Weyerhaeuser, after looking around for a while and taking a trip to Alaska, announced in 1900 the purchase of 900,000 acres of timber country from the Northern Pacific Railroad for six dollars an acre. This was a transaction of staggering magnitude, one of the biggest single land transfers in national history. It involved lands given to the railroad under grants made by Congress in 1864.[1]

The Weyerhaeuser Company established the first tree farm in the United States in 1941 at Gray's Harbor in Washington State.[2] By 1974 the company owned outright some 5,719,000 acres, a total holding bigger than Massachusetts. Of that, 1,699,000 were in Washington, 1,090,000 in Oregon, and the remainder in Oklahoma, Arkansas, North Carolina, Mississippi, Alabama, California, and the Canadian provinces of Ontario, British Columbia, and Quebec. In addition to land it owned, the company had harvest rights on another 10,723,000 acres it did not own, all in Canada except for nearly 2,000,000 in the Far East. It sold 2.7 billion board feet of lumber in 1973, a figure that may be compared with about 12 billion board feet harvested and more than 10 billion sold for future harvest in the federally owned National Forest System the same year. One board foot is a piece of wood twelve inches square and one inch thick, or the equivalent.

When concern about a lumber shortage arose during the Nixon administration, about 80 percent of the nation's commercial timberlands were in private ownership, and the remainder were publicly owned, chiefly by the federal government. There was no federal control over management of private timber holdings, but the industry—by means of traditional political pressures—had a great deal of control over what the public owned. The national forests had about ninety million acres of commercial timberlands, or 18 percent of the total, and were producing about one-fourth of the annual timber harvest, chiefly from the Pacific coast and the Rocky Mountains. The $35 billion forest industry—that is, timber and paper companies and the like, as opposed to farmers—had more than sixty-seven million acres, or 14 percent, and was turning out 28 percent of the wood supply. In general, the industry owned a larger proportion of high-quality timberland than the federal government. The chief remaining supply of large-size, high-quality timber was in the softwood—coniferous—forests of the Pacific.

Weyerhaeuser as the giant of the industry had rich and abundant timberlands of its own, as did some other companies, but the large concerns and countless small operators had a direct stake in the availability of timber from the federal forests. Timber interests that had overcut their own holdings had to look elsewhere. Federal logging rights, auctioned off by the Forest Service or the Bureau of Land Management, came to have increasing importance as the lumber squeeze grew worse and the housing industry cried out for wood. For small logging towns deep in the federal forests, access to federal trees was a life-or-death matter.

Standing next to Weyerhaeuser in sales volume in 1973 was Georgia-Pacific, which began life as a small lumber company in Georgia in 1927, with $12,000 capital.[3] It flourished during World War II and shortly after the war expanded into the Pacific Northwest. Its offspring company, Louisiana-Pacific, formed under a settlement with the Federal Trade Commission late in 1972, was a protagonist in the controversy over enlarging Redwood National Park, as we shall see.

In 1981 there was controversy over President Reagan's nomination of John B. Crowell Jr., former general counsel for Louisiana-Pacific, to be assistant secretary of agriculture for natural resources and environment, with responsibility for overseeing the national forests.

Third among the giants in the 1973 time frame was Champion International, which increased its United States timber holdings by more than one-third in 1972 when it bought a sawmill and 670,000 acres of Montana timberland from the Anaconda Company. Much of that had been acquired from the Northern Pacific in 1904, only a few years after Weyerhaeuser's big deal with the same line.

In the early 1970s, Champion International was involved in legal difficulties with environmentalists about timber contracts with the Forest Service in Alaska and Wyoming. The Alaska controversy involved the hauntingly beautiful Tongass National Forest. Here the Forest Service in 1965 sought bidders for an estimated 8.75 billion board foot of timber, the largest sale in its history. Three years later, Champion agreed to an arrangement under which it was to build a pulp mill and related sawmills and cut the timber over a fifty-year period. In 1970 the Sierra Club and others brought suit, terming the sale "the single largest act of wilderness destruction ever contemplated." Legal action held up the logging, and in March 1976 the company requested that the contract be canceled, citing delays caused by litigation and confusion arising from native claims. Forest Service Chief John R. McGuire expressed regret. Most of the pulp and lumber would have gone to Japan.

The industry's fourth largest company in 1973, Boise Cascade, noted soberly in its annual report that year the nation's continuing uncertainty about whether adequate timber would be available from government lands. It complained that the Forest Service could not manage national timberlands fully because the agency was "critically underfunded," which was true. Not enough money was being made available for preparing timber sales and for essential reforestation and the improvement of timber stands.

Keep in mind that the timber industry people and the conservationists do not always mean the same thing when they speak of a need for "good management" in the national forests, even while agreeing that the forests are financially down-at-heel. To the skeptical conservationist, industry's use of the word *manage-*

ment is simply jargon for getting out more logs, producing more timber. In this context, *management* means logging roads, reforestation to increase growth so that more of the old virgin timber can be cut, and fertilization and spraying for the same purpose. The public's forests, critics of the loggers point out, are dedicated by law to multiple uses of which timber production is only one.

Similarly, the skeptical conservationist does not swallow the assumption that industry's private forests have been superbly managed while those in federal hands have been run inefficiently. The cause of the "lumber squeeze," he will tell you, is that the timber industry overcut its own lands, an assertion he says is supported by many studies and admitted by the industry itself.

A Sierra Club official, Brock Evans, also objected to the jargon term *timber harvest* and said he would prefer to call a spade a spade.

"The word 'harvest' implies they did something to get it where it was," the official explained. "Until they start 'harvesting' second-growth timber which they did in fact 'manage', I don't think the logging of big, old trees deserves to be called anything but just that—logging."[4]

Like thousands of other lumber companies large and small, the four largest all had dealings with the Forest Service in fiscal 1974 through successful bidding for timber contracts. Boise Cascade led the group, obtaining rights to 446.4 million board feet, all but 17 million of it in the West. Georgia-Pacific bought only 23.4 million, all in the southern states, but its corporate scion, Louisiana-Pacific, bought 159 million, of which all but some 13 million were in the Pacific states and Idaho and Montana. Champion bought 134.7 million, mainly in California and the Pacific Northwest. Weyerhaeuser was the lightest purchaser—3.2 million board feet in Oregon and Washington and 26.4 million in the South.

These figures vary from year to year, of course, and we look at them briefly only to get an idea of the pattern and dimension of these transactions, from which much of the nation's lumber flows.

When the nation observed its Bicentennial in 1976, the gloomiest pessimist could not deny that things had come a long way, in the right direction, since the cut-and-run days of the nineteenth century when few seemed to care what happened to the forests. Where once there had been no federal timber reserves in protected status, hundreds of millions of acres had been stashed away. Where once the logger took little thought of tomorrow, he now perforce had become a tree farmer, a careful planter of seedlings. What formerly had been a criminally wasteful business now was marked by nickel-nursing husbandry, a trade in which even the sawdust and scraps were put to use and profit—everything but the sigh of the pine, as the saying went. And the federal government could look back on seventy-five years of safeguarding the public's trees. Surely, the federal groves must be in good shape.

Unfortunately, there was no basis for complacency. What remained of the virgin, or "old-growth," timber was virtually all in the West and was being laid low at a rate that would exhaust it within decades. Noble stands of trees averaging 250 or 260 years in age were going down, and their likes were not to be seen again. In places, new growth was planted and taking hold, but it was not the same. Anybody with eyes could see that. One did not have to be a John Muir or a poet to perceive the difference. Trees were being sawed down and dragged from the forests much faster than they were being replaced by man or nature. On national forest lands, removal of softwood sawtimber was exceeding growth by 48 percent, and millions of acres needed replanting. On the acreage owned by the forest industries, removal in 1970 was running 63 percent ahead of growth. Cheerfully admitting to these figures, the Forest Service made a virtue of the sacrifice. It explained that the old-growth timber of the West grew but slowly, being old, and that it must be replaced with new crops of young, thrifty, fast-growing trees.[5] In time, the Congress was assured, growth and harvest would be brought into balance to achieve a sustained yield.

What was in store for the residue of uninvaded Douglas fir, ponderosa pine, and other coniferous giants could be guessed from the difficult rearguard action that was fought to save for posterity a small acreage of California's immense redwoods in the wet, misty country north of San Francisco. This struggle, taking place in the 1960s and 1970s, looked like a cliff-hanger at times and had a somber interest, if only because it might fairly be said that a citizenry that would not preserve these magnificent and unique trees would not, in the end, preserve any trees.

From the day western man first set eyes on the great stands of Sequoia sempervirens, probably late in the sixteenth century with the brief sojourn of Sir Francis Drake, the coastal redwoods have been seen as remarkable. They are primordial trees, dream trees, which extend upward nearly out of sight, poking a hole in the sky. The tallest tree in the world is said to be the Howard Libbey Redwood, which towers about 367 feet on Redwood Creek in Humboldt County. Originally, it is thought, California had nearly 2 million acres of coastal redwoods, scattered in quiet, cathedrallike groves for a distance of 500 miles along the Pacific slope, from the Santa Lucia Range south of Monterey to southern Oregon. Some were there a century or two before the birth of Christ.

By the 1970s, when a fight raged to keep the Libbey and other prize trees from being ruined by upstream logging, the Save-the-Redwoods League at San Francisco put the total remaining virgin redwood timber in California at about 186,000 acres, of which 66,000 were in federal- or state-protected status and the rest in private hands. This was being cut at the rate of about 10,000 acres a year.

The Humboldt County battleground had been logged since before the Civil War. As has been mentioned, timber operators got hold of some of the redwood lands fraudulently by hiring sailors to file homestead claims and paying them $50 for the

271

rights thus obtained. During Cleveland's administration, the frauds were investigated, and federal officers canceled some 200 homesteads and reclaimed timberland said to have been worth $20 million. As the great trees began to fall to the logger's axe and saw, the literate and sensitive rose to defend them. The loggers themselves were not immune to the mystique of those trees. In gold-rush days, there were cries that the redwoods must be spared. In 1879, Interior Secretary Schurz recommended that 46,000 acres be set aside.[6]

Nothing was done by Congress, and citizens of California, amid recurring predictions in the late nineteenth century that the redwoods could last only a few decades longer, took effective action. Private philanthropists and lumbermen—William Randolph Hearst, Col. James B. Armstrong, Henry L. Middleton, William Kent, and others—bought up and donated redwoods acreage to the state. When the Save-the-Redwoods League was formed in 1918 with Woodrow Wilson's Interior Secretary Franklin K. Lane as its president, about 5,000 acres had been reserved for public purposes. The league thumped the tambourine. It got excellent cooperation from lumber companies, many of which donated valuable tracts and went along with the effort to save the best. As late as 1969, Georgia-Pacific donated two groves of redwoods in northern California, valued at $6.2 million, to the Nature Conservancy, which welcomed the donation as "the largest single gift ever made by an American firm for conservation purposes."

Nevertheless, despite all the private and corporate generosity and a national interest that sometimes burned intensely, the movement toward a federal redwoods park bogged down in a quagmire of conflicting economic considerations, claims and counterclaims, greed, and the anxiety of local interests. One argument against federal intervention at the time was that state parks, already set up, would protect representative forests, and there was not enough good virgin timber left to make a proper federal park. Anyway, it was said, the area was too cold and wet to attract visitors. In 1963 the Sierra Club came out with its evangelical coffee-table book, *The Last Redwoods*, flaying the timber companies, the foresters, and the politicians.[7]

President Johnson was persuaded to take up the cause in earnest. What followed, during more than ten years of savage wrangling, was a federal save-the-redwoods campaign that was fought in two phases. The first culminated in a Pyrrhic victory for the conservationists—the setting aside of the small and inadequate Redwood National Park in 1968. The second ended in 1978, under Carter, when Congress authorized a larger, more nearly adequate park, tidying things up. The failure to provide a substantial park in the first place, the lack of attention paid to the frantic urgings of conservationists, resulted in the waste of large sums of money and threatened a priceless national resource.

This is not to say that the task of wresting the original park from the grasp of the loggers was an easy one. Industry fought it tooth and nail. Johnson pleaded for it from 1965 onward, and in 1968 he went so far as to mention it in his State of the Union address.[8] There was a ferocious battle in which the conservationists were at times divided among themselves and in which they saw arrayed against them a formidable host—the timber workers and their bosses, the state's conservative Republican Gov. Ronald Reagan, local citizens fearful of a park's impact on jobs and the tax rolls, and House Interior Committee Chairman Aspinall himself.

The Johnson administration sought a total park of more than 41,000 acres, which it estimated would cost about $60 million. The Sierra Club and like-minded groups pleaded for a very different and more generous and ecologically sensible proposal— 90,000 acres and $200 million. Both these plans contemplated the federal enfolding of the existing state parks and the purchase of additional tracts to round them out. Foes were against any substantive expansion.

What finally emerged from the pulling and hauling in September 1968, as President Johnson was leaving office, was a forceps-delivery compromise that turned out to be a monstrosity.

273

The 1968 law authorized a redwood national park of 58,000 acres in Del Norte and Humboldt counties. This involved federal acquisition by "legislative taking" of about 28,000 acres of private land containing some 10,000 acres of old-growth timber. Private lands within the new park boundaries thus became federal property without delay.[9]

The private owners—four lumber companies, chiefly—were to be compensated, of course. But whereas past practice had been that the secretary of the interior might undertake condemnation of private land, if purchase efforts failed, at a cost determined by district federal court juries, the new law sought to avoid the inflation in land prices that had often made such procedures unreasonably expensive for the government. Private owners within the redwoods park could obtain payment either in cash or by exchange for lands in the Forest Service's Redwood Purchase Unit or public lands in California administered by the Bureau of Land Management. If not satisfied, private owners could file suit in the United States Court of Claims, a remedy that does not involve jury trial. The 1968 law was the first in which Congress had taken private property for a park by simple declaration. To pay the tab, an appropriation of $92 million was authorized from the Land and Water Conservation Fund, created in 1965 and fed by federal mineral revenues. It seemed a painless approach, but turned out not to be.

As a Washington correspondent assigned to cover the Western White House in the summer of 1969, I was present when former President and Mrs. Johnson visited President and Mrs. Nixon at San Clemente on August 27 and flew some 800 miles into northern California for dedication of the Lady Bird Johnson Grove in the brand-new Redwood National Park. It was a charming and reassuring occasion. The day was hot. The logistics of the trip were nerve-racking. The climax came at last in a setting that seemed to calm everybody down. It was a clump of redwoods of indescribable majesty. The soft forest floor deadened the sound of trooping feet, and the grandeur of the sight awed visitors and made them silent. In addition to the president and the former president and their wives, the notables assembled to do honor to Mrs. Johnson and the trees included the Reverend Billy Graham, evangelist; Governor Reagan; and Interior Secretary Hickel, who had more than another year to serve before Nixon fired him.

Speaking in the cool depths of the grove, the Reverend Mr. Graham said in his invocation that some of the oldest trees were 2,500 years old and had been there before Christ. The average age was 500 years, before the coming of the white man. Noting this antiquity, President Nixon recalled that he had been reading a biography of Theodore Roosevelt, a great Republican conservationist who liked to visit such forests. Former President Johnson, whose sixty-first birthday it was, paid tribute to the Democratic Roosevelt, Franklin D. Somewhat prophetically, as it turned out, Johnson said a president's problem was not in doing what was right, but "in knowing what was right." Reagan spoke of the devotion of Californians for their redwoods and said many people might be surprised that so many were left standing. Reporters were careful to point out in their stories that it had been Reagan who, addressing a lumbermen's convention in San Francisco in 1966, received warm applause with a quip along the lines of "If you've seen one redwood, you've seen them all."[10]

What I remember best was standing next to a tall, white-haired man whom I recognized as David Brower, then of the Sierra Club, later of Friends of the Earth. He was listening to the speeches. I introduced myself and was surprised to find him unimpressed by the oratory. He told me that if I listened carefully I could hear the saws whining among the redwoods just out of view, in an area known as Skunk Cabbage Creek.

Brower's insistence on pointing out the realities served as a reminder that the original park's boundaries had been drawn in so cramped and skimpy a fashion that they did not protect watersheds where some of the best trees within the park are situated—the treasured Tall Trees Grove, for example. In the Redwood Creek area, through a piece of environmental idiocy that conservationists blame on Aspinall, the 1968 park included only a slender "worm" of land along the creek bottom leading to the grove, leaving timber operators in possession of the slopes above and upstream. The worm was half a mile wide, seven miles long.

As had been warned against in the clearest terms and was to be expected, the companies—principally Arcata Redwood, Rellim Redwood, and Louisiana-Pacific—proceeded to log their property. The Sierra Club in the summer of 1973 reported appalling devastation caused by clear-cutting along the edge of the park. By that time, some 7,560 acres of virgin timber out of 14,620 standing in 1968 had been sawed down, leaving scrofulous bald spots crisscrossed by tractor trails. Nothing effective was done by the Interior Department to halt this Verdun-like devastation. The Sierra Club took the department to court and fought and pleaded for action. As the price of the original taking escalated, park proponents urged that more land be bought. It was obvious that logging, if permitted to go on, might ruin the existing park by causing siltage and erosion. Also obvious was the aesthetic damage.

Whatever the magnitude of the threat, which the park opponents heartily discounted, the cost of the original "taking" as the land-acquisition cases dragged on in the court of claims was so horrendous that the heavy federal investment already made lent weight to pleas by environmentalists for a more comprehensive, more viable park. The loggers sent in whopping bills. In mid-1977 the General Accounting Office reported that payments totaling nearly $190 million had already been made to the private landowners, of which about $181 million went to four timber companies—Arcata, Georgia-Pacific, Simpson Timber, and Harold A. Miller et al. The total was more than twice the $92 million authorized by Congress. It included some $52 million in swapped federal timberland and $27 million in interest. Inasmuch as $70 million in claims were still unsettled, the total cost of acquiring less than 30,000 acres of land threatened to approach $250 million dollars. What the public had obtained in return was, as had been foreseen, a disaster.

Nevertheless, as Rep. Leo J. Ryan, California Democrat, noted in releasing the GAO report, the timber people were struggling against expansion of the dearly bought parklet in the 1970s, just as they had fought its establishment in the 1960s. Ryan said the government had been outmaneuvered and had paid more than was necessary. The companies, he added, "have literally cried all the way to the bank."

Led by two other California Democrats, Rep. Phillip Burton and Sen. Alan Cranston, Congress undertook early in 1978 to redress the errors it had made ten years earlier. Carter signed into law a bill authorizing a taking of an additional 48,000 acres to extend and protect the existing holding in the Redwood Creek watershed, enlarging the park from the original 58,000-acre federal-state enclave to 106,000,000 acres.[11] In addition, Congress set up a 30,000-acre "buffer zone" that could be purchased if necessary to safeguard the park.

The 1978 bill avoided the court of claims, where the government side had fared so poorly, and provided instead that any claims were to be adjusted in federal district court. Even so, the estimated costs were high. Acquisition of the 48,000 acres—containing only about 9,000 with virgin redwood stands—would run to about $359 million, it was thought. Land rehabilitation would cost $33 million. The standby acquisition authority for the 30,000 buffer acres would, if fully used, cost another $60 million.

Furthermore, Congress, at the insistence of the House, wrote into the second-phase redwood law a complexity of detailed job and economic security measures aimed at cushioning such impact as the park expansion might have on the locality and its citizens. It was believed this economic package might cost $90 to

277

$100 million. In the redwoods country of northern California, already a distressed area, there had been a bitter controversy over the expansion. Timber production, the backbone of the economy, was in decline. Loggers and business interests staged a 3,000-mile march on Washington in May 1977 to protest enlargement of the park. They feared loss of jobs and an onset of hard times. Environmentalists promoting a larger park encountered overt hostility. Organized labor joined industry in opposition.

President Carter had pledged full effort to soften the economic impact, and support was firm for federal intervention to assist people displaced by federal action, but the new law's income maintenance for loggers and others thrown out of work caused misgivings in Congress because it would give these people privileged status not enjoyed by unemployed workers elsewhere. Sen. Ted Stevens, Alaska Republican, commented that Alaskans affected by pending federal parklands proposals would expect similar consideration. In the case of Alaska, of course, the federal government already owned the land being proposed for parks. Congress may have gone too far in its rescue effort for alleged victims of redwoods survival, but at least the nation now had a viable park—at a cost far exceeding total outlays for all the nation's parks in the past.

As the redwoods price tag moved toward $1 billion, it was interesting if irrelevant to recall that Mexico in 1848 received only about $16 million from the United States for a vast territory that included the whole of what are now California and Nevada as well as most of Arizona and Utah. And one could ponder wistfully the fact that much of the redwoods land went out of federal hands in the late nineteenth century for a few dollars an acre or for nothing, through various abuses of the land laws.[12]

The emphasis on economics and bookkeeping and cost accounting which hampered efforts to salvage a small remnant of California's Sequoia sempervirens had been prevalent for many years in the management of federal commercial forests. That emphasis became more decisive as the pressure for more timber mounted after World War II, and it became a subject of lively controversy when the hunger for increased yield from the government forests clashed with mounting conservationist sentiment during the Johnson and subsequent administrations. The timber industry and the home builders demanded more logs. Conservationists said the national forest lands were being over-cut—and cut savagely and wrongly—to meet short-term needs.

A question that loomed large in the public mind in the late twentieth century involved the extent to which the publicly owned forests should be regarded primarily as a source of lumber. Many Americans had come to think of the national forests, when they thought of them at all, as places where trees were protected against the rapine that had gone on outside the federal reserves. Among people with that viewpoint, indignation and outrage were natural reactions when it became clear through public discussion or personal observation that the federal forester was hand in glove with the timber industry and that the national forests were not, in fact, getting much protection.

Closely aligned with the view that the federal attitude toward trees should be one of benevolence was the rapidly developing concept that the remaining wilderness in the federal reserves— places not yet penetrated by man to any extent—ought to be safeguarded and held inviolate for a while.

It is true that Congress, when it established the forest reserves, said in 1897 that one purpose was "to furnish a continuous supply of timber for the use and necessity of citizens of the United States," but Congress also ordained that the forests be protected.[13] In the early years, timber production was not massive. World War II brought an orgy of overcutting and waste. The postwar flowering of outdoor recreational activity, along with increased population and use of the automobile, sent millions into the forests. In 1960, Congress approved the Multiple Use and Sustained Yield Act, which welcomed the visitors and mandated twin objectives that were easier to talk about than to achieve.[14]

Congress laid it down that the Forest Service's lands "shall be administered for outdoor recreation, range, timber, watershed, and wildlife and fish purposes." Timber was one of five multiple uses. Mining, of course, already had an assured position. The law directed the secretary of agriculture to develop and run the national forests not only in accordance with the "multiple use" principle, but also for "sustained yield," as far as renewable resources like timber were concerned.

Multiple use was defined somewhat laboriously in the law as follows: "the management of all the various renewable surface resources of the national forests so that they are utilized in the combination that will best meet the needs of the American people; making the most judicious use of the land for some or all of these resources or related services over areas large enough to provide sufficient latitude for periodic adjustments in use to conform to changing needs and conditions; that some land will be used for less than all of the resources; and harmonious and coordinated management of the various resources, each with the other, without impairment of the productivity of the land, with consideration being given to the relative values of the various resources, and not necessarily the combination of uses that will give the greatest dollar return or the greatest unit output."

With no better language than that for guidance, the local Forest Service ranger might have been hard put to resolve a dispute without telephoning his superior, but at least the law established that the poet, the backpacker, and the family seeking recreation had rights that had to be weighed against the demands of grazing and the extractive industries.

Congress was more succinct in its definition of *sustained yield*. What the term meant, the law said, was the "achievement and maintenance in perpetuity of a high-level annual or regular periodic output of the various renewable resources of the national forests without impairment of the productivity of the land."

Initially these two broad principles applied only to the lands administered by the Forest Service. With the Classification and

Multiple Use Act of 1964, Congress applied them also to the huge holdings of the BLM.[15]

In September 1964, a year after President Kennedy was assassinated, conservationists won a hard-fought victory in gaining approval of the Wilderness Act.[16] Essentially, this was an effort to designate wild, remote, and as-yet-unspoiled areas already in federal hands and give them a quality of protection they would not otherwise have. These were places back of beyond, in the fastnesses of existing national forests, parks, wildlife refuges, places where a tree might fall in the woods and nobody would be there to hear the sound. The idea for setting aside a portion of the nation's remaining wilderness—that is, for organizing to do it—evolved at a roadside discussion in the Great Smoky Mountains in 1934. From the roadside talk, at which Benton MacKaye, Robert Marshall, Harvey Broome, and Bernard Frank were present, came a conservationist organization known as the Wilderness Society. It was formed at Washington, D.C., early in 1935.

The struggle was a difficult one. In a nation that less than 200 years earlier had been almost entirely wilderness, only about 4 percent remained in the state of nature. A group that included David Brower of the Sierra Club and Howard Zahniser, Olaus Murie, and George Marshall of the Wilderness Society drafted a model bill. In 1956, legislation was introduced. The timber, mining, oil, and cattle interests saw it as an effort to close off to their activities large tracts that should, they believed, remain available for exploitation. Vehement objection was raised to the notion of sealing off wilderness without first searching it for minerals. Nevertheless, the wilderness concept, dear to the heart of the great John Muir, generated great enthusiasm. It had the firm support of the Kennedy and Johnson administrations.

A cardinal virtue of wilderness to the less poetically inclined was that it did not cost the government anything. The land involved was already federal, and by its nature it required little upkeep or surveillance. Wilderness advocates were relatively few, but they were passionate, determined, and caustic. Brower, testifying before a House interior subcommittee late in 1961, said he found "something appalling about the scramble for the last five percent of the original American wilderness by those too accustomed to living off federal subsidy to stop coveting wilderness. . . .

"I hope the American people will note well and remember well," Brower continued, "who the groups are who think so much of their present, and so little of everyone's future, that they fight and stall this bill—the dammers, the sawlog foresters, the graziers, the miners, and strangely, the oil men who above all should know the importance of keeping America full of beautiful places to drive to or to drive near."[17]

There was a high-hearted spirit at large in the opening period of the Johnson presidency, before the Vietnam War overshadowed talk of the Great Society. Although House Interior Committee Chairman Aspinall insisted that wilderness be left open to mining, prospecting, and oil and gas development for another nineteen years, and although hostile forces saw to it that the conferring of wilderness status was made difficult, the Wilderness Act finally passed.

And Congress, as Congress sometimes does, rose to the occasion and put its imprimatur on some exalted and imaginative language.

"In order," said the lawgivers in their preamble, "to assure that an increasing population, accompanied by expanding settlement and growing mechanization, does not occupy and modify all areas within the United States and its possessions, leaving no lands designated for preservation and protection in their natural condition, it is hereby declared to be the policy of the Congress to secure for the American people of present and future generations the benefits of an enduring resource of wilderness."

Congress put into the act a legal definition of *wilderness*, as follows: "A wilderness, in contrast with those areas where man and his own works dominate the landscape, is hereby recog-

282

nized as an area where the earth and its community of life are untrammeled by man, where man himself is a visitor who does not remain."

Later on, there were arguments over whether a cabin and road or two disqualified an area for wilderness status. The Wilderness Act signed by President Johnson established a repository to be called the National Wilderness Preservation System, to consist initially of 9,000,000 acres and fifty-four areas in the national forests. As time went by, additional tracts were to be added from a potential total estimated at some 66,440,387 acres. The law set up a ten-year program for review, by federal agencies, of 150 or so other areas for possible wilderness protection. Congress was to have the right of final action in each instance, and the wilderness areas were to be open to mineral activity through 1983. The secretary of the interior was to comb the National Park System and the wildlife refuges and game ranges for suitable wilderness.

Despite the chivying of wilderness advocates, things moved very slowly. Public hearings had to be held. The built-in procedures were tedious, and the federal agencies seemed unenthusiastic. By late 1974, when the act was ten years old and the initial appraisal period was over, only 3.8 million additional acres had been placed in the system. Wilderness supporters found encouragement, however, in the fact that the procedural mill was grinding and that in 1974 Congress extended the possibility of wilderness protection to certain forests and other federal lands in the eastern United States, lands that had been cut over and otherwise exploited but had reverted to a wild state.

Sigurd F. Olson of the Wilderness Society, urging favorable action on the eastern forests the previous year before a Senate interior subcommittee, said that when the work had been completed there would probably be no more than fifty to fifty-five million acres in the National Wilderness Preservation System. This, he pointed out, is less than 3 percent of the land mass.

"The people who say we are trying to sew everybody up and the people who accuse us of trying to bankrupt our economy," Olson told Public Lands Subcommittee Chairman Floyd K. Haskell of Colorado, "do not seem to realize that 97 percent of the United States of America is open for grabs. We are not asking for very much. We are asking for very, very little, a minimum."[18]

The Wilderness Society, the Sierra Club, and other conservationist groups badgered the Forest Service for dragging its heels. Ed Cliff, then chief of the Forest Service, organized a 1972 study called the Roadless Area Review and Evaluation, or RARE, in which fifty-six million acres were inventoried and twelve million selected for wilderness study. At that time, the eastern forests were not included. The Sierra Club challenged the Cliff study. When President Carter assumed office, one of the environmentalist luminaries he brought into the government was M. Rupert Cutler, formerly an official of the Wilderness Society, who became the new assistant secretary of agriculture with suzerainty over the Forest Service. Cutler ordered a new study, called RARE-II, from which wilderness proponents hoped to recoup a substantial part of what they called "the missing 44,000,000" acres denied under Cliff. When the Agriculture Department made its new recommendations to Congress in January 1979, based on the Cutler review, disappointment and dismay struck the wilderness camp.[19]

RARE-II proposed that fifteen million acres of the Forest Service's roadless land be set aside as wilderness and that thirty-six million be classified as nonwilderness, suitable for development. Conservationists raised a howl. A Sierra Club representative said the fifteen million acres approved for wilderness status "really amounted to about 8,000,000 or 9,000,000 of *new* areas . . . that they hadn't already recommended for protection; and most of that was 'rock and ice' that was already *de facto* protected anyhow. . . . The fact that timber operators complained was pro forma, for the record; they have been secretly delighted."[20]

Even so, the National Wilderness Preservation System had grown by the end of 1980 to a holding of about twenty million acres, and a great deal more was in prospect. Some 89 percent of the total came from the Forest Service. Wilderness allocation was the major issue among conservationists throughout the 1960s. It gave force and focus to the battles of the 1970s over sustained yield and clear-cutting in the federal forests. As the 1980s began, the BLM under its new organic act was studying sixty-one million acres of BLM land as potential wilderness. Meanwhile, the Sierra Club, Wilderness Society, and Friends of the Earth joined in denouncing what they called an "extreme anti-wilderness bill" introduced by Rep. Thomas Foley, Washington State Democrat, chairman of the House Agriculture Committee.[21]

Closely related to and paralleling the struggles over wilderness preservation were the broils of the 1970s over what was going on in those segments of the federal forests which were undergoing routine commercial exploitation. There were two major issues. One was the question of whether the commercially attractive forests managed by the Forest Service and the BLM were being cut at an excessive rate. Another was the debate over clear-cutting, an unsightly but relatively cheap and efficient logging technique in which all trees in an area are razored off the land, leaving none standing.

It was not until 1968 that conservationists in the Northwest, where the principal forestry battles were being fought, began attacking the forest industry on its own grounds—that is to say, on forest management and clear-cutting. One scarred veteran of those future wars recalled sitting in a hotel room at Coeur d'Alene when the Idaho Environmental Council was being organized and listening to Guy M. Brandborg of Montana, retired from the Forest Service, saying, "Well, . . . they're clear-cutting too much in the Bitterroot National Forest, and we're gonna take them on." And that, said the veteran, is how it all began. A significant number of the critics of Forest Service practices were men who had worked for the service.

The pressure on the national forests had come gradually. For nearly fifty years after Gifford Pinchot organized the Forest Service in 1905, its lands produced only about 5 percent of the nation's logs, and the agency's paramount role was that of guardian and protector. With World War II and the heightened building activity that followed, private timber supplies began to show signs of playing out. The annual timber harvest from the national forests rose from only 1.5 billion board feet in 1941 to 4.7 billion in 1951. At the height of the Vietnam War it reached 12.1 billion, and in the 1970s it fluctuated uneasily between 10 and 12 billion or thereabouts. Forty percent of the federal logged area was being clear-cut. The money rolled in. In the period between 1968 and 1977, annual Forest Service receipts from timber rose from $206 million to $652 million, more than tripling.

Meanwhile, the Forest Service's "allowable harvest"—the ceiling that is imposed to ensure a sustained yield, over time—was edging up from about 12.8 billion board feet in 1969 to 13 in 1974 and 16.2 in 1977. When the Nixon and Ford administrations sought to drive the federal timber cut higher in order to ease soaring lumber prices, the Forest Service and other federal land managers were widely suspected to be abandoning sustained yield and going hell-for-leather for greater log output. This they denied, but the government's credibility was low, and the traditionally pristine Forest Service no longer was thought to be above politics.

President Nixon entered the White House at a time of great concern—one that was reflected at hearings before the Senate and House committees on banking and currency—about rising lumber prices and their impact on the housing industry. Nixon had been in office only a few weeks when he named the Special Task Force on Lumber and Plywood under the chairmanship of Robert P. Mayo, director of the Bureau of the Budget. Meanwhile, Congress's agriculture committees wrestled with a lumber-producing proposal known as the National Timber Supply Act of 1969.[22] The conservationist lobby rallied against the bill, which would have directed the secretary of agriculture to change harvesting rates in the forests to fetch greater timber yields. "Optimum timber productivity," it was called. Secretary of Agriculture Clifford M. Hardin endorsed the measure, as did George Romney, secretary of housing and urban development.

Another advocate, Rep. Al Ullman, a Democrat from Baker, Oregon, said the western forests were losing as much as ten billion board feet of timber annually through mortality. The old "even flow" concept of sustained yield is obsolete, he explained, and has made the American people custodians of a "static resource" when good conservation cries out for a more positive program of "thinning and salvage," such as were making private forests more productive than public forests. He saw a double benefit from cutting the old trees: "It increases the immediate supply through the harvest of overcrowded, overmature or diseased timber," he said, "and provides a greatly increased growth rate for the healthy standing timber."[23]

A great many people argued that the national forests could produce much more timber if managed efficiently and that the private timber holdings, meaning those of the big, well-organized companies, were better managed than those of the government. There was some basis for these contentions, although they were applicable only if one assumed that the forests were managed for efficient timber production alone. For one thing, company budgets were not subject to the whim of Congress or responsive to the winds of politics. For another, private forests are not dedicated to multiple use.

Ullman's statement about the desirability of harvesting "overmature" timber reflected a viewpoint that was widely shared not merely among politicians seeking to assist the timber and housing industries but also among timber-oriented professionals in the Forest Service and in the groves of academe. It was being pushed as a matter of faith, among some of the nation's eminent silviculturists, that it would be a glad day when the so-called virgin or old-growth forests were gone. These forests, it was

287

said, were cluttered up, slow growing, diseased, unproductive, wasteful. Once they were removed, then younger, more vigorous stock would take over, and the annual growth would scale upward, justifying a larger annual cut. Here again, of course, there was more than a grain of truth. Those espousing these views included Marion Clawson, of Resources for the Future.

There is more to a forest, however, than seedlings and sawdust. Despite the plausibility of the drive to wring more lumber from the national forests in time of apparent scarcity, and despite a powerful alliance among the timber lobbyists, the housing-construction industry, and representatives of the poor in urban ghettos, Congress proved reluctant to force a speedup in federal log production. Timber prices eased somewhat, reducing the pressure. The standard-bearers for the timber supply bill were the National Forest Products Association and the National Association of Home Builders. Opposing was a spirited and active coalition of environmental groups joined by the United Auto Workers. Brock Evans of the Sierra Club, a principal spokesman, said passage of the timber supply legislation would mean the logging off of more than twenty million acres of federal reserves classified as "commercial" but possessing high aesthetic, scenic, and wilderness value. The Sierra Club, the Wilderness Society, the National Audubon Society, Friends of the Earth, and Trout Unlimited dispatched volunteers to Capitol Hill to plead their case. Late in January 1970, eight groups sent legislators a telegram saying the timber proposal "threatens America's national forests, scuttles historic multiple-use practices and undermines prospective parks, wilderness, open space and recreation areas."

Stewart M. Brandborg, son of Guy M., mentioned earlier, and then executive director of the Wilderness Society, telephoned White House Special Counsel Charles W. Colson and warned him that two of the president's cabinet officers—Hardin and Romney—had endorsed what Brandborg later described as "this lousy, industry-sponsored bill." Brandborg and C. R. Gutermuth

288

of the Wildlife Management Institute went to see Colson and told him the bill would harm the forests and that President Nixon, who then was making friendly overtures toward the conservationist cause, ought to be advised to pull away from it.[24] For whatever reason, the president apparently did not put his weight behind the legislation. As the crucial time came on, the environmental coalition organized a campaign that brought in 100,000 to 150,000 letters and telegrams within a few days. In February 1970, the House killed the bill by rejecting a rule under which it was to be considered.[25]

The pressure to convert more of the forest primeval to cellulose did not abate, however. In June 1970, the president released the Mayo task force report, which said the timber harvest from the national forests could and should be increased by seven billion board feet by 1978 "without impairing sustained yield and environmental objectives."[26] The president issued a statement in which he fully endorsed the findings, noted the importance of adequate housing for the American people, and directed the secretaries of agriculture and interior to get cracking.

Only a few days later, on June 23, the insistence on timbering as the dominant use for productive federal forest lands got a powerful further boost when Chairman Aspinall unveiled the long-awaited report of the Public Land Law Review Commission, discussed in chapter 6. It was plain as a pikestaff. The commission, on whose advisory council Weyerhaeuser and other timber interests were represented, advocated that public lands highly productive for timber—mainly in Alaska, the West, and the South—be classified for commercial timber production and given special management, with lumber output the dominant use. It spoke of "liquidating" old-growth trees over a period of time.[27]

Neither the president's call for more than one million additional board feet from the federal forests nor the note sounded by Aspinall's group sat well with those who saw a threat to the forests. Gutermuth, who served on the Aspinall commission's advisory council, pointed out that two billion board feet of lumber from private forests was being sold to Japan. He charged, in a comment quoted in the *New York Times*, that timber operators "have been cutting the hell out of their own lands and depending on the government to bail them out by permitting excessive cutting in the national forests." Representative Saylor of Pennsylvania, a commission member, said Nixon's timber order was an attempt "to do by executive fiat what could not be done legislatively." Saylor added that the Aspinall commission "conveniently substantiates the President's action." He asked why Nixon had not blocked the industry's export of logs to Japan and why timber companies were holding a backlog of twenty-seven billion board feet of federal timber they had bought, but not harvested.

"What's wrong basically," Brandborg of the Wilderness Society said, "is that pressures brought by industry—by way of the White House—have been so intense that the cutting and road building have gone forward under conditions in which regulations have been so relaxed that industry has had nearly a wide-open opportunity, no holds barred, in taking the remnant of old growth trees. Industry has cut its own old growth. It wants to go into national forests and cut essentially without regulation. Massive clear-cutting."[28]

In this early-1970s period, critics of the Forest Service led by Sen. Gale W. McGee, Wyoming Democrat, and others stimulated a lively debate in Congress on the clear-cutting issue while President Nixon, without much success, kept pushing for more logs. Nixon followed a suggestion of his 1970 Mayo task force by creating the President's Advisory Panel on Timber and the Environment, headed by Fred A. Seaton of Nebraska, who had been secretary of the interior during Eisenhower's second term. Among the members was timber lobbyist Ralph D. Hodges, Jr., of the National Forest Products Association.

By the time the Seaton panel brought in its report in September 1973, Nixon was mired in the revelations of Watergate, and environmentalists were briskly pursuing the Forest Service in the courts. Seaton and his associates came down heavily for an increased cut from the public's forests. The annual harvest from such lands, it was said, should be raised by 50 to 100 percent on old growth. The government ought to spend $200 million a year more on forestry programs. Excellent conservation methods should be practiced, but fears of enduring or widespread environmental damage due to timber harvesting were, as Nixon put it, "unfounded, misleading, or exaggerated."[29]

Undaunted by this, the environmentalists concerned about the forests, who had already held up Champion International's mammoth 1968 purchase in the Tongass by litigation, took legal action on the expanded timber production issue. Nixon's directives were challenged. The Natural Resources Defense Council and the Sierra Club forced an agreement that the Forest Service would prepare environmental impact statements on timber sales contracts after mid-1973.[30] In February 1974, the council, the Sierra Club, and the Wilderness Society obtained a federal district court order in Washington, D.C., imposing a 10 percent reduction in the Forest Service's planned timber sales for fiscal 1974. This meant holding sales to about 10.8 billion board feet and eliminating an extra billion to which the Forest Service had agreed as part of an administration effort to bring lumber prices down.

The Natural Resources Defense Council, a public-interest law center organized early in 1970 with assistance from the Ford Foundation and a staff composed chiefly of young Yale Law School graduates, put out a triumphant press release in which it pointed out that a large quantity of lumber was involved in its victory, however transitory. One billion board feet of timber, said the NRDC, "covers approximately 40,000 acres and when cut, would fill 150,000 logging trucks."[31]

For a person who admires trees in their natural state and who likes to believe that in the back country there are dark and brooding primeval forests protected by the federal writ, it is a traumatic experience to come suddenly upon an area that has been subjected to the lumbering tactic called clear-cutting. I remember a water journey up the Inside Passage to Alaska in the late autumn of 1969. We were threading our way toward Sitka. All day the Alaska ferry had been moving past thick forests of spruce and fir that came down to the water's edge on either side. I was standing on the upper deck when we passed a segment of forest which had been razored of its trees, with nothing left but a gray stubble of fallen trunks and brush. It ran for miles and miles along the bank and as deep as the eye could see. I remembered something I had studied in an army course on nuclear warfare, about what happens to trees in a blast area. "Blowdown," the army called it.

The advantages and disadvantages of clear-cutting were explored by Congress in a series of hearings in April, May, and June of 1971 before the Senate Interior Subcommittee on Public Lands, presided over by Sen. Frank Church, Idaho Democrat.[32] The subcommittee's purpose was to find out whether the practice resulted in intolerable damage to the federal forests.

It is obvious that a cheap and easy way to log a tract of timber is to clear-cut it—that is, saw down all the trees at one time. With this method there is no need to send experts through the forest to make decisions as to which trees are ripe for harvest and which are not, no need for the sawyers and machinery operators to be careful not to knock down or damage timber that is to be left for another time. All of it goes. Clear-cutting is a form of "even-aged" management. The alternative is uneven, or "all-aged," management, in which it is assumed that the forest consists of various types, sizes, and ages of trees, and the logging is done selectively, one tree here and one there.

Fallen Timbers

The abrupt mowing down of a stand of large and beautiful trees, as if by a giant scythe, is emotionally and aesthetically objectionable to many people, regardless of the rationale. Pushing emotional and aesthetic considerations aside, there was no substantial disagreement between conservationists and forestry experts in the 1960s and 1970s that clear-cutting was an acceptable method of harvest, if done properly and within limits. Certain trees, like Douglas fir, for example, need full sunlight for development. Where trees are infected by disease, such as dwarf mistletoe, a clear-cut may be the only way to get a healthy regeneration, and so on. The argument against clear-cutting was not that it was never in order and should never be done, but rather that the practice had been grossly abused. In a sense, the clear-cutting controversy was part of the larger indictment against ruthless and excessive cutting of any kind.

Before the Church subcommittee held hearings, there had been agonizing and complaining over a period of years about clear-cutting and overcutting in the forests. In four of them—the Tongass in Alaska, the Bitterroot in Montana, the Bridger in Wyoming, and the Monongahela in West Virginia—clear-cutting stirred up laments that were heard in the nation's capital. The complaints became audible in 1964, when the Forest Service began razing the hardwoods of the Monongahela and other eastern forests. There was an outcry from West Virginians. Sen. Jennings Randolph of that state, a Democrat and chairman of the Public Works Committee, took up the cause.

Senator Metcalf of Montana, hearing from constituents about clear-cutting in the Bitterroot and about what appeared to them to be a Forest Service policy that stressed timber production to the detriment of other values, wrote to Dean Arnold Bolle of the University of Montana's School of Forestry late in 1969. Metcalf, one of the hardy liberals Montana has sent to the Senate, asked Dean Bolle to undertake a study. Dean Bolle and six other faculty members formed a select committee that delivered a note-

293

worthy report in November of 1970. It was printed as a Senate document, 10,000 copies. The professors, whose expertise and qualifications were difficult to fault, indicted the Forest Service for what it had done to the Bitterroot but went far beyond that to write a general condemnation of the agency's timber-oriented, bureaucratic ways. Their report critiqued the service's own in-house study of the Bitterroot, completed a little earlier, and castigated the Public Land Law Review Commission for trying to erode the spirit and intent of the Multiple Use and Sustained Yield Act.

"Multiple use management, in fact, does not exist as the governing principle on the Bitterroot National Forest," Dean Bolle and his colleagues concluded. ". . . Quality timber management and harvest practices are missing. Considerations of recreation, watershed, wildlife and grazing appear as afterthoughts. . . . The management sequence of clearcutting-terracing-planting cannot be justified as an investment for producing timber on the BNF. We doubt that the Bitterroot National Forest can continue to produce timber at the present harvest level."[33]

The Forest Service was seen as an archaic bureaucracy, resistant to change and measuring success chiefly by the amount of timber produced.

It was one thing for tree lovers or do-gooders or backpackers to lament the arboreal slaughter but quite another when the Bolle select committee complained of overcutting and mismanagement. Indignation was not confined to conservationist publications. Local and national newspapers took up the cudgels. Dale A. Burk, state editor of the *Missoulian* in Montana, kept the issue at white heat. James Risser of the *Des Moines Register* wrote a hard-hitting series that found its way into the *Congressional Record* in March 1971 and was widely circulated. Senator McGee of Wyoming, who had been listening to ululations from citizens of his state for several years, had toured the Bridger National Forest near the incomparably lovely Jackson Hole area in 1968. He said he was staggered, almost unbelieving:

it looked "as if Hiroshima had suddenly been transplanted to the pristine Wind River Mountains."[34]

Such was the background for the Church subcommittee's hearings on clear-cutting in the spring and early summer of 1971. The first witness was Senator McGee himself, a personable western progressive, former professor of American history, and the 1966 recipient of the Golden Fleece Award of the National Association of Wool Manufacturers. McGee declared that the nation could produce adequate housing without destroying its forests. He called clear-cutting an assault on the mountainsides. What had taken place on the Bridger was a disaster, he said, because it would take a century—perhaps 130 to 140 years—to replace the trees shorn from the clear-cut areas. In any event, there was doubt that replanting would succeed.

Senator McGee announced that he was introducing a bill providing for a two-year moratorium on all clear-cutting while a national committee of stature assessed the policy. He did in fact introduce the bill, but it gathered dust.

Horror story followed horror story. David H. McGinnis of the West Virginia Forest Management Practices Commission told the Church panel about the Forest Service's practices in the Appalachians. When part of the forest was clear-cut, McGinnis said, trees worthless as lumber were not felled but were "girdled" with an axe and left to die, so that their shade would not interfere with young, shade-intolerant growth that would be clear-cut later, in its turn.[35] This kind of thing maddened sojourners in the woods. It was enough, McGinnis said, to make conservationists sick to their stomachs. Guy M. Brandborg of Montana, already introduced, who supervised the Bitterroot National Forest until his retirement from the service in 1955, complained of shortsighted timber management and what he called "cut and get out" policies on the Bitterroot.

Striking testimony came from Robert Curry, a professor of environmental geology at the University of Montana. Curry, who held a doctorate from the University of California at Berkeley, summarized a five-year study he had made of forest soil degradation. He warned that current timber operations not only were "absurdly expensive, ugly and destructive," as he called them, but threatened to turn parts of Wyoming, California, Oregon, Washington, Idaho, Utah, Colorado, New Mexico, Arizona, the Virginias, and the northeastern states into the kind of bleak, treeless, scrub-covered hills that are found in Greece, Yugoslavia, Italy, Spain, and the Middle East.

"As a geologist," Curry said, "I view forest soils as nutrient reservoirs which take tens of thousands of years to form and which are now being lost through faulty logging practices at rates hundreds to thousands of times faster than their formation."[36]

When Chief Cliff of the Forest Service and the industry representatives had their day in court, they found themselves in no great disarray despite the dramatic evidence that had been given of grievous malpractices here and there. After all, everybody knew the nation had to have timber and that 30 percent of softwood harvest came from the national forests. Chief Cliff sturdily insisted that, despite the impression created by Nixon's timber directives, nobody had told him to increase the actual cut and that it was not, in fact, being increased. The Forest Service's position, Cliff said, was that the output of logs could not be stepped up unless more money was spent for reforestation and the like.[37]

As for the Forest Service's little brother, the Interior Department's BLM, the subcommittee was told by Director Rasmussen, a former Forest Service man, that matters were under firm control. Of the BLM's 23 million acres of commercial or potentially commercial forest, Rasmussen said about 4 million were producing commercially. Nearly all the rest, about 19 million acres, were in Alaska. Of the timber-producing BLM lands, some 2.5 million acres, or more than half, were in the rich western Oregon country—the so-called O & C revested lands. BLM was putting up for sale about 1.4 billion board feet of timber a year,

90 percent of it in western Oregon, and was yielding about 3 percent of the nation's softwood timber supply, compared with the Forest Service's 30 percent. About half of BLM's Oregon holdings—mainly Douglas fir with hemlock and cedar—were trees 100 to 400 years old, but most of these relics of an inefficient and cluttered past were being "converted" by chain saw to what Rasmussen called "a younger and managed forest."[38]

As was made abundantly plain at the hearings, the attitude of the modern slide-rule forester toward old-growth, or virgin, timber was that of Joshua toward the inhabitants of Jericho. None were to be spared. Loggers made a virtue of the slaughter. It was creating order out of chaos. Until the saw and heavy machinery had removed what nature put on the land, man's more orderly handiwork could not replace it. Cliff spoke of an increase in timber growth which would follow "as overmature and decadent timber stands are regenerated." Lowry Wyatt, president of the National Forest Products Association and senior vice president of Weyerhaeuser, said that "forests consigned to the whimsical attention of nature alone fall into neglect and ultimate disaster."[39] Noting that less than 7 percent of the revenue from sale of national forest timber was being reinvested in growing new trees, Wyatt also stated the public ought to know that its forests were losing almost as much timber every year to fire, insects, disease, old age, and natural disaster as they were producing through harvest.

As has been said, Senator McGee's proposal for a moratorium on clear-cutting did not catch fire, and the Church subcommittee, when it finally issued its report, managed to come down on all sides of the burning issues it had so usefully explored. The report did lay down some sensible guidelines on federal timber management, expressing hope that the executive branch would quickly adopt them. The Council on Environmental Quality, urged on by conservationists, proposed to the president in January 1972 an executive order limiting clear-cutting on public lands. The draft was kicked around in the White House for some time. Industry objected, and the project was abandoned. Sen. Fred R. Harris, Oklahoma Democrat with Populist leanings, charged "blatant collusion" involving government officials and the timber lobby.

Nevertheless, the Forest Service and the Bureau of Land Management got the message that many Americans were disturbed at what had been going on in the public's forests. The Forest Service received a bad press. Not a few of its critics, including retired men of the Forest Service itself, appeared to know what they were talking about. Chief Cliff, a tough logger not beloved by conservationists, was succeeded in April 1972 by John R. McGuire, regarded as more gentle, scholarly, and sensitive to aesthetics. In June, McGuire sent out new instructions on clear-cutting in response to the Church subcommittee's guidelines. On the legislative front, things also looked up.

To improve the nation's ability to look ahead with confidence, Congress passed the Forest and Rangeland Renewable Resources Planning Act of 1974.[40] This provided for periodic assessments of such assets as timber and grass, whether under public or private ownership. The Forest Service, while playing the major role in the assessment, ran into trouble the following year when its timber-sales policies for the Monongahela National Forest in West Virginia were held to be illegal. In an action brought by the Izaak Walton League of America, federal courts held the policies, which involved clear-cutting and the like, violated the 1897 organic act under which the Forest Service operated. The only timber that could be sold, it was decreed, was timber that was dead, physiologically mature, and of large growth.[41] Furthermore, each tree had to be individually marked and removed. The same ruling was soon made applicable to a sale in the Tongass Forest in Alaska.

Amid the consternation caused by the Monongahela case, which stopped the Forest Service in its tracks, Congress bestirred itself to pass a new and comprehensive Forest Service law, as the fourth circuit court of appeals had suggested be done. Thus in the Bicentennial Year came another round of fisticuffs between the conservationists and the timber lobby. The Sierra Club denounced early versions of the bill as weak, ruinous, disastrous. Club members were told the forests were in jeopardy. Letters and telegrams from environmentalists flooded in. Finally, shortly before Carter defeated President Ford, the National Forest Management Act of 1976 emerged in a form the Sierra Club conceded was "a net plus."[42] It required timber harvesting on a sustained-yield basis and set guidelines on clear-cutting. The Council on Environmental Quality reported with satisfaction that with the passage of the new law "comprehensive legislation for better forestry management on federal lands is complete."

The true controversy over logging in the publicly owned timberlands in the 1970s centered on objectives, quality of management, integrity. Responsible conservationists did not oppose the harvesting of timber. Rather, they objected to the way it was being done, to what they saw as the emphasis on sawdust over all else. They suspected that economic factors were being overemphasized at the expense of wise husbandry. They were right, of course.

"When you get home to America you must manage a forest and make it pay," young Gifford Pinchot was told by one of his professors at the French *Ecole nationale forestiere* at Nancy. Pinchot, the first head of the Forest Service and long its guiding spirit, had the liveliest interest in harvesting timber. One of his missions was to convince private lumber interests like the Weyerhaeusers that "practical forestry" was practical. Men who were accustomed to cutting and getting out had to be persuaded that the time had come to manage the forests, cultivate them, and make them pay over the long haul. Pinchot believed in producing wood.

But Pinchot would fight like a tiger for what he conceived to be the public interest. He fought Big Money, predatory westerners, people with political pull. He had the backing of President Theodore Roosevelt. He built the Forest Service into a marvelously effective agency, manned by nonpolitical professionals with high morale.

"Big Money was king in the Great Open Spaces, and no mistake," Pinchot recalled in his autobiography, written in the fullness of his years.

"But in the National Forests," he said proudly, "Big Money was not king. Every member of the Forest Service in the office and in the field knew that the President was with us. Everyone knew that neither money nor political influence could dictate to the Forest Service or secure or endanger his advancement or his job."[43]

Pinchot's was a golden time, like the early days of the civil rights movement, when so many dragons roamed the land that the sword arm of the righteous became weary and every blow found its mark.

And as the first chief, Pinchot had the kind of easy access to power not enjoyed by his successors. In his prime, he used to think nothing of dropping by the White House in the afternoon, joining the president in a long walk along the Potomac, staying for tea.

Steam tractor of 1894 hauling logs. It was built by the Best Manufacturing Company, one of the predecessors of the present Caterpillar Tractor Co. *Courtesy U.S. Department of Agriculture.*

CHAPTER 12

COME BLOW YOUR HORN

How do the beasts groan!
The herds of cattle are perplexed,
Because they have no pasture;
Yea, the flocks of sheep are made desolate.
— BIBLE, JOEL 1:18

Grass is the forgiveness of nature—her constant benediction. Fields trampled with battle, saturated with blood, torn with the ruts of the cannon, grow green again with grass, and carnage is forgotten. Forests decay, harvests perish, flowers vanish, but grass is immortal.
— Sen. JOHN JAMES INGALLS

Of all the causes that disrupt the delicate balance between the native vegetation and its environment, man himself has been the most devastating and continuously destructive—and always with increasing effectiveness.
— *Yearbook of Agriculture*, 1948

Grass has often moved men to poetry and lyrical prose. It has also been a cause of bloody conflict. The struggle for power over the federal grazing lands in the West is a romantic and exalting story as well as a distressing one. By this time, the United States should have a well-managed federal range on which the number of grazing animals has been adjusted to the carrying capacity of the land. This has not been achieved, largely because of politics.

To understand why so much of the federal range has been overgrazed and otherwise abused and neglected, one must look back at the development of western ranching and then follow in some detail, tedious though the procedure may be, the efforts that have been made to put the range under meaningful control and curb the abuses. Such efforts often have been frustrated. They rate in difficulty somewhere close to the task of snatching a side of beef from a Bengal tiger.

In the early days, the very early days, there was plenty of grass and plenty of land, but seldom enough water. Later on, there was not enough of any of the three. In the early days, the federal government owned most of the range land but did not control it. In the late 1970s, after decades of persuasion and struggle in good times and bad, the government's managers were asserting more authority over public grazing but still were not masters in their own house. Like the federal timber and mineral managers, they were not fully in charge. The Forest Service sat more firmly in the saddle than the BLM, but both had to reckon with a politically powerful and headstrong clientele. It is not overstating the case to say that the livestock industry did as it wished with its own grazing lands and also, in effect, ran the federal range.

The issues concerning management and use of publicly owned grazing lands in the 1970s were similar to those that arose in the care and use of the federal timberlands. Was the federal range being overgrazed? The answer was yes. Was the range being properly cared for and replenished? The answer

303

was no. Was the government receiving fair value for the use of the range? Again, the answer was no. As was the case with the timberlands, it was a matter of insufficient funds and inadequate personnel, a curious combination of lopsided politics and neglect.

This is not to suggest that the federal range either should have been or ought to be managed in an arrogant, arbitrary manner, wtih no thought for the welfare of those dependent on the public grazing lands and no participation by them in the making of decisions. It is simply to assert that federal managers, responsible for federal property, ought not to be made helpless.

The independent spirit of the Golden West, when the range was free and unfenced and the drovers could move stock from Texas to Missouri without seeing a federal officer, did not die easily. As sodbusters—the hated "nesters"—moved onto the prairies and built their legal fences, the cattlemen reacted by building illegal fences of their own, enclosing large tracts of federal land to which they had no right or title. The struggle between farmers and ranchers for what was left of the open range continued over a period of years, against the background of the fabled 1880s, which opened with a tremendous boom in the cattle trade but ended in a bust following the harsh winter of 1886–87. It was a back breaking winter, leaving thousands of cattle dead when the spring thaws came. Ranchers lost half their herds. Many lost heart. Many others figured they must acquire and fence their own pastures, before somebody else got ahead of them. Barbed wire had come on the market in 1874.[1]

Big ranchers in many parts of the West formed protective associations and took high-handed measures they considered to be in their own interest. President Theodore Roosevelt, who had operated a ranch in the Dakota Badlands and lost 60 percent of his herd in the 1886–87 blizzard, ordered the illegal fences taken down. The cattlemen backed a lease bill under which they could make their holdings legal. Congress dutifully approved it, whereupon there was jubilation in the cattle kingdom. Roosevelt vetoed the bill. The president had resisted the blandishments of livestock delegations that called upon him in Washington.[2] He told them, "Gentlemen, the fences will come down." In the early 1900s, Roosevelt, striving to round up illegal fencers of government land, managed to put a few of the wealthy and arrogant in jail. A rich Nebraska and Wyoming operator, Bartlett Richards, died before serving out his term under Taft, Roosevelt's successor.[3] He had been allowed to choose his place of confinement, and he and his colleagues enjoyed special privileges, but he did serve time. It was a lesson to scofflaws on the range.

Homesteading's inexorable breaking up of the vast common pastureland was delayed by illegal fencing and by abuse of the land laws. In the period when Roosevelt was instituting his reforms, around 1901, a federal agent was reporting from Nebraska that big ranchers, as a means of keeping their fences and barring intrusion by settlers, had been hiring dummy entrymen—"loafers, tramps, railway graders, Negroes"—to file for homesteads along the fence lines.[4] It took years to run down or circumvent these frauds, all too reminiscent of what had gone on before.

To an extraordinary degree, the malefactions of the big ranchers had the support of the newspapers and many members of Congress. Among the Wyoming ranchers who encroached on federal land were Republican United States Sen. Joseph M. Carey and Sen. Francis E. Warren, both of whom also served as governor of the state. Roosevelt backed the small settlers against the cattle kings but did not hide his scorn for so-called homesteaders who took up a claim and then sold or "relinquished" it for a price, often to cattle or timber operators. A man of that sort, argued Roosevelt, was not entitled to sympathy and was not the man who settles down, tills the soil, and builds up the country. "This is the man who skins the country and moves on," he said.[5]

In the Wyoming of today, a century of history and the erosion of harsh frontier attitudes have made a difference. For example, the state's Republican United States Sen. Clifford P. Hansen, when taken to task in 1972 for running his cattle in Grand Teton

National Park, explained patiently through his office on Capitol Hill that he and later his wife held valid grazing permits there, dating from before the park was expanded.[6] It was all perfectly legal and proper, whatever the cosmic propriety of a senator's Herefords cropping grass in a federal park. This was a pastoral scene indeed compared to the situation when Wyoming stockmen were warring with Federal Land Commissioner William A. J. Sparks in the 1880s. Sparks had reports that Territorial Delegate Carey and Governor Warren were among the many illegal enclosers of public land. Sparks gave ranchers a painful rawhiding, and he was finally dry-gulched.[7]

When Roosevelt took up the fencing crusade in the 1900s, he did not press it against his friend, Senator Warren, whom a Senate colleague once called "the greatest shepherd since Abraham." An Interior Department inquiry egged on by Democrats brought evidence that the Warren Livestock Company had wrongfully fenced seventy-three square miles and maintained the fences for twenty years. Settlers trying to invade Warren's public pastures, it was reported, had been persecuted and driven away. Roosevelt sent the report to the Justice Department, which discredited it.[8]

The offenses laid at the door of Senator Warren, a towering hero of Wyoming's early years, were mild, however, compared to what had gone on in the so-called Johnson County War that raged between well-to-do stockmen and small settlers and ranchers early in the 1890s. In an earlier episode to the south, referred to by T. A. Larson in his *History of Wyoming,* a party of cattlemen aroused public indignation by lynching a woman named Ella Watson or "Cattle Kate," and her homesteader consort, James Averell. She had the distinction of being the first and last woman hanged in the state. Six men were arrested but released after witnesses failed to appear before the grand jury. The *Salt Lake City Tribune* deplored the lynching of Watson, terming it something of which Wyoming men would not be proud. "That is about the poorest use that a woman can be put to," the *Tribune* said.[9]

Governor Warren was appalled by the massacre at Rock Springs in 1885, when some twenty-eight Chinese were slaughtered and hundreds forced to leave town. The Chinese had been brought in to work at the Union Pacific's coal mines some years earlier when white miners were on strike. They stayed on and were resented. Governor Warren took a strong stand for law and order and came to be called "Chinese" Warren for his pains. Grand jury indictments could not be obtained. The perpetrators of the massacre, whoever they were, went unpunished.[10]

The struggles of the West's unfettered cattle and sheep magnificoes when the federal gyves were being put upon their wrists had a sweep and grandeur that were lacking in the subsequent wrangle over grazing fees. Hollywood could make motion pictures about longhorns and sheep, fences and nesters, cow towns and the Chisholm Trail, mortgages and widows and fights over water, but no plot could be built around the government's charging a nickel a month for grazing a steer. This was ribbon clerk stuff, something for country lawyers to argue about. Nevertheless, the principle was important, and both the federal officers and the western ranchers knew it. The government wanted to assert sovereignty and get enough revenue to pay for maintaining the range. The ranchers wanted to establish a property right—not ownership, perhaps, but a right.

The National Forest System began charging a small fee for grazing when the agency was established in 1905, but the forage on the unappropriated public domain, under the General Land Office, remained free for three decades longer. The Forest Service's audacity in attempting to control the number of animals feeding in designated areas did not sit well with the livestock industry.[11] Fees in the first few years never totaled more than $1 million annually, but stockmen chafed and agonized under the supervision. In some cases the Forest Service dared to order a reduction in the number of livestock. Its authority to impose fees was upheld by the United States Supreme Court in 1911.[12] The view was spreading that the Forest Service's prim surveillance was preferable to the chaos still prevailing on the pub-

307

lic domain. A disastrous drop in cattle and sheep prices on the eve of the Great Depression of the 1930s contributed to a willingness to accept regulation. Finally, in 1934, Congress acted to bring the rest of the federally owned range into some semblance of order.

The legislative vehicle was the Taylor Grazing Act, which we have encountered earlier.[13] It was named after Edward T. Taylor, Democratic congressman from Colorado, schooled in law at the University of Michigan and former high school principal at Leadville. The Taylor Act was an important conservation law. Recognizing that the primary economic use of the broad federal domain was grazing and the cultivation of forage crops, it set up a formula for distribution of federal grazing privileges at a modest fee to ranchers who, generally speaking, already were enjoying those privileges gratis. It vested the grazing mission in Secretary Ickes's Interior Department and not in the Forest Service, just as Ickes had urged be done. It authorized the secretary to set up grazing districts and to make rules and regulations for them, but it also laid down that he must provide for "cooperation" with local stockmen's associations, state land officials, and official state agencies engaged in conservation or propagation of wildlife. The broad objectives, as stated in the new law, were "to stop injury to the public grazing lands by preventing overgrazing and soil deterioration; to provide for their orderly use, improvement, and development; and to stabilize the livestock industry dependent upon the public range."

As was mentioned earlier, the Taylor Grazing Act contained language in its first sentence which reflected the uncertainty of the ultimate fate of the federal domain—that is, whether the federal government would keep the lands or allow them to move into state or private ownership. "That in order to promote the highest use of public lands *pending its final disposal*," the law started out, "the Secretary of the Interior is authorized . . . " The question of the future was left open, and it remained open for many years.

308

The law called for the "payment annually of reasonable fees" to be determined from time to time, and gave preference in issuance of grazing permits, as was inevitable, "to those within or near a district who are landowners engaged in the livestock business, bona fide occupants or settlers, or owners of water or water rights, as may be necessary to permit the proper use of lands, water, or water rights owned, occupied, or leased by them." This put propertied ranchers in the catbird's seat and settled the hash of the itinerant, nomadic sheepmen who had grazed their animals on the public range but had no land base of their own, or none to speak of.

Although the imposition of a monetary charge for grazing generated bitter controversy, the fees amounted to very little in the early days, and they had not been allowed to come within roping distance of the fair market value of forage by the late 1970s. When the Forest Service began levying a fee in 1906, the charge averaged only five cents for cattle and a penny for sheep for a standardized measure that came to be known as an "animal unit month"—that is, the forage needed to sustain one animal unit for a month. An AUM was equivalent to one cow, one horse, five sheep, or five goats, all more than six months of age. The Interior Department's original fee in 1936 was five cents, compared with thirteen for the Forest Service at that time. Interior held to the five-cent level for another ten years.

The law clearly stated that the issuance of a permit did not create any right, title, interest, or estate in the federal lands, but it recognized that permits had economic value. In fact, the law provided that renewal of a permit should not be denied if the rancher's grazing unit had been pledged as security for a loan. The initial permittees got their permits without charge, but from then on the permits figured in the sale of ranch properties and could be said to represent—and, of course, did represent—an investment on the buyer's part, even though, theoretically at least, the grazing privilege could be curtailed or entirely cut off at the government's whim.

309

Obviously, the rancher with a small private "base" property touching a broad expanse of the public lands depended on the accessibility of the federal range to his livestock. Theoretically he had no legal right to grazing privileges. As a practical matter, he and everybody else knew that certain grazing permits ran with his property and that he might well have made an "investment" in those permits and, further, that it would be no easy matter for federal officials to deprive him of them. The question of the rancher's investment grievously complicated the federal effort to move toward fair market value in grazing fees.[14] The rancher argued that because he had already paid a great deal for what he was getting, the fees should be low. Those pressing for higher charges contended that low fees encouraged overgrazing and abuse of the federal pasture.

The grazing-fee issue plagued the Forest Service from the outset, as has been seen. It continued as a burr under the saddle of Secretary Ickes's new Grazing Division, which the ambitious Ickes had condemned to penury by telling Congress that his department could manage the grasslands for $150,000 a year. Ickes based his estimate on 80 million acres rather than on the 140 million he soon had under his wing, but even so, his appraisal of the cost was only about one-tenth that of the Forest Service.

By that time, of course, the Forest Service had acquired experience in dealing with the cattlemen's and wool growers' associations and with ranchers out in the gulches and mountain valleys. It is recounted that Pinchot's rangers in Utah once played a lighthearted game with cattlemen, in which the rangers daubed a special paint on the flank of each animal permitted to graze in the forest, and the ranchers quickly obtained the same kind of paint and marked the nonpermit animals the same way.[15] The Forest Service learned that control of grazing was a difficult business that took a lot of time and patience and effort, particularly when the West's leading ranchers were so often its leading politicians as well. Senator Warren of Wyoming, for example, was the first president of the National Wool Growers Association.

Drought and depression gripped the scenic and pastoral western landscape when the Taylor Grazing Act became law. Uncurbed use of the federal range over many years had taken savage toll. Drought had made things worse. The Forest Service's restraints had driven animals elsewhere, increasing the burden on the general public domain to which the new grazing law applied. It was estimated in 1932 that the western range—meaning the range outside the forests—had lost nearly half of its original productivity. Not since domestic animals first began cropping grass in the West, said the experts, had the range been in a more miserable state.[16]

The first director of the Interior Department's Grazing Division was Farrington R. Carpenter, a Harvard lawyer and stockman from Colorado.[17] At Harvard, Carpenter had sat at the feet of the eminent historian Frederick Jackson Turner, whose *Significance of the Frontier in American History* illuminated discussion of the national expansion westward. The first grazing director was an able man whose education and background enabled him to see the broader dimensions of his task. He headed a sadly inadequate little band that later became the Grazing Service and ultimately, after the reorganization of 1946, the Division of Range Management in the BLM. Initially, Carpenter had a staff of seventeen from the Geological Survey, the General Land Office, and the Forest Service, along with experienced stockmen, some of whom had gone broke in hard times.

Carpenter, by all accounts a happy warrior who had been a homesteader himself and knew the West and its ways with the public lands, faced the colossal job of setting up grazing districts and allocating the first permits. Not only did he have to carry out the task inexpensively, thanks to what Secretary Ickes had promised, but he had to live with Ickes's pronouncement that grazing fees should not be imposed for the purpose of making money for the federal government. The fees, Ickes had said, should only be such as might cover the cost of running the range. The Taylor Act itself, it may be remembered, provided for "reasonable" fees but did not define what Congress meant by *reasonable*.

A good hand at swinging the federal lariat that was now to be tossed over the necks of the quivering but depression-tamed ranchers, Carpenter sneaked up on their blind side as best he could. He advocated a self-rule system that gave the stockmen a loud voice in the operation of their grazing districts.[18] Advisory boards had, of course, been built into the law. It was judged that local people would recognize their stake in range conditions in their own areas and would help keep one another honest.

Carpenter strongly encouraged state and local participation as the federal government sought to assert its authority over grazing on land that was then—and always had been since the nation obtained it—the common property of the people of the United States. He called the organization of grazing districts "our attempt to regulate the last of the free-loading on the public domain by the cowboys and sheepherders." As a practical matter, he did get valuable on-the-ground assistance from local advisory boards in deciding on a fair allocation of range privileges based on the history of use between 1929 and 1934.

"It is harder to lie in front of your neighbors," he said, "than to a government official far removed from the scene."

The first allocations were made and permits issued during what was called the "adjudication" period. Lengthy and tedious legal proceedings were common. Ranchers and companies with a property base were taken care of. The death knell was tolled for tramp herdsmen who had driven bands of sheep where they willed and whose animals—"hoofed locusts," John Muir called them—cropped the vegetation down to its very roots. It was the end of the open range and the end of homesteading, or nearly so.

All flesh is grass, says the Bible. There had been a time, not so long past, when grass grew belly-high to a horse in parts of the western plains. This was by no means true of all public domain, but it was true of much that had been damaged by decades of neglect and overgrazing. The carrying capacity of wild federal range varies a great deal, but generally it is nowhere near as great as that of cultivated, farmed pastureland. Six acres of good short-grass land in Montana may support a cow for a month, while an animal grazing in Nevada's desert shrub country may need nearly twenty-two. Abuse of the drier, poorer land has disastrous consequences.

Born to weakness, Secretary Ickes's Grazing Division was soon in the same kind of trouble with western stockmen and politicians that the Forest Service had run into much earlier. In 1940, by which time the Grazing Division had been renamed the Grazing Service and Carpenter had been replaced by Richard H. Rutledge, the Interior Department was proposing to double fees in its grazing districts. Another Forest Service career man, Clarence Forsling, succeeded Rutledge in 1944 and stirred up the ranchers by trying to triple fees. Already, as World War II came on, the Grazing Service had needed more funds and was being chivied by the House Appropriations Committee to raise the charges for grazing. Pat McCarran of Nevada and the Senate Interior Committee did not want higher fees. Beginning about 1940, Senator McCarran roasted the Grazing Service at a series of hearings during which the fury of his attack reminded Marion Clawson of the vendetta waged against the Forest Service in the 1920s by Republican Sen. R. N. Stanfield, an Oregon livestock man and banker.[19] McCarran had great staying power. He kept after the Grazing Service for years and ultimately was credited by Bernard DeVoto with having given brilliant leadership to the western bloc that emasculated it. "Senator McCarran," DeVoto wrote in January 1947, "has been the ablest representative of cattle and sheep interests in Washington, against the West and the people of the United States."[20]

The coup de grâce for the Grazing Service, followed by a reincarnation of sorts, came immediately after the war, in 1946. In

313

that year the service's appropriations were axed so grievously that it was impossible to keep a field man and a clerk in each of the grazing districts, some of which contained several million acres of land. Also in an ossified condition, thoroughly subdued and demoralized, a jungle of paper work, was the old General Land Office. President Truman in May 1946 sent to Congress Reorganization Plan 3 in which, by executive order, he consolidated functions of the Grazing Service and the General Land Office to form the present Bureau of Land Management.[21] The director was to be appointed by the secretary of interior and was to receive $10,000 a year. The BLM thus began life without statutory authority from Congress. It had no stated mission, broadly speaking, beyond what had been set forth in the Taylor Grazing Act twelve years earlier. It was under the thumb of Senator McCarran, the livestock interests, mining companies, and other users of the public lands.[22]

Nothing in the BLM's genes justified an assumption that it would prove a lusty infant. Interior Secretary Julius A. Krug, who had succeeded Ickes, reported to President Truman and to Congress that more money was going to have to be spent if the land was to be conserved. He estimated that 115 million acres of federally owned rangelands stood in need of restorative attention, while 46 million were in critically bad condition, all but destroyed by erosion and overgrazing. The Krug statement was another alarm bell that went unheard. The same kind of report was being made a quarter century later, haunting and familiar, like the "On the Trail" part of Grofé's *Grand Canyon Suite* played by a high school band.

With the pickets of a demoralized federal officialdom driven in, the cow lobby, backed by powerful conservative forces, mounted its final onslaught in the period from 1946 to 1953 and was, strangely enough, whipped. The stockmen overextended themselves—or, more properly, some of them did—by trying to make the public's range their private property. Wyoming Sen. Edward V. Robertson, a Welshman and Republican, greeted the

314

fledgling BLM in 1946 with a legislative proposal under which the federal grazing lands would be conveyed to the states and ranchers would be enabled to buy them on concessional terms. The livestock industry and its spokesmen in Congress made other crippling proposals, including one that would have stripped the Forest Service of its pastures and left them to the mercy of permit holders. The arrogance of the effort caused widespread resentment. In the Forest Service, with its proud tradition of professionalism, the cow lobby found that it had taken on a formidable foe. There was a stinging reaction in the press and in national magazines, led by DeVoto in *Harper's Magazine* and Lester Velie in *Collier's*. The cattlemen and wool growers were seen as trying to devour the public domain. A great many people in the West, including smaller ranchers and other users of the lands, did not want that to happen and said so.

DeVoto knew the West as a native and was a magnificent free-style barroom brawler in debate. An aficionado of the martini cocktail and a scholar turned polemicist, he put a sharp knife into Senator Robertson. He regaled his readers with the fact that Robertson owned a big Wyoming sheep and cattle ranch and held a grazing permit for 2,400 sheep in the Shoshone National Forest. DeVoto exposed the flagrantly one-sided character of hearings conducted in the West by Wyoming Rep. Frank A. Barrett, Republican, then chairman of the House subcommittee on public lands and also a stockman in his own right.[23] Basically, as DeVoto described them, the hearings were an assault on the Forest Service.

There was a drumhead court-martial quality about the scene, with Forest Service witnesses herded together and given short shrift, while their indignant adversaries were suffered to rail on at length. At Grand Junction, in Western Colorado, Barrett was said by a representative of the Izaak Walton League to have "launched into a shouting, fist-clenching outburst that was intemperate in language and at times reached screaming intensity." The spectacle of cattle-running politicians toadying up to

315

the local magnificoes and trying to intimidate federal officials did not please all westerners. The *Denver Post* referred to the barnstorming subcommittee as "Stockman Barrett's Wild West Show."[24] In the end, the tactics of stridency backfired.

DeVoto found the cattlemen to be his meat. In a series of pieces that appeared from time to time, up through the beginning of the Eisenhower administration, he gave his select audience a liberal education on the grazing issue, the public lands and their importance, and the groups seeking to exploit them. Never before or since, it might be said, has the nation's intelligentsia learned more about cows, sheep, and the public grass. DeVoto applied his scourge with a remarkably effective mixture of humor, sarcasm, and gentlemanly abuse.[25] The "Cattle Kingdom," as he called it, roared in anguish and charged that the Forest Service was feeding material to DeVoto. When the industry sought to get back into the feed bin, he was there with his prod.

Badgered in the press and fighting a rising tide of competitive uses for the federal range, including the increasingly lucrative recreation and tourist trade, the livestock industry went through what appeared to be its last hurrah in 1953, the year President Eisenhower entered the White House. The effort was boldly made. As Farrington Carpenter had said: "These were the men who did not want to stick their necks into the government collar and who did not want to pay a fee for grazing their livestock." The American National Livestock Association and the National Wool Growers Association had the satisfaction of seeing some of their views reflected in the 1952 Republican platform. One of the planks in that document urged an impartial study of "tax-free federal lands" and favored legislation to "define the rights of grazers and other users" and to protect those rights against "administrative invasions" by means of a system of independent judicial review.[26] This meant pouring concrete around the privileges enjoyed by ranchers and giving those privileges the status of rights while placing the final decision in grazing matters out-

side the province of the Forest Service and the BLM. Such a proposal, which critics denounced as a giveaway, was indeed
introduced early in 1953 by Montana Republican Rep. Wesley
D'Ewart.

Notwithstanding the stockmen's assault on the federal citadel
in the 1940s and the renewed thrust when President Eisenhower
took office, the Bureau of Land Management and the Forest Service contrived to raise the fees. Common sense demanded it.
Early in 1963 under Kennedy, Interior Secretary Udall, who said
the subject had been "studied to exhaustion," increased the BLM
fee to thirty cents, closer to the Forest Service's forty-nine.
Ranchers protested. At a hearing of the Senate public lands subcommittee, Chairman Alan Bible of Nevada termed the long-
suffering BLM "one of the most browbeaten agencies of the government." Assistant Secretary of the Interior John A. Carver told
Bible that the fees were indefensibly low, that to fail to raise
them would be a dereliction of duty. Western states with grazing
lands, Carver said, were charging two to eighteen times the BLM
fee. Private charges were much higher. The government was
spending four times as much for range improvements as it was
collecting in fees. Reminded that some ranchers were in hard
times, Carver said the law did not authorize the secretary to run
the Taylor Act on a welfare basis.[27]

In response to pressure for a uniform solution of the fee issue,
the Johnson administration in 1966 established an interdepart-
mental committee to study the charges imposed on users for
livestock grazing on all federal lands. It involved the Budget Bureau and Defense Department as well as the Agriculture and Interior departments. This was carefully done, with a study design
approved by the Budget Bureau. There were interviews with
10,000 people and 218 financial institutions. The surveyors pored
through more than 14,000 questionnaires. What was the real difference between what ranchers were paying for grazing an animal unit for one month on federal lands and what was being
paid for comparable privileges on private lands? It was calcu-

lated that the fair market value of federal grazing was $1.23, or 90 cents more than the 33 cents then being charged by BLM. The word *calculated* is used advisedly, since the figure for fair market value would have been much higher had it not been whittled down by elaborate computations and deductions.

However realistic, the market value was thus set, and late in 1968, with President Johnson about to be replaced by Nixon, the Agriculture and Interior departments announced a joint decision to raise fees by nine cents a year for the next ten years, thereby moving toward the full value goal by incremental stages.[28] Budget officers said the government would not be getting what the forage was worth for a while. A considerate government, it was suggested, had chosen to inch the fees up year by year, rather than taking the full advance immediately, "to minimize the effect on stockmen." Ranchers and their spokesmen were not mollified.

Senator Church of Idaho, chairman of the interior subcommittee on public lands, called the increase "the most drastic adjustment of grazing fees ever imposed." He sent a sharp letter to his fellow Democrats, Interior Secretary Udall and Agriculture Secretary Orville Freeman, who, of course, were on their way out. The attempt to fix a policy that would bind the incoming Republicans was an attempt at the impossible and would be regarded as presumptuous, said Church, who had been the National Jaycee Outstanding Young Man in 1957. He called hearings for February 27 and 28.[29]

At the Church hearings, stockmen and western politicians gave federal officials a drubbing, but were not vituperative. They argued that it would be only fair to count the rancher's investment in his grazing permits—then reckoned to have a sale value of $25.35 for Forest Service land and 6 percent on $14.41 for each animal unit month if one holder transferred them to another—as part of his cost of doing business on the public domain. For this purpose 6 percent of the "permit value" would be added to what he was assumed to be paying.

318

However audacious their reasoning may seem, there could be no doubt that many stockmen believed it was only fair to take "permit value" into account. Reuben Pankey of Truth or Consequences, New Mexico, the chairman of the forest committee of the American National Cattlemen's Association, went to the witness table accompanied by Darwin B. Nielsen, professor of ecomnimics at Utah State University. A study by Nielsen, estimating the permit value on BLM and Forest Service lands at $343 million, had argued that the government's announced fee increases would wipe out all permit values, an outright confiscation and a blow to an already depressed industry.

When livestock men cooperated in the federal data-gathering effort in 1966, Pankey testified, their understanding was that the capitalized permit value—4½ percent on $25.35 for Forest Service land and 6 percent on $14.41 for BLM land—would be included in operating costs. Had that been done, little or no fee increase would have been justified. The government, however, despite the acknowledged dollar value of the grazing permit, threw it out as a factor. "We consider it a repudiation of their word to us," Pankey said.[30]

From the National Wool Growers Association the story was the same. M. Joseph Burke, a Wyoming sheep operator and chairman of the association's federal lands committee, noted that the Internal Revenue Service, the Defense Department, the Federal Land Bank, and other agencies had recognized the value of grazing permits, and it was inconceivable that eliminating them as a cost factor could be justified.

The general counsel of the Public Lands Council, Joseph H. Tudor, followed with a statement he said he had been authorized to make on behalf of the cattlemen and woolgrowers associations and the council itself. Tudor had resigned within the year as assistant solicitor in the Interior Department, where he had served some thirty-five years. He said the issue of vested rights was a "bugaboo" and should be put aside in the discussion.

319

"The western livestock industry," Tudor said in carefully phrased legalese, "disavows and denies any intent or desire to claim or assert as against the United States directly or indirectly, any proprietary interest in or to the public lands or national forest lands purportedly arising out of the recognition by the Federal agencies of 'permit values' as a cost factor in any comparison of costs of using or grazing on the public lands compared to private lands as in the 1966 western grazing lands survey except as to any rights arising under the public land laws of the United States in the same ways as they would apply to all other citizens."[31]

The position taken by the ranchers, however, had in it elements of the ridiculous, as their opponents pointed out.

Rasmussen of the BLM made a stout defense of the fee increases. So did Chief Cliff of the Forest Service. Rasmussen said that giving permittees credit for interest on permit value in assessing fees "would recognize that the permit gives the operator a proprietary interest in the public lands." This, he went on, would clearly violate the Taylor Act, which provided that issuance of a permit "shall not create any right, title, interest or estate in or to the lands." It was brought out by Rasmussen that 52 percent of the BLM's forage was going to only 5 percent of the agency's permittees, or about 700 ranchers. That is to say, most of the gravy was going to the large operators who would be paying most of the increase.

Chief Cliff, in his turn, argued that granting special rights to the ranchers would impair the capacity of the public lands to serve other uses and would convert grazing privileges in the national forests to grazing rights. If the value of grazing permits were ground into the fee-setting mix, Cliff said, then logically the holder of permits could demand compensation from the government for any curtailment, and that would inhibit decisions to protect or improve the range.

Despite the sympathetic cluckings of Senator McGee of Wyoming, Senator Church, Senator Bible of Nevada, and many others, and despite much talk about the plight of the small rancher in a cost-price squeeze—a hazard that seemed to be chronic whenever higher fees were under debate—the stockmen got the worst of it.

Not all the western senators went along with the cow and sheep lobby, and not all the ranchers agreed with it. Senator Metcalf of Montana, sympathetic but stubbornly honest and realistic, reminded all present that Congress had never recognized that a grazing permit was anything more than just that—a permit, subject to withdrawal. He introduced a letter from a constituent, Robert C. Lynam of Miles City, who had served for many years on a BLM district advisory board. It was a trenchant, closely reasoned, and caustic document supporting the $1 million grazing survey and the action federal officials were taking in the light of its conclusions.[32]

If the permit value that thousands of operators had gotten for nothing were allowed to be capitalized and subtracted from grazing fees, Lynam said, a rise in value of less than eight dollars could eliminate the charges, and a rise beyond that could, in theory at least, result in "the Federal government actually paying a rancher to graze livestock on the public lands."

"I suggest," Lynam continued, "that any such arrangement is untenable and grossly unfair to the American taxpayer."

In eastern Montana, Lynam informed the Church subcommittee, low grazing fees on the federal range had encouraged widespread subleasing, with the result that some 60 percent of the BLM's forage was being channeled to individual operators through middlemen. The rates being charged for it were as much as fourteen times the BLM rate. Lynam knew of a banker who had bought four ranches with grazing permits attached. The banker was running no stock himself but was subletting the grazing privileges, not for 33 cents, but for an average of $4.50 a cow month. The banker got the difference and was paying for the ranches with the money.

The nickel-a-month ranchers took a severe hiding from conservationist and wildlife organizations. Vice President Gutermuth of the Wildlife Management Institute praised the Johnson and Nixon administrations for having the gumption to raise fees. He said the arguments being made by stockmen had been heard before.

A western senator who followed the grazing-fee struggle with sardonic interest, nagging Interior Secretary Hickel for postponing the 1970 increase, was Metcalf. In the period from September 1969 through January 1971, the Montanan put in the *Congressional Record* a series of ten packets of information.[33] He stressed the parlous condition of the range and the miniscule amount the government was getting for its forage. Nowhere else could the feed for an animal be purchased for forty-four cents a month, the Senate and the public were told. "A rancher cannot feed his 50-pound dog for so little," the senator said. In virtually every western state, he noted, a sportsman will pay more for a license to hunt or fish for one day than it costs to graze a cow for one month on the public lands.

Senator Metcalf, who knew how to use the weapon of ridicule, badgered Hickel unmercifully for yielding to the political winds and putting off the 1970 hike in fees. He said he had never seen such "delaying tacttics and confusion." He submitted evidence that the Montana Public Land Council, trying to raise contributions for its Washington campaign, was claiming credit for persuading Hickel to the stockmen's viewpoint.

"This Administration," Metcalf said, "has the issue squarely in its lap. It has a choice to make—improve the range, conserve the soil, restore the environment, or peel the fragile headwaters and let streams run brown with mud. It may increase the grazing fees and plow more of the revenue back into the depleted range, or starve out the livestock and the game on the eroded range."

Secretary Hickel chose to postpone the 1970 escalation, saying he wanted to wait and see what the Public Land Law Review Commission would recommend. The commission supported "fair market value" but was otherwise ambivalent on grazing. Hickel's tempering of the wind was followed by other delays, ordered by Congress or the executive branch. Each postponement meant that millions that might have been used to restore the land went instead into the pockets of ranchers. Each was lamented by conservationists.

The federal grazing lands suffered neglect during the Vietnam War and its aftermath, just as did other nonmilitary and postponable affairs of the government. The BLM's thin line of permanent employees actually declined from 1968 to 1972. At appropriations hearings, agency spokesmen complained that they were expected to manage the public domain, and the Outer Continental Shelf as well, with not many more people than the Smithsonian Institution. They got sympathy and encouragement.

"I think it is tragic that the richest nation on earth can't manage its land," said Julia Butler Hansen, Washington State Democrat and chairwoman of the House subcommittee. She kept urging them to raise their sights. Meanwhile, better information was coming to light on the dismal state of the range.

In a study called *The Nation's Range Resources,* the United States Forest Service reported in 1972 that the forty-eight contiguous states had a total of 1.2 billion acres of forest-rangelands, of which 69 percent was grazed by livestock in 1970.[34] The federal government had jurisdiction over 373 million acres, or 31 percent, of the total. Some 166 million acres of the federal holdings were in the National Forest System, mainly in the West, and about the same acreage was being administered by the BLM. Most of the western forest and the western range was in federal hands, while private ownership dominated in the Great Plains and eastern forests. Federal lands were providing about 14 percent of the forage consumed by livestock.

The great preponderance of the nonforested western range, public and private, was in poor or only fair condition, and its productivity was low. About one-fourth of the total range was estimated to be in poor condition. Although millions of acres of federal grazing land were in bad shape, the Forest Service and BLM together were budgeting only about $27 million for "range

323

management" in the mid-1970s, and their total grazing receipts—fees charged to ranchers at far below fair market levels—were running less than $21 million. Perplexed by the failure of the Interior Department and the Office of Management and Budget to seek more funds for BLM's activities, the Senate Appropriations Committee added $1 million in fiscal 1975 for range management and in doing so denounced the $10 million level thus achieved as "grossly inadequate." The committee said range conditions were getting worse at an alarming rate. It directed the Interior Department to study the matter and make a full report.

A glimpse of the deplorable state of affairs had been provided in 1974 when BLM Director Berklund made public an in-house BLM study on livestock grazing's impact on wildlife, watershed, recreation, and other resource values in Nevada. The study complained of ranchers' failure to cooperate with the BLM's "allotment management plans." Under such plans, BLM officials work in partnership with stockmen and agree on a system for the best use of an area. It was found that some Nevada stockmen ignored what had been agreed upon—they let their cattle run in pastures that were to be given a rest, for example. As the study pointed out, BLM supervision was too thin. What could be expected when four people were looking after 4.5 million acres of BLM land, as was the case in one area? Livestock operators dominated the grazing advisory boards. BLM personnel were reflecting too closely the rancher viewpoint. Once again it was a case of too few people, too little money, not enough muscle.

Many months later, in an unusually frank talk before the Nevada Public Land Users, BLM Director Berklund protested the one-sided local news coverage that the agency's range reforms had been getting and reminded Nevada stockmen that one-fourth of the livestock grazing trespass cases detected in the past year had occurred in their state.

"Obviously," Berklund said, "unauthorized grazing use has been a serious problem in Nevada and elsewhere in the West. It can't continue. It won't."

In response to the instructions of the Senate appropriations panel, the BLM early in 1975 submitted a report on range conditions, a fat volume that drew conclusions strikingly similar to those that had been drawn for three decades.[35] Eighty-three percent of the bureau-managed western grazing land was in only fair to bad condition. More than sixty-two million acres—an area larger than Wyoming—was in "unacceptable condition." In essence, the BLM's report to the senators said that the range would continue to deteriorate at the current level of spending, about $10 million annually. If that rate were doubled, the decline might be halted in twenty years, and if the rate were tripled, to about $28 million or more annually, substantial improvement might be expected.

Only a few weeks earlier, at the end of December 1974, the BLM came forth with a three-volume "programmatic" environmental impact statement on its livestock grazing management. It said about the same thing. The range would support much larger numbers of cows, sheep, and wildlife than it did currently, but better planning and more money would be required. Various alternatives were proposed. The production of more forage, it was said, might require the building of more water sites for stock and a quadrupling of the fencing on the public range, a measure essential to the rotation of pastures.

A preliminary draft of the BLM's impact statement on grazing had been attacked vigorously in 1974 by the National Resources Defense Council, the National Wildlife Federation, and other conservationist organizations as "fundamentally inadequate." It was already apparent that conservationists would not be satisfied with one statement covering the entire federal range. The NRDC took the issue to court. The Pacific Legal Foundation of Sacramento and the Public Lands Council intervened on the other side. On December 30, 1974, United States District Judge Thomas A. Flannery in Washington, D.C., ruled for the environmentalists and against the government and the stockmen. Flannery found that "grazing clearly may have a severe impact on

325

local environments." The law, he said, required the BLM to prepare "geographically individualized" impact statements when it issued permits to private owners of livestock for grazing. He said the BLM's "programmatic" assessment was not sufficient. It was not clear where the bureau would find the money for preparing the statements.

Meanwhile, as the nation went through the presidential election of 1976, with President Ford under challenge by Democratic contender Jimmy Carter of Georgia, Congress labored over passage of the long-awaited organic act that would give status and mission to the Bureau of Land Management. Sentiment was well-nigh universal that such a law was needed, but action was delayed by a recrudescence of the ancient and still unsettled battle over special rights for the livestock industry on the western range.

The smoke of combat was thick, but the battle lines were clear enough to conservationists if not to the general public. The livestock industry, assisted by Senator Hansen of Wyoming and Rep. Jim Santini, Democrat, of Nevada and Sam Steiger, Republican, of Arizona, wanted a new federal fee formula for grazing, based on the market value of beef and differentiating between good and poor federal lands. The industry also wanted to restore rancher dominance over BLM advisory committees and extend the duration of grazing leases. In short, it sought for grazers a firmer and more advantageous tenure on the public lands.

On the other side, conservationist groups and the Interior Department opposed with vigor any built-in provision of the new law which would interfere with the right of the federal government to manage the public lands in the general public interest, block the effort to bring grazing fees to fair market value, and give stockmen vested rights in property owned by all Americans.

The Bicentennial Year debate over the BLM's organic act revealed that the nation had not fully resolved some very old issues respecting ownership of the public domain. In the Senate, the livestock lobby was defeated. In the House, it prevailed. On February 25, 1976, the Senate, under the generalship of Senator Jackson, approved legislation that conservationists considered good and constructive. An effort by Senator Hansen to change the grazing-fee formula was beaten. In the House, where Rep. John Melcher, Montana Democrat, headed the Interior Subcommittee on Public Lands, special interests succeeded in making the bill a Christmas tree for cattlemen and for others. The House voted on July 22, producing what environmentalists and the Interior Department regarded as a monstrosity. The Sierra Club termed it disastrous. Interior Secretary Kleppe said it was simply not acceptable.

The Senate, however, prevailed in conference, and the livestock industry was very unhappy with the Federal Land Policy and Management Act of 1976, as the BLM's organic act was formally titled.[36] In a compromise, a new study of grazing fees was ordered, with a one-year moratorium on higher fees. Stockmen won mandatory ten-year grazing permits, but federal land managers received the right to insist on tighter controls and limited duration. Grazing advisory committees were created but given only limited authority. "The livestock industry ended up only with crumbs," said a spokesman for the Sierra Club, which reported exultantly that the industry was so disenchanted that it sought a presidential veto. The effort to tie grazing fees to livestock prices failed, at least for the time being.

It was the Federal Land Policy and Management Act, with its aura of permanence and its tightening of federal management, that seemed to set off the western effort to assert control over federal lands known as the Sagebrush Rebellion. Nevada livestock men led the charge. The movement, stimulated by various factors, spread to other states. The Interior Department under Secretary Andrus reacted strongly, seeking to put the controversy in historical context. Andrus invited Nevada to submit the legal issues to federal court. He charged that the rebellion developed, in part, from the irritations of groups that had long had their own way on the public lands and now felt the impact of new laws requiring better management.

"It is my personal belief," Andrus told an audience at Carlsbad, New Mexico, "that much of the momentum in the Sagebrush Rebellion comes from those who want to profit—those who hope to convert the public lands to their own use for economic purposes. Many of these people have done just this in the past and don't want to stop now. This is why I have said the Sagebrush Rebellion is an attempt to hornswoggle Americans out of a precious portion of their natural heritage."

Assistant Secretary Herbst, speaking at Rapid City, South Dakota, in June 1980, warned that a successful Sagebrush Rebellion would mean "you could write the obituary to the democratic right of all Americans to enjoy or to share in the bounty of these lands which have been traditionally and historically and rightfully theirs.

"You could kiss goodbye millions of acres of our best hunting, fishing, and hiking territory, because it would soon be fenced and posted 'no trespassing,' 'private property—keep out.' "

Congress, which itself had been responsible for much of the neglect of the public's grazing lands, continued to press for better management, more spending, and higher productivity. It had become increasingly clear that something had to be done. In mid-1977, the General Accounting Office came out with a report saying the rangelands had been deteriorating for years and were, for the most part, not improving. It said the damage could be attributed chiefly to poorly managed livestock grazing. Some 49 million acres were being subjected to continuous grazing throughout the forage-growing season, the GAO said, and although the BLM considered this destructive of vegetation, it was not moving effectively to stop it because of the possible financial effect on livestock operators.

The BLM was hampered by court order, it was pointed out, from moving ahead with its "allotment management plans"—a term referring to documents looking toward improvement of relatively small, specific parts of the range. Furthermore, the agency was not enforcing the grazing regulations that existed. It had the authority to do so but was hindered by a requirement that violations had to be proved to be intentional and damaging. This was time-consuming and difficult, even when violations were flagrant.

In October 1977, the secretaries of interior and agriculture sent Congress the grazing-fee report called for in the Federal Land Policy and Management Act of the previous year.[37] This was a thick volume prepared after extensive public participation. The secretaries declined to yield to the livestock industry. They steadfastly held to the principle that the government should impose fees aimed at fair market value, and they opposed the effort, defeated the year before but still very much alive, to hitch fees to fluctuations in the livestock business. Attempts to stabilize farm income, they argued, should be left to separate programs designed for that purpose. The secretaries proposed a 1978 grazing fee of $1.89 per animal unit month for both the BLM and the Forest Service. This was nearly 50 cents below fair market value, which was determined at $2.38, but would raise the fee from the 1977 average of $1.51 and $1.60 charged by the two agencies. It should be noted that the "fair market value" figure of $2.38 had been watered down by various deductions purporting to reflect the difference between leasing federal and private land. Actually, the private lease rate in the western states was more than $7.00.

Considering the obvious and long-standing disparity between what the public was getting for its grazing lands and what private owners were charging, it is amazing how tenaciously the permittee stockmen resisted fair market value or anything like fair market value for federal forage. The increase sought by the secretaries for 1978 would have fetched only about $6 million over the $28 million collected in 1977, but Congress turned down the increase, granting instead another moratorium in fees.

The rationale was that ranchers were having hard times. In the period from 1936 to 1977, federal grazing fees had gone up by only about $1.50 and more than $1 of the increase had come since 1968. If the proposed 1978 increases had been put into effect, the cost to nearly three-fourths of the 25,000 total federal permittees would have risen by an average of only $60 for the year. For the big operators, the estimated cost of the increase would have been about $3,800. Not very large sums, surely.

Aside from the politically supercharged issue of who would foot the bill, there was substantial support in Congress, expressed in session after session, for finding money with which to arrest the deterioration of the public grazing lands and make them more productive. These objectives suited the permittees, provided the funds came from elsewhere. A likely vehicle came along in 1978 in the form of a bill pressed by Rep. Teno Roncalio, Wyoming Democrat and chairman of the House Interior Subcommittee on Indian Affairs and Public Lands. Interior Secretary Andrus and BLM Director Gregg put their shoulders to the wheel. The Forest Service was supportive. Thus was enacted into law, in June, the landmark legislation known as the Public Range Lands Improvement Act of 1978.[38] It authorized the spending of nearly two billion federal dollars over twenty years for rangeland improvement, the money to come from earmarked grazing receipts and general appropriations.

There was one major catch to this quantum escalation, from the viewpoint of the Interior Department, the Forest Service, and other parties concerned with putting grazing rights on a market-value basis, as Congress had said should be done. The catch was that the Roncalio bill embraced the "ability to pay" principle that had been rejected in 1976. It laid down that the grazing fee would be modified on the basis of total profitability of all cattle or sheep production, rather than on the market value of the forage. As BLM Director Gregg commented, this was not fair to livestock operators who did not have access to public lands and who did have to deal with normal market forces. Nor

330

was it fair to the taxpayers generally, who were being asked to put up a large part of the money to be used for range improvement and maintenance. In short, it meant that grazing permittees would continue to enjoy a subsidy at public expense.

At the 1978 House appropriations hearings on the Bureau of Land Management, Rep. Sidney R. Yates, Illinois Democrat, wanted to know why the BLM's intricately calculated "fair market value" for grazing—still unachieved, of course—was far below what ranchers were paying for private and other forage.

Gregg and the BLM's able and veteran associate director, George L. Turcott, patiently sought to explain the thirteen-factor formula used in melting away the value of the public's forage.[39] They did not mention a fourteenth factor—western politics.

To those familiar with it, the story of the federally owned pasturelands conveyed a sense of frustration, even though progress was slowly being made. It brought to mind the biblical story of Nebuchadnezzar, who went mad and fell to cropping the grass in the fields outside Babylon.

CHAPTER 13

TO HAVE AND TO HOLD

Those profs are the snakes to be scotched—they and all their milk-and-water ilk! The American business man is generous to a fault, but one thing he does demand of all teachers and lecturers and journalists: if we're going to pay them our good money, they've got to help us by selling efficiency and whooping it up for the national prosperity! And when it comes to these blab-mouth, fault-finding, pessimistic, cynical University teachers, let me tell you that during this golden coming year it's just as much our duty to bring influence to bear to have those cusses fired as it is to sell all the real estate and gather in all the good shekels we can.

—GEORGE F. BABBITT in Sinclair Lewis's *Babbitt*

The middle-American dream of owning land at the right place at the right time to make a big profit is part of the old pioneering homestead philosophy that promoters have exploited.

—Rep. MORRIS K. UDALL in *Field and Stream*, December 1972

They're nothing but canned sardines, and all the bait you need to catch 'em is a pocketknife and a soda cracker.

—JEFF PETERS in *The Gentle Grafter*

In the West, because the federal government owns so much of the land, development is the handmaiden of federal decisions. When federal policies run counter to development, or seem to, the reaction may be very intense. President Carter's attempt at water and reclamation reforms—none too diplomatically presented at the outset—helped stir up the so-called Sagebrush Rebellion. A state like Nevada, 87 percent in federal hands, talked darkly about taking over most of the public domain.

President Carter was fortunate to have a secretary of the interior who understood well the ambivalence of the western attitude toward the federal bureaucracy and the public lands. Cecil D. Andrus, trout-fishing former governor of Idaho and onetime lumber operator, had only limited sympathy for the attitude, but he knew what he was up against. Loosening the reins has always been easier than trying to gather them up again.

"The general public doesn't understand what it is all about now," Andrus said in an interview in the summer of 1979. "You've got to go back into the 1800s, when we as a nation were trying to develop. There were proposals to get people to move West. The Homestead Law. The Mining Act of 1872. They were trying to entice people to move West and build up the country.

"We have matured and developed into the strongest nation on earth. Congress has said we are no longer holding lands for disposal. Now we say the problem is management, a stewardship program."

Andrus pointed out that the public lands are owned by all the people of the United States. He suggested that because the Interior Department had begun to manage the lands, insisting on restrictions, some of the users had grown unhappy.

"The Sagebrush Rebellion is based on emotionalism and not legal fact," the secretary said. "They want the old days of rip and tear, and do what you please. . . . And those days are gone."

These struggles are inevitable when federal, state, and local activities are so closely intertwined, with Uncle Sam representing a national interest not always clearly defined and sometimes at odds with local aspirations. Uncle Sam as a fat boy with a bag of candy, bearing gifts to be had for the taking, is more popular than Uncle Sam, the stern lawgiver and landlord. In the latter role, he can be depicted as a meddler and red-tape artist, if not as a twentieth-century Captain Boycott, kicking his Irish tenants around.

In contrast, conservationists in the West and elsewhere are inclined to see federal ownership of the West's scenic areas and leftover marginal lands as a godsend. This attitude does not grow out of naive illusions about the high quality of federal management, nor does it necessarily reflect hostility toward free enterprise. It exists simply because many conservationists see Uncle Sam as the strongest available guardian of a disappearing heritage.

The federal record may be bad, but the record of state and private owners is worse. There are notable exceptions, but the smaller, weaker entities of government have been unable or unwilling to stand up firmly against development pressures. Many westerners realize this. In the December 1972 issue of *Field and Stream* magazine, Arizona's Representative Udall, then looking toward the presidency, lambasted land sharks who were peddling raw and waterless desert plots to urban innocents in faraway places.[1]

"America is running out of land," Udall wrote. "And the land still left is taking a beating so a few speculators and high-pressure salesmen can become wealthy."

The West's rocks and arid scenery, he said, were being "merchandized in eastern cities like deodorants or magazine subscriptions with bonus prizes of silverware, green stamps, or small appliances for early bird buyers." He asked all Americans to help stop what he called the rape of the western land.

What Udall decried was not only the systematic flimflamming of simple people and the harm done them as individuals but also the damage done to the ravaged, checkerboarded, carved-up acreage and to prospects for proper planning as to its future use. This was grievous. Congress had already mandated a federal effort to tidy things up in the jackrabbit and alligator-swamp segments of the real estate business, and it was doing some good.

There were many quality developments, put forward by reliable sponsors, in which purchasers got what they paid for. No basis exists for thinking that honesty and integrity are less abundant among dealers in land than in the generality of mankind. But the folklore of knavery associated with land dealings has been hard to live down. When Sinclair Lewis created his prototype of the all-American booster and morally imprecise supersalesman, he made George F. Babbitt a real estate promoter and put him in the town of Zenith—"Zenith the Zip City—Zeal, Zest and Zowie."[2]

Land being a great deal more than just a vendible commodity like a rifle or sleeping bag, waffle iron or automobile, the proponents of land-use planning in the United States were interested in a much broader question than the simple issue of honesty or dishonesty in sales promotion. A development scheme might be pure as new-fallen snow in the Rockies and yet harmful. On the other hand, an outright swindle might do little damage except to the guileless victims who had fallen for it. The attention paid by the press to the lurid activities of fly-by-nights was in that sense a divertissement, off the main point. Sound planning at the federal, state, and local level, if it could be achieved, would create an atmosphere in which land sharks would find life more difficult, but it would also, in its main thrust, inhibit and circumscribe the legitimate real estate dealers whose handiwork was everywhere to be seen. The industry knew that and fought hard to escape the net.

To those Americans seeking to make a case for more intelligent planning, as Udall was, the foibles of the hotshot entrepreneur trying to make a killing were Tin Pan Alley aspects of a larger trouble. More important were the great symphonies of land development in which the federal government had a major role—works of art in which whole regions have been transformed and masses of people shifted to areas where such numbers did not, indeed could not, live before.

An example of such a symphony, in which the orchestra was not together, may be seen in the exploitation of the mighty Colorado River, which rises in the Rocky Mountains and flows a distance of some 1,440 miles through the Southwest to the Gulf of California, where what is left of it finds the sea. Along much of its course the Colorado winds through country that gets considerably less than the twenty inches of annual rainfall John Wesley Powell said was required for nonirrigated farming. The river drains a basin extending for 243,000 square miles, and the average rainfall for the whole of it is, as a matter of fact, only about fifteen inches. It is now one of the nation's most regulated rivers, having been plugged and encrusted with many dams and works. It exports large quantities of water across mountains to other drainage areas, particularly to southern California. In terms of population, for that reason, more than half the West depends directly on the Colorado River as a water source. This is a heavy responsibility.

The Colorado's development since the Bureau of Reclamation came into existence after the turn of the century has been a history of achievement, struggle, political trading, and man-made arrangements that did not take all factors into account. The sequence of events was complex, involving agreements between states, acts of Congress, and court rulings as well as the pouring of great quantities of concrete.

In what is known as the Colorado River Compact of 1922, the four states of the Upper Basin—Colorado, New Mexico, Utah, and Wyoming—got together under federal supervision with the three states of the Lower Basin—California, Arizona, and Nevada.[3] They divided the beneficial use of the river waters between the two basins. The federal representative and chairman was Herbert Hoover, then secretary of commerce under President Harding. At that time the river was substantially unharnessed, and it was necessary to reach an interbasin agreement before major federal works could proceed. The Lower Basin, growing more rapidly, wanted the issue settled so that the Upper Basin, fearful of losing its share of the water, would not block federal assistance downstream.

River experts assumed in 1922 that the Colorado's virgin or undepleted flow might be as high as 18 million acre-feet a year, an acre-foot being a hydrologist's way of saying the amount of water that will cover an acre of flat ground to a depth of one foot. It was agreed under Hoover's chairmanship that each of the basins could use 7.5 million acre-feet a year and, more specifically, that the Upper Basin states, whose snowcapped mountains produced most of the water, would be prohibited from causing the river's flow to the Lower Basin to run less than 75 million acre-feet over a ten-year period, or an annual average of 7.5 million acre-feet. The division point between the two basins was set at Lees Ferry, a point in northern Arizona a short distance above where the river enters the Grand Canyon.

It is at Lees Ferry, about sixteen miles below what was to become the Reclamation Bureau's Glen Canyon Dam, that the Upper Basin "delivers" water to the Lower Basin. The place has an interesting history, with curious similarities to that of John Brown and Harper's Ferry on the Potomac River in the East. Major Powell, after his first exploration trip down the Colorado in 1869, returned in 1871 and made a crossing at Lees Ferry, where he met the Mormon farmer and leader John D. Lee, after whom the crossing came to be named.[4] Lee called it Lonely Dell. At the time of his encounter with Powell, which was a pleasant one, Lee was in deep trouble.

Much earlier, in 1857, Lee had taken part in the infamous Mountain Meadows Massacre, in which Mormons and Indians attacked an Arkansas wagon train in western Utah. That was a time of strife between Brigham Young's followers and intruders from the outside, including federal troops under Albert Sidney

Johnston. The Civil War intervened, bringing on larger bloodshed during which General Johnston was killed on the Confederate side at Shiloh, the same engagement in which Major Powell lost an arm for the Union. Afterward, public outrage demanded that someone pay the piper for what had happened at Mountain Meadows long before. The man who eventually paid was Lee. He was sought out in his remote refuge on the river, tried, and convicted.[5] In early 1877 he was taken to the scene of the massacre, placed blindfolded at the edge of his coffin, and shot by firing squad. So much for drama.

The years since the 1922 compact in which the upstream and downstream states agreed on a division of the Colorado's waters have brought great change to the river, to the region around Lees Ferry, and to the Southwest as a whole. The Bureau of Reclamation erected its works along the river. The vast wilderness and desert region of which Lees Ferry is a part suddenly blossomed in the 1960s as a place where the nation wanted to generate electricity by burning cheap Indian and federal coal. The dry Southwest, eminently habitable where water can be made available, attracted increasing numbers of new citizens, particularly in California and Arizona. To an extent these developments could be described as planned, but it was a loose, fragmented kind of planning that overlooked the hard choices that one day were going to have to be made.

Another change since 1922 was a gradual realization that the Colorado's flow was not nearly as abundant as some had assumed.[6] Instead of having a virgin flow at Lees Ferry of eighteen million acre-feet, as was thought, the river was estimated a half century later at somewhere between 13 and 14 million acre-feet. The virgin flow is the undepleted flow. Obviously if the Upper Basin began taking out 7.5 million acre-feet a year—which it was not yet anywhere close to doing—there would not be enough water to supply the Lower Basin with its entitlement of 7.5 million acre-feet. This was not to mention the additional 1.5 million acre-feet a year that the United States agreed to deliver to Mexico by a treaty executed in 1944.

338

Through aeons of time the Colorado had been a fearsome, leaping torrent in its flood season and a torpid, dwindling stream when water was slack. "The unregulated Colorado was a son of a bitch—it wasn't any good," former Reclamation Commissioner Floyd E. Dominy told John McPhee.[7] The flow has varied greatly from year to year. It was twenty-four million acre-feet in 1917 and was down to six million in 1934. The task of damming the Colorado along its length and establishing impoundment reservoirs was a stupendous one that only the federal government could undertake. Flood control. Hydroelectric power. Irrigation water and water for municipal and industrial use. Blue lakes in a parched country, boating and fishing in the desert, recreation for millions of people. The achievement was admirable. It compelled admiration. It was admired. Yet there were haunting misgivings.

Development of the Colorado's Lower Basin came first, once the seven river states had made their compact. Ever since the 1890s, private capital had been tapping the lower Colorado for irrigation waters to be used in the Imperial Valley of California. Floods and the river's erratic ways buffeted the Imperial Canal in the early 1900s. In 1905 the river broke through the canal headworks and poured itself for sixteen months into the fertile valley and the Salton Sink, creating the Salton Sea. The river also punished Yuma and the Yuma project, where under authority obtained in 1904 the Reclamation Bureau furnishes water to irrigate a countryside that gets only about three inches of rain but has a growing season of 365 days. These early troubles generated pressure for federal harnessing of the river and for reaching an interbasin agreement that would permit the Lower Basin to go ahead while assuaging the fears of the Upper Basin that the upriver states might, under the law of the river, be euchred out of their share of the water by the Lower Basin's prior use.

The pressure became intense, as witness President Harding's appointment of Hoover, a Californian and an engineer of towering prestige, to handle the federal end of the state river compact. Metropolitan Los Angeles outgrew the Los Angeles River early in the century, when it had only 160,000 people. Then, in one of the bold and Homeric sagas of southern California, the Belfast-born Irish engineer William Mulholland reached northward to build the 238-mile, $23 million Owens River Aqueduct that still brings most of the city's water from the remote and beautiful Owens Valley in the Sierras. Not without strife that finds echo in the present day, the aqueduct was finished in 1913.[8] By 1920, having tapped the mountains to the north, Los Angeles was looking toward the Colorado River. It was already clear that the Imperial and Coachella valleys, Yuma, and other places in the desert needed only steady irrigation to make them agricultural Edens. A search for dam sites quickened in 1919 and soon fastened on an ideal plugging point in the hard volcanic rock at Black Canyon, in the Lower Basin. At Black Canyon, some 350 miles upriver from the Mexican border, the Colorado's major gorges ended, and the river descended in flatter, more gentle terrain.

At that point, where the river has finished its race through the Grand Canyon and forms the boundary between Arizona and Nevada, the United States government was to build a dam high enough to store the Colorado River's entire flow for two years—6.6 million tons of concrete holding back a volume of water that would cover an area the size of Pennsylvania to a depth of one foot.[9] This Brobdingnagian project, together with a related proposal that the federal government undertake construction of the projected All-American Canal to California's Imperial Valley, had been put before the Senate nine months before commissioners for the seven states, under Hoover's guidance, signed the compact at Santa Fe in November 1922.

Congress and President Coolidge approved the Boulder Canyon Project Act late in 1928, Boulder being just upstream from Black Canyon.[10] The legislation authorized both the big dam and the All-American Canal. Expenditures were to be $165 million for building the entire project. Revenues were to pay for the dam and power plant, with interest, in fifty years. The Bureau of

Reclamation rose to an unprecedented challenge. It hastily rushed the specifications through at its design office in Denver, awarded the labor contract to Six Companies Incorporated of San Francisco early in 1931, and set up a government town on federal land at Boulder City, Nevada, on a high plateau seven miles southwest of the dam site—a new town, created out of desert and thin air. Fearsome structural problems were solved, and in twenty-one months a force of about 5,000 men had built a structure of greater volume than Egypt's largest pyramid. The last concrete was poured in May 1935, and in late September that year President Franklin D. Roosevelt helped dedicate the 726.4-foot-high dam.

With the Hoover Dam, a wonder of the engineering world, in place, southern California and other parts of the Lower Basin proceeded to reap advantages from the Colorado which were not yet available to the Upper Basin states. A veritable terrace of federally constructed dams extended downstream from the mighty Hoover. Through 1950 the Lower Basin got Davis Dam, Parker Dam, Imperial Dam, and others, largely through federal financing. The Metropolitan Water District of southern California put up funds with which the Reclamation Bureau built Parker Dam, 155 miles downstream from Hoover, to provide a forebay from which the famed Colorado River Aqueduct, finished in 1941, could take water across mountains and desert to the semiarid coast. Later the bureau and the navy built the first San Diego Aqueduct. In the 1970s the Colorado was supplying three-fourths of the water used in southern California.

All this was well enough, no doubt, but what about the Upper Basin states, for which little had been done? And what about Arizona, which had no federal straw with which to suck up its share of the river? A provision for studies had been tucked into the 1928 Hoover Dam legislation. Various river projects were investigated, and after World War II Interior Secretary Krug made a report in which he said that the individual states had to settle their water disputes among themselves before Congress could approve any further construction. The 1922 compact had divided the water between basins but had avoided a state-by-state allocation. Taking Krug's hint, and eager to get on the move, Arizona and the upstream states of Colorado, New Mexico, Utah, and Wyoming consulted together and agreed on what might be a fair apportionment of the Upper Basin's share. This was called the Upper Colorado River Basin Compact of 1948.[11] It was decided that Arizona, partly in the Upper Basin, was to receive 50,000 acre-feet annually. The balance of consumptive use was to be shared as follows: Colorado, 51.75 percent; Utah, 23 percent; Wyoming, 14 percent; and New Mexico, 11.25 percent.

In the Lower Basin the United States Supreme Court made the apportionment in a 1963 ruling that meant substantial victory for Arizona in a long and bitter legal struggle with California. The Supreme Court decided that California was to get 4.4 million of the 7.5 million acre-feet deliverable at Lees Ferry and rejected California's claim to a larger share. Arizona was to get 2.8 million acre-feet, and Nevada 300 thousand.[12]

These laboriously worked out determinations, dealing with the distribution of federally supplied water over what still were or until recently had been federally owned lands, were essential to further federal action. Seeking to make up for lost time, the Upper Basin asked for and eventually got its own upriver version of Hoover Dam and related works. In addition, Arizona sought and got, more than ten years later, a federal project for moving water eastward into the central part of the state, much in the manner that California had been helped in moving it westward to the coast.

With the enthusiastic, dedicated assistance of the Bureau of Reclamation, the Upper Basin states mapped out the political and geological terrain and moved toward passage of what came to be known as the Colorado River Storage Project Act of 1956, consisting essentially of the Glen Canyon Dam.[13] It was widely believed that the Upper Basin had something coming, in view of what the federal authority had done for the Lower Basin. Nevertheless, the fight was difficult. California water interests were strenuously opposed for patently selfish reasons. Any delay in creating works upstream would give California more time to dip freely into the Colorado and work out alternate solutions. David Brower and the Sierra Club fought a shrewd, effective campaign to prevent construction of a dam at Echo Park in the Dinosaur National Monument on the Utah-Colorado border.

When conservationists made it clear they would not tolerate the invasion of national park territory at Echo Canyon, near the confluence of the Green and Yampa rivers, the Echo Canyon proposal was thrown out. Brower and his forces tried to put off for a time the inundation of Glen Canyon, a place of haunting beauty which was destined to vanish forever under the slowly rising waters of Lake Powell. It was, as the book of photographs by Eliot Porter suggested, the land that nobody knew.[14] Brower and others raised questions regarding the strength of the Glen Canyon rock and the water-holding capabilities of the shale and porous sandstone of the proposed reservoir. An Interior Department geologist testified that Glen Canyon was an excellent dam site, with rock of sufficient strength, and that the reservoir was not too porous.

The debate over feasibility of the site became dramatic. Rep. Craig Hosmer of southern California, a Republican, made it known that he personally had visited the proposed reservoir site with two consulting geologists. They had collected samples of Chinle shale, he said, and learned that the material would disintegrate in water. In House debate early in 1956, Rep. James A. Haley, Florida Democrat, put a piece of the shale in a glass of water and watched the shale fall apart, whereupon Udall of Arizona, supporting the project, dropped another sample of shale in water and said he would drink the water when he had finished his speech.[15]

Bureau of Reclamation engineers had enough confidence in the Glen Canyon site to build a dam there rising 710 feet above bedrock and 583 feet above the original river channel. The dam, containing nearly five million cubic yards of concrete, was constructed between 1956 and 1964. Glen Canyon Dam in northern Arizona and its Lake Powell reservoir backing deep into Utah were the principal elements of the Colorado River Storage Project when finally sorted out by Congress and approved with the strong encouragement of President Eisenhower. Three other water-storage reservoirs were authorized—Flaming Gorge in Wyoming, Curecanti in Colorado, and Navajo in northern New Mexico. The authorization was $760 million. Glen Canyon Dam plugged the Colorado at a point just above Lees Ferry and the eastern entrance to the Grand Canyon, about 370 miles upriver from Hoover Dam. Containing more concrete than Hoover Dam and nearly as tall, Glen Canyon was designed as the Upper Basin's "cash register," generating 900,000 kilowatts of electric power and earning revenue.

Thus did the Upper Basin struggle against adversity and pry from the federal government a major Colorado reservoir at Lake Powell and a scattered brood of related water impoundments higher up in the drainage area. Arizona's turn came next. While Lake Powell slowly filled, its waters turning blue as they lost their silt, Arizona undertook to make good the promise of its 1963 Supreme Court victory over California and obtain a government-financed infrastructure for making use of the Colorado. The state's pleas for the Central Arizona Project, as the proposal was called, had reached Washington shortly after World War II, but Congress served notice in 1951 that no action could be taken until the Lower Basin states had settled their dispute.[16] In the 1960s, with *Arizona v California* out of the way, it was now or never. President Johnson, a man who understood dry-country politics, was in the White House. Carl Hayden of Arizona was a power in the Senate. Arizonan Stewart L. Udall was secretary of the interior, and his younger brother, Mo, an able advocate, thirsted for water and glory in the House of Representatives.

There was no doubt that Arizona desperately needed water. The state had been growing rapidly, moving from an agricultural to an industrial economy, but it was running dry because of the heavy drawdown for farming. Representative Udall put the case neatly in a letter to his constituents. Arizona was using a total of 4.3 million acre-feet a year, he said, but only 1.3 million came from rivers or other surface sources, while fully 2.3 million was an "overdraft" on the state's declining water table. The water table was dropping ten to twenty feet a year, and in some places the water quality became poor at great depths because of salt. Udall said the state's growth would come to a halt unless more water was supplied, especially in the central area, where 75 percent of the people lived.[17]

Those who strove for the Central Arizona Project had to hoe a long and hard row before they reached the cooling federal bucket and dipper—or, at least, the promise of them—in 1968. The greatest difficulty was the implacable hostility of the California delegation. Another hurdle was the desire of Upper Basin states—notably Colorado, New Mexico, and Utah—to broaden the legislation in such a way as to further their own objectives. A third was the outcry of the conservationists, who rose up against a proposal that the Bureau of Reclamation construct dams on the Colorado at both ends of the Grand Canyon. The new dams, at Marble Canyon going in and Bridge Canyon going out, would generate power to finance the Arizona works.

In the deadly struggle for the river, Arizonans had to make concession after concession. Secretary Udall and his brother on the Hill, members of a politically prominent Mormon family in the state, did their best to put a deal together. Victory seemed to elude them.

It finally became clear that the proposed Grand Canyon dams, an outrageous insult to one of the great natural wonders of the world, would not be tolerated. In this fight, which was touch and go for a while, the Sierra Club lost its tax-exempt status but won a doubling of membership. "Should we also flood the Sistine Chapel," a Sierra Club advertisement asked, "so the tourists can get nearer the ceiling?"[18]

Secretary of the Interior Udall supported both dams in the first half of the 1960s but switched to one dam in 1965 and then, early in 1967, to a position that no dams be built. In lieu of the offending dams, it was proposed that the Arizona project obtain pumping power from a coal-fired generating plant to be built and operated by an industry combine, with federal participation. This materialized as the Navajo Power Plant, on the Navajo reservation just southeast of Lake Powell in northern Arizona.

During the months prior to September 30, 1968, when Representative Udall stood at the White House as President Johnson finally signed the Central Arizona Project legislation, the congressman had gone through a trying period. Udall expressed some of his frustration in a speech he called "Countdown on the Colorado," delivered before the Town Hall of California at Los Angeles the previous December.[19] It was a very frank speech, full of humor. Udall took Californians to task for their obstructionism. Obstacle after obstacle had been thrown across the way, he said, with new ones always ready when the old had been overcome. He likened the situation to the fairy tale in which a youth, seeking to wed the king's daughter, is given an impossible task to overcome and, having achieved it, is confronted by another, and another. Udall told the Californians there would be a vote the next year—as indeed there was—and that "we intend to try to win it—either with your help or over your dead bodies."

The Central Arizona Project was the major nugget in the bill Congress eventually passed, which was entitled the Colorado Basin Project Act and came freighted with other things as well.[20] Basically, Arizona was authorized to build a series of pumping plants and aqueducts that would lift Colorado River water from Lake Havasu, behind Parker Dam in the Lower Basin, to Maricopa, Pinal, and Pima counties along the Phoenix-Tucson axis in central Arizona. The estimated cost was more than $832 million. In addition, California was to be assured its full allotment of water in time of possible shortage, western Colorado was to receive five projects, and various other Upper Basin works were authorized. The law provided that what was due to Mexico under the Mexican Water Treaty was "a national obligation" rather than one to be shouldered by the basin states alone—a significant change. The secretary of the interior was directed to make a westwide study of water availability and requirements. He was forbidden for ten years to make reconnaissance studies of any plan for importing water into the basin, a point insisted on by Northwest interests led by Senator Jackson of Washington state.

"There was little to tell us in 1963," Representative Udall wrote in 1972, "that the great ecology-environment movement would take center stage by the end of the decade. In retrospect, it is clear that the battle of the Grand Canyon dams was a central, symbolic event which played a major role in awakening environmental awareness in America."[21]

It was Udall's opinion, he said, that if Arizona had settled with California a decade earlier the dams would have been constructed without furor, since until the 1960s dams were regarded as good, while undammed, turbulent streams were bad. In view of the change in attitude, he was inclined to doubt whether another sizable dam would ever be built on any American river.

Against a backdrop of six or seven decades of heavy federal construction along the Colorado, causing movement of people and affecting the value of millions of acres of federal and private lands, the stage was set for another titanic struggle. It took place in high, remote, arid country around the Four Corners, the point where Utah and Colorado meet Arizona and New Mexico. The point falls in the 24,000-square-mile Navajo Indian reservation, the largest in the nation. Within the Navajo is the Hopi reservation, with another 2,100 square miles. Inasmuch as there was plenty of coal beneath the Indian lands and the public domain, the availability of river water made it possible for giant power plants to spring up in the desert. Such plants did indeed spring up, with the hearty encouragement of federal, state, and local officials. The stacks sent up plumes of smoke into what had been clean air.

But of course giant utility complexes do not appear overnight, as if by magic. They must be designed. The financing must be arranged. Coal and water rights must be in hand. Land must be leased or purchased. Workers must be housed. Rights-of-way for transmission lines must be cleared. The Four Corners development was carefully planned, in the sense that the short-term logistics were worked out by skilled and intelligent and doubtless well-intentioned people. It is fair to say, however, that the planning was inadequate. Only in the 1970s, when the smoke and environmental degradation could no longer be ignored, did the national public become thoroughly aware of what was going on. Only then did Congress and the Interior Department undertake massive studies that purported to weigh the desirability of the dramatic change in land use which had taken place. The soul-searching, if it could be described as such, was valuable for future decision making, but the horse was already out of the stable as far as the Four Corners region was concerned. By the time the review took place, one huge plant in New Mexico had been operating for nearly a decade and was estimated to be pouring out 320 tons of sulfur oxides a day, more than any other plant in the nation.

Thus it was late in the day when Senator Jackson's Interior Committee held public hearings from May through November of 1971.[22] The focus was on six major generating stations generally associated with the Four Corners area. Two were finished and operating, three others were under construction, and a sixth was only proposed. Altogether, Senator Jackson observed, they would ultimately generate enough power to serve nine million people, and they were being built in a sparsely populated country having about four persons to the square mile, excluding metropolitan areas. As Jackson said, the imposition of stringent pollution regulations in urban America had tended to drive power development to the desert, where, in this instance, there was coal and sufficient water, at least for the time being.[23]

The two existing plants were the Four Corners plant near Farmington, New Mexico, which got into operation in 1963, and the Mohave plant, at the southern tip of Nevada near Davis Dam, which had just come on-line in 1971. The three then under construction but destined to be operating by 1975 were the San Juan plant in New Mexico, ten miles north of the Four Corners facility; the Navajo plant mentioned earlier as part of the Central Arizona Project near Lake Powell; and the Huntington Canyon plant in central Utah. In the planning stage was the largest of the six, the Kaiparowits generating station. This was to be built on a high plateau in Utah, across Lake Powell from the Navajo plant.

Various combines undertook to build and operate the plants with a high degree of cooperation and in accordance with the regional blueprints credited to the Western Energy and Supply Transmission Associates, or WEST, a planning consortium of twenty-three privately owned and public utilities in seven states, formed in 1964. Seeking to anticipate and meet the energy demands of their service areas, they worked closely with the Reclamation Bureau and other federal agencies. The origins of the initial Four Corners plant, whose emissions brought down the wrath of conservationists, went back to the 1950s, when Arizona Public Service Company, a private utility, and Utah Mining and Construction Company began activities that led to the leasing of Navajo land and coal rights. The plant, using strip-mined coal, started up in 1963. Southern California Edison and several other companies later joined in expanding it. Secretary Udall approved arrangements for additional coal and water. At the end of 1970, Utah International was trucking 20,000 tons of coal a day to the plant.

The second plant of the Four Corners complex, the Mohave in southern Nevada, was a product of the WEST consortium's planning. Southern California Edison and three other utilities built it 270 miles west of the Four Corners plant and about the same distance from its coal source at Black Mesa, where Navajo and Hopi coal was strip-mined and pulverized and sent to the plant in the largest, longest slurry pipeline that had been constructed up to that time. The combine began negotiating with the Colorado River Commission of Nevada in 1965. Under the congressional Mohave Development Act, sponsored by Nevada's Senator Bible, the federal government made 15,000 acres of land available for sale to the state. The combine gave the state funds with which it purchased 4,000 acres, enough to provide a 2,500-acre plant site bought by the combine and leave a large acreage for state parklands and other development. Mohave began operations in 1971, using water charged against Nevada's share of the river. Black Mesa coal was mined by the Peabody Coal Company of St. Louis. To some Indians the mesa had religious significance. If anything kicked up a greater row than the Four Corners smokestacks, it was the strip-mining at Black Mesa, which also supplied the Navajo plant at Lake Powell.

"Coal can play a crucial role in helping to bridge the time gap until nuclear energy can be brought on the line to carry an increasing share of western energy to man," Howard P. Allen, Southern California Edison vice president, told the Jackson committee in his testimony at Las Vegas.[24]

There could be no doubt at all, of course, that the Interior Department had invited private industry to the Four Corners feast, if feast it was. Or that Congress had gone along with it. The Bureau of Reclamation was a direct participant in the Navajo plant, which the government helped build in connection with the Central Arizona Project and in which the bureau was senior partner along with the Salt River Project, the plant's operator, and four other sharers in the costs and benefits. The San Juan plant, owned by Public Service Company of New Mexico and the Tucson Gas and Electric Company, had a contract with the secretary of the interior for water from the Navajo reservoir, and its coal came from leases issued by the Bureau of Land Management. Utah Power and Light Company's Huntington Canyon plant in Utah, using coal deep mined on private land, involved use of reclamation water and action by the BLM in shaping up a land deal with the state.

When the environmental storm broke, only the Kaiparowits giant was caught at a stage where construction had not begun. It was held up by the Interior Department and still had not received a green light in April 1976 when its sponsors announced they would not proceed. In some respects the Kaiparowits, which took its name from the high and lonely plateau on which it was to rest, was the most interesting of the projects, just as it was the largest. Southern California Edison, with a 40 percent interest, had put the proposal forward in alliance with Arizona Public Service, San Diego Gas and Electric, and the Salt River Project.

The Geological Survey had long known there was coal under Utah's Kaiparowits Plateau but was in no hurry to make a thorough investigation. After all, coal was plentiful elsewhere, closer to market. The utilities combine obtained federal prospecting permits in 1963, sought and found the coal it wanted, and in 1965 asserted its right to preferential leases at one dollar an acre rental to 39,350 acres of federal and 6,212 acres of state land. Royalties were to be fifteen and seventeen and a half cents a ton. The combine arranged with the Interior Department in 1969 to obtain large quantities of water from Lake Powell—up to 102,000 acre-feet a year. Such plants have a large thirst, gulping six tons of water for each ton of coal they consume.

After the Kaiparowits coal had been leased without competitive bidding, the Geological Survey got around to finding out how much coal was there, but not until June 1974 was official action taken to make parts of the plateau a "known coal leasing area," thereby closing off further preferential leasing. Meanwhile, the official estimates of coal that could be recovered by deep mining had increased to staggering proportions—conservatively, about four billion tons, the energy equivalent of eight billion barrels of crude oil.

Interior Secretary Udall had pledged fealty to the proposed Kaiparowits plant during the House Interior Committee's 1968 hearings on the cherished Central Arizona Project, also known as CAP.[25] Rep. Laurence J. Burton, Utah Republican, sought and got assurance that the Navajo plant for CAP would not prejudice

351

plans for Utah's Kaiparowits. Udall explained that the WEST group felt the Navajo plant should be built first, but the WEST planners were "very enthusiastic" about the Utah deep-coal development across the lake. Udall talked about the "first Kaiparowits plant," indicating there would be more than one. "We are going to get to the Kaiparowits development and I expect it to move forward right on schedule," the secretary told Burton.[26]

The Southern California Edison combine applied to the Interior Department in May 1971 for right-of-way permits, but the companies were doomed to an initial disappointment and to further setbacks. The wind had shifted strongly toward the environment and, as Udall's Republican successor after Hickel, Rogers C. B. Morton, would say, it was a new ball game.

While Senator Jackson's committee explored the situation, Secretary Morton himself, hearing the rumble of none-too-distant drums, had organized a Southwest power development task force in May 1971 under chairmanship of his under secretary, the late William T. Pecora.[27] The task force produced a summary report, which Morton made public in December of the following year. It was a thick, informative study that projected a four-phase power development of which the existing five plants were only the first. The Kaiparowits plant would be in Phase II and might be doubled in capacity in later phases, at which time a second Kaiparowits plant also would be built in the northern part of the plateau. The Southwest's energy needs were expected to be more than double the 1970 demand by 1980 and nearly four times the 1970 figure by 1990, with southern California accounting for about 60 percent of the use. The Colorado basin's coal-fired generating plants as then envisaged, it was said, could supply 23 percent of the 1980 demand and 28 percent of the 1990 demand. There was plenty of coal—100 billion tons of it reasonably accessible—and enough water to service an eventual Phase IV development more than four times the size of the Four Corners plants already built.

On the minus side, Morton's Southwest energy study reported that the coal-fired plants constructed so far had sent up objectionable amounts of smoke and had reduced visibility. It spoke of various impacts, including a sevenfold increase in the population of Kane County, and acknowledged a possibility that under certain weather circumstances some of the effluent from the Navajo or Kaiparowits plants "could be trapped in the Grand Canyon."

The secretary thought it over and on June 13, 1973, announced rejection of the Kaiparowits applications "for environmental reasons." The rejected site was Nipple Bench, about fifteen miles from Glen Canyon Dam and dangerously close to several national parks. In turning it down, Morton followed the recommendations of an interagency task force that he endorse the five plants already finished or under construction but reject Kaiparowits and help the companies find another site "more consistent with environmental quality standards and sound resource conservation practice."

Secretary Morton could hardly have gone against the existing plants in view of the Interior Department's history of helping to create them. That omelet could not be unscrambled. The secretary's thumbs-down on Kaiparowits brought a protest from the utilities combine, which complained that he had not waited for its own $1 million, two-volume "environmental report" explaining in detail its plans for the plant and mine and what both would do to stimulate the economy of struggling Kane County and the region thereabout—6,300 new jobs, a new community of 13,700 people, 4,600 new housing units, annual property tax revenues of nearly $29 million, and so on. Utah's Sen. Frank E. ("Ted") Moss, a Democrat of excellent repute, voiced his concern and shock at Morton's action and urged him to await the companies' study, which was to be available in a few days, and reconsider.[28]

"All this was done through consultation with state, federal and local officials as well as private industry," said Moss, speaking of a nine-year process of planning for and choosing the rejected site. "Every conceivable problem has been carefully considered.

353

"For Interior to now suggest that a new site be selected is tantamount to killing the project."

Senator Moss and Gov. Calvin L. Rampton of Utah, also a Democrat, called on Secretary Morton the following week to do what Moss's office called "a little arm twisting." The upshot was that Morton did agree to look at the tardy study, and a task force was set up under Deputy Under Secretary Jared G. Carter for that purpose. Late that year, at a December press conference, Morton volunteered to the press that a new Kaiparowits site, fifteen or sixteen miles north of the Nipple Bench area, was being assessed and that it appeared to be free of the problems that had led him to turn down Nipple Bench. The combine felt confident enough to move forward with arrangements for the deep mine that would supply its $2 billion plant. It estimated that moving to the new site, at a place called Fourmile Bench, would cost an additional $130 million.

The environmental issues Morton had raised, though, were heavy and complicated ones, hanging over the entire 108,000-square-mile Four Corners region like the yellow gases pouring from the stacks. For one thing, there were the Indians for whom the government held much of the land in trust. President Chester A. Arthur had established a reservation for the Hopis in 1882, and the Navajos, under pressure from white settlers, had moved there too. The Indians, like many others, were divided in their attitude toward the strip-mining and the power plants. The development meant 500 jobs and some $10 million in annual benefits to them, the department estimated. The Indians and others did need employment. It was never easy to figure out when the Indian was truly in favor of something and when he was being pushed into it by white boosters.

For another thing, the plants were accumulating in a region studded with priceless scenic and recreational places which the United States had put aside for present and future public enjoyment, and in an area where the United States was the major landowner. Within or bordering the region were six national parks, twenty-eight national monuments, and three national recreation areas, including Glen Canyon. A circle of 100 miles in radius, drawn around the Navajo and proposed Kaiparowits plants at Lake Powell, would impinge on Grand Canyon, Bryce Canyon, and Zion national parks. Morton, in rejecting Kaiparowits, noted a danger that the Navajo plant alone might reduce visibility in the Grand Canyon. He did not say what the two of them might do. In general terms, the federal government owned more than 50 percent of the land thereabouts and held another 16 percent in nineteen Indian reservations totaling 27,000 square miles.

A third factor facing Secretary Morton was the necessity for compliance with the National Environmental Policy Act and with the clear-air and clean-water legislation policed by the Environmental Protection Agency. Secretary Udall, a few years earlier, was not impeded by these laws because they did not exist. In the case of Four Corners, for example, Morton had to reckon with the consequences of a Supreme Court decision on clean air handed down two days before he announced his own decision not to grant the Kaiparowits permits. The Supreme Court affirmed lower court decisions in a lawsuit brought by the Sierra Club against EPA in 1972.[29] It was contended by the Sierra Club that the law required EPA to prevent "significant deterioration" of clean air. That position was upheld, which meant, if it meant anything, that industry penetrating an area like the desert Southwest would not have carte blanche to pollute the atmosphere to the point where it reached the dirtier levels set as minimum national air-quality standards.

This was a difficult hurdle for Morton and the utilities, and there were others. In the same month that the Supreme Court acted in the "significant deterioration" case, June 1973, the secretary and various federal officials were named defendants in a Sierra Club action brought to hold up federal coal development in the northern Great Plains until there had been full compliance with the National Environmental Policy Act.[30] Coal and

355

water and the environment were the burning issues in the coal-rich northern Great Plains, just as they were in the Four Corners region and elsewhere in the Colorado River basin.

As aforesaid, much of the sober federal analysis and investigation of the southwestern power development took place after the horses were out of the stable and running. In April 1976, after Secretary Morton had gone and shortly before Secretary Thomas S. Kleppe was to make a decision on Kaiparowits, the three utility concerns that were proposing to build the plant announced that they had suspended their plans. A spokesman said that cost estimates had escalated in twelve years from about $750 million to a current figure of $3.5 billion or more. "It was no longer economically feasible," he said, even if federal approval could be assumed and no further delays encountered.[31]

"The radical environmentalists have won their victory," said Sen. Jake Garn, Utah Republican.

It was indeed a new ball game. Interior Department studies seeking a focus on water and energy in the West poured out in profusion as the national energy shortage wore on. They tended to be long on statistics and short on conclusions. In general, they became less optimistic about the Colorado River's ability to meet the drawdowns that were in prospect.[32] Something, it was said, had to be done.

But what? Did the answer lie in the Bureau of Reclamation's cloud-seeding experiments in the Rockies, thickening the winter snowpack in the mountains and thereby increasing the flow? Could water eventually be brought from other basins? Was it feasible to desalt water on the Pacific coast and pipe it up to Hoover Dam's Lake Mead? The last course seemed ridiculous but was discussed. Who was it that decided, in the first instance, that the bleak Four Corners region would be the furnace room for southern California, Phoenix, and Tucson?

The thing that could be concluded with a degree of certainty was that, thanks to the reclamation program and the energy squeeze, irrevocable changes had been wrought in the West over a period of years, adding up to a momentous decision of which the American people had been largely unaware.[33]

When President Carter came to power as a Galahad from the rainy Southeast, national misgivings over water policy and the federal role in it had been in evidence for decades. Critics of the Bureau of Reclamation and the Army Corps of Engineers had been saying for years that projects undertaken at huge public expense often were wasteful, if not harmful. Too many, it was said, were boondoggles pure and simple, reeking of the pork barrel. The Reclamation Bureau's shining achievements and promises for the future, once taken as an article of faith, were put in question. It was charged that the objectives of the 1902 Reclamation Act, aimed at benefiting the family farmer, had been subverted. This was demonstrably the case.

Environmentalists joined heartily in the hue and cry against the Reclamation Bureau in the 1960s and 1970s, but they were not alone. Individuals and groups pleading for the small farmer swelled the chorus. During the Johnson administration, the Interior Department went to court to enforce the 160-acre limitation in California's Imperial Valley, where landowners had been allowed to consider themselves exempt. The old law, the landowners said, was out of date and hopelessly out of step with modern agriculture. In 1967, Johnson's National Advisory Commission on Rural Poverty published a report called *The People Left Behind*. The commission recommended, among other things, that the acreage limitation be enforced throughout the western reclamation empire and that the sale of "excess lands" receiving federal water be expedited, so that the little man could benefit from the federal subsidy Congress meant him to have.

These were by no means pinpricks, but the unkindest cut suffered by the Reclamation Bureau, an organization proud and sturdy in its righteousness, came from a different quarter entirely—the National Water Commission. This was a panel of presidential appointees authorized by Congress in 1968 and allowed $5 million to study water-resource needs and problems.

The chairman was a businessman, Charles F. Luce, chief executive officer of Consolidated Edison Company of New York and former under secretary of the interior.

In 1973 the commission, which expired when its work was done, made a long and detailed report that alarmed proponents of reclamation projects and comparable activities of the Army Corps of Engineers, the Agriculture Department's Soil Conservation Service, and the Tennessee Valley Authority.[34] The panel had no enthusiasm for more and bigger projects. It saw no need in sight, at least through the year 2000, for additional federally financed irrigation works that would put more land into farm production. It said beneficiaries of projects should pay for what they get, to the maximum extent possible. The commission made a case for putting federal water undertakings on a tough, cost-effective basis and requiring that states and localities share the expenses.

No sooner was the report out in draft form than it began catching heavy flak. Water politicians raked it on Capitol Hill. The National Water Resources Association denounced the report, saying that "many of its conclusions and recommendations, if accepted as valid, would have widespread and damaging effect on the nation as a whole." The commissioners were flayed for their assumption that the United States, then being pressed to export food and fiber for the world, had plenty of farmland. Water zealots linked the commission with social critic Ralph Nader, suggesting that both were guilty of similar heresies.

As might be expected, the National Water Commission report found favor in the sight of environmentalists. The National Resources Defense Council, while not praising the report *in toto*, rejoiced that "the federal agencies which ditch, dam and divert our nation's streams have been dealt sharp blows." Noting that beneficiaries of the status quo were scurrying to gut the report, the major conservationist groups sent out a brochure urging the faithful to back it, in a selective way.

"A tremendous public response ... will make it more difficult," the brochure said, "for public servants who have traditionally been partial to the special interests of water resource developers to ignore some of the report's key recommendations for curtailing destructive water projects."

In the light of all this, President Carter's famous "hit-list" initiative shortly after taking office, when he decided to cut nineteen water-resource projects from the fiscal 1978 budget, may be seen as a reasonable if imprudent move. They included eight Reclamation Bureau projects and eleven being built by the Army Corps of Engineers. Carter estimated 1978 budget savings of $289 million. The potential long-term savings in construction costs was put at more than $5 billion.

The president's attack on the entrenched interests of the water kingdom was ineptly handled. It showed little sensitivity to the feelings of Congress. Even Secretary Andrus was taken somewhat by surprise. Small fry from the White House staff, youngsters fresh from the environmental wars, were put forward to explain the deletions to indignant water proponents who converged on Washington.[35]

As Andrus explained, when he got a chance to explain, the president's review involved the reevaluation of 327 projects nationwide, and only 19 had been chosen for the axe. Among factors arguing for rejection were adverse environmental impacts and poor economic justifications.

The president's emissaries got a hostile reception on Capitol Hill and in the West, which felt itself much abused. He finally trimmed his sails and went along with a Senate compromise in which all but nine of the projects he wanted to delete were restored. But he did not give up the struggle.

Although the president was castigated for awkward management of the hit-list affair, even by those sympathetic to his aims, he had shown political courage in attacking head-on a formidable giant with which others had been reluctant to cross swords.

In June of 1978, an undaunted President Carter announced new policies following a comprehensive review by the Water Resources Council, the Office of Management and Budget, and the Council on Environmental Policy.[36] The following October, he vetoed a $10.1 billion public-works bill because it contained thirty-three water projects he considered "wasteful" and "inflationary." The House overrode its own leadership to sustain the president's veto.

"Carter is not only serious but also right about the need to start screening out water projects that cannot meet the test of national interest," said an editorial in the *Los Angeles Times*.[37] It gave the president credit for being the first chief executive in many years to try to tip over the pork barrel.

It was not only Carter's struggle against inefficient or damaging federal irrigation and water-storage works that got him into difficulties with reclamation beneficiaries in the West. He and Andrus also were identified as villains and meddlers in seeking to straighten out long-standing, much-cherished abuses in the enforcement of the 1902 Reclamation Act.

A whole book could be written about the vagaries of the old law, as it worked out on the ground, but the essential elements can be set down in brief space.

As noted in an earlier chapter, the law's legislative history leaves no doubt that Congress and President Theodore Roosevelt intended to subsidize the small landowner and rule out the possibility of seeing the benefits concentrated in the hands of speculators or big interests. Toward that end, the original law specified that individuals would be limited to 160 acres. This was not a limitation on land ownership, it might be noted. It was a limit on the land that could be served with federally subsidized project water. In addition, the law set up a "residency requirement." The benefits were for farmers living on the land.

There were early abuses. Congress tightened up the law in 1914 and again in 1926. What emerged was a requirement that a landowner, if he wanted federal water for more than 160 acres, had to agree to sell his "excess" land within ten years—not at the going market rate, but at a price that did not reflect the availability of low-cost federal water.

For various reasons, not necessarily the fault of current landowners or current officials, the acreage limitation has not been enforced with any rigor, while the residency requirement, since 1926 at least, has been ignored.

The consequence of lackadaisical adherence to what the reclamation law said, more or less throughout the West, was a buildup over the years of big landholdings and corporate farming, coupled with a squeeze-out of small farmers lacking capital. This trend did not go unnoticed. It was protested by such critics as Paul Taylor, professor emeritus of economics at the University of California, Berkeley, and Paul W. Gates, former professor of history at Cornell.

California's rich Central and Imperial valleys were high-visibility trouble spots, from the standpoint of those concerned with enforcement of the law. Here were big landowners and corporations getting rich on a federal subsidy intended for others.[38] Here the disparity between law and practice generated lawsuits as well as millionaires.

When Andrus became secretary of the interior, he did not plunge himself into the acreage-limitation controversy entirely by choice. He inherited a 1976 federal court order in a California Central Valley case called *National Land for the People* v. *Bureau of Reclamation et al.* The court instructed him to publish regulations for enforcement of the 1902 law.

Secretary Andrus duly proposed the new rules in August 1977. They caused an uproar, and a group of landowners and the Pacific Legal Foundation in California brought suit under the National Environmental Policy Act of 1969, contending that the federal proposals would have "devastating environmental consequences" for eleven million acres of irrigated farmland. A federal judge ruled in December that Andrus must file an environmental-impact statement before clamping down. Andrus bowed to the court and set about preparing the statement, which was to take about three years and cost $2.5 million.

Meanwhile, the frustrated secretary was also involved, indirectly at least, in landmark litigation involving the Imperial Val-

361

ley, a huge expanse of flat and productive farmland lying east of San Diego, west of the Colorado River, and north of the Mexican border.

The Imperial Valley was considered a special case because private developers there were already tapping the Colorado for irrigation water before the Reclamation Act was passed and long before the river was tamed by Hoover Dam and federal water began flowing into the new All-American Canal in 1940.

Another unusual factor was that in 1933, in the final days of the Hoover administration, Secretary of the Interior Ray Lyman Wilbur—a medical man rather than a lawyer by training—wrote a letter saying the acreage limitation did not apply to the Imperial Valley. The landowners had sought the ruling and relied upon it.

Interior Department lawyers doubted the soundness of the Wilbur judgment, but it was not officially repudiated until late in 1964, when Johnson's interior secretary, Udall, and the department's solicitor, Frank J. Barry, decided the time had come to bite the bullet. Barry issued an official opinion that the excess-land laws did apply to the Imperial Valley. He had been asked about the matter by Sen. Clinton B. Anderson, Democrat of New Mexico, then chairman of the Interior Committee.[39]

The Justice Department accordingly brought suit in 1967 against the Imperial Irrigation District, seeking to impose the acreage limitation. The landowners girded for battle. Dr. Ben Yellen, a valley physician and champion of poor people and Chicanos, intervened in the case on the government's side. He also brought an action of his own to enforce the residency requirement. The state of California and Gov. Ronald Reagan sided with the landowners.

Early in 1971 the federal district judge, Howard B. Turrentine, decided the *United States* v. *Imperial Irrigation District* case against the government, as some of the Justice Department attorneys had expected he might. They thought they would win in appellate court, which might take a broader view.

In a dramatic turn of events, however, the Justice Department,

362

by then under President Nixon with John A. Mitchell as attorney general, decided to accept defeat without appeal. This was to the chagrin and disgust of subordinates, some of whom soon left.

The decision to drop such an important case—in effect, throwing the fight after a bad first round—was highly unusual. It was the responsibility of the solicitor general, former Harvard Law School Dean Erwin Griswold, who said he had tried to rule on the merits without yielding to pressures from either side.

In a long memorandum, Griswold held no brief for the quality of the Turrentine opinion, later upset, but felt the thrust of it was right. Griswold gave great weight to the 1933 Wilbur letter. He said it was not "good government" to try to reverse things after thirty-eight years had passed.

"It is not just that I think an appeal . . . would be unsuccessful, but that I think it ought to be unsuccessful," Griswold wrote.[40]

Undaunted, Dr. Yellen, an elderly man who was born in Brooklyn but had lived in the valley since the 1940s, got permission to take over the government's drooping battle flag and make the appeal Griswold had rejected. In 1977, he won the case in the Ninth Circuit Court of Appeals. The defeated landowners sought a rehearing. This was turned down in 1979, and the issue seemed on its way to the United States Supreme Court.

Carter's assistant attorney general for land and natural resources, James W. Moorman, could be counted on to take a lively interest in the outcome of the litigation. As a young Justice Department lawyer in the 1960s, Moorman helped work up the federal case against Imperial Irrigation District. Later he organized the Sierra Club's legal arm.

While the lawyers argued, Secretary Andrus grappled with the task of persuading Congress to amend the Reclamation Act in such a way as to adapt it to modern conditions, without gutting the law and killing its social objectives, in which Andrus firmly believed.

As John W. Gardner of Common Cause wrote to John Mitchell in urging appeal of the Imperial Valley case, a lot was at stake: "The large landowners, with their subsidized water, electricity and crops, reap the rich harvest of socialism while the poor are, in effect, told to be satisfied with the benefits of the free enterprise system."

The Imperial Valley subsidy was estimated by the federal government at about $260 million to nearly $770 million over a fifty-year period. In June 1980, the United States Supreme Court decided the case in favor of the landowners.[41] The court construed the Boulder Canyon Project Act, which authorized Hoover Dam and the All-American Canal, to mean that acreage limitations did not apply to lands that were already receiving Colorado River water in 1929 via the old privately constructed canal.

Thus was the matter settled, as far as the Imperial Valley was concerned. There were no dissenters. In the opinion delivered by Associate Justice Byron R. White, named to the court in 1962 by President Kennedy, no time was wasted agonizing over the social objectives of the 1902 Reclamation Act. The decision left the big landowners in unchallenged possession of their federal subsidy.

Hoover Dam from a visitor's viewpoint on the Nevada side of the dam. More than 600,000 people take the conducted tour of the dam and power-plant each year. *Courtesy Water and Power Resources Service, U.S. Department of the Interior.*

14

A PILGRIM'S PROGRESS

Every separate government agency having to do with natural resources was riding its own hobby in its own direction. Instead of being, as we should have been, like a squadron of cavalry, all acting together for a single purpose, we were like loose horses in a field, each one following his own nose.

—GIFFORD PINCHOT, *Breaking New Ground*

... To create and maintain conditions under which man and nature can exist in productive harmony, and fulfill the social, economic, and other requirements of present and future generations of Americans.

—NATIONAL ENVIRONMENTAL POLICY ACT of 1969

Is it meet to think that a little child should handle Goliath as David did? Or that there should be the strength of an ox in a wren? Some are strong, some are weak; some have great faith, some have little. This man was one of the weak, and therefore he went to the wall.

—JOHN BUNYAN, *The Pilgrim's Progress*

B efore we move from the battles fought over the Colorado River in the Southwest to the struggle over the partitioning of Alaska, the nation's last frontier, it is appropriate to devote some attention to the American conservationist movement. We should also take a closer look at the National Environmental Policy Act of 1969, also known as NEPA. In our earlier discussions of mining, logging, and grazing on the public lands, we have made frequent mention of the conservationists and their interventions. In Alaska, as we shall see, the conservationists have played a bold and often a decisive role.

No matter how one may feel about the wisdom of the movement's position on this or that specific issue, it is beyond question that the conservationists have performed—and do perform—an essential public service in throwing the spotlight on public-lands questions. The activist organizations among them— notably the Sierra Club and a number of others—make it their business to keep a vigil. They know what is going on, and they pass the information along. If anybody represents the public interest and the public conscience, they do.

Thanks to the vigilance of the active conservationists and their willingness to do battle in the lobbies of Congress and in the courts, the United States had in place by the end of the fractious 1970s a block of relatively sound legislation on the management of the federal forests, the grazing lands, and other federal holdings. The general public at large had little awareness of these struggles. Newspapers and the electronic media illuminated the scene only fitfully, if at all. In the end, the approved laws fell short of the conservationist ideal but were much better, it is safe to say, than if the shaping of them had been left entirely to the commercial interests, their political allies, and the bureaucrats.

A great deal of arrant nonsense has been put forward to the effect that conservationists in their various modes are impractical idealists, do-gooders who impede national progress. Actually, the nation owes them much. The American people have always been and still are conspicuous wasters as far as natural resources are concerned. In matters of money, they have cherished a tradition of thrift, making use of a hog down to the squeal and bristles, tearing down good buildings because the tax laws encouraged it. They have not behaved, however, at least until recently, as if they recognized a need or obligation to leave anything for the next generation. When Alexis de Tocqueville paid his call in the 1830s, seeing the new country through the eyes of an aristocratic young Frenchman, he found Americans admirable in many ways but acquisitive as individuals and "insensible to the wonders of inanimate nature." They could not see the mighty forests that surrounded them until those forests fell to the axe. De Tocqueville noted how quickly the green wilds returned when intruding man had moved on; but that was before the age of steel and concrete.

In some contrast to the older cultures in Europe, whose domestic resources were well staked out and not so abundant in the first place, the new Americans were inclined to grow up greedy but not stingy. There was always a better place, if not in the next valley, then beyond. Each generation expected to be better off than the preceding one. The son had to have more than his father had. It was a formula that dictated voracious consumption. President Truman's Materials Policy Commission, headed by William S. Paley, reported in 1952 that "the United States appetite for materials is Gargantuan—and so far, insatiable." When the Paley report came out, half the world was scattered with the World War II output of American mines and factories, and American shell fragments were manuring the soil of Korea. Vietnam was yet to come.

Noting that the United States was using up its reserves faster than any other country, the commission expressed faith in the principles of growth and free enterprise. It favored a minimum of interference with the patterns of private enterprise, but not zero interference. Of the cold war, then raging, it said: "The United States, once criticized as the creator of a crassly materialistic order of things, is today throwing its might into the task of keeping alive the spirit of man and helping beat back from the frontiers of the free world everywhere the threat of force and of a new dark age which rise from the communist nations."

The most electrifying statement in the Paley commission document, called *Resources for Freedom*, had to do with the astounding pace at which the use of materials by this country had escalated since the early twentieth century. It was mentioned in chapter 1 and is repeated here for emphasis.

"There is scarcely a metal or a mineral fuel," said the report on page 5, "of which the quantity used in the United States since the outbreak of the first World War did not exceed the total used throughout the world in all the centuries preceding."[1]

To most citizens of this much-blessed nation, an ever-expanding economy seemed the normal state of affairs, and there was little apparent awareness of the moral issue raised by a situation in which 6 percent of the world's people were taking one-third of its resources. The danger of running out of materials—a different matter—did come to mind, however. Concern evidenced itself in the 1960s not only about supply but also about a problem of pollution, particularly in air and water, which was becoming intolerable. Both supply and pollution were genuine problems, of course, but the pressure for increasing supply clashed with the drive to do something about pollution, and vice versa.

As we have seen, Truman's Paley commission had its counterpart under President Nixon when Congress in 1970 set up the National Commission on Materials Policy, of which James Boyd was the executive director. The Boyd study, which came out in final form in 1973, pointed to prospective shortages but was not alarmist in tone. It called for further federal encouragement of the American mining industry.

Although presidential commissions assemble useful information and frequently represent the considered, composite opinion of able people, they seldom reach dramatic heights in stating

369

their conclusions. The dry reports and statistics gather dust on library shelves or hit the wastebasket after being thumbed through by a newspaper reporter on a dull afternoon.

Wayne Aspinall, in an interview following his defeat for re-election to the House in 1972, came closer to the heart of the materials issue when he said that Americans had become profligate. "We let the private enterprise system run wild," he pointed out. "Like anything else running wild, it made mistakes, some of them intentional, and some unintentional. . . . We had too much. We didn't protect what we had."

To understand the dimensions of waste and built-in profligacy in the American society, it is useful to travel in other countries more thickly populated or less well endowed by nature than ours. During World War II, before the invasion of southern France, I was in Algiers for a while, and I remember walking through the streets in the early morning as poor people were looking through the refuse bins of the well-to-do. What impressed me was that every object of possible utility was picked out. The matter left behind after such a winnowing was not garbage by American standards, but a quintessence. At a street market, where farmers were selling vegetables from wagons, small children crept under the horses to pick up vagrant bean pods, not minding the manure and urine.

In India, a traveler from the United States, where gleaming refrigerators are junked for small defects, the intricate metal carcasses of automobiles are not worth hauling off, and superbly fashioned cans and bottles are simply thrown away, found himself in a land where everything—or nearly everything—had a resale value.

The fact is, of course, that we do not know poverty in the United States as poverty is known in many parts of the world. We are not as close to the bone. We have more margin for error. The conservationist reaction to the wanton abuse of the land

and its resources in the United States began with the razing of the forests and had become a powerful force by the late nineteenth century. It was intense at the time of Theodore Roosevelt and Gifford Pinchot. When the nation reached its two hundredth anniversary in 1976, conservation had leaped to the forefront of public discourse. The word was on every tongue. Nearly everybody regarded himself as a conservationist, or at least would deny not being one, but there was wide disagreement as to what the articles of the true faith were and how they should be applied to specific situations.

In Alaska, for example, both the forces backing the oil pipeline from the North Slope and those against it called themselves conservationists. Nobody in public life in the 1970s cared to say what was attributed to old Senator Clark of Montana many decades earlier—"Those who succeed us can well take care of themselves."

Conservation, however, was a house of many mansions, and Americans of widely different persuasions saw the word in different contexts. The house gave shelter to groups as diverse as rod-and-gun clubs and zealots against nuclear power. The variety of motivations and attitudes is well described in Lynton Keith Caldwell's 1970 book, *Environment*.[2] Caldwell, professor of political science at Indiana University, had a part in shaping the NEPA and was a member of Nixon's National Commission on Materials Policy. He observed that George Perkins Marsh's *Man and Nature*, published in 1864, might be considered the opening note in a new chorus of environmental awareness among Americans, who theretofore had tended to regard the subduing of the wilderness as a God-given task, wholly without sin. Caldwell pointed to the difference between economic conservationists, who want to husband resources carefully, and aesthetic conservationists, who seek the protection of scenic values and the natural state of things, sometimes to the point of ruling out change altogether. As a classic example of the clash in these attitudes, he cited the falling out of John Muir and Pinchot over the flooding

371

of Hetch Hetchy Valley in Yosemite National Park to provide water power for San Francisco.[3] Muir fought to keep the valley the way it was. Pinchot said it should be put to use.

With the Muir-Pinchot controversy in mind, no doubt, Under Secretary of Interior John C. Whitaker said in a speech in California in October 1974 that the current surge of interest in the nation's natural surroundings was different from the one that took place earlier when the conservationist movement, as expressed by Roosevelt and Pinchot, had its primary focus on utilitarian objectives.

Whereas the old conservation movement left a legacy of dams, irrigation projects, and forests managed for lumber production, Whitaker said, and whereas it was worried not so much about pollution as about the possibility that industrial progress might be limited one day by an inadequate supply of resources, the new movement that arose in the 1960s and crested on Earth Day in 1970 arose from problems created by abundance rather than scarcity. It came, he suggested, when well-heeled and mobile Americans traveled around their country and did not like the ugliness and desolation that confronted them. Affluence had given people time to think. Some had become angry. Whitaker believed two landmark events had stirred the new breed of environmentalists to action: publication in 1962 of Rachel Carson's eloquent *Silent Spring,* warning of the damage man's intervention was doing to the ecological systems of the earth, and the Santa Barbara oil spill in January 1969.[4]

Whitaker's address was intelligent, witty, and a good deal more friendly to the conservationists than were some administration spokesmen. He gave the environmental revolutionaries credit for steering a stable course. Other leaders, including Secretary Morton himself, found the harassments of NEPA intolerable at times as they sought to solve the energy and other shortages, real and imagined. They allowed themselves to slap and swear a bit, like men beset by hornets while at the milking stool. At Spokane in August 1974, Morton had given the back of his hand

372

to "well-meaning" people who advocated "zero growth." It was unreasonable, Morton said, to think the environment could be the controlling factor in every decision.

An earlier, more memorable example of Nixon administration irritation over what it considered rampant environmentalism was Commerce Secretary Maurice Stans's speech in July 1971 to the Interior Department's National Petroleum Council. Stans entitled his speech "Wait a Minute."

By all means curb pollution and clean up the water and air, Stans counseled, but let the nation pause before it makes decisions that might harm the economy, cause loss of jobs, and even impair national security. He applied his "Wait a Minute" admonition to a variety of problems, including the proposed trans-Alaska pipeline.

"Are we so afraid of what might happen," he asked the oil executives serving on interior's advisory group, "that we will sacrifice the enormous new sources of oil which we need for our homes and our cars and our jobs and our country? Will we sacrifice potential jobs for thousands of people who need work in the shipping industries, in Alaska and elsewhere—will we turn our backs on all the economic benefits to that state and to the country?"[5]

Stans had great prestige at the time as a self-made man from Shakopee, Minnesota, who had worked his way through college, done well as a certified public accountant, become the head of a New York investment banking firm, taken up big-game hunting in Africa, and emerged as a cabinet officer and chief money raiser for Nixon. Not until later, after the 1972 fund-raising effort, did he fall into difficulties related to the Watergate disclosures. His speech struck some as amusing because it reflected the discomfort that environmentalists were causing for a business-oriented administration. Stans's "Wait a Minute" theme, one that recurred in administration utterances, was excellent counsel as far as it went. The conservationists were saying precisely the same thing, but on the opposite side of the table.

They were not impressed by assurances that the nation need only put its fears aside and plunge ahead, leaving private industry and industrial know-how to take care of Spaceship Earth.

In fairness to the Republicans holding power in the 1970s, trying to grapple with an energy shortage and various complex environmental problems, one must add that many held aloft the conservationist standard set for the party by the first Roosevelt. These certainly included Nixon's appointees to the chairmanship of the Council on Environmental Quality, Russell E. Train, the first to hold that post, and Train's successor, former Gov. Russell W. Peterson of Delaware. Another was William D. Ruckelshaus, Nixon's administrator of the Environmental Protection Agency.

It is true, as Under Secretary Whitaker suggested, that since 1900 time had wrought significant changes in the conservationist movement and in national attitudes. In the 1970s the movement had better legal weapons, a more sophisticated and better-educated citizenry, friendlier courts. The environmental organizations were more activist in style. Nevertheless, the broad nature of the clash between conservation and development changed little from the day of Theodore Roosevelt to that of Richard M. Nixon, Gerald R. Ford, and Jimmy Carter. Teddy Roosevelt and his equally assured and self-confident friend Pinchot fought for the public interest against the private interest, for long-term planning against short-term exploitation. In the 1970s the struggle had become less simplistic and the stakes higher. The enemy as seen in the gunsights of the environmentalists was more shrewd, subtle, complex—at times, indeed, the enemy seemed to be society itself. The issues in their larger dimensions, however, remained what they had been—public interest versus private interest, intelligently guided growth versus runaway expansionism.

If conservationists were invariably enlightened, unselfishly motivated, and correct in their judgment of what should be done on specific problems, and if their opponents were invariably wrong, then the management of public affairs would be much simpler than it is. The movement, though, whatever other burdens it may have imposed on constituted authority, has never claimed for itself the attributes of unanimity or infallibility. It speaks with many tongues and with the usual variety of motives, some of them excellent. An oil-company official may, as an individual, be a superb and dedicated conservationist. A backpacker who rails at the Establishment may, for all the paperback of Keats in his pocket, be an inconsiderate oaf who leaves beer cans for others to clean up. A person whose heart leaps up when he beholds a deer may hate wild horses, and so on.

The *Shorter Oxford English Dictionary* defines the word *conservation*, in part, as follows: "preservation from destructive influences, decay, or waste; preservation in being, health, etc." In the 1975 edition of the National Wildlife Federation's *Conservation Directory*, a stout volume of some 220 pages with an eagle on the cover, the section for international, national, and interstate organizations lists more than 280, beginning with the African Wildlife Leadership Foundation and ending with Zero Population Growth. It includes the American Forest Institute, the Boy Scouts of America, the Brotherhood of the Jungle Cock, the Camp Fire Girls, the Good Outdoor Manners Association, Keep America Beautiful, the National Prairie Grouse Technical Council, the National Rifle Association, and many others, not to mention Trout Unlimited and the Society of Tympanuchus Cupido Pinnatus.

It is a broad tent, conservation, broad enough to cover anyone who ever burned a thumb at a campfire or looked through *National Geographic* magazine at the dentist's office. In this book, the word *conservationist* is meant to apply loosely to any individual or group characterized by an interest in and regard for the land and its creatures and a desire to protect both from needless disturbance and insult. The word *environmentalist* has a somewhat different origin and emphasis, of course, but in com-

375

mon usage has come to be a handy synonym for *conservationist*. That is to say, a writer or speaker who has used one of these terms to the exhaustion point will tend to throw in the other, to vary the monotony.

Used thus broadly, the words describe the attitude of the large majority of people in this or any other country when made aware of an issue affecting their quality of life. The number of Americans who are active conservationists, keen and interested in protecting the land from being laid waste and abused, has always been a very much smaller number—possibly not more than three to five million people, if that many.

Among conservation organizations, as with individuals, the range of interests and degree of intensity cover a wide spectrum. Some are little more than professional societies putting out learned papers. Some, such as the American Forest Institute, organized in 1941, frankly represent an industry viewpoint. Some reflect the kind of concern for the land which grows out of a fondness for the outdoors and for hunting and fishing. Some concentrate on scholarly research and education, like Resources for the Future Incorporated, formed in 1952 with the help of the Ford Foundation and late in 1974 the recipient of a $12 million, four-year grant from Ford. Charles J. Hitch, retiring as president of the University of California, was its new head. A somewhat similar group was the Conservation Foundation, founded in 1948 by Fairfield Osborn of the New York Zoological Society and supported by the Ford and Mellon foundations and others.[6] Both Resources for the Future and the Conservation Foundation occupied offices in the same block of Massachusetts Avenue in Washington as the Brookings Institution. Like Brookings, each had enough throw weight intellectually to influence national policy in a quiet way.

Ever since the beginning of the conservationist movement in the United States, it has been supported to a great extent by wealthy and influential people, frequently by businessmen and outdoors enthusiasts who were socially prominent in their day.

Teddy Roosevelt and Pinchot were American blue bloods. Of similar kidney is the aforementioned Train, the Rhode Islander and Princeton graduate who headed the African Wildlife Leadership Foundation and later the Conservation Foundation before Nixon, seeking such credentials, picked him to back up Hickel in the Interior Department and, after that, to be first chairman of the CEQ. In the mid-1970s the Conservation Foundation's president was William K. Reilly, who had been executive director of Laurance S. Rockefeller's Task Force on Land Use and Urban Growth Policy. The foundation's board of trustees was joined in 1974 by William D. Ruckelshaus, first administrator of the Environmental Protection Agency.

The influence of well-to-do sportsmen has always been strong in the conservation movement in the United States. As is recalled by Jerry A. O'Callaghan, public-lands scholar associated with the BLM, the wildlife-refuge movement had solid and enthusiastic backing from the Boone and Crockett Club, a group of prosperous amateur sportsmen and scientists founded by Theodore Roosevelt. And it was Edward H. Harriman, the railway magnate, who took a shipload of scientists and naturalists to Alaska in the famous Harriman expedition of 1899. The party included John Muir and John Burroughs. Muir and Harriman were friends. Muir named a glacier after Harriman, and Harriman, later on, encouraged Muir to dictate his boyhood memoirs while Muir was a guest at Harriman's Pelican Lodge on Klamath Lake.

There has been cooperation and joint effort among the major conservation groups as well as among conservation lobbyists, federal and state officialdom, and Congress. Men who agreed on nothing else might find common ground in talking about duck hunting and trout fishing. The Wildlife Management Institute, whose president, Ira N. Gabrielson, clashed with Senator Gruening in the 1950s over oil exploration in the Kenai Moose Range, grew out of a game protective association backed by titans of industry. The National Wildlife Federation, a large and success-

377

ful organization headed by Thomas L. Kimball, was established in 1936 following the first North American Wildlife Conference, a White House meeting called by Franklin D. Roosevelt. C. R. ("Pink") Gutermuth of the Wildlife Management Institute and Howard C. Zahniser of the Wilderness Society called a meeting of the heads of national groups at Mammoth Cave, Kentucky, in October 1946. A need for swapping information about legislation and other matters was felt. At Gutermuth's suggestion, the resulting federation came to be called the Natural Resources Council of America. The word *conservation* was avoided in the title because, as Gutermuth remarked, the term had been abused. The council in the 1970s was an alliance of forty-two national organizations with a combined membership of more than six million people. It was this council, we may remember, which, when the Public Land Law Review Commission made its industry-oriented report in 1970, published a 343-page critique and review called *What's Ahead for Our Public Lands?*

Pink Gutermuth, to whom the critique was dedicated, had long been a tough, resilient fighter against abuse of the federal domain. In 1975, he was interviewed when he had moved on to serve as president of the National Rifle Association. In a fashion typical of such spirits, he was anything but radical or unfriendly to industry but bold in calling the shots as he saw them. The Bureau of Land Management had been, among other things, "thoroughly and completely and destructively dominated by the user groups—from the beginning," he said.

The six largest citizen conservation organizations during the Nixon and early Ford administrations were the National Wildlife Federation, claiming more than 2,000,000 members and associated persons; the National Audubon Society, with more than 250,000; the Sierra Club and the Wilderness Society, each with more than 100,000; the Izaak Walton League, with some 56,000; and the American Forestry Association, with about 50,000. All but the last were heavily involved in the public confrontations of the early 1970s. The American Forestry Association, formed in

1875, had a long and respectable history as a conservationist group but in recent years had come to be regarded as being too "middle of the road" to suit some critics.

Among the activists, the Sierra Club and the Wilderness Society served in the front lines almost continuously as Congress and the administration shaped legislation affecting the nation's air and water and the public lands. Both had elite troops that knew what they were doing. John Muir, a Scotsman preaching the gospel of wilderness, joined with others in 1892 to form the Sierra Club.[7] The pioneer members were distinguished and highly placed Californians, most of them educated at the University of California and Stanford. Following World War II, the club under David R. Brower extended its influence, issued a series of beautiful publications that displayed the scenic splendors of the land, fought the Reclamation Bureau, and joined the Wilderness Society in pushing through the Wilderness Act, which was approved by Congress in 1964. Under Michael McCloskey, who succeeded Brower as executive director, it has remained the most prestigious and perhaps the most effective of the conservationist groups.

In 1966, following the insertion by the Sierra Club of advertisements in major newspapers urging the protection of the Grand Canyon, the Internal Revenue Service ruled that contributions to the Sierra Club were no longer tax deductible.

The Wilderness Society, under the spur of Stewart N. Brandborg, until 1976 its outspoken and unabashed executive director, rivaled the Sierra Club as a force in the national capital, at least for a time. It was a leading voice in the battle for Alaska. Two veterans of the United States Forest Service, Robert Marshall and Aldo Leopold, organized the society in 1935, along with six other men. Their immediate objective was to provide protection, as was mentioned earlier, for a remnant of the vanishing American wilderness. As has been noted, even though the federal government already owned the wilderness and most was inaccessible to industry, the enactment of a law took eight years. Congress

379

made the protection of wilderness a long, difficult, and perilous process. It was the primary mission of the Wilderness Society, of course, to try to safeguard what remained of the remote and pristine places.

William A. Turnage, an outdoors enthusiast with a Yale and Harvard background, became executive director of the Wilderness Society in November 1978. He said he would try to keep the society on the cutting edge of the conservation movement. When Gaylord Nelson of Wisconsin, organizer of the 1970 Earth Day observance and a leading environmentalist in the Senate, went down to defeat in 1980, Nelson accepted the chairmanship of the Wilderness Society and, as a spokesman for the society, testified against Senate confirmation of James C. Watt to be secretary of the interior under President Reagan.

Often ranked with the Sierra Club and the Wilderness Society in the litigation, oratory, and propaganda wars of the 1970s was Friends of the Earth, a smaller and younger but no less militant organization founded by Brower in July 1969, after his resignation from the Sierra Club. Friends of the Earth went through a personnel shake-up early in 1972. Several staffers resigned to form a new organization called the Environmental Policy Center. By that time, the band of militants had grown to include a new phenomenon: the public-interest law firm. Several of these—the Center for Law and Social Policy, the Natural Resources Defense Council, and the Environmental Defense Fund—sprang up in the 1960s and later, with the support of philanthropic foundations and some encouragement from the government itself. They played a crucial role in enabling conservationists to seize the opportunities for court action provided by the National Environmental Policy Act.

Time and again, when Congress and the administration went about reshaping the public land laws in response to the Aspinall commission's 1970 report, the conservationists rushed to the barricades. They found ways to rally support for what they thought was constructive and opposition for what they considered wrongheaded. They poured out press releases, kept their membership informed through bulletins, gave in-depth treatment of complex issues in their magazines. One of the most widely respected groups, the National Audubon Society, founded in 1905, presented in its handsome, slick-paper magazine, *Audubon*, a detailed analysis of Secretary Morton's Alaskan withdrawal proposals. The analysis was written by Robert Cahn, a Pulitzer Prize–winning *Christian Science Monitor* reporter who had served as one of the first three members of the Council on Environmental Quality. With it were printed stunning pictures of Alaska. Many other such conservationist magazines went regularly into American homes, among them the Sierra Club's *Bulletin*, the Wilderness Society's *Living Wilderness*, and the National Wildlife Federation's *National Wildlife*. The Izaak Walton League, organized in 1922 at the Chicago Athletic Club, published *Outdoor America*.

Armed with the bright new sword of NEPA, the conservationists seemed at times to be triumphing over their foes—or, at least, to be on an equal footing with them. None knew better, however, than these valiant pilgrims that for every Apollyon laid low and every Slough of Despond safely crossed, there would be others beyond.

In the conservation business, beating back the forces of darkness took a lot of time and attention. Meetings. Court cases. Testimony on the Hill. Strategy sessions. Appointments with federal officials, friendly and unfriendly. Putting the flat of the sword to lagging troops. Having sandwiches and beer with newspaper reporters and other media people.

Some conservationist organizations were more keen for the fray than others.

"Within the movement, there is a high degree of ossification," a major conservationist leader, one of the activists, said to me one day. I asked him which organizations he considered most effective. He ticked off seven, including one not mentioned above, Environmental Action, a spirited and youthful band that developed from among the organizers of Earth Day in 1970. Environmental Action, calling itself a Washington Citizen's Lobby, enlivened the capital with a sprightly and irreverent magazine. It began to formulate each election year a "Dirty Dozen" list of House members it regarded as most antienvironmental in their voting and therefore deserving of defeat. In November 1974, eight of the dozen nominees were not returned.

The militant conservationist I was talking to, a veteran of many battles won and lost, told me that victory could not be achieved for what he considered the forces of right and justice unless conservationists were willing to get involved,—get their shoes muddy and their feet wet. He was a little scornful of the ones who held themselves above the fray and were, as he said, content to philosophize and safeguard their tax-exempt status.

"Some are safe," he said with sarcasm. "They will sit here and ruminate. Drink a lot of whiskey and go home and forget the whole damned mess. They talk about the problem, but avoid all effective action. They won't do a damned thing. They won't even come to a meeting."

In Arkansas, there is a saying that even a blind hog picks up some acorns. Another homely way of putting it is that the sun does not shine on the same dog all of the time. For Americans who wanted their decision makers to pause a bit before inflicting further wounds on the earth and air and water, the year 1969 brought a bountiful and unlooked-for harvest. This was the year that yielded the enactment in late December of the National Environmental Policy Act, or NEPA, as it soon came to be called. Here was a barbed-wire fence that a good lawyer could throw in front of the thundering herd. The fence might not hold forever, but it would do for a while.

Congress is capable of noble actions that are quite intentional and carefully considered, but sometimes it is at its best when it does not fully realize what it is doing. Such was the case with

NEPA, a law that, like the Bill of Rights in the Constitution, might have had more trouble winning approval had the consequences been anticipated. The interesting thing about NEPA is that the provision that turned out to be most important—the famous section 102, requiring environmental impact statements—crept into the legislation with very little formal attention or discussion.

This is not to say that nobody in the Senate or the House knew what was in the bill. It is probably accurate, however, to say that even those involved in the drafting of the substantive portions could not foresee how seriously they would be taken or how the courts would construe them.

What the act did was to go beyond fine words about harmony between man and his environment to require that federal agencies give a public accounting of planned actions affecting the environment in a major way. It enabled citizens to challenge the adequacy of these analyses, or impact statements, and to take the government to court.

During the Johnson administration, there had been an outpouring of the spirit, much talk about "beautification" of the nation, and a striving toward a better quality of life in Johnson's Great Society. Sensitivities sharpened by the Vietnam War heightened public concern about the environment. In July 1968, the Senate Interior Committee and the House Committee on Science and Astronautics held a joint colloquium to talk about a national policy.

At the colloquium, Senator Jackson, Interior Committee chairman and the architect of the bill eventually passed the following year, argued that new approaches to environmental management were needed. He spoke of "action-forcing" processes to make the system work.

The importance of putting into the law a requirement for action was emphasized at the colloquium and elsewhere by the aforementioned Lynton K. Caldwell of Indiana University, an astute and broad-gauged man. He made the point in a paper

383

prepared late in November 1968 for Laurance Rockefeller, chairman of the Citizens Advisory Committee on Recreation and Natural Beauty. The paper was submitted as part of a package being prepared for the incoming President Nixon.

"To obtain a national policy for the environment will not be easy," Caldwell wrote. "The short-term and particular interests of influential agencies and organizations inside and outside of government would be opposed to it. For this reason a mere hortatory statement of intent would very likely remain inoperative. It could be ignored with impunity and would thus be open to ridicule, contempt, or relegation to political oblivion."

More than twenty environmental policy bills were before the Ninety-first Congress, but Jackson's was the chosen vehicle. When the Interior Committee of the Senate held hearings in April 1969, the measure was still more or less toothless. Concerned about that, Jackson consulted with committee Chief Counsel William J. Van Ness and Daniel A. Dreyfus, of the staff. They had the advice of Caldwell.[8]

Van Ness and Dreyfus sat down and did some thinking and writing. They wanted to fix the law in such a way that the responsible federal agency would be required to put on paper everything about a pending decision, including possible alternative actions. They wanted to provide time for review and rigorous analysis and give people a right to sue.

The putting together of all the elements in a major decision had been a practice in some parts of the bureaucracy—the Bureau of Reclamation, for example—but was by no means standard practice. Van Ness recalled that in the environmental tussle over the Central Arizona Project several years earlier, Jackson had asked Secretary Udall to come up with alternatives to the building of dams near the Grand Canyon. It turned out that building a dam was only one of six options, whereupon the controversy melted away.

"You can solve most problems if you know what the problems are," Van Ness said. "The trouble is, people seldom know enough about the alternatives to make a decision."

In any event, the new "action-forcing" provision was prepared, and on June 5 Senator Jackson put it in the *Congressional Record*. His committee approved it unanimously, without further hearings, and on July 10 the Senate whipped it through without debate.[9]

On September 23 the House passed a different version of the bill by an overwhelming margin, 372 to 15.[10] The measure had been delayed on the House side by a jurisdictional dispute between the merchant marine and the interior committees. It contained nothing comparable to Jackson's amendment. The leading proponent in the House was a dauntless conservationist, Rep. John D. Dingell, Michigan Democrat, chairman of the merchant marine subcommittee on fisheries and wildlife conservation and the environment.

There remained the task of the Senate-House conference—to iron out differences in the two versions of the bill. The Jackson "action-forcing" provisions survived. The Senate quickly passed the final bill, and the House took its own final action—swallowing section 102—in the rush just before Christmas 1969.[11] It was amazing that neither in the Senate nor in the House did the environmental impact statement part of the bill generate substantive discussion. In a capital crammed with power-conscious bureaucrats and lobbyists paid to look out for industry, the entire legislative history of NEPA reflects little or no awareness that it would be a blockbuster.

Senator Jackson was correct when he called the completed bill, with its fateful section 102, "the most important and far-reaching conservation-environmental measure ever enacted by the Congress."[12]

"The future of succeeding generations is in our hands," Jackson said in the Senate. "It will be shaped by the choices we make. We will not, and they cannot, escape the consequence of our choices."[13]

Within about one week, President Nixon had signed the new law, and within another month Russell E. Train was being shifted from the Interior Department to the new Council on Environmental Quality. Within four months, the gigantic Alaska pipeline project had been stopped cold by the *Wilderness Society* v. *Hickel* lawsuit alleging, among other things, failure to comply fully with NEPA.

The federal agencies did not realize at first, but soon learned, that the conservationists would insist on adequate studies of actions significantly affecting the environment and that the courts would back them up. By April of 1972, when the pipeline had been blocked for two years, there had been more than 17 federal appellate court decisions and 50 district court decisions applying the NEPA. In all, there were at that time about 160 NEPA cases, of which 17 were against the Interior Department and 15 against the Department of Agriculture.

Litigation in the public interest, under NEPA and other laws affording a foothold, required money and legal talent. Who was to pay the cost? Following a successful challenge to Federal Power Commission licensing of a pumped storage power installation on Storm King Mountain on the Hudson River in 1965, the field of environmental law began to grow apace, attracting many bright young lawyers.[14] The Environmental Defense Fund was organized on Long Island in 1967. It was the first organization of its type. In 1969, the Center for Law and Social Policy was created at Washington, D.C., with former Supreme Court Justice Arthur Goldberg as its first board chairman. The National Resources Defense Council came along in 1970, opening offices in New York, Washington, and Palo Alto, California. The Sierra Club Legal Defense Fund was established in 1971. Its executive director was James W. Moorman, the Duke University law graduate who had handled the pipeline delaying action. Later, Moorman became Carter's assistant attorney general for land and resources.

The environmental law effort had the early and generous support of the Ford Foundation and other contributors. In the period between 1969 and 1978, the Ford Foundation made grants totaling nearly $10 million for environmental law and mediation. This included sizable sums in support of the Environmental Defense Fund, the Natural Resources Defense Council, the Sierra Club Legal Defense Fund, and the Environmental Law Institute, which published the *Environmental Law Reporter*.[15] Late in 1979, however, the *Washington Post* carried a story indicating that the Ford Foundation had decided to "virtually eliminate" the future funding of public-interest law firms.[16] This was bad news, inasmuch as the Ford Foundation had been far and away the heaviest contributor to these enterprises.

Money was a problem, and so, early in the game, was the question of tax-exempt status for public-interest law firms, which affected the flow of funds to them. In October 1970 the Internal Revenue Service caused a furor by issuing an announcement that cast doubt on tax-exempt status for the firms, which the IRS described as a "new phenomenon rapidly proliferating on the American scene." CEQ Chairman Train rushed to the defense, pointing out that litigation by private groups relying on contributions for their support was regarded as essential to environmental protection. Within a few weeks the black clouds disappeared. IRS Commissioner Randolph Thrower said tax-exempt status would continue to be granted to public-service law firms.

The NEPA did not ensure decisions favorable to the environment once all the legally required studies had been made, and it was a two-edged sword that could also be used by forces opposing the environmentalists. The public-interest law groups championing the environmental side, as it was perceived, did not have the field to themselves. There was a vigorous countermovement heartily applauded by business interests. The pioneer public-interest law firm of the new type was the Pacific Legal Foundation of Sacramento. It was organized in 1973 through the efforts of J. Simon Fluor, retired chairman of Fluor Corporation, with the backing of the California Chamber of Commerce and others. Later, additional groups were set up to reflect the business-industry viewpoint. Early in 1975 came the

National Legal Center for the Public Interest, a Washington, D.C., headquarters for six regional legal centers of a conservative stripe.[17] As we have seen, James G. Watt was director of one of these, the Mountain States Legal Foundation, when he was chosen to succed Andrus as secretary of the interior.

Despite difficulties, the story of the conservationist pilgrims as they went through the 1970s was one of success. To a greater extent than earlier, they were able to get a hearing before Congress and the executive branch and in the courts. They had a growing constituency among the citizenry at large. They could whip up powerful pressures on Capitol Hill, and the politicians knew it.

Under NEPA and other laws, the conservationists were able to hold up—at least temporarily—not only the Alaska pipeline but the sale of timber in the Tongass National Forest. They blocked the Nixon speedup in the allowable timber cut in the national forests generally, the accelerated leasing of offshore oil lands, the surge toward coal development in the Great Plains and the Southwest. There were many other cases.

We now turn to Alaska. Here in the North was a magnificent and largely untouched land empire to be divided up. It would be a testing ground for the conservationists and their foes and for the attitudes of a still young but aging nation that had made many errors in the past and would make more.

Theodore Roosevelt and Gifford Pinchot on a trip down the Mississippi in October 1907 made as a means of awakening interest in the development of our inland waterways. *Courtesy of U.S. Forest Service.*

CHAPTER 15

OIL, ICE, AND POLITICS

Russia has sold us a sucked orange.
        —*New York World*, April 1, 1867

Alaska entered the oil industry on July 19, 1957, when the Richfield Oil Company struck oil in the Swanson River field on the Kenai Peninsula.
        —ERNEST GRUENING, *The State of Alaska*

Now, to be specific, I think that the territory up there belongs to the people of Alaska and not to the people of the present 48 states. I think that you have to have those resources if you are going to develop and control your own destiny as a state.
        —Sen. FRANK A. BARRETT at Senate Interior Committee hearing on Alaska Statehood, 1957

What must be kept in mind about Alaska is that it is very large, very beautiful, very thinly populated, and, until recently, almost all owned by the United States government. Homesteading never worked up there. There is little good farmland. Construction is difficult. Most of the things Alaska consumes have to be shipped in at high cost. Because of climate, terrain, and remoteness, vast tracts are hostile to year-round human habitation.

Alaska was the nation's last frontier, the last blank tablet upon which to write. It was a bright new copybook, now somewhat soiled but not yet ruined, thanks in large part to gallant and determined efforts by those in Alaska and elsewhere who did not want to see the errors of the national past repeated.

The United States bought Alaska from Imperial Russia in 1867, paying $7.2 million. An immense and spectacular land far to the north, largely unexplored, came under the American flag. Early in 1959, having languished for nearly a century as a district and later as a territory, Alaska entered the Union as the forty-ninth state. After that came what might be called a second Alaska Purchase, when the oil industry "bought" the state again at a cost of some billions of dollars in cash and the promise of more money and jobs to come.

Still later, near the close of the 1970s, the conservationist war to protect choice fragments of Alaska as federal parklands led to a third Alaska Purchase. This was a purchase in the sense that the United States paid a heavy price in compromise for the federal holdings it wanted to safeguard from development.

The great expanse of Alaska has other riches besides oil, but it was oil that ended the years of neglect and put Alaska back on the bonanza trail. Nothing was quite the same after Atlantic Richfield struck oil on the North Slope in February 1968. ARCO and Humble Oil and Refining Company, later Exxon USA, confirmed the discovery that summer. It was a very big strike, estimated at 9.6 billion barrels or more, the biggest ever made on this continent, bigger by far than the East Texas strike.

As the smell of oil rose from the Prudhoe Bay strike, which Luther J. Carter of *Science* magazine said might make Alaska the Kuwait of the Arctic, wheels began to turn more rapidly than before in Alaska, in Congress, and in the federal bureaucracy. The state had received only about $12 million in bonus bids in the mid-1960s for leases on lands involved in the 1968 strike, but in September 1969 it got more than $900 million for additional leases in that area. The state did not yet have clear title to these tracts, but the federal landlord had no great reason to quibble over ownership, since even if the land remained in federal hands, the generous statehood law gave Alaska nine-tenths of any revenues.

The Statehood Act was generous in other respects. In addition to allowing Alaska 90 percent of federal mineral revenues, compared with 37½ percent for states previously admitted, the law allowed the state the right to select 103,350,000 acres from federal lands within twenty-five years. This would leave 70 percent of the state in federal ownership, but the grant was a much greater quantity than any other entering state had received. As for national forest revenues, Alaska was to receive a 37½ percent share, or 12 ½ percent above the share that had been granted to other states. These points were frequently cited, but sometimes lost sight of, in the subsequent debate over the disposal of Alaska's back country.

In writing the statehood law, Congress was aware, of course, that Alaska as a state would have financial difficulties because of the vast area to be governed. Here was a land mass of prodigious dimensions and untold mineral wealth, encompassing more than 375 million acres of land and water, an area twice the size of Texas with a good deal to spare. Its population at admission was estimated at only 212,500, including about 50,000 Eskimos, Aleuts, and Indians—or "natives"—and some 50,000 military personnel. Alaskans had been paying under $21 million a year in territorial and about $45 million in federal taxes. The territory's total bank deposits were only $160 million. An issue of long standing was the multiplicity of native land claims, based on aboriginal rights. The statehood law left this issue in status quo. It was understood that the United States would continue to provide services to the native population.

The small size of Alaska's population detracted nothing from Alaska's status as a sovereign state, but the miniscule number of the state's citizens, in relation to the great size and potential wealth of their state, may lend perspective and a touch of sardonic humor to the forensic struggles over native claims and the North Slope oil pipeline project. By 1970, the population had grown substantially but still was only 302,173, a little less than the number living in Norfolk, Virginia, a little more than the number in Birmingham or Rochester, New York, about one-tenth of 1 percent of the national total. Of the Alaskan total, natives accounted for one-fifth to one-sixth, and the Defense Department for 73,200, including military and civilian personnel and their dependents. There were about 28,000 nondefense government workers. Alaska's principal industry, in fact, was government. Alaska had a population density of 1 person to two square miles, while New York State had more than 380 to the square mile. In the late 1970s, the population of Alaska was well past the 400,000 mark. The mammoth oil pipeline brought many thousands to the northernmost state, of course, and some of them would stay on.

As a Russian possession and later as a fiefdom of the Interior Department and the mainland port of Seattle, Alaska had been ransacked in the past by hunters, trappers, commercial fishermen, and seekers of gold and copper. The gold brought thousands to Skagway and Nome and the Yukon in the late 1890s. The miners came and went, making no great impact on the lonely and forbidding wastes of the North. World War II caused a boom of sorts. Construction of the cold war's Distant Early Warning line helped the economy along. Copper and coal had played out, not because they were exhausted, but because of economic factors outside Alaska's control. The fisheries were rich and productive. Lumber was produced in the Chugach and Tongass national forests in the more temperate south and southeast, mainly for export to Japan.

The Alaskan role, however, had traditionally been that of an exploited colony, run from the outside, not getting much from the extractive industries that took its resources, until the petroleum boom raised the ante.[1] It was faraway and forgotten, and its climate and terrain tended to defy settlement. Not until the oil industry came in did Alaskans begin to see much real money. In the light of the region's history of poverty and omnipresent federal meddling, the hearty enthusiasm for oil development was not surprising. Oil began making its contribution after the day in July 1957 when the Richfield Oil Company made a strike in the Swanson River Field on the Kenai National Moose Range, a 2,700-square-mile federal reserve below Anchorage, established by Secretary Ickes in 1941. The range was opened to oil exploration in 1955 by Secretary McKay, a move that dismayed wildlife enthusiasts but mightily pleased Alaska's Gov. Ernest Gruening, soon to enter the Senate. He was an able intellectual and a towering figure in the state's politics for many years. There was no sensible reason, he insisted, for the federal withdrawal of two million acres from development to provide habitat for moose.

In his history of Alaska, Gruening noted that the state was producing no oil commercially in 1955 but that by 1966 oil and natural gas accounted for 60 percent of mineral output and generated $19 million in lease rentals and royalties for the state. "A great new industry had been brought to Alaska," Senator Gruening wrote, "saving the state from bankruptcy."[2]

The town of Kenai, on the eastern shore of Cook Inlet, was the "Oil Capital of Alaska" at the time of the Prudhoe Bay strike far away in the trackless North. Along with its old Russian church and magnificent marine view, it offered a brand-new Tulsa-style motel in the middle of a shopping center, a long strip development, and a cluster or two of oil company suburban homes. A

394

line of big oil rigs stood out in the blue inlet, each of them with its corona of flaring natural gas, and north of town were a helicopter pad and a dock complex servicing the offshore rigs. Out in the water, the nine-knot current and the ice in winter, which can be four or five feet thick, made life interesting for the men on duty.

Kenai was not the center of interest for long. The presence of large quantities of oil lying beneath the North Slope had long been suspected. In World War II, the Navy had undertaken exploration of its ice-locked Petroleum Reserve Number 4, usually called Pet 4, a bleak, 37,000-square-mile wilderness around Barrow set aside in 1923 by President Harding and turned over to the Interior Department in June 1977. Oil and gas were found, but there was no production. The Prudhoe Bay find was made just to the East, in a strip of two million acres of state land selected from the federal domain in 1964. It runs for about 100 miles along the shore of the Arctic Ocean, from the eastern edge of the navy's reserve at the Colville River to the western edge of the 14,000-square-mile Arctic National Wildlife Range, which was established in 1960 from the Canning River to the Canadian border and became more interesting to oil geologists as time went by.

Although the Prudhoe Bay country was a traditional fishing and hunting ground for Eskimos, the land had changed from federal to state hands without more than pro forma notice to them. Alaska's natives became more assertive with their land claims as the state selected choice parcels, and in consequence Interior Secretary Udall in 1967 put a "freeze" on the selection process to safeguard native rights. The clampdown came at a time when less than ten million acres had been transferred to the state, and it was widely protested in Alaska as a freeze on development. Udall, however, persevered. He insisted he had no choice.

For Alaska, the Cinderella among states, still sweeping up after its terrifying 1964 earthquake and hemmed in by the

395

federal presence, the North Slope was a vision of infinite riches. A fever of euphoria and excitement seized the state from its mountain-fringed southern capital at Juneau to the faraway northern slope, which hummed with activity. The Big Three on the North Slope—Atlantic Richfield, Humble, and British Petroleum—held out a cornucopia of riches. The University of Alaska estimated that state revenues from Prudhoe Bay could be running close to $1 million a day when the proposed pipeline was operating at its full capacity of two million barrels daily. Such a flow of dollars would run up a larger sum than the state's total general fund expenditures at the time. A difficulty was that the state's natives, well represented by lawyers, were asserting "Indian title" to about 80 percent of the state.

The North Slope's Big Three among the exploring petroleum giants announced in February 1969 their plans for getting the oil to market, a problem that had to be solved before the new field could yield a dollar in profits or a penny in revenue. They proposed building a forty-eight-inch pipeline running from Prudhoe Bay across three mountain ranges to Valdez, a distance of nearly 800 miles. It was described as the largest single private construction project in the free world. The early cost estimates were in the $900 million range, but inflation and other factors pushed them skyward.[3]

Secretary Hickel, who had shown a keen interest in the incipient Prudhoe Bay bonanza when he was governor of Alaska, reacted to the pipeline proposal by creating the North Slope Task Force in his department. He gave it the mission of making sure that the environment was safeguarded and native rights protected. President Nixon, newly ensconced in the White House, was not oblivious to what was going on. He ordered Hickel to enlarge the task force in May 1969, bringing in the Departments of Defense, Transportation, Commerce, Health, Education, and Welfare, and Housing and Urban Development. In June the oil industry consortium, known then as the Trans-Alaska Pipeline System, or TAPS, and later as Alyeska Pipeline Service Company, filed application with the Bureau of Land Management at Anchorage for a right-of-way across federal land for the pipeline and an associated construction road. In July the state of Alaska, seeking to help the enterprise along, asked the Interior Department to modify the land freeze to permit construction by the company of a fifty-three-mile secondary highway paralleling the pipeline route from Livengood, a hamlet north of Fairbanks, to the Yukon River. This highway into a roadless wilderness was the first element of the titanic project.

In the light of the furor that had raged over the spilling of oil into the Santa Barbara Channel from a blowout of an offshore drilling rig on January 27, 1969, only four days after Secretary Hickel had been confirmed, the TAPS combine was amazingly unrealistic in its expectation of prompt federal action on the pipeline right-of-way. Equally unrealistic was the confidence of state and federal officials, along with the state's delegation in Congress, that the enterprise would go smoothly. TAPS in its June application to BLM asked a favorable response "by July." With permit in hand, the companies intended to build their haul road that autumn (as they in fact did), make arrangements with contractors before the snow flew, and begin actual pipeline construction in the early spring of 1970. For a time that gung-ho schedule found acceptance. Alaska Sen. Ted Stevens, Republican, and Sen. Mike Gravel, Democrat, were impatient of delay. Even the levelheaded under secretary of interior, Russell E. Train, was telling the Senate Interior Committee in mid-October that "we in this department believe that there is sufficient knowledge at this time and sufficient assurance that unresolved questions will be answered satisfactorily in due course, to permit a deliberate, careful going ahead with this project."[4]

Back in April 1969, the combine had ordered its pipe from Japan. The pipe was already being delivered at the port of Valdez. Its cost was put at about $100 million. This and other busy preparations had the effect of crowding the decision makers. Conservationists saw it as the time-honored industry tactic of

presenting government red-tape artists with a *fait accompli.*
Hickel's jarring brush with the environmentalists at his confirmation hearings, however, had taught him a lesson. He demonstrated in the Santa Barbara pollution mishap that he was not
the bat boy for the oil industry some had suspected he might be
when Nixon chose him for the cabinet. He did not hesitate to
tell the TAPS people, publicly, that it was ridiculous to expect
the government to act on a matter of such magnitude within a
few weeks. It would take more time than that, said he, to get a
permit to tear up a street in Anchorage.

But nobody seems to have foreseen, in the frantic summer
and fall of 1969, the dimensions of the engineering and environmental problems that the giant oil pipeline faced, or the tenacity
and effectiveness of the conservationist campaign that would be
launched against it. None could have anticipated, of course, that
Congress would approve late in December the historic National
Environmental Policy Act, which Nixon signed into law at San
Clemente on the very first day of the new year, 1970. During
most of 1969, the go-ahead spirit was strong. While conservationists were bringing up their troops, hoping for delay if nothing else, Congress labored with the native claims and pipeline
issues while the Interior Department sweated over "stipulations" for construction and operation of the pipeline. Meanwhile, Alaska, on September 10, had its internationally publicized day of rejoicing when oil titans vied with one another to
pay the state nearly $1 billion for leases on half the amount of
North Slope land that had been let earlier for only $12 million.

There were whistles and cheers as the bids were opened. It
was a lot of money for a state that had little. The bidding companies went through dramatic gyrations as they worked out
their combinations. A "mystery train" shuttled back and forth
between Calgary and Edmonton in Canada, with oil executives
aboard to formulate joint bids. News reporters gathered in
Alaska for the fun. The lease sale was conducted by Thomas
Kelly, who had been appointed state commissioner of natural

resources by Governor Hickel. Kelly was a former oil-industry geologist, a transplanted Texan, and the stepson of Michael Halbouty, head of Halbouty Oil Company. Large though the state's take from the sale was, critics said it should have been larger. Kelly favored bids with the largest cash bonuses and the standard 12 ½ percent royalty, which was small compared to the 25 percent being paid in Oklahoma and the even larger royalties elsewhere. Bidders who offered smaller bonuses but larger royalties—27 ½ to 37 ½ percent—filed suit after Kelly decided to take the cash and let the royalties go. The dissidents contended the state would gain more in the long run from larger royalties. Therefore, they said, a gift of public money had been made to the winners, and the state constitution had thereby been violated. Kelly, a good-humored young man, said he thought the state had come out very well. An oil scholar who encountered Kelly in Alaska quoted him as remarking, "I know how to deal with vultures—I am one of them." The scholar's comment was that in the past the industries that came to Alaska had taken money out. "The illusion is that oil is going to be different," he said. Time would tell.

A few weeks after the lease sale, I visited Alaska on a reporting trip and talked to dozens of people in various walks of life. Most of them strongly favored the pipeline. Some deplored it. Virtually all assumed it was going to be built. Conservation-minded Alaskans, of whom there were many, seemed to regard the pipeline as inevitable and were concerned about taking the time to iron out the problems and do the job safely and correctly, with minimum damage. Among intellectuals and professionals, it was not uncommon to find a euphoric vision of what Alaska's future might be now that its fortune seemed secure. Limitless oil in the North. The Northwest Passage opened to commercial shipping. Alaska at the hub of world commerce, a center of international trade. Oceans of oil on top of the world. Alaska with 69 percent of the nation's Continental Shelf. Delicate negotiations between the United States and Canada over policing and ownership of the Arctic. And so on. It was heady stuff.

I traveled to Alaska the long and slow way, a good introduction for the newcomer because it gave an idea of the country and the distances. Sailing at 6:00 in the evening from Seattle on the motor vessel *Matanuska*, owned by the state of Alaska. Up the foggy and haunting Inside Passage along the Canadian shore. Three days and four nights via Ketchikan, Wrangell, and Sitka to Juneau, a capital locked in by coastal mountains and 573 air miles from the state's principal city at Anchorage. Then northwest by plane to Skagway, the old gold town, and from there northeast over the mountains by the White Pass and Yukon Railroad to Whitehorse in Canada. From there by rented car on the graveled Alaska Highway to Tok Junction in Alaska, and thence to Valdez and finally Anchorage on a better road. With Anchorage as a base, side trips to the North Slope, Fairbanks, and Nome by air and to the Kenai Peninsula by car. I was in the state a little more than three weeks. I never visited a place where the people seemed warmer or more friendly or more generous. At times it seemed well-nigh impossible for a stranger to pay for his own drink at a bar.

"The ordinary guy in Alaska," I had been told by a federal official in Washington, D.C., who had a long familiarity with the state and its politics, "is all for development and to hell with conservation."

That was during a conversation of the kind a newspaper reporter tries to have, by way of briefings, before going to a new place. My informant, a Democrat, told me the second team was in, politically, all the way around in Alaska. He characterized Gov. Keith Miller, who stepped into the office when Hickel entered the cabinet, as a lightweight. Miller had been a holly and mistletoe dealer and had settled on a homestead in the Susitna Valley in the 1950s. He had decided to run for secretary of state in 1966 and was dragged in with Hickel, who ran an excellent race and came from behind to beat Democrat William A. Egan, the state's first elected governor, by 1,080 votes. Miller was behaving like a governor and trying to do a good job. The first team in Alaska, in my informant's opinion, would have included Egan, former Senators Gruening and Bob Bartlett, and perhaps Hickel. All had been active in the statehood fight. The aging but still active Gruening had been beaten in 1968 by Mike Gravel, an Anchorage real estate developer and agile Democratic politician. Gravel defeated Gruening in the primary with the aid of a thirty-minute campaign film. The immensely respected Senator Bartlett died, creating a vacancy that Governor Hickel filled in December 1968 by appointing Ted Stevens, an Anchorage Republican who had served as assistant to Interior Secretary Seaton during the Eisenhower administration.

As for the Alaska natives, my informant said that five years earlier he would have answered that they did not have a legitimate claim. He would guess that fifteen years ago any claim they might have could have been bought up for $100,000. Now it was different. Most Alaskans thought the natives probably had something coming, although many of the whites could not see why a racial group that enjoyed full citizenship—voting, paying taxes, serving in the legislature—should receive a huge settlement. The general hope was that Congress would quickly settle the claims issue, with the federal government paying the bill.

Another point emphasized—significant to one trying to sort out the rights and wrongs as Alaska cashed in on some of its natural wealth—was the malaise among citizens there about what Senator Gruening used to call "American colonialism" and what some considered to be the dead hand of the federal bureaucracy, a hand that chilled development and enterprise.

"All the mistakes made in the south forty-eight," my informant said in our not-for-attribution talk, "were overcorrected in Alaska. It has been almost impossible to do anything in Alaska."

In that autumn of 1969, Udall's freeze was still effective. It was holding the state back, in a sense, but it was also keeping Alaska from being invaded and ruined overnight. It was a good and necessary thing. I could understand, though, the attitude of a young trucker with whom I had a drink one night at Hickel's Traveler's Inn in Fairbanks. He had led a truck convoy the previous winter on the controversial "Hickel Highway," a $1.4 million ice road built by the state. The convoy made Prudhoe Bay in eight days, taking up groceries, tractors, prefabricated buildings, and the like. The trucks ran eighteen hours a day. Engines going all night while the drivers slept. Twelve-volt coffeepots in the cabs. Macaroni and cheese warming on the manifolds. Radio contact between the trucks. It got down to sixty-nine below zero. The trucker said the trucks would roll the coming winter whether or not the state kept up the ice road, with its ice bridge over the Yukon.

"If you don't need a road to the North Slope, the biggest oil boom in the world, then you don't need a road anywhere," he said emphatically.

I returned from Alaska fascinated by the state's grandeur and convinced that the pipeline would become a reality regardless of what the conservationists might do. The question on the minds of many sophisticated Alaskans was not whether the project would be built—they assumed it would be—but whether an essentially weak and geographically balkanized state government could deal with the pressures that were building up. From the 1920s until statehood, Alaska felt itself under the thumb of an absentee salmon industry whose lobby had great power in the state legislature and in the Interior Department. With the oil industry riding high, some in Alaska feared a return of that kind of thralldom.

In the year of the billion-dollar North Slope bonus bidding, two things had to be done before oil could move from Prudhoe Bay. One was the settlement of native claims, which encumbered the titles to land. The other was the construction of the pipeline, which required a federal permit because the right-of-way lay across federal land. Congress dealt with the claims issue first and, in doing so, laid the foundation for a general land settlement in Alaska.

Many white Alaskans regarded the native-claims issue as a nuisance, a shakedown, a lawyer's dream, a piece of romantic blackmail. From a broader perspective, the claims were a matter of highest importance, involving the nation's honesty and integrity in dealing with a minority of some 60,000 to 90,000 Eskimos, Aleuts, and Indians, many of them poor and ignorant. In any event, until Congress had extinguished by fair means or foul the vague but all-pervasive claims of the aborigines to nearly all of Alaska, including the oil-rich North Slope, the state's development could not proceed. Private interests could not determine who owned what. The state could not go ahead with selection of the 103 million acres granted at statehood, and the federal government itself was unable to decide what federal lands should be retained for national parks and other purposes.

In former days, most of the federally owned lands in Alaska had been protected from invasion by their very inaccessibility, if not by their climate and their uselessness for agriculture. Statehood and the opening up of corridors to the North Slope and elsewhere were rapidly changing that situation, bringing a clash of interests that impelled the Udall land freeze in the late 1960s. Of Alaska's 375 million acres—bought from Russia 100 years earlier for two cents an acre—only 125 million were below the 1,000-foot level, and only 1 percent were arable.

It had already been well established in the courts that aboriginal claims were a moral rather than a legal right and that Congress had exclusive power to deal with them—in fact, could extinguish them without compensation if it chose. Putting rhetoric and sentimentality aside, the questions to be answered in the settlement were, in their broad terms, fairly simple. How much land and money should the Alaska natives—many of whom had adapted themselves to the general Alaskan culture—receive in return for the relinquishment forever of their traditional rights? Should the federal government shoulder the burden of compensation, or the state, or both? What about mineral rights?

The concept of a fair settlement escalated in price, nudged upward by the oil fever. Early in 1968, President Johnson had urged settlement in his message entitled "The Forgotten American."[5] In 1967, under Udall, the Interior Department had proposed about ten million acres of land and a cash payment based on what Russia received, $7.2 million. In 1968 the Interior Department's proposal was ten million acres and $180 million.[6] In 1969 it was fourteen to sixteen million acres and $500 million from the federal treasury, spread over twenty years.

When Hickel as governor of Alaska spoke in terms of $1 billion at House Interior Committee hearings in 1968, Chairman Aspinall noted that it would be a handsome sum for the less than 60,000 natives then in Alaska, inasmuch as all Indian claims thus far granted to Indian tribes in the lower forty-eight states had at that point amounted to only $251 million, and it was likely that all claims outside Alaska would not exceed $500 million. The Alaska natives had national public sentiment behind them, though, and they had good lawyers and mentors, not only those they retained privately but eminent public figures who volunteered their services, including former Supreme Court Justice Arthur Goldberg and former Attorney General Ramsey Clark. Americans had become sensitive to the great injustices done to native peoples in the past. There was a widespread feeling that, in the case of Alaska at least, a fair and equitable bargain should be struck.

At a Senate hearing early in the discussion, Secretary Udall observed that the native claims problem had been swept under the rug when the Statehood Act was passed, "and now we have lifted the rug and here it is."[7] A liberal western senator could not resist carrying the analogy a bit further. "After you lifted up the rug, you found an attorney, did you not?" remarked Sen. Clinton P. Anderson, Democrat of New Mexico.

After several years of debate and study, enlivened by humor, sentiment, and some hard bargaining, Congress agreed late in

1971 to award the waiting Alaska natives full title, including minerals, to forty million acres and a grant of $962.5 million, including $462.5 million to be paid from the United States Treasury over eleven years.[8] The other $500 million was to come from mineral revenues flowing from state and federal lands. This was largely a state burden, since the state received 90 percent of federal mineral revenues and would have gotten most of the $500 million if it had not been earmarked for the regional development corporations set up for benefit of the natives. It was laid down that state selections made before the Udall freeze, about twenty-six million acres, would be protected against native selection. That, of course, included the North Slope area, where the big oil strike was made.

A cynic might have observed that if the Alaskan Eskimos, Aleuts, and Indians had a valid claim to most of the state, they were poorly compensated. If their claim was not valid, they did quite well. They had been and remained, of course, an active and powerful force in state politics.

Thanks to conservation-minded members of the Senate and House, the claims bill as finally enacted contained safeguards against pell-mell exploitation. It established the Joint Federal-State Land Use Planning Commission for Alaska. This body was given advisory powers only but received a broad mandate for making recommendations about the parceling out of the state's extensive land riches. In addition, the bill provided machinery for orderly selection by the United States of choice areas suitable for national parks and other purposes in which Americans as a whole had an interest.

Here was a case in which the House, with Representative Aspinall still in charge of the Interior Committee, turned in a lackluster performance from the standpoint of intelligent land planning while the Senate did a better job and ultimately prevailed.

In the House, Representatives Saylor and Udall met defeat in a bitter fight to win passage of a conservationist-backed amendment that would have mandated comprehensive land planning

405

and reserved "national interest" lands in Alaska for possible use as parks or wildlife refuges. They lost by forty votes. Saylor, a committee member, warned that a great opportunity was being passed up. There would be no point in closing the gate after the horses were gone, he said, and the committee was "ignoring the real issues and placing its head in the oil." Saylor had a sharp tongue.

In the Senate's version of the bill, which came along later, Senators Jackson and Bible succeeded in adding, during floor debate, an amendment that provided for review by the secretary of the interior for possible parks, forests, and wildlife refuges. When the differences between the House and Senate bills were reconciled in conference, Jackson, Bible, Saylor, and Udall all served on the conference committee. The compromise bill emerged with a new provision directing Morton to withdraw "for study" as much as eighty million acres of federal land that he considered most suitable for national parks, forest, wildlife refuges, or wild and scenic rivers.[9] In effect, all unreserved federal public lands were to be protected for ninety days from all forms of entry, except for hard-rock mining, so that the secretary could make his review.

Again the land seekers and entrepreneurs were staved off, for the time being. Secretary Morton hailed the review provisions as an unprecedented opportunity—quite correctly—and set about the work with a flourish.

In the meantime, solving the problems that beset the proposed oil pipeline and its related federal permits and environmental safeguards turned out to more laborious and drawn out than quieting the native claims.

Despite the smooth, self-assured, steamrollerlike impression made by the drive to construct the pipeline, during the first months of public discussion it became apparent late in 1969 that Hickel and the Interior Department were seriously dissatisfied with the TAPS plan for the project. Hickel had asked the late William T. Pecora, the director of the Geological Survey and later

406

the under secretary, to make detailed studies directed toward finding out whether a hot oil pipeline could be built between the North Slope and Valdez and, if so, whether the line should be buried or built above ground. The oil would enter the pipe at temperatures between 158 and 178 degrees Fahrenheit and would remain at about the same heat during its entire journey through or over terrain that was mostly permafrost—that is, rock or soil material that remains frozen throughout the year. Inasmuch as Alaska's permafrost region includes 85 percent of the state and had already been a cause of notorious construction difficulties, a permafrost problem with the pipeline had been anticipated. In response to a set of questions posed by Train as chairman of the federal task force in June, R. G. Dulaney, chairman of the TAPS management committee at Houston, said about 95 percent—all but forty or fifty miles—would be buried. Burial was the established technique in normal climates, safer and cheaper than aboveground construction.

Late in the fall, Hickel got a report from Pecora which summarized a computer study estimating the thermal effects of a heated pipeline in permafrost.[10] It was written by Arthur H. Lachenbruch, a senior geophysicist at the Menlo Park, California, office of the Geological Survey. Lachenbruch's findings alarmed Hickel, who sent a letter to Senator Jackson on December 3 in which he said that certain major environmental and technological problems still remained to be answered with regard to the pipeline route, particularly with regard to permafrost engineering in the Copper River Basin between Fairbanks and Valdez.

Hickel called Jackson's attention to the following excerpt from the Lachenbruch summary as a matter of serious concern: "A four-foot pipe line buried several feet in permafrost and heated to 80 degrees Centigrade (176 degrees Fahrenheit) will thaw a cylindrical region 20 to 30 feet in diameter in a few years in typical permafrost materials. At the end of the second decade of operation, typical thawing depths would be 40 to 50 feet near the southern limit of permafrost and 35 to 40 feet in northern Alaska where permafrost is colder. In general, equilibrium conditions will not be reached and thawing will continue throughout the life of the pipe line, but at a progressively decreasing rate. If the thawed material or the water within it flows, these amounts of thawing can be increased several fold."

Also enclosed with Hickel's letter was a copy of the Train task force's preliminary report to President Nixon, submitted September 15 but not previously made public. Among other things, the Alaska task force said that TAPS had not yet prepared adequate final plans, on a technological level, for construction either of the pipeline or of ancillary projects. The task force listed outstanding problems still to be solved. It mentioned permafrost and the necessity of finding an acceptable source of gravel—more than thirteen million cubic yards of it—for insulation of construction over the ice. It also mentioned seismic activity along the route—after all, Valdez had been well-nigh swept away in the destructive earthquake and tidal waves of 1964—the disposal of solid and human waste, the danger of water pollution, and possible adverse effects on fish and wildlife.

Pecora was a competent geologist holding degrees from Princeton and Harvard. Capitol Hill had great confidence in him, as did Hickel. In a foreword to the Lachenbruch report, Pecora summed up the situation in six terse, clear paragraphs. He explained that until a year or so earlier, the pipeline concept had been considered in terms of transporting cold oil, but that subsequently TAPS had announced that, with a throughput of two million barrels a day, kicked along by pumping stations, the oil would be maintained at a high temperature.

"To bury a hot pipeline in hard rock or in coarse rocky terrain does not cause concern," Pecora said, "because the foundation is firm enough to support the pipeline without danger of disturbing it. But to bury a hot pipeline in permafrost ground composed of unconsolidated sediments with relatively high ice content could give us grave concern, not because of the melting

by itself, but because of the consequences of the melting if safeguards were not designed into the engineering system."

Pecora went on to express the belief that rapid thawing of the
permafrost in critical areas—the major one apparently being the
Copper River Basin—"could have most significant effects on the
local environment and upon the security of the pipeline itself."
He spoke of the importance of accommodating the problem by
proper engineering design, either above or below ground, or
else by "selection of alternative routes." The Copper River Basin
was the bed of an ancient lake, and in some parts the frozen
sediments were hundreds of feet thick. The pipeline would be
composed of mile after mile of heavy steel tubing, formed by a
succession of forty-foot joints, each weighing five tons when
empty, welded together end to end. Where the tube with its
cargo of hot oil had the support of rock or frozen gravel, there
was reasonable guarantee of stability. The old lake bed and certain other points along the route, however, conjured up a frightening image of a hot metal hose full of oil slipping and sliding
around in a soup of muck. Lachenbruch's term was "a semi-
liquid slurry."

The Lachenbruch analysis was in fact a nightmare, with its
dry, dispassionate discussion of what might happen to the
pipeline under this circumstance or that. Flow, and stress, and
shear. Ice-wedge networks melting away and leaving the pipe
unsupported. Seismic vibrations. The difficulty of detecting trouble in advance, even by drilling holes every 1,000 feet along the
way. It was like a medical description of the fate awaiting a
gutshot polar bear, which walks away after receiving the slug
but has within it the seed of its ultimate destruction.

Thus as 1970 began there were very real technical and engineering difficulties standing in the way of the trans-Alaska
project. Secretary Hickel on January 7 signed an order modify-
ing the Alaska land freeze in such a way that the right-of-way
for the pipeline could be granted, but he cautioned that approval
would not be forthcoming until "all geological and engineering

conditions have been met." Both the Senate and House interior committees had gone along with the action, but both took pains to tell Hickel formally that the responsibility for approving or disapproving the permit was his own. Although the secretary's modification of the freeze made it appear that issuance of the permit itself might come any day, the reality was that Hickel had no intention of allowing himself to be rushed into a disaster. The be-it-on-your-own-head attitude of the congressional mentors could be read in the same way.

Secretary Hickel met with the TAPS executives in his office in mid-January. It was unofficially reported to have been a stormy session, a meeting of a type in which the feisty and ambitious Hickel—who, whatever his other shortcomings, did not lack courage—was at no disadvantage. His official version of the meeting was that the parties had reached full understanding about the permafrost difficulty and that he, Hickel, stressed that "the pipeline will indeed be built." He said the project was a joint venture in which the cooperation his department had established with industry was of landmark quality. He did not say who his visitors were, but elsewhere it was learned they included Dulaney of Atlantic Richfield, George G. Hughes, Jr., of Humble, and Edward Wellbaum of British Petroleum.

All in all, the winter of 1969-70 was a chilly one for TAPS, even though the barrage of propaganda favoring the project never faltered. If the industry really thought it was going to get started in the spring with federal blessing, it was sadly disappointed. TAPS had not yet completed an expensive core-drilling program in the Copper River Basin. The Interior Department hinted at doubts regarding whether that part of the route was feasible at all. Hickel had already suggested that TAPS might avoid the treacherous basin by seeking an alternative port to Valdez, in the Whittier-Seward area closer to Anchorage. Jack Horton, the executive secretary of Train's federal task force, said Hickel wanted to "make damned sure this thing is built right."

"He has more at stake than any of us," Horton noted. "He has deep concern to make sure there is not an environmental catastrophe."

While Hickel held up the permit for the pipeline itself, he did nearly approve, in the spring of 1970, a right-of-way for a 390-mile haul road from the Yukon River to Prudhoe Bay. There were no roads up there. TAPS had already built the road from Livengood to the Yukon, and extending the road to the North Slope would be the next step. Hickel told the Associated Press late in March that he was ready to give permission for the road "momentarily." TAPS had proceeded to let certain contracts for construction work, and heavy machinery had been deployed along the route during the winter freeze. The go-ahead had to be given, it was argued, before the spring thaw about April 1 caused machinery to bog down and made work impossible.

At that point, TAPS and the Interior Department and the state of Alaska began running into a different type of roadblock: court action. Delays caused by litigation were to provide a cushion and a barrier that gave the engineers time to work out the permafrost problem at more leisure.

Two lawsuits, both of them brought in federal court in the District of Columbia, blocked Interior Department approval of the pipeline from April 1970. The obstacle remained in place until Congress acted to remove it more than three years later, in the autumn of 1973. Seldom has the power of the law and of the federal courts been demonstrated in a more dramatic fashion. The state of Alaska was in a tearing rush to get the oil out; the nation's most powerful industry underwent costly delay; the Interior Department and the president himself chafed at the bit. What stood in their path was a federal court order. A piece of paper.

The first of the two legal actions was brought against Secretary Hickel by the Alaskan Indian village of Allakaket and other villages and Indian individuals living along the proposed

411

pipeline route north of the Yukon, not far from the Arctic Circle. Represented by the prestigious Washington law firm of Arnold and Porter, the plaintiffs based their case on the absence of consent to the project rather than on environmental grounds. They sought a preliminary injunction against issuance of permits for a pipeline or road passing through a twenty-four-mile-long area of native-claimed land. They asserted a right of possession and of free enjoyment of their lands which was guaranteed, they said, by the purchase treaty with Russia in 1867 and by an 1884 act of Congress and affirmed by another in 1900. United States District Judge George L. Hart, Jr., set April 1 for the hearing date, and the Interior Department agreed to hold up permits until that date.

On April 1, 1970, Judge Hart lent a sympathetic ear to the Indian plea. He granted the restraint they sought and was deaf to Justice Department arguments that prompt action was needed because 700 to 800 pieces of equipment and heavy machinery, costing more than $40 million, had already crossed the Yukon on the ice and were incurring standby costs estimated at $120 thousand a day. When told that only about 400 Indians were living in the five villages figuring in the petition, Judge Hart said: "If there were only one in each village, and the law applied, the law would apply." He also remarked that granting the permits would take away the Indians' bargaining power, "and Heaven knows they've got little enough to start with."[11]

Daniel A. Rezneck, attorney representing the Indians, called attention to a significant affidavit filed in the case by Pecora of the Geological Survey. Pecora's statement was another dash of cold water on the huge project. He said a hot oil pipeline could be built *above* ground from the North Slope to Valdez and that a road could also be built safely. Pecora added, however, that the survey's Menlo Park office had reported that TAPS had not yet provided enough information to support a decision as to which parts of the pipeline could be buried with safety.

412

About a week before Judge Hart ruled for the Indians, the Wilderness Society and two other environmental groups, Friends of the Earth and Environmental Defense Fund Incorporated, entered the federal district court in Washington, on March 26, and asked for an injunction barring Secretary Hickel from issuing permits for the right-of-way, both for the pipeline and the haul road.[12] This action, the second of the two mentioned, was brought on environmental grounds, and it invoked the new NEPA, which Nixon had signed on the first day of the year. In this and other cases, NEPA was to prove a powerful weapon. The three plaintiffs cited the permafrost hazard, the mountains and numerous streams, the high-risk earthquake terrain, and other perils that might cause a pipeline break and a resultant oil spill, which would surely damage "part of the last great wilderness in the United States and one of the few remaining major ecosystems left on the earth in a relatively unspoiled condition."

The Wilderness Society and the others alleged that issuance of the permits would be unlawful because the Interior Department had not made the detailed impact statement required by section 102 of the NEPA, had not explored alternative actions to the proposed pipeline as the law dictated. Furthermore, the rights-of-way sought were wider than the fifty-four feet—that is, twenty-five feet on either side of a four-foot pipe—authorized by the Mineral Leasing Act of 1920. Building the pipeline would require thirteen to twenty-one million cubic yards of gravel, the taking of which could do harm to moose and other animals, fish, and birds. If the pipeline were built with large segments above ground, it was said, the raised structures would interfere with migratory movements of caribou and moose. Judge Hart agreed that NEPA had not been fully complied with, and the width of the right-of-way sought was not authorized. He granted the injunction sought.

In a telegram to the president dated April 1, nine conservation organizations asked Nixon to prevent the Interior Department from going ahead. The nine supported the Wilderness Society lawsuit. They said the pipeline could bring "devastating" consequences to Alaska and told the president, "The Alaskan environment is a natural resource which dwarfs in value the investment made in Alaska by the oil companies." Former Under Secretary of Interior Train, who had been named by Nixon to be the first chairman of the Council on Environmental Quality, created by NEPA, said publicly that he thought the TAPS haul road could wait until the route of the pipeline across the tundra had been determined. Train said the Interior Department's insistence on getting the facts before approving the pipeline itself would pay off, particularly in relation to the TAPS plan to bury the line along substantially the entire route.

"If we had accepted the companies' assurances," Train said in his makeshift temporary offices at the fledgling CEQ, "we could have been in a hell of a mess."[13]

The state of Alaska, though, was in no mood for dillydallying. Hardly was the ink on Judge Hart's injunction papers dry before Governor Miller gave TAPS permission to proceed with its haul road. The legality of that was questioned, and TAPS did not move. Miller then led a delegation of about 120 Alaskans on a pipeline-boosting jaunt to Washington.[14] The Alaskans arrived late in April 1970, on a state-chartered aircraft, to beat the drums, whoop things up, and present "the positive side of the pipeline problems." At the Interior Department the delegation received a sympathetic briefing. Alaskans consulted with members of Congress and blew off steam.

At a Washington luncheon of his "task force" before taking the plane back to Alaska, Governor Miller announced that he would ask the Alaska legislature to approve state construction of the 390-mile road that TAPS wanted from the Yukon to Prudhoe Bay. The task force seemed in hearty agreement, but in the end nothing came of it. Miller's high-hearted expedition was an exercise in futility. The thaws came, the ice on the river broke up, and the machinery spread along the roadway remained idle.

414

TAPS, a loose consortium without formal corporate structure, was joined by five other companies early in 1970. In his book written later, Hickel complained that TAPS was "seven Indians and no chief," with no single spokesman who could speak for all. It could take weeks, he said, to reach agreement on "what color to paint the toilets in the construction camps." In August, to Hickel's satisfaction, TAPS was replaced by the Alyeska Pipe Line Service Company, a legal corporate entity. In addition to Atlantic Richfield, British Petroleum as operator for Standard of Ohio, and Exxon (Humble), the companies involved were Mobil, Phillips, Union of California, and Amerada Hess. Home Oil was in for a while but eventually sold out to the others.

It was also in August that Secretary Hickel, whose star was declining faster than he knew, made a five-day tour of the Canadian and Alaskan Arctic with his opposite number in Canada, Minister of Indian Affairs and Northern Development Jean Chretien. They made one of those sweeping, broad-brush forays that occasionally reward men in public service. Chretien took Hickel to see Frobisher Bay above Hudson Strait, then to Melville Island and on to Inuvik, regarded by Canadians as a model Arctic community. In his turn, Hickel escorted Chretien to the Arctic Wildlife Range, Prudhoe Bay, and Barrow. The secretary spoke to the chamber of commerce at Anchorage. The North Polar ice cap, he told his audience exultantly, could become "the unifying bridge which brings mankind together." He said the way to develop the North's riches was to proceed slowly and do it right the first time. He pointed admiringly to the Russians, who had developed cities of more than 300,000 people north of the Arctic Circle. "Let us not fall into the trap of building now and mending later," he said in what became a litany of his public discourse.

There was a feeling among some Alaskans at the time, particularly in academic circles, that the Northwest Passage through Canadian waters would become a busy trade route. In 1969, the year following the Prudhoe Bay strike, Humble Oil had modified the 115,000-ton tanker *Manhattan* as an icebreaker and had sent it on an adventurous three-month passage from the East Coast to Prudhoe via the Northwest Passage. Early in 1970 the *Manhattan* made a second voyage. A suspicion frequently encountered among Alaskans was that for high diplomatic reasons, and perhaps others, the potential of the Northwest Passage for shipping was being played down.

In any event, the great Alaska pipeline controversy seemed to burn with a quiet fuse once the state and the industry failed to take the citadel by storm and became reconciled, more or less, to indefinite delay. Hickel had issued no permits when President Nixon fired him on Thanksgiving Eve of 1970, naming Morton in his place. In that same autumn, Egan regained the governorship of Alaska, and Democrats took over the state government. They were no less enthusiastic about the pipeline than the Republicans had been. The struggle over North Slope oil development warmed up again in January 1971, when another spring thaw on the Yukon was approaching and the Interior Department published its "draft" environmental impact statement as required by NEPA and the court.

Section 102 of NEPA laid on federal decision makers the obligation of making a detailed analysis of major federal actions significantly affecting the quality of the human environment. It required a study of alternatives to the course of action proposed. Nobody knew at first how seriously this might be taken. Interior's early faltering effort on the Yukon–North Slope road ran only eight pages and had been dismissed by Judge Hart as inadequate. Bestirring itself, the department returned to the battle on January 13, 1971, with a 196-page draft in which it purported to weigh the diverse factors. It concluded that the proposed pipeline could be built without unacceptable damage to the environment, that getting the North Slope oil out was essential to the nation's strength, growth, and security, and that the Prudhoe Bay–Valdez route was the best way to go.

At his confirmation hearings in late January, shortly after the draft was published, Morton finessed the issue of ultimate pipeline approval as a foregone conclusion but recognized that it must be safe and compatible with other land uses. "This pipeline won't be built on a Sunday afternoon, by a long shot, and we are going to have to monitor it as the work progresses," he said.[15]

At Washington hearings held by the Interior Department in mid-February 1971, chaired by Horton, the draft impact statement—which had been described as "impressive" in a *New York Times* editorial of January 26—got a savage mauling from conservationists. It had not, they said, paid enough attention to the earthquake peril; it had glossed over the hazards associated with tanker traffic over rough waters south of Valdez; it did not give proper consideration to choice of an all-overland pipeline route running down the Mackenzie River valley in Canada. The proponents also were out in force. Governor Egan led a state delegation. He pointed out that financially impoverished Alaska, facing grievous human problems of want and ignorance and disease, would have spent its $900 million by mid-1976. "We must have royalty oil flowing before that time or face bankruptcy," he said.[16] Egan contended that the North Slope oil belonged to the people of Alaska and that its development should be a choice for them to make.

What Governor Egan was saying was that the 302,000 or so people then living in Alaska could not make a living in that vast area without the North Slope's oil, the existence of which was not known when the state entered the Union.

The case for the conservationists against the Interior Department's draft was well and coldly put by James W. Moorman, the young lawyer who had figured in the *Wilderness Society et al.* lawsuit against Hickel. Moorman, speaking for the scientist-organized Environmental Defense Fund, complained that the department had not made the kind of statement required by

417

NEPA. Rather, he said, the statement simply offered "the Secretary's proposed final decision with his findings and conclusions set forth in detail."[17] Moorman felt there should be no decision until after a final environmental statement had been made available to the public, the Council on Environmental Quality, and the president.

"A reading of the draft," he continued, "suggests that the foreshadowed decision approving the pipeline has infected and corrupted the entire draft with an inappropriate spirit of advocacy for the pipeline. The result is that the environmental harm is understated throughout in order to expedite building the pipeline."[18]

Moorman was correct, of course. Former Interior Secretary Udall, speaking for the Wilderness Society, charged that the department had "largely ignored" the counsel of some of its own bureaus and experts.[19] He challenged Egan's statement that Alaska faced bankruptcy. Alaska was in fact, he said, the wealthiest among states. He urged that the burden be put upon the state, while the federal government still had the authority, to make a comprehensive land-use plan for the North Slope area. Congress, said Udall, had been "super-generous" with Alaska in the dowry provided with statehood, making concessions not offered in the cases of states admitted earlier.

There was a lot more said on both sides. At the hearing on the draft statement, the British Columbia opposition to the proposed increase in tanker traffic along the unspoiled Pacific coast emerged as a cardinal issue, along with consideration of the so-called Canadian alternative—putting the pipeline through Canada to the Midwest, thereby avoiding marine pollution and seismic hazards endemic to the North Slope–Valdez–West Coast route. David Anderson, a Canadian parliament member from Victoria, testified. He considered it "quite unworthy of the United States" that the country was going ahead with the tanker route without consulting its friendly neighbor to the north.

418

"We are not told what will happen after the oil leaves Prince William Sound," Moorman said, speaking of the succession of tankers loading at Valdez. "Yet we know that each tanker that leaves Prince William Sound must cross the stormy Gulf of Alaska and proceed down the yet unspoiled Pacific Coast of the Alaska panhandle and British Columbia. . . . We can look forward to massive oil spills along literally thousands of miles of the Pacific Coast of both the United States and Canada and in Washington's priceless Puget Sound."[20]

Secretary Morton gave assurance that the final draft statement would be "an objective, carefully weighed and balanced discussion of the environmental impact of the proposed project."[21]

With the complex native claims settlement out of the way at Christmas 1971 and the pipeline issue still tied up in court and unsettled as President Nixon's reelection year began, Morton's Interior Department made public on March 20, 1972, the long-awaited final environmental impact statement required by the NEPA.[22] The barbs directed against the previous year's unsatisfactory draft analysis had been effective.

The final impact statement on the Alaska pipeline set a new standard—in terms of physical dimensions, at least. The department obviously intended it to be overwhelming, a document so comprehensive and ponderous that no sane or sober person could challenge it. It consisted of six green-bound volumes for the impact statement itself plus three more slender volumes in yellow, the latter called *An Analysis of the Economic and Security Aspects of the Trans-Alaska Pipeline*, prepared by the department's Office of Economic Analysis. The total package weighed close to thirty pounds. It was given to the press in cardboard boxes at a briefing handled by Pecora, then under secretary. He said federal experts alone had put at least 175 man-years of work into it since the previous March.

"Certainly this is the most thorough, complete environmental impact statement ever prepared," Pecora said. Avoiding pitfalls of the earlier draft, the final statement carefully shied away from conclusions, and it devoted an entire volume to the problem of tanker traffic between Valdez and the West Coast ports, which earlier had been ignored. Reporters staggered away with their boxes of documents, about 3,550 pages of reading matter, a blockbuster of an impact statement. Unimpressed, the environmentalists vigorously denounced it. They urged President Nixon to allow new hearings. When Secretary Morton announced on May 11 that he had decided, on the basis of "our best national interest," to grant right-of-way permits as soon as that could be done without violating any court order, his decision was attacked as "capricious in the extreme." Critics complained about the $42.50 price put on the department's statement. They said additional copies should be made available to the public. The Wilderness Society and the two other plaintiffs in the injunction action—Environmental Defense Fund and Friends of the Earth—hastily put together a four-volume set of comments nearly as weighty as the department's and sent this answering salvo to Morton in May.

In the courts, in the newspapers, in the conservationist bulletins and magazines, and in advertisements taken by the oil industry and their opponents, the battle raged back and forth. *Wilderness Society* v. *Hickel* became *Wilderness Society* v. *Morton*. Morton could not issue the permits until the litigation was cleared up. The federal appellate court did not rule until February 1973, when it held that Morton lacked authority to grant permits of the width sought by the pipeline applicants. Under the law, fifty-four feet was all that could be granted, which meant Congress would have to act. Thus it was Congress that ultimately decided the pipeline would be built, in a specially tailored bill signed into law the following November. In the same law, Congress also squelched further conservationist action against the pipeline under NEPA. Opponents put up a hard fight. In the Senate, Vice President Agnew cast the deciding vote.[23]

420

This meant defeat for a coalition of midwestern members of Congress, conservationists, and others who wanted further study of the trans-Canada alternative and had pressed vigorously for a one-year independent review. One of the sponsors was the future vice president of the United States, Sen. Walter Mondale of Minnesota. Support for going across Canada was very strong but was overridden.[24] Ironically, Congress and President Carter in 1977 approved a route across Canada, roughly paralleling the Alcan Highway, for the multi-billion-dollar pipeline that had to be built to deliver the North Slope's natural gas to the United States.

In the case of the much more controversial oil pipeline, President Nixon signed the bill in November 1973, and Secretary Morton, with a flourish, issued the permit on January 23, 1974.

"Signing this permit," Morton said, "is deeply gratifying to me and to many other Interior Department officials, past and present, who labored through nearly five years of the most intensive environmental and technical studies, complex litigation, and legislative effort."[25]

Late in April the dirt began to fly. The pipeline consortium started work on the long-delayed road from the Yukon River, north of Fairbanks, to Prudhoe Bay. The first section of welded pipe was put into the ground beneath the Tonsina River, northeast of Valdez, about a year later. Construction of the line was a monumental undertaking that required as many as 21,600 people at one time. Rapid progress was made. Nine years after the Prudhoe Bay oil discovery, the first crude entered the pipeline on June 20, 1977, to begin the long journey south. It began pouring into the storage tanks at Valdez on July 29. The 883-foot tanker *Arco Juneau* delivered the first cargo of North Slope oil on August 5 to the refinery at Cherry Point, Washington. The *New York Times* front-paged a photograph of the tanker moving through Rosario Strait near the end of its voyage.

Alyeska had won victory after a long struggle. The conservationist side had suffered a Waterloo, but it could take consolation in the fact that the pipeline had been built in a safer fashion than if the battle had not taken place. Whereas initially the TAPS plan was to bury all but 40 or 50 miles of the nearly 800-mile length, at a total cost of less than $1 billion, the outcome was that more than 422 miles were put above ground. At the time of completion, the company estimated the cost at $7.7 billion. Some said it was $10 billion or more. Meanwhile, the world price of oil had quadrupled.

The terminal port of Valdez had grown from 1,000 residents to 10,000 during the oil boom, had seen its share of prostitutes and high jinks, and was down again to about 3,500.

Valdez is and doubtless always will remain a place where the works of man are dwarfed by the majesty of the natural setting—the great reach of the waters, the clouds and fog, and the mountains beyond. It is a scene that encourages the imagination to think of cataclysmic events to come, perhaps even primordial movements of earth and water such as did indeed take place in 1964.

The pipeline boosters in Alaska had waited a long time. Late in 1969 I drove over the Keystone Pass to the lovely little deep-water port of Valdez, where the Good Friday earthquake of 1964, centering beneath Prince William Sound, had left the town a pathetic litter. I had a cup of coffee with Mayor George Gilson, a Republican who ran the major clothing and grocery store. Mayor Gilson, who had attended the Naval Academy at Annapolis, spoke of the arrogance of the conservationists. He said a high-school biology teacher there had objected that a tanker might flood the harbor with oil. "Yes," the mayor had replied, "but what if the sun doesn't rise tomorrow? It's a cruel world, and you've got to take your chances."

Still awaiting Alaskans and the nation was a public question of greater importance than the pipeline. It was the issue of land disposal in Alaska, for which Congress set the stage in the Native Claims Act.

Bigfoot

Engelhardt in the St. Louis-Dispatch.

CHAPTER 16

CARVING THE LAST MELON

I'll tell you what is going to happen.—The State of Alaska will select all the valleys and they will leave the federal government the mountains.

—Former Interior Secretary Stewart
L. Udall in early 1971

The Alaskans sure as hell don't want to destroy Alaska. They love it. They just want to make a living.

—George C. Cheek of the American
Forest Institute in 1978

It is not our intention to "lock up" the State of Alaska, and our plan provides sufficient latitude for needed development.

—Interior Secretary Cecil D. Andrus
in September 1977

S eeing is believing, but seeing is not always possible. A small and fortunate band of reporters, traveling at their own or their employers' expense, accompanied Secretary of the Interior Cecil D. Andrus to Alaska in the summer of 1978. They traveled by light plane and helicopter, looking at certain "crown jewels" Andrus wanted to save for posterity. Many of the enchanting places they visited could be reached by the average American only with considerable cost and difficulty, if at all.

One of the not easily forgotten experiences was a brief glimpse of the Arrigetch Peaks in the Central Brooks Range, in the company of Ray Bane, a cultural anthropologist for the National Park Service. Helicopters set them down in a remote mountain valley above the Arctic Circle, a wild and silent place, miles from road or river.

It was very beautiful. The intruders were awed. Conversation was at a subdued level. Bane, a small and wiry West Virginian given to speaking his mind, knew all about the spot. He seized the opportunity to preach a sermon about the wilderness.

"I'll be very honest with you," Bane told those circled around him. "I don't like coming in here like this. I think you have to earn it."

Explaining this pronouncement, Bane said it was only right to establish parks that were readily accessible, where mom and dad and the old folks and little kids generally could view the scenery, but he regarded the Arrigetch Peaks to be at the other end of the natural spectrum: "This is where you come and earn it."

"I'm hoping to get in here next winter by dogsled, which means I'll snowshoe every mile of the way from Bettles," Bane went on. Bettles, where Bane lived, is about 100 miles from the Arrigetch Peaks as the crow flies. His winter journey, which his wife, Barbara, vowed to share, would take him along the frozen Kobuk River and then up-country through the snow.

Bane had formerly taught school. He had developed rapport with the Kobuk River Eskimos and had written about them. He flew his own plane, and in it he carried a folding boat. He was an excellent hand with sled dogs. On favorite subjects, such as the Eskimos and their land, he spoke quietly but with passion.

"Let's save real parts of Alaska—not just postage stamps," he was heard to say. "This country has a right to be, because it is."

Under Andrus's federal blueprint, which was hanging fire in the Senate at that time, the proposed Gates of the Arctic National Park in the Brooks Range would enfold the Arrigetch Peaks and some eight million acres of trackless wilderness besides. None could call that a postage stamp. It would be about four times the size of Yellowstone National Park.[1] In fact, Andrus's plans for protecting ninety-two million acres of federal land in Alaska would create five other parks, each dwarfing Yellowstone, the largest in the existing federal system.

Not every American might embrace Bane's views about keeping some of the places beyond easy reach or be able to follow him across the snow, but there can be no argument that the pristine back country will never be the same once it is penetrated by roads and exposed to mining and various forms of public entry. In this perspective, ease or difficulty of getting into an area is of the greatest importance.

Looking back, it is easy to grasp that, from a practical standpoint, there never was a chance that the development of Alaskan oil and natural gas would not take place. The federal and state governments promoted it from the start. Oil was the light at the end of the tunnel. It was oil bonus money that rescued the financially hard-pressed state from "bankruptcy," and it was oil money, or the promise of oil money to come, that formed the keystone for federal-state planning for Alaska's future. The smell of oil stirred up the native-claims issue, then helped put the issue to rest. Long before the pipeline finally was approved, Congress extinguished the native claims with a generous monetary and land settlement based on anticipated oil revenues.

But Congress also was persuaded, by farsighted members, to put into the settlement a mechanism whereby the United States as a nation could, if it wished, keep for the benefit of all the nation's citizens a goodly heritage in Alaska. This involved much more complex questions than the simple decision as to whether a pipeline should be built. In effect, it set the stage for a more or less final dividing up of Alaska's land. Historian Parrington, had he lived, might have put it another way. He might have called it the most glorious barbecue of all.

To the extent that Americans in the lower forty-eight states thought much about Alaska before and during the heyday of Watergate, they became vaguely aware of an interminable squabble over the pipeline. The post-Watergate period brought cryptic headline references to another titanic struggle: Alaska's "D-2" lands.

The focus of environmentalist concern in Alaska, once it was clear the drive to tap the North Slope's energy could not be blocked, was on the effort to preserve choice federal lands under terms of the Alaska Native Claims Settlement Act of 1971. In writing that law, it will be remembered, Congress in section 17 (d) (2) directed the secretary of the interior to withdraw no more than eighty million acres of public lands in Alaska for study as possible additions to the national park, national forest, wildlife refuge, and wild and scenic rivers systems. These lands were to be considered for additions to or creation of new units in the "four systems." Meanwhile, they were protected from all forms of appropriation under the public-land laws, including mining and mineral leasing.

This was a magnificent opportunity to reserve choice scenic and wildlife areas in public hands before they became hopelessly encrusted by private claims. Secretary Morton described himself as "excited about it because land use planning of this magnitude is the key to the quality of American life." He announced preliminary set-asides on March 15, 1972, and quickly found himself in a court battle with Alaska and Governor Egan concerning 40 million acres sought by both the state and the Interior Department. Early in September, Morton revealed that a lawsuit filed by the state in May had been settled by an agreement under which the state received prior right to 1.9 million acres of the disputed lands.[2] The Sierra Club called the settlement "a bad deal for the American people," contending Morton had yielded areas that should have been kept in federal ownership.

At a news conference, Morton and his aides were subjected to close questioning about the surrendered acreage. The land involved included mineral areas around the Alatna River in what would have been a southern segment of the proposed Gates of the Arctic National Park and also tracts on the southern slope of Mount McKinley, near Anchorage.[3] These were not the only concessions, to put it mildly, that would be made as the gigantic federal protection plan, through the Nixon, Ford, and Carter administrations, underwent the surgery of federal-state discussion and congressional scrutiny.

Morton persisted in his task of refining the federal choices for submission to Congress. There was a lengthy and largely unpublicized tussle between the Interior Department and Alaska, and among various agencies in the federal government, over colossal tracts of scenic Alaskan real estate in places still largely roadless and little penetrated. Morton completed his withdrawal of nearly seventy-nine million acres under the law in mid-September 1972.[4] This withdrawal was again preliminary and subject to further study. As critics of the withdrawals pointed out, Alaska already had more than forty-six million acres dedicated to federal management as national parks, forests, and wildlife refuges.

When Morton came up with his final, concrete recommendations to Congress on December 18, 1973, he proposed that more than eighty-three million additional acres of federal land in the state receive more or less permanent protection in the four systems,[5] noting that this would involve an approximate doubling of the acreage in the government's existing national park and national wildlife refuge systems. He asked Congress to more than double the size of Mount McKinley National Park and to establish three entirely new national parks, two of which, Gates of the Arctic in the Brooks Range and Wrangell–St. Elias in the mountainous southeast, would be larger than the nation's oldest and then largest park, Yellowstone. The third proposed new park was Lake Clark, in southern Alaska west of Anchorage. Three new national forests were recommended, along with numerous federal wildlife and scenic river areas.

Morton's proposals came under heavy fire from conservationists who complained that even though his plans were of gargantuan dimensions, he had been overly considerate of state, mining, and lumber interests. Morton was charged with having been too generous to the Agriculture Department's Forest Service, which was to have two new forests in interior Alaska, where the timber is poor, and a third adjacent to the proposed Wrangell–St. Elias National Park, in mineral-rich lowlands that the federal government wanted to leave open to mining entry. Morton, it was said, was asking that natural ecosystems be fragmented in order to permit them to be exploited by waiting entrepreneurs.

Inevitably, there had been bargaining and trading. More was to come. Secretary Morton's package had been put together by the Alaska Task Force, a federal interagency group headed by Assistant Secretary of the Interior Laurence E. Lynn. It included representatives of the Agriculture Department, whose Forest Service had vital interests at stake, and of the President's Office of Management and Budget. The Interior Department worked closely with the Joint Federal-State Land Use Planning Commission, which had been set up under the Alaska Native Claims Act. Interior's Jack Horton was the federal cochairman. Alaska's cochairman was State Sen. Joe Josephson.

From the standpoint of those seeking to open Alaska up for development, of course, there was more to consider than simply whether a block of land went to the state or remained in federal hands. Also of crucial importance was the type of federal ownership. A tract that went into a national park, for example, would be essentially "locked up" as far as mining and hunting were concerned, while land in a national forest or under the Bureau of Land Management would not. And leaving state aspirations aside, there was competition among federal agencies for a suitable share of the Alaskan feast.

Robert Cahn, one of the original members of the Council on Environmental Quality, wrote a comprehensive article in the July 1974 issue of *Audubon* magazine, in the course of which he described trade-offs between Morton and Earl L. Butz, the secretary of agriculture.[6] Agriculture's Forest Service already held virtually all the heavily forested country in southeast Alaska, but it sought an additional 42.5 million acres. Butz agreed to stay out of the Gates of the Arctic region, where the Forest Service had a proposal overlapping the proposed national park. After three meetings with Morton, he was offered and accepted a package of eighteen million acres, including the three new forests mentioned above plus a small addition to the existing Chugach Forest. The bonus for the Interior Department was retention under BLM control of the Fortymile River system along the Canadian border, which the Forest Service wanted.

Under the law, Congress had five years to act after Morton made his withdrawal proposals—that is, until December 1978. The federal lands in question were protected and could be studied at leisure.

President Ford, shortly after his nomination by the Republican party in 1976, paid a visit to Yellowstone Park, where he had served as a ranger in his youth. It was a beautiful day in late August. Standing with the Old Faithful geyser at his back, Ford unveiled a $1.5 billion proposal for expanding and improving the federal system of parks, recreation areas, wildlife refuges, and similar facilities over a ten-year period. The system would be more than doubled. Much of the expansion would consist of the growth already anticipated for Alaska.[7]

"Being alone with nature strengthens our love for one another and for our country," the president told a large crowd. The only dark cloud was projected by conservationists, who were on hand to give news reporters the view that, while Ford's new program was excellent, it came late in the game—considering the sorry state of parks and refuges—and was not consistent with his past policies.

"President Ford and his predecessor, Richard Nixon, have kept our wildlife refuges and national parks in the breadlines for years," said John W. Grandy of Defenders of Wildlife, a conservationist group. Montana's Democratic Gov. Tom Judge, who welcomed the president, commented that both the national parks and the national forests had been underfunded. He said he hoped the Ford proposal would be a serious effort to help the parks.

With the change in administrations from Republican to Democratic in 1977, President Carter and Interior Secretary Andrus pledged that the Alaskan four-systems land selections would receive highest environmental priority. Andrus put Cynthia Wilson, who had been the National Audubon Society's representative in Washington, in charge of the Interior Department task force shaping new proposals. On September 15, 1977, there was submitted to Congress a plan that fell well short of the 115 million acres proposed in the House bill sponsored by Democratic Rep. Morris K. Udall of Arizona but went well beyond what Morton had suggested in his package of December 1973, in terms of both size and the quality of federal protection sought.

Backed by President Carter, Andrus asked that 92 million acres be protected for the benefit of the American people as a whole. He proposed 41.7 million acres for ten new units of the National Park System and for expansion of three existing parks. He put another 45.1 million acres into the National Wildlife Refuges System and 2.45 million acres into the National Wild and Scenic Rivers System. He wiped out Morton's proposals for new national forests but added 2.5 million acres to existing forests in Alaska.

"Through enactment of our proposals," Andrus told the House interior subcommittee on general oversight and Alaska lands, "we can be certain that the crown jewels of Alaska—its most spectacular natural environments, recreation areas, and wildlife habitats—will remain intact for the benefit of our nation's citizens."[8]

In President Carter's environmental message the previous May, the president had said: "No conservation action the Ninety-fifth Congress could take would have more lasting value than this."[9]

Secretary Andrus's proposals affected an area nearly as large as California. His recommendations for additions to the national park and wildlife refuge systems were larger than Morton's by nearly 23 million acres, an area comparable to Ohio or Virginia in size. Andrus inclined toward the higher level of protection advocated by conservationists. For example, Morton urged a Wrangell–St. Elias National Park in south central Alaska of 8.64 million acres but flanked the spectacular mountain park with a two-unit Wrangell Mountains National Forest of 5.5 million acres in the lowland approaches. Morton mentioned the copper and other mineral deposits. Andrus wiped out the forest and proposed a 9.56-million-acre park, buffered by a less-protected National Park System "preserve" of another 2.49 million acres. These were tracts of stupendous size, totaling an area in the Wrangells alone about twice the size of Vermont.

"Let me suggest this," Secretary Andrus said on Capitol Hill as he presented his plans. " —If we err in this decision and exclude some precious and delicate areas from the four systems, these areas could be lost forever. Americans in the future could never enjoy them nor benefit from production from them. Alaska would be left with devastated areas rather than with preserved treasure, with a liability rather than an asset.

" —But if we err by conserving too much, this can always be changed in the future. Our system of government—as I needn't remind Members of Congress—responds to pressures from the people."[10]

This was a point Andrus was to make frequently as the legislation was shaped, twisted, and shaped again. He was not above pointing out, when accused of trying to put Alaska into cold storage, that his own state of Idaho received a federal grant of only 4,254,000 acres at statehood—8 percent of Idaho'a area—while Alaska was granted more than 104,000,000 acres, nearly one-third of Alaska's available land. In Alaska there would be, he kept saying, plenty of room for miners, loggers, hunters, fishermen, and others trying to make a living or enjoy life.

The Andrus proposals did not entirely satisfy the Alaska Coalition, a conservationist group organized to push for preservation of Alaska's "national interest wildlands," but the coalition gave him a commendation. It noted that some key areas omitted by Andrus could be restored by congressional action, which was to be completed by the end of 1978. Congress might also, of course, make decisions less palatable to conservationists than what Andrus proposed. But Andrus had been pragmatic about omitting known mineral areas, as was Morton, and he had worked closely with Alaska's Republican Gov. Jay S. Hammond, a former bush pilot and state senator, elected in 1974. There was optimism that Andrus would prevail.

As Secretary Andrus said, Alaska was an opportunity for avoiding the rash mistakes of the past. It was, he said, a kind of rejuvenation for the country, a chance to do things right. It was an opportunity that would not come again.

Conservationists and proponents of more or less unfettered Alaskan development girded for battle. The Sierra Club, the Wilderness Society, the National Audubon Society, the National Wildlife Federation, and other conservationist groups, large and small, organized their coalition and issued bulletins to their troops. Studies were made and articles written, with key areas of a glorious wonderland depicted in vivid color photographs. On the other side, those who took a dim view of the four-systems movement, in whole or part, also got ready. They included the

433

obvious extractive-industry groups, Alaska's delegation in Congress, the state's political leaders almost without exception, and doubtless the great majority of Alaskan citizens. A leading oppositional role was taken by Citizens for Management of Alaska Lands, or CMAL, formed late in 1976.[11]

Both these armies faced a difficult, expensive, and time-consuming task. They had first to get the attention of the American public in the lower forty-eight states, then attempt to put across their rival points of view. Neither could hope to explain all the details. Each insisted that Alaska's future was at stake.

At this point chronologically, while the hearings and the infighting over Alaskan land disposal were going on, it is appropriate to make a digression and return to Prudhoe Bay, which, having won a means of shipping out its oil, now needed a pipeline for natural gas.

There remained the problem of bringing to market the huge quantities of natural gas available on Alaska's North Slope, the largest reserve yet discovered in North America and estimated at more than twenty trillion cubic feet, or 5 percent of the nation's gas consumption for twenty-five years. In the 1960s in Cook Inlet, gas produced in association with oil was simply "flared" or wasted. With the Prudhoe Bay wells it was possible to reinject the gas for three or four years, but a way of getting it out had to be found. The first private industry application to the Federal Power Commission came in March 1974, shortly after Interior Secretary Morton had issued the permit for the hot oil pipeline. In due course the FPC had before it three competing proposals for delivering natural gas from Prudhoe Bay to markets in the lower forty-eight states, where it was in short supply. These would be cold pipelines, an important difference.

Earliest in the field, close on the heels of the trans-Alaska oil project, was the Alaskan Arctic Gas Pipeline Company's proposal for building 3,600 miles of new pipeline from Prudhoe Bay east across the Interior Department's Arctic National Wildlife Range into Canada and then down the Mackenzie River valley into Alberta, where it would divide, with one leg going into Montana and southeast into Illinois, the other into the Pacific Northwest into California. To be built by a consortium of United States and Canadian companies, the line was estimated to cost $6.73 billion in 1975 dollars and would deliver some 2.2 billion cubic feet of gas a day to United States markets. For a while the Arctic project looked like a winner.

Six months later, on September 24, 1974, El Paso Alaska Company sought FPC permission for an 809-mile pipeline that would follow the Alyeska oil pipeline corridor down through Alaska to Point Gravina on the coast just southeast of Valdez, the oil terminal. At Point Gravina the gas would be liquefied and shipped 1,900 nautical miles south by a fleet of eight cryogenic tankers to Point Conception in California, where it would be re-gasified. The estimated cost was $6.57 billion and the capability about 2.1 billion cubic feet daily. In Alaska, which needed gas-distribution facilities and stood to benefit from the economic activity, the El Paso plan had substantial support.

It was not until nearly two years later, on July 9, 1976, that a third application was filed which soon moved to the front as a sort of compromise. Alcan Pipeline Company and Northwest Corporation proposed 3,000 miles of new pipeline that, like the Arctic plan, would deliver the gas overland via Canada. Instead of trespassing on the wildlife range, however, Alcan proposed following the Alyeska route in Alaska, like El Paso, to a point south of Fairbanks, where it would swing east into Canada and follow the World War II Alcan Highway corridor. The original plan was later revised to call for 3,900 miles of new line, with an estimated cost of $6.76 billion and a delivery capability of at least 2.2 billion cubic feet a day.

These were gigantic enterprises, but they generated nothing like the controversy that attended the genesis of the long-debated oil pipeline. Environmentalists did warmly oppose Arctic's plan for crossing the virtually untouched, 8.9-million-acre wildlife range east of Prudhoe Bay, and they preferred the Alcan compromise to the El Paso plan. In contrast, members of Congress from upper midwestern states got behind the Arctic proposal initially, because it would deliver gas to their region. The rival entrepreneurs and their supporters vigorously thumped the tub for their competing blueprints for delivery. To put the decision in an orderly framework and push action, Congress passed the Alaskan Natural Gas Transportation Act of 1976, forcing a presidential choice by September 1, 1977, or, at the latest, by December 1.[12]

At the FPC, hearings had been going on since April 1975 before Administrative Law Judge Nahum Litt. The judge sat for 253 days and assembled 44,458 pages of transcripts together with numerous exhibits. On February 1, 1977, he issued an initial decision recommending approval for Arctic's trans-Canadian application. The FPC staff, meanwhile, favored Alcan. The commission itself then received briefs, heard oral arguments, and came out on May 2 with a recommendation to the president favoring an overland route but indecisive as to which one. Commissioners Don S. Smith and John H. Holloman III favored Arctic. Chairman Richard L. Dunham and a fourth commissioner, James G. Watt, later to be secretary to the interior, favored Alcan. The commission members found all three proposals technically and economically feasible, and they concluded a system should be built.

In the case of the oil pipeline, with its threat of oil pollution along Canada's west coast, there had been complaints that the United States moved ahead in high-handed disregard for Canadian attitudes. National-security reasons were often cited as a factor weighing against choice of a route across Canada. By this was meant not only that the nation could not afford to risk delays and uncertainties in getting the oil out but also simply that the line across Canada would be subject to the whims of a foreign state. Even President Ford himself, when he was in Congress, had hinted darkly—and publicly—that the United States could not assume there would always be a friendly government in Canada.[13] As to the long sea journey involved in the selected route, there was evident a touching faith in the ability of the American navy to guard against submarine interdiction.

The gas pipeline proposal, for reasons that were not made entirely clear, was a different story. Cooperation between the two countries was excellent, the security consideration was muted, and common sense prevailed. Canada was busy in the spring of 1977 with gas pipeline studies, as was the United States. A Royal Commission of Inquiry headed by Justice Thomas R. Berger looked at the proposition as it might affect crown lands and native peoples in the upper Yukon and Northwest territories. The Berger commission, set up in 1974, examined the socioeconomic and environmental impacts, and in May it issued an initial report throwing cold water on any immediate construction in the Mackenzie River valley. In July, Canada's National Energy Board rejected the northern route proposed by Arctic but gave its qualified blessing to Alcan's route along the Alaska Highway. Alcan also received qualified support from two other Canadian panels, including one chaired by British Columbia Law School Dean Kenneth Lysyk. Parliament debated the issue, after which the Canadian government announced its approval of a line through the southern Yukon—that is, Alcan's proposal.

The midwestern members of Congress who earlier had backed Arctic's plan for cutting across the wildlife range switched to the front-running Alcan plan for swinging well to the south before entering Canada. Arctic Gas's participants abandoned their own project perforce and got on the Alcan bandwagon. Senator Stevens of Alaska held out stubbornly for the El Paso trans-Alaska route, but in vain.[14] Finally, on September 8, President Carter and Canadian Prime Minister Pierre Elliott Trudeau appeared together at the White House and made a joint statement.[15]

"Today we have agreed in principle," they announced, "on the elements of a joint proposal to construct the Alcan-Foothills pipeline along the Alaska Highway to transport Alaskan natural gas through Canada to the lower forty-eight states and at a later time Canadian gas to Canadian markets.

"This joint undertaking will be the largest single private energy project in history."

It was said that the Alcan plan would save American consumers $6 billion during the project's life, as compared to the El Paso alternative. Daily deliveries of more than 3.5 billion cubic feet of gas a day could be expected. Both countries insisted the project be financed entirely with private funds. Total cost estimates were $13 to $14 billion at the time of the 1977 agreement, but by 1979, with no actual construction yet undertaken, the figures had moved upward to $15 billion. About 735 miles of the 4,800-mile pipeline system would be in Alaska.

Congress approved President Carter's decision with alacrity. The president made his recommendation on September 21, and the Senate and House of Representatives approved it by joint resolution on November 2. Alaskans were not unhappy with the decision once it had been made. The state would benefit from the estimated $3.4 billion cost of the Alaska leg, which would employ 9,000 workers at the peak of the construction phase. As Senator Stevens explained, most Alaskans originally favored the El Paso proposal because it would have created a large capital investment in the state and would have made gas available in the southern tidewater region, which has a good industrial potential. Alcan would deliver gas to Fairbanks, however, if not to Anchorage.

As can be seen, the intensity of conservationist fury over the natural-gas pipeline was not great, compared to what had been generated by the oil pipeline. Once the threat to the Arctic National Wildlife Range had been averted, relative calm prevailed. The oil, after all, was now flowing southward, and it was difficult to argue that the natural gas should be wasted or left untapped. Moreover, the gas line would be cold and therefore less subject to permafrost troubles.

Leaving the gas-pipeline planners to find the money, do their planning, and wend their way through the United States–Canadian regulatory tangle with the objective of completing the project by 1984 or 1985, Congress snipped and fiddled with the "D-2" land proposals for Alaska. The lobbying was intense.

Early in 1978, Rep. Mo Udall, chairman of the House Interior Committee and Rep. John Seiberling, the Ohio Democrat who headed the Alaska lands subcommittee, strove heroically to push the bill through. They found it necessary to do a great deal of compromising.

"You throw them a little meat, and they want the whole body," Seiberling was heard to remark after a brush with a mining magnate. It was, he said, like dealing with sharks.

On March 21, Udall managed to steer a badly mauled but still recognizable and generally satisfactory bill through his committee with a favorable vote of thirty-two to thirteen. The bill also got through the Merchant Marine and Fisheries Committee. Udall had proposed originally that 147 million acres of federal Alaska be given protection under the 1964 Wilderness Act. His committee cut the figure down to about 73 million.

Udall had to delete a plan to give wilderness status to the Misty Fjords area in southeastern Alaska, a matter of 2.34 million acres. It is a remote and beautiful place where molybdenum had been found. The committee also agreed to a special oil and gas study of the cherished Arctic National Wildlife Range, east of Prudhoe Bay.

Alaska's Republican Rep. Don Young, an Interior Committee member, worked effectively against the bill, as did Washington State Democrat Lloyd Meeds.

Despite the cross fire, the House as a whole passed the Alaska national interest lands bill overwhelmingly on May 19, 277 to 31.[16] The bill had the administration's support and was roughly equivalent to what Andrus had sought. It offered enhanced protection for about 100 million acres.

Alaska's Senator Stevens was ready on the other side of Capitol Hill with a counterproposal, introduced a year earlier, that conservationists and Secretary Andrus did not consider satisfactory. Stevens wanted to put only 25 million acres into the federal four systems—about one-fourth of the acreage in the House-approved bill. In addition, he would place some 140 million acres of federal and state lands under a cooperative management status, for multiple-use purposes.

Stevens made a tough fight. In June he summoned Interior Secretary Andrus to the Hill and grilled him about the administration's "lobbying" and public-relations campaign in support of the massive Alaskan land set-asides. Andrus stood his ground.

As minority whip and the ranking Republican on the appropriations subcommittee handling Interior Department matters, Senator Stevens had a powerful position. He had the support of Majority Leader Robert C. Byrd of West Virginia, who said he would not call the bill to the Senate floor if Stevens and the Alaska Democrat, Mike Gravel, were against it.

The result was that Congress went home in 1978 without Senate action on the Alaskan lands. Stevens wanted to compromise, but Gravel threatened a filibuster, and the Senate, busy as always, went on to other things. President Carter immediately took executive action to hold the issue in status quo until the Congress could express its will.[17]

In the spring of 1979, Representative Udall's committee got out of hand and approved by narrow margin, twenty-three to twenty, a substitute Alaskan bill that Udall, other like-minded colleagues, the administration, and the conservationist forces found unacceptable. The Udall forces rallied and backed an alternative sponsored by Udall, Seiberling, and Illinois Republican John B. Anderson, who would become a candidate for the presidency in 1980. The conservationists turned the tide and won a remarkable victory on May 16 when the House adopted their version, 360 to 65.[18]

In a number of respects, the 1979 House bill was an improvement over the 1978 one from the standpoint of the conservationist lobby. The Arctic National Wildlife Range would be placed in the wilderness system *in toto,* as would Admiralty Island, in the southeast, and the aforementioned Misty Fjords.

"The victory in the House this year was even more remarkable than last year because opponents of a good conservation bill had been geared up and working so long," said Edgar Wayburn, chairman of the Sierra Club's Alaska Task Force.

"They had poured immense amounts of money into their campaign and attempted to match our work in the grass roots. In Washington, their lobbyists were all over the 'Hill' —the oil and lumber interests, the Chamber of Commerce, the Committee for Alaska Lands, the State of Alaska, and others. However, the size of the vote demonstrated conclusively that the American people value most highly their stake in Alaska's wilderness and are determined to protect it."

The spotlight turned to the Senate, where the Energy and Natural Resources Committee under Senator Jackson, formerly the Interior Committee, made slow progress and finally, on October 30, reported a bill that conservationists found very disappointing. They considered it too soft on mining in the Wrangells–St. Elias and Gates of the Arctic national park proposals, too encouraging of private exploration of the Arctic National Wildlife Range, and too stingy in allocating wilderness acreage.[19]

This was a setback for proponents of the Carter administration viewpoint. However, the Jackson committee report contained a series of strong dissents signed by Democratic Senators Paul E. Tsongas of Massachusetts, Howard M. Metzenbaum of Ohio, and others. Senate Majority Leader Byrd of West Virginia said the bill would not be brought up on the Senate floor until after the July 4 recess of 1980, an arrangement both Alaska senators approved as a delaying tactic. Senator Tsongas protested the delay.

Meanwhile, conservationists and a bipartisan group of senators led by Tsongas took advantage of the opportunity to drum up support for five "strengthening" amendments that were formally introduced in the Senate on May 22. Those who felt that the committee-approved Senate bill was unsatisfactory believed the amendments would bring it closer to the House version. On

441

July 21, the Senate floor debate got underway, and it quickly became apparent that the conservationist position might prevail. Senators Stevens and Gravel fought desperately, but on August 19 the Senate passed by vote of seventy-two to sixteen a substitute Alaska bill that bore the names of Tsongas, Jackson, Mark O. Hatfield of Oregon, and William V. Roth, Jr., of Delaware, Hatfield and Roth being Republicans. Earlier, the Senate had voted sixty-three to twenty-five in a move to invoke cloture and end a filibuster by Gravel.[20]

A sophisticated comparison of the House and Senate bills is impossible in brief space, but Representative Seiberling estimated the Senate version "probably represents about 85 percent of what we had hoped to achieve when we passed the House bill."[21] Conservationists were hopeful that House spokesmen might be able to gain more ground in the Senate-House conference to iron out differences. Plans were made to bring about such an outcome, but the 1980 presidential election, with the landslide victory of conservative Republican candidate Ronald Reagan and the Republican capture of the Senate, intervened.

When the Congress returned to Capitol Hill after the election recess, advocates of a larger and better-protected federal domain in Alaska had no difficulty reading the handwriting on the wall. They decided it would be wiser to accept a large part of the loaf than to risk the possibility of getting much less. Thus on November 12 the House accepted the Senate version without change, passing by voice vote the Alaska National Interest Lands Conservation Act. The bill went directly to the White House without hazard of further action by the Senate.

What the Congress approved was a measure that put 104.1 million acres of federal land into various types of protected status, compared to about 128 million acres in the House bill. As to wilderness acreage, the Senate provided 56 million, compared to the House bill's 67 million. There were many other differences, some of them very significant.

Alaska is such a huge place, with so much to offer, that both opposing sides could say at the end, in the spirit of Tennyson's poem *Ulysses*, "Tho much is taken, much abides . . ."

Notwithstanding any shortcomings, the conservationist forces gave a party at a Washington, D.C., hotel to celebrate what had been achieved, and a large assemblage gathered in the East Room of the White House to witness President Carter's signing of the new law. The outgoing president called the bill "one of the most important pieces of conservation legislation ever passed in this nation."

"In the decade past," Carter said, "we've worked hard to build strong programs to protect the environment and, where there was damage, to clean our skies and waterways. We have made some progress. It has not been easy. Human greed is not an easy foe to conquer."[22]

Representative Udall, whose labors on the Alaska lands bill had been prodigious, spoke in humorous vein. He had been returned to Congress, but the election had been a narrow squeak for him.

"I remember, Mr. President, up in Fairbanks [Alaska] last summer, they had a fair and exhibits and booths and the Junior Chamber of Commerce got 2,000 empty beer bottles and they had four pictures on the wall that you could pay a quarter and throw a beer bottle at—Jimmy Carter, Cecil Andrus, Mo Udall, and the Ayatollah " (The Ayatollah mentioned by Udall is the Iranian leader who was not popular in the United States at the time.)

In a more serious mood, Udall said Americans had been poor judges of contemporary presidents. He said he thought Carter would in time be ranked with Theodore Roosevelt as a conservationist.

The carving up of Alaska was a truly mammoth undertaking and a fascinating public spectacle. As an example of land planning on a large scale, it had major shortcomings. It reminded one of the situation in Shakespeare's *Henry IV*, when Hotspur, Mortimer, and Owen Glendower are quarreling over the division of England.

"I do not care," Hotspur exclaims.

I'll give twice so much land
To any well-deserving friend;
But in the way of bargain, mark ye me,
I'll cavil on the ninth part of a hair.

John Wesley Powell

John Muir

Thomas Ewing

William A. J. Sparks

Stewart L. Udall

Walter J. Hickel

444

Russell E. Train

Morris K. Udall

Gaylord Nelson

Ted Stevens

Mike Gravel

Major figures
instrumental, either
as conservationists
or legislators, in
the development of
land utilization policies.

445

EPILOGUE: LOOKING TO THE FUTURE

Your Constitution is all sail and no anchor.
> —THOMAS BABINGTON MACAULAY to Henry S. Randall, an American friend, 1857

It is better for the government to help a poor man to make a living for his family than to help a rich man make more profit for his company.
> —THEODORE ROOSEVELT, *Autobiography*

No matter how the dissection of Alaska turned out, the United States as the 1980s began was moving perforce toward a greater degree of planning for the future. This would occur regardless of the sharp resurgence of the laissez-faire spirit manifest in the election of Ronald Reagan to the presidency. The old, hit-or-miss ways were simply not good enough. The country had a tremendous amount of building and rebuilding to do. Space and materials were less abundant than in the past. What still was left of the great public-land heritage was immense, but it no longer offered an open frontier.

New concepts of private land ownership, impinging painfully on the old, were being advanced without trembling, apology, or embarrassment—and by respected national leaders. The new concepts, often touching on government's powers over the fate of private holdings, stirred up fear and anger in some quarters. But the country had become so crowded, relatively speaking, and its industrial system so complex and pollution ridden, that there necessarily followed an erosion of the brave old notion that individuals and corporations ought to be able to do what they please with their own property. The notion already has been greatly eroded, of course. It will suffer more.

As for the public's land, we have seen in earlier chapters that political and other pressures frequently get in the way of intelligent decision making. Sight of the public interest, which could be called the long view of things, often is lost in the dust kicked up by conflicting interests that know what they want and want it desperately. In mining, in the extraction of fossil fuels, in logging and grazing and water development, the special, regional interests have tended to be paramount. There are hopeful signs that this tendency is diminishing. The basic legislation pushed through Congress in the 1970s is generally constructive. It may have ushered in a better time.

The pressures will always be there, of course. They are normal and understandable. Students of American history and government are familiar with James Madison's famous *Federalist* essay number 10, first published in New York in 1787.[1] It deals with the advantages of a republic over a raw democracy in coping with the threat to popular government posed by partisan rivalry. Madison's point was that a republic like the proposed Union, broadly based and with powers delegated to elected representatives, would be better able than a democracy to smother harsh discord and act in the public interest. Surely one of the problems with the public lands over the years was that in their case Madison's benign principle did not work well. Decisions too often were left to a narrow clique with an axe to grind, while other citizens stood by in ignorance or apathy.

Madison's paper also sheds light on the unending debate over whether federal, state, or local control is best for this or that aspect of government. For some aspects, of course, the more local the control, the better. Madison believed, however, that the same advantage a republic has over a democracy, in controlling partisan discord, was enjoyed by the Union over the States. Similarly, the modern conservationist inclination to prefer federal control stems from the conviction that the federal authority is less vulnerable than the state to being pushed around.

Nearly as familiar as Madison's essay are the famous negative views expressed by Thomas Babington Macaulay, the British historian, on Thomas Jefferson and the American Constitution, already touched on in chapter 3. Lord Macaulay had said that Jefferson was not one of his heroes, despite the admiration for Jefferson in the United States, and he explained why in a letter written in 1857 to an American friend, Henry S. Randall. Macaulay had long been convinced, he said, that "institutions purely democratic must, sooner or later, destroy liberty or civilization or both." In such a state, either the poor would plunder the rich or the military would take over.

"You may think that your country enjoys an exemption from these evils," Macaulay wrote. "I will frankly own to you that I am of a very different opinion. Your fate I believe to be certain, although it is deferred by a physical cause. As long as you have a boundless extent of fertile and unoccupied land, your laboring

448

population will be far more at ease than the laboring population of the Old World, and, while that is the case, the Jefferson politics may continue to exist without causing any fatal calamity."[2]

There would come a time, however, Macaulay predicted, when New England would be as thickly settled as Old England, and hundreds of thousands of artisans would be out of work. When these unsettling conditions prevailed, said Macaulay, then the proud new nation's vaunted institutions would be fairly put to the test, and they would not, in his opinion, stand up. In England, on the other hand, power was not in the hands of the poor and ignorant, as in the United States, but in those of a select and educated class by which malcontents were "firmly yet gently restrained." Macaulay's thesis is subject to challenge on a number of grounds. It is drawn in here to emphasize the special character that an open land frontier has given to American development.

What needs emphasis is that the open frontier is now long gone, but the mystique and the myths persist as if it were still there. Before and immediately following the Civil War, in the Gilded Age, the massive giveaways of the public lands—to the railroads, the timber interests, the mining interests, the ranchers—took place against a background of apparently limitless resources and a thinly spread population that included authentic pioneers who were ready to stick it out and do battle with the elements. Nearly everybody got something, or could get something if he wished. The open land was there, and the nation then was very close to the state of nature described in John Locke's treatise on civil government, wherein he was discussing man's right to subdue a piece of land and improve it with his labor.

In these bustling, hectic, and in some ways more perilous modern times, Locke's seventeenth-century language falls pleasantly on the ear, calling up the image of a pastoral Eden as yet unravaged.

"Nor was this appropriation of any parcel of land, by improving it, any prejudice to any other Man, since there was still enough, and as good left; and more than the yet unprovided could use," Locke wrote nearly 300 years ago. "So that in effect, there was never the less left for others because of his inclosure for himself. For he that leaves as much as another can make use of, does as good as take nothing at all. No Body could think himself injur'd by the drinking of another Man, though he had a good Draught, who had a whole River of the same Water left him to quench his thirst. And the Case of Land and Water, where there is enough of both, is perfectly the same."[3]

The idyllic state of affairs described by Locke did not exist in the England of his time, but he imagined it to obtain in the Americas, which he described as rich in land but poor in the conveniences of life because the land here had not been improved by labor.

In the United States at its two hundredth anniversary, when the nation celebrated the survival and flourishing of a constitutional government based in part on Locke's teachings, the amount of tillable but unappropriated land had for many years been insufficient to satisfy the wants of newcomers. The "still enough, and as good left" condition assumed by Locke for his rural utopia could not be met. The good farmland had already been taken up, and the loss of about three million acres a year to urban sprawl, highways, and other uses had been recognized as a national problem. An increasing number of people were competing for a small plot on which to live. Pressures were fierce on what Locke might have called the Common—that is, the public domain and the reserved federal lands owned by all citizens.

It is worth recalling that in England, from which this country drew so much of its legal and social tradition, there had been a long, complex history of public use of "commons," or common fields, from early times. Most of the farming once was done on common fields, at times tilled and at times thrown open to cattle or other use. A gradual diminution of the commons, often to advance sheep raising and the wool trade, took place in the period of Henry VIII and subsequently. This process, called "inclosure," caused hardship and resentment. In the nineteenth century the movement toward fencing of the commons subsided, and it is to the survival of some of the commons that England owes much of its present-day open space.

In this country, as has been noted frequently throughout this book, there was marked and early concern for providing the small farmer and his family with land they could call their own. This was the emphasis of the Homestead Act during the Civil War and of much subsequent legislation. We have seen that Congress's solicitude for the small farmer, the family farmer, did not always benefit him to the extent intended and resulted in windfalls for land speculators or the well-to-do. Nevertheless, Congress remained loyal to the small farmer in theory, if not in practice. The policy of the nation was clearly one of putting sturdy yeoman settlers on the land.

Championship of the small farmer or settler over the rich and the corporations was characteristic of Theodore Roosevelt. The principle finds vigorous expression in Roosevelt's autobiography when he discusses the Reclamation Act of 1902 and the establishment of the United States Forest Service.

"This principle was too sound to be fought openly," Roosevelt wrote. "It is the kind of principle to which politicians delight to pay unctuous homage in words. But we translated the words into deeds; and when they found that this was the case, many rich men, especially sheep owners, were stirred to hostility, and they used the Congressmen they controlled to assault us—getting most aid from certain demagogues, who were equally glad improperly to denounce rich men in public and improperly to serve them in private."[4]

These small settlers became the best friends the new Forest Service had, Roosevelt said, "although in places their ignorance was played on by demagogues to influence them against the policy that was primarily for their own interest."

Despite the traditional eloquence about the virtues of the small, independent farmer and the national stake in putting

451

people on the land, the American experience since 1935 has been a marked decline in the number of farms and an increase in average farm size. From a 1935 peak of 6,800,000 farms, the total had declined by 1978 to 2,672,000.[5] The average acreage per farm increased from 278 in 1960 to 401 in 1978. The Department of Agriculture reported early in 1980 that the largest 50,000 farms accounted for more than one-third of all farm sales.[6] Corporate ownership was increasing. One percent of farm and ranch landowners had 29 percent of the land.

It is all but impossible to get precise information about ownership of private land holdings in the United States, but Gene Wunderlich of the United States Department of Agriculture pulled together and published a useful broad survey late in the 1970s. As of that time, private owners held 60 percent of the nation's total 2.3 billion acres, the federal government owned about 33 percent, and state and public agencies and American Indians owned the rest. There were 1.3 billion acres of private lands, and these were held by sixty to seventy-seven million owners in fourteen to seventeen million parcels. In the private sector, some forty-seven to fifty-eight million persons owned land used for housing, accounting for 2 percent of the private land, or 25 million acres.

What about the farms and woodlands in the countryside away from the towns and cities and rural residences? Wunderlich estimated that more than 63 percent of all privately held land was in farms and ranches, and another 32 percent was in forests. Thus he concluded that about 95 percent of private land was devoted to agricultural and forest use. It was held by seven to eight million owners, in parcels ranging in number from fourteen to seventeen million acres.

Taking the Agriculture Department's estimates as reasonably accurate and based on the best available information, which is all that was claimed for them, one saw that in 1980 the ownership of privately held lands in the United States was concentrated in the hands of a relative few. James A. Lewis of the

Department of Agriculture, in his 1978 study, estimated that 1 percent of the nation's adult population owned 75 percent of the land. Somewhat wistfully, the Wunderlich report pointed to the passage from Jefferson's letter to Bishop Madison: "it is not too soon to provide by every possible means that as few as possible shall be without a little portion of land."

The references in this book to the ideas of Locke, Jefferson, Madison, Henry George, and others may seem presumptuous and out of place to some readers. Such references may serve, however, to recall to our minds the freedom and flexibility with which our forefathers discussed the nature of government and the propriety of property rights in the ownership of land. We are in a time when many citizens coming of age find themselves excluded from living space and from employment. If the counsel of the past tells us anything, it is that a government that does not find remedies for such evils will go down.

American agriculture is a tremendous success in terms of efficiency and size and quality of harvest. It is the envy of the world. In human and social terms, however, the farm sector has not worked out in the way that idealists had envisaged. There is a wilderness of machinery out there, along with an impressive accumulation of wealth and skill, but relatively few people. This is a profound change, one to which attention has been called repeatedly by presidential commissions and various studies of Congress. As manifest from the chronic failure to enforce the acreage limitation and residency requirements of the reclamation law, the small and poor farmer no longer has the national appeal he once had. He is considered inefficient.

The attitude of the modern conservationist toward the small farmer is, it must be confessed, ambivalent in the extreme. Where the antagonist is agribusiness, or big landowners, or industry, the conservationists may well find themselves in alliance with small holders or the poor or landless. Good use has been made of the myth that native peoples, for example, never do violence to the land. But obviously the conservationists would not favor the throwing open of the rural West to a new tide of marginal settlers. This does not apply, of course, to resettlement where the land is good and the cause of exodus has been mechanization and federal farm policies that favor the rich.

Although most of the remaining public domain is of only marginal utility for farming, if that, the public lands will inevitably be affected by the frightening loss of prime and other farmland to urbanization. To curb such losses, amounting to a total of several million acres annually, the National Agricultural Lands Study was set up in June 1979. Secretary of Agriculture Bob Bergland and Chairman Gus Speth of the Council on Environmental Quality were cochairmen.

"The United States is losing one million acres of the best and flattest agricultural land each year to urban sprawl," Bergland said. "In my lifetime, we've paved over the equivalent of all the cropland in Ohio. Before this century is out, we will pave over an area the size of Indiana."[7]

A continued squandering of good farmland, an irreplaceable resource, would of course increase pressures on the public lands in addition to causing damage to the nation's ability to produce food for domestic and foreign needs. It is but one of the areas in which the national land-planning policy rejected by Congress in the early 1970s would be helpful. The statement has been made frequently by planning advocates, and appears to be true, that good planning for the federally owned lands will not be possible except in the broader context of good planning for all lands, public and private.

General land planning is a subject in whose upper reaches eagles may soar and poets may sing but which tends to be deadly dull and very difficult when things get down to the nitty-gritty. It involves interference by government with what people want to do with their own. Shall Farmer Jones, a good and kindly man who has operated a dairy farm for decades and now wants to retire, be permitted to sell his acreage to a housing developer? If not, he is damaged. Who compensates him? And if houses are not to be built on the pastures and grain fields of Farmer Jones, where shall they be built? These are questions that try men's souls and pocketbooks in stressful ways. It is no wonder that conservative demagogues have found land planning an easy, attractive target. Let it go, they say. Leave it alone. Free enterprise will work it out.

With regard to privately held lands, many people simply do not believe that the federal government should be meddling in any way with state or local planning of land use. They question whether federal officials "back in Washington" are wise enough to do this, and in any event they consider it inappropriate. On the other hand, proponents of a strong federal leadership role contend that the destructive forces at work are so powerful and pervasive that local agencies alone cannot deal with them effectively. In these circumstances, many states have been driving ahead on their own to solve such problems as the steady attrition of agricultural or coastal land. Various federal agencies are assisting with these procedures, and it appears to be only a matter of time before a federal or national policy act is approved to pull it all together.

Leaving this aside for the moment and getting back to John Muir's wilderness and the woods and pastures and deserts and mountain heights of the public lands, whose history and future have been the narrower focus of this book, there was reason in 1980 for guarded optimism. In the main, they have now been adopted by the federal government as a holding in perpetuity. They are not to be given away, or so it appeared. The framework for properly looking after them is in place.

And the federally-owned lands offer a simpler planning challenge than do all the nation's lands taken as a whole, if only because the public lands are already in a common ownership. In our dealing with them, it is not necessary to sort out, mollify, and otherwise contend with a complexity of diverse owners. What is required of us in this case is to seek out the public interest—not always an easy task, to be sure—and adhere to that.

Much has been said in earlier chapters about the profligate, careless ways of past generations of Americans, and the wholesale land frauds that were suffered to go on, more or less cheerfully, by those responsible for preventing them. Officials who tried to enforce the law had a hard time. They were unpopular. "Efforts made to release it [the public domain] from the grip of its despoilers have met with every embarrassment that human ingenuity could devise," said Interior Secretary Ethan A. Hitchcock in his annual report of 1909. Where dishonesty was so widespread and complacently accepted among people otherwise trustworthy, the natural inclination was to blame the system, the laws themselves.

Thus the stouthearted Texas historian Walter Prescott Webb offered an apologia in his excellent book on the Great Plains, already referred to, in which he contended that "the land laws were persistently broken in the West because they were not made for the West and were wholly unsuited to any arid region. The homestead law gave a man 160 acres and presumed that he should not acquire more. Since a man could not live on 160 acres of land in many parts of the region, he had to acquire more or starve. Men circumvented this law in every possible way, and managed at least to build up estates sufficient to earn a living."[8]

Webb said the rancher's rights on the public lands should have been recognized, as those of the miner had been. "The blame for a great deal of western lawlessness," he suggested, "rests more with the lawmaker than with the lawbreaker."[9]

Doubtless Webb was correct in saying that a perceived injustice and impracticality of the land laws in the West had a lot to do with the breaking of them, but surely there were other factors, including greed and confidence that nothing would be done about it. Under our system, there are legal ways by which men can bring about changes in laws of which they disapprove.

As we look to the future of the land laws, we must find ways to guard against the selective disobedience that has marred the past. Even though charity for the departed is never out of place,

456

and a certain broad tolerance for sinners is one of the great American virtues, we must create an atmosphere in which the federal writ is obeyed.

One of the essentials is the building up of a corps of dedicated professionals in the land-managing agencies. We already have a goodly battalion, but not a big enough one. It must consist of people who are educated, know the law, and know their jobs. They must be aware of their mission and proud of their organizations. They must have an esprit de corps, like the original foresters under Pinchot.

These federal land managers ought to be well paid and generously deployed in the field, with tours of duty long enough to enable them to know the terrain and the people well. All ought to be as well insulated from politics as is possible. One of their cardinal duties always should be maintenance of full and friendly relations with the local community, but they must be shielded from intimidation.

In the Congress and in the higher reaches of the executive branch, where the decisions are made, there is need for development of a greater respect for the facts about the public lands and less sensitivity to the political and economic demands, mostly short term, being made upon those lands.

It would help greatly if decisions about the public lands, and about money for their care, were not so often made hastily or pushed aside by other business regarded as more pressing. Presidents are very busy. So are members of Congress. A lands bill finally comes up and is deferred again. As the Bishop of Canterbury said in Shakespeare's *Henry V*, "the scambling and unquiet time did push it out of further question."

Unfortunately, there are things that will not wait and reckonings that must be paid regardless of whether they are politically convenient, in this country and elsewhere. Adversity has a way of turning nations and people inward, toward their own immediate concerns. The United States in 1980, racked by inflation and frustrated by economic woes, was in no mood to take on new international commitments or hearken to global doom-sayers. Nevertheless, there was some concern in July 1980 when President Carter released *The Global 2000 Report to the President: Entering the Twenty-first Century*, prepared by the Council on Environmental Quality and the Department of State.

"If present trends continue," the report said, "the world in 2000 will be more crowded, more polluted, less stable ecologically, and more vulnerable to disruption than the world we live in now."

S. Dillon Ripley, secretary of the Smithsonian Institution in Washington, D.C., took a pessimistic view when asked in an interview in November 1980 whether he thought people—the world at large—were going to solve their environmental problems.

"I don't really think we are," he said. "The whole history of the exploitation of land is a one-way street, so I hesitate to be optimistic. . . . I think it is going to be downhill for the next 200 years, if we survive that long."

The American environmental concern that swelled at the beginning of the 1970s does not appear, at the end of the decade, to be a mere temporary thing, a false sunrise quickly to be eclipsed by a frantic search for more oil, more minerals, more timber. Surely not. But, as has often been remarked of the National Environmental Policy Act and its ubiquitous environmental impact statements, there is no guarantee the conservationist spirit will keep the ascendancy. Here the important factor is the attitude of the public at large.

This crucial factor—the existence or nonexistence of a strong and supportive public opinion in good times and bad—has been brought up time and again in the mea culpa, "We have sinned in the dark days of the past against our land and now we've got to do better" type of environmental speech made by national leaders. The collective *we* is a useful device. It indicts nobody, offends nobody, and ensures a consensus. Such speeches, which serve to promote a receptive and cooperative spirit, often invoke the memory of the great conservationist Aldo Leopold, the United States Forest Service professional who died in 1948. He met his death fighting a grass fire on a neighbor's farm.

Aldo Leopold wrote a valuable essay called "The Land Ethic," published in 1949 as part of a set of Leopold's writings known as *A Sand County Almanac*. In the essay, he thoughtfully pointed out that man had embraced a code of conduct governing relations between individuals, and between an individual and society, but that "there is as yet no ethic dealing with man's relation to land and to the animals and plants which grow upon it."[10] When there is a land ethic, he said, society will affirm that the abuse of land is not only an unwise practice but a wrong one, and the land will be kept in better shape.

Leopold worked out his thesis very carefully. His essay should be read. He regarded the conservationist movement as the embryo of an affirmation by society of a land ethic. It is not remarkable that Leopold's land-ethic idea has been referred to so frequently in addresses and books concerning the fate of the land, including this one. There can be no negating the broad point—that progress toward wise land use depends on the support of society. Laws are not enough.

Progress has been made on the development of a land ethic. The tenth annual report of the President's Council on Environmental Quality, reviewing the last ten years, speaks of a "new ethic" and says the commitment to environmental progress seems to be here to stay.[11] An optimist can bring himself to believe it may be farther advanced than realized, like the subtle and slow-moving but mighty and inexorable flow of tidal waters in Sidney Lanier's poem "The Marshes of Glynn."

In President Carter's foreword to the CEQ's tenth annual report, the President—soon to meet an overwhelming defeat at the polls—noted with approval that a change in the nation's collective consciousness had taken place and that it had been "not only remarkably swift, but remarkably broad." A decade of environmental progress, he said, began with the signing of the Na-

459

tional Environmental Policy Act of January 1, 1970, and "the environmental record of the Congress and the Executive Branch during these ten years has been exceptional."[12]

The council's eleventh annual report, made public as the Democratic administration was about to leave office and President-elect Reagan's forces were waiting at the door, remained optimistic but was not quite so upbeat as the previous one.

"The signs are unmistakable," said the outgoing president's message dispatching the report to Congress, "that we in the United States are learning how to live in balance with nature and beginning to find sustainable ways to exist on this Nation's plentiful but finite resources. Yet there are also undeniable signs that in many parts of the world the Earth's carrying capacity—the ability of biological systems to meet human needs—is being threatened by human activities."[13]

Carter wound up his remarks by noting that the 1980s were presenting new challenges. He urged that the nation "must continue to move forward and extend the progress we have made—progress for which we are being repaid many times over."[14] The report itself gave emphasis to signs of a degraded world environment and a dwindling of resources. It pointed out that, although hopeful new policies have been established, there has been no vanishing of controversy and tensions as to how public lands should be managed. Brief mention was made of the effort to transfer federal lands to the states.

"In the West," said the report, "individuals engaged in ranching and in oil, gas, and mineral development have recently launched the 'sagebrush rebellion' in reaction to federal restrictions on their access to and use of federal lands."[15]

There are interesting times ahead, in which the environmental wars will continue, with neither side likely to succumb to a whiff of rhetorical grapeshot, and neither likely to prevail wholly. An impressive machinery for the defense of the environment and the public lands unquestionably has been built, in the government and outside. Until it is more firmly in place

460

and has the steady acceptance of the American people, we shall owe a heavy debt—as we do now—to the corporal's guard of environmental lawyers and professional conservationists who man the ramparts while others sleep.

461

NOTES

PROLOGUE: FROM SEA TO SEA

[1]See Gilbert White, *The Natural History of Selborne* (London and New York: John Lane, 1900), passim, and Thomas Jefferson to Dr. John P. Emmett, April 27, 1826, in *The Writings of Thomas Jefferson* (Washington, D.C.: Thomas Jefferson Memorial Association, 1903), 16:163–167.

[2]*Resources for Freedom*, a report to the President by the President's Materials Policy Commission (Washington, D.C.: Government Printing Office, 1952). See also *Material Needs and the Environment Today and Tomorrow*, final report of the National Commission on Materials Policy (Washington, D.C.: Government Printing Office, 1973).

[3]In the early 1970s, the newly organized President's Council on Environmental Quality gave high priority to national land-use policy and showed lively interest in legal problems relating to land-use planning. The subject is discussed by Fred Bosselman and David Callies, Chicago lawyers, in *The Quiet Revolution in Land Use Control* (Washington, D.C.: Government Printing Office, 1971), and by Bosselman, Callies, and John Banta in *The Taking Issue*, (Washington, D.C.: Government Printing Office, 1973), a study prepared for the CEQ on the constitutional limits of government authority to regulate the use of privately owned land without paying compensation to the owners. Also published in 1973, under sponsorship of the Rockefeller Brothers Fund, was *The Use of Land: A Citizen's Policy Guide to Urban Growth* (New York: Thomas Y. Crowell Co.), a task force report of the Citizens Advisory Committee on Environmental Quality edited by William K. Reilly, executive director of the task force, who had been borrowed from the staff of CEQ.

[4]"In short, between now and the year 2000, we must build again all that we have built before. We must build as many homes, schools, and hospitals in the next three decades as we built in the previous three centuries." — Sen. Henry M. Jackson, Washington Democrat, during remarks on introducing the Land Use Policy and Planning Assistance Act of 1973 on January 9, 1973. U.S., Congress, Senate, *Congressional Record*, 93d Cong., 1st sess., 1973, 119, p. 1:654.

[5]Reilly, *The Use of Land*, pp. 172–175; and Bosselman, Callies, and Banta, *The Taking Issue*, p. 324.

[6]Public Law 91-190. President Nixon signed the NEPA on January 1, 1970, as his first official act of the new year. U.S., Statutes at Large 83:852.

[7]Special message to the Congress proposing the 1971 environmental program, February 8, 1971, *Public Papers of the Presidents: Richard Nixon, 1971* (Washington, D.C.: Government Printing Office, 1972), pp. 134–139.

[8]The Nixon administration's reversal became apparent in February 1974, when the House Rules Committee voted nine to four against allowing the land-use measure to reach the House floor for a final vote. This ac-

tion was taken following a formal request from Minority Leader John J. Rhodes of Arizona, who asked the committee not to grant a rule, explaining that the president now favored a substitute bill. See Leonard Downie, Jr., "The Ambush of the Land Bill," *Washington Post*, March 10, 1974.

[9]For example, James W. Moorman, formerly director of the Sierra Club Legal Defense Fund, named by President Carter to be assistant attorney general, Land and Natural Resources Division, U.S. Department of Justice; and M. Rupert Cutler, assistant executive director of the Wilderness Society in the 1960s, who became Carter's assistant secretary of agriculture for conservation, research, and education, a position that includes supervision of the Forest Service.

1. THE PUBLIC LANDS

[1]*Resources for Freedom*, report of the President's Materials Policy Commission (Washington, D.C.: Government Printing Office, 1952), p. 5. The chairman, William S. Paley, board chairman of the Columbia Broadcasting System, was an organizer of Resources for the Future, a conservation group formed the year the Paley report came out.

[2]The National Commission on Materials Policy, of which the chairman was Jerome L. Klaff of Baltimore, was established under terms of the National Materials Policy Act of 1970 (Public Law 91-512). U.S. *Statutes at Large* 84:1234.

[3]*The Limits to Growth*, a report for the Club of Rome's Project on the Predicament of Mankind, 2d ed. (New York: Universe Books, 1974).

[4]*Material Needs and the Environment Today and Tomorrow*, final report of the National Commission on Materials Policy (Washington, D.C.: Government Printing Office, 1973), pp. 7–13; and *One Third of the Nation's Land*, a report to the president and to the Congress by the Public Land Law Review Commission, made public June 23, 1970 (Washington, D.C.: Government Printing Office), pp. 28–29, 41.

[5]See observations of Michel Guillaume Saint Jean de Crèvecoeur in his *Journey into Northern Pennsylvania and the State of New York*, trans. Clarissa Spencer Bostelmann (Ann Arbor: University of Michigan Press, 1964), passim.

[6]Thaddeus Mason Harris, *Journal of a Tour into the Territory Northwest of the Alleghany Mountains* (Boston: Manning & Loring, 1805), pp. 50–61.

[7]A. M. Sakolski, *The Great American Land Bubble* (New York and London: Harper & Brothers, 1932), passim.

[8]George Washington to Jacob Read, Nov. 3, 1784, in *The Writings of George Washington*, ed. John C. Fitzpatrick, 39 vols. (Washington, D.C.: Government Printing Office, 1931–1944), 27:486.

[9]Ibid., p. 487.

¹⁰*Journals of the Continental Congress, 1774–1789*, 34 vols., reprint ed. (New York and London: Johnson Reprint, 1968), 25:694. Also quoted, as is the material in the two preceding notes, by Paul W. Gates in his *History of Public Land Law Development* (Washington, D.C.: Government Printing Office, 1968), a useful and comprehensive book written for the Public Land Law Review Commission.

¹¹Charles A. Hanna, *The Scotch Irish or the Scot in North Britain, North Ireland, and North America*, 2 vols., reprint ed. (Baltimore: Geneological Publishing Co., 1968), pp. 62–63.

¹²James Madison to James Monroe, May 29, 1785, in *Letters of Members of the Continental Congress*, ed. Edmund C. Burnett, 8 vols., reprint ed. (Gloucester, Mass.: Peter Smith, 1963), 8:viii.

¹³Sakolski, *The Great American Land Bubble*, pp. 106–110.

¹⁴Malcolm J. Rohrbach, *The Land Office Business* (New York: Oxford University Press, 1968), pp. 15–16; and Gates, *Public Land Law*, p. 67.

¹⁵Quoted in Gates, *Public Land Law*, p. 62. See Thomas Jefferson to Rev. James Madison, Fontainebleau, Oct. 18, 1785, in *Papers of Thomas Jefferson* (Princeton: Princeton University Press, 1953), 8:682.

¹⁶Sakolski, *The Great American Land Bubble*, p. 37.

¹⁷Abraham Bishop, *Georgia Speculation Unveiled* (Ann Arbor: University Microfilm, 1966), foreword.

¹⁸Ibid., p. 38.

¹⁹Sakolski, *The Great American Land Bubble*, p. 141.

²⁰See *Lewis and Clark*, prepared by Roy E. Appelman for the National Park Service as part of a series edited by Robert G. Ferris (Washington, D.C.: Government Printing Office, 1975). See also the expedition's journals, edited by Bernard DeVoto.

²¹To be precise, total income from Texas public lands for the period from 1835 to 1970 came to $1,683,203,639.98. Thomas Lloyd Miller, *The Public Lands of Texas, 1519–1970* (Norman: University of Oklahoma Press, 1972), p. 285.

²²Charles R. Beard, Mary R. Beard, and William Beard, *The Beards' New Basic History of the United States* (Garden City, N.Y.: Doubleday & Co., 1960), p. 184.

²³Gates, *Public Land Law*, p. 84.

²⁴Baron Edouard de Stoeckl to Prince Gorchakov, July 12–24, 1867, in *An Alaska Reader*, comp. and ed. Ernest Gruening (New York: Meredith Press, 1966), pp. 41–48.

²⁵See Samuel Eliot Morison and Henry Steele Commager, *The Growth of the American Republic*, 2 vols. (New York: Oxford University Press, 1950), 2:176–188.

²⁶*Public Land Statistics, 1976*, U.S. Interior Department, Bureau of Land Management (Washington, D.C.: Government Printing Office, 1976), p. 10, table 7.

27Ibid. The BLM's annual *Public Land Statistics* is a handy compendium of data on the federally owned lands.

28Bob Bergland, secretary of agriculture, took considerable interest in the plight of the rural poor.

29*One Third of the Nation's Land*, p. 1.

2. LAND GRABBERS, THE LAW, AND THE PROPHETS

1See William Sidney Porter [O. Henry], *Stories of the Old Texas Land Office* (Austin: Daughters of the Republic of Texas, Museum Committee, 1964).

2In George Rothwell Brown's introduction to *Reminiscences of Senator William M. Stewart of Nevada* (New York and Washington, D.C.: Neale Publishing Co., 1908), which Brown edited.

3Ibid. Brown also said: "Probably no man in the United States has won and lost more fortunes than William M. Stewart."

4Stewart wrote of Clemens: "I suppose he was the most lovable scamp and nuisance who ever blighted Nevada" (*Reminiscences*, p. 220).

5See Carl B. Glasscock, *The War of the Copper Kings* (New York: Grosset & Dunlap, 1935), passim, and William Daniel Mangam's critical *The Clarks of Montana: An American Phenomenon* (New York: Silver Bow Press, 1941).

6U.S., Congress, Senate, *Congressional Record*, 56th Cong., 1st sess., May 15, 1900, pp. 5531–5536.

7Mangam, *Clarks of Montana*, p. 69.

8Richard Hofstadter, *Social Darwinism in American Thought* (New York: George Braziller, 1959), passim.

9Anecdote recalled by Benton J. Stong, an aide of United States Sen. John Melcher, Montana Democrat, in an interview with the author in the early 1970s. Also, for a discussion of "claims clubs," see Everett Dick, *The Lure of the Land* (Lincoln: University of Nebraska Press, 1970), chap. 5.

10See Mark Twain and Charles Dudley Warner, *The Gilded Age* (New York and Toronto: New American Library, Signet Classics, 1969), chap. 17.

11Morris Birkbeck, *Notes on a Journey in America* (New York: Augustus M. Kelley, 1971), p. 69. Also quoted in A. M. Sakolski, *The Great American Land Bubble* (New York and London: Harper & Brothers, 1932), p. 174.

12Birkbeck, *Letters from Illinois* (New York: DaCapo Press, 1970), p. 81, letter 13.

13See Charles Dickens, *American Notes* (Penguin Books, 1972), p. 160, and *Martin Chuzzlewit* (New York: Alfred A. Knopf, 1947), the American chapters, particularly chap. 23.

14Rudyard Kipling, *From Sea to Sea* (Garden City, N.Y.: Doubleday, Page & Co., 1918), p. 431.

15Theodore Roosevelt to Kermit Roosevelt, February 29, 1908, in *The Works of Theodore Roosevelt*, memorial ed., 24 vols. (New York: Charles Scribner's Sons, 1923–26), 21:601.

[16]*One Third of the Nation's Land*, a report by the Public Land Law Review Commission (Washington, D.C.: Government Printing Office, 1970), p. 244. See also Interior Department press release dated April 5, 1972, in which Secretary Rogers C. B. Morton, announcing that his department would expedite transfer of lands to Alaska, pointed out that Alaska's 103-million-acre allotment exceeded the total amount of land granted to seventeen of the states west of the Mississippi River. A table of state allotments was supplied with the press release.

[17]Paul W. Gates, *History of Public Land Law Development* (Washington, D.C.: Government Printing Office, 1968), p. 328.

[18]Ibid., p. 329. See also Dick, *Lure of the Land*, pp. 214 ff.

[19]Land Grant College Act of 1862, U.S., *Statutes at Large*, 12:503.

[20]Gates, *Public Land Law*, p. 338.

[21]Homestead Act of 1862, U.S., *Statutes at Large*, 12:392.

[22]Gates, *Public Land Law*, p. 392.

[23]Ibid., p. 400.

[24]John Ise, *Sod and Stubble: The Story of a Kansas Homestead* (New York: Wilson-Erickson, 1936), particularly pp. 35–37, in which a boy dies of hydrophobia after having been bitten by a rabid wolf.

[25]See Yasuo Okada, *Public Lands and Pioneer Farms, Gage County, Neb.—1850–1900* (Tokyo: Keio Economic Society, 1971). Okada's study indicates that 40 percent of the county's land was entered by holders of agricultural college scrip—issued by non-public-lands states under the Morrill Act—compared with 15 percent taken up under the homestead act. About one-third of Gage County homesteaders stayed on as stable farmers, he found (p. 92).

[26]Gates, *Public Land Law*, p. 364. For a discussion of the railroad grants, see pp. 356–386.

[27]David Lavender, *The Great Persuader* (Garden City, N.Y.: Doubleday & Co., 1970), pp. 241–242. Lavender refers to letters to E. B. Crocker, May 17, 1869, and to Leland Stanford, August 2, 1870, in Collis P. Huntington, *Collected Letters* (New York: John C. Rankin Co., 1892), vol. 2.

[28]See J. B. Crawford, *Credit Mobilier of America* (Boston: C. W. Calkins & Co., 1880), passim; also, Charles R. Beard, Mary R. Beard, and William Beard, *The Beards' New Basic History of the United States* (Garden City, N.Y.: Doubleday & Co., 1960), p. 307, and James D. McCabe, *Behind the Scenes in Washington* (New York: Arno Press, 1974), chap. 8.

[29]Crawford, *Credit Mobilier*, pp. 214–219. Crawford defended Ames and wrote: "There is no doubt but the disgrace thus put upon him ended his life" (p. 217).

[30]*Public Land Statistics, 1976*, U.S. Interior Department, Bureau of Land Management (Washington, D.C.: Government Printing Office, 1976), p. 9, table 6.

[31]U.S., *Reports*, 1875, 88:44.

[32]U.S., *Statutes at Large*, 30:36. See Gates, *Public Land Law*, pp. 569–592.

[33]Gates, *Public Land Law*, p. 591.

[34]Hamlin Garland, *A Son of the Middle Border* (New York: Macmillan Co., 1962), p. 309.

[35]Ibid., p. 311.

[36]O. E. Rolvaag, *Giants in the Earth: A Saga of the Prairie* (New York, Evanston, and London: Harper & Row, Harper Torch Books, 1946). Vernon L. Parrington deals at some length with Hamlin Garland and Rolvaag in his *Main Currents in American Thought*, 3 vols. (New York: Harcourt, Brace & Co., 1927, 1930). In the addenda to his book, see the introduction to the 1929 text edition of *Giants in the Earth*, pp. 387–396.

[37]Henry George, *The Complete Works of Henry George*, vol. 3, *The Land Question*, reprint ed. (New York: Doubleday, Page & Co., 1906), p. 52.

[38]George Perkins Marsh, *The Earth Is Modified by Human Action* (New York: Scribner, Armstrong & Co., 1977), p. 33. This is a new edition of *Man and Nature.*

3. CONGRESS GUARDS THE LAND

[1]Interview with the author, New York City, 1971.

[2]See Carl Schurz, "The Need of a Rational Forest Policy," an address delivered Oct. 15, 1889, before the American Forestry Association and the Pennsylvania Forest Association, in *Speeches, Correspondence, and Political Papers of Carl Schurz*, ed. Frederic Bancroft, 6 vols. (New York and London: G. P. Putnam's Sons, 1913), 5:22–33.

[3]Malcolm J. Rohrbach, *The Land Office Business: The Settlement and Administration of American Public Lands, 1789–1837* (New York: Oxford University Press, 1968), pp. 176–179, and E. Louise Peffer, *The Closing of the Public Domain* (Stanford: Stanford University Press, 1951), p. 16.

[4]Charles R. Beard, Mary R. Beard, and William Beard, *The Beards' New Basic History of the United States* (Garden City, N.Y.: Doubleday & Co., 1960), p. 281.

[5]Vernon Louis Parrington, *Main Currents in American Thought: An Interpretation of American Literature from the Beginnings to 1920*, 3 vols. (New York: Harcourt, Brace & Co., 1927, 1930), 3:23 ff.

[6]Ibid., p. 25.

[7]Alexis de Tocqueville, *Democracy in America* (New York: Washington Square Press, 1964), 2:273. It is interesting that this frequently cited observation is followed by the statement, "Nowhere does the majority display less inclination for those principles which threaten to alter, in whatever fashion, the laws of property."

[8]Macaulay to H. S. Randall, May 23, 1857, in G. O. Trevelyan, *The Life and Letters of Lord Macaulay*, 2 vols. (New York and London: Harper & Bros.,

1875), 2:452. He had long been convinced, Macaulay confided, that "institutions purely democratic must, sooner or later, destroy liberty or civilization or both."

9See Charles E. Wallace, *Creation of the Department of the Interior*, Office of Communications, U.S. Interior Department (Washington, D.C.: Government Printing Office, 1976). Also, U.S., Congress, Senate, *Congressional Globe*, 30th Cong., 2d sess., March 3, 1849, 18:671–673.

10U.S., Congress, Senate, *Congressional Globe*, 35th Cong., 2d sess., February 25, 1859, pp. 1353–1354.

11Walter Prescott Webb, *The Great Plains* (New York: Ginn & Co., 1931), pp. 496–502.

12Paul W. Gates, *History of Public Land Law Development* (Washington, D.C.: Government Printing Office, 1968), pp. 413–414. See U.S., *Statutes at Large*, 14:66–67 for the law as enacted June 21, 1866, and U.S., *Statutes at Large*, 19:73–74 for the repeal. This law, called an Act for the Disposal of the Public Lands for Homestead Actual Settlement in the States of Alabama, Mississippi, Lousiana, Arkansas, and Florida, provided that no discrimination be made on the basis of race or color and excluded for one year all who had "borne arms against the United States, or given aid and comfort to its enemies." For a more extended discussion of the failure of land reform in the postbellum South, see also Gates, "Federal Land Policy in the South, 1866–88," *Journal of Southern History* 6 (August 1940):303–330, and Kenneth M. Stampp, *The Era of Reconstruction: 1865–1877* (New York: Alfred A. Knopf, 1970), passim.

13Gates, *Public Land Law*, p. 552.

14Ibid., pp. 464–466.

15U.S., Congress, House, Committee on Indian Affairs, *Lands in Severalty to Indians*, 46th Cong., 1st and 2d sess., 1879–1880, H. Rept. 1576, 5:10.

16José Marti, *Obras completas: edition commemorativa del cincuentenario de su muerte*, with a prologue and biographical notes by M. Isidro Mendez (Havana: Editorial Lex, 1946), 1:1942–1949. See also Everett Dick, *Lure of the Land* (Lincoln: University of Nebraska Press, 1970), chaps. 16–17.

17U.S., *Statutes at Large*, 19:377.

18Ralph Nader Study Group, *Politics of Land: Report on Land Use in California* (New York: Grossman Publishers, 1973), pp. 18, 164.

19U.S., Congress, Senate, *Farmworkers in Rural America, 1971–1972: Hearings before the Subcommittee on Migratory Labor of the Committee on Labor and Public Welfare*, 92d Cong., 1st and 2d sess., July 22, 1971–June 20, 1972.

20California accounts for about 30 percent of the total acreage irrigated by Reclamation Bureau projects. Some 80 percent of the lands receiving water in excess of the law's acreage limitation were in California.

21Wallace Stegner, *Beyond the Hundredth Meridian: John Wesley Powell and the Second Opening of the West* (Boston: Houghton Mifflin Co., 1954), chap. 3 and passim.

[22]See Henry Nash Smith, *Virgin Land: The American West as Symbol and Myth* (Cambridge: Harvard University Press, 1950), chap. 16, "The Garden and the Desert." See also Dick, *Lure of the Land*, pp. 319–320.

[23]Stegner, *Beyond the Hundredth Meridian*, p. 303.

[24]Ibid., p. 333. Stegner gives a detailed account of the rawhiding suffered by Powell at the hands of Senator Stewart and others in Congress.

[25]Gates, *Public Land Law*, pp. 644–645.

[26]Lawrence Clark Powell, *Arizona: A Bicentennial History* (New York: W. W. Norton & Co., 1976), p. 43.

[27]*Messages and Papers of the Presidents*, comp. James D. Richardson (New York: Bureau of National Literature, 1897–) 13:6656–6658.

[28]U.S., *Statutes at Large*, 32:388.

[29]Gates, *Public Land Law*, pp. 661–666.

[30]U.S., Interior Department, Bureau of Reclamation, *Summary Report*, 1977.

[31]Ibid., p. 1.

[32]Richard O'Connor, *The Oil Barons: Men of Greed and Grandeur* (Boston and Toronto: Little, Brown & Co., 1971), pp. 139–143. Also see W. A. Swanberg, *Citizen Hearst* (New York: Charles Scribner's Sons, 1961), pp. 257–264.

[33]See John Ise, *Our National Park Policy: A Critical History*, Resources for the Future (Baltimore: Johns Hopkins Press, 1961), pp. 232–235, 303–307.

[34]Cameron's vendetta with the National Park Service, sometimes amusing in view of the favorable outcome, is further detailed in Robert Shankland's *Steve Mather of the National Parks* (New York: Alfred A. Knopf, 1954), chap. 17, "Mammon and the Bright Angel," p. 225 ff. The toilet facilities supplied by Cameron at his Bright Angel camp are described as unspeakable. Complaint was made on the floor of the House, Shankland reports, that "women in whom modesty has restrained obedience to demands of nature have suffered permanent and severe injury" (pp. 229–230).

[35]In another version of this theme, Train said that "improved land use is the No. 1 environmental priority facing the nation today." This was in testimony before Senate Interior and Insular Affairs Committee on February 6, 1973. U.S., Congress, Senate, *Hearings on Land Use Policy and Planning Assistance Act*, 93d Cong., 1st sess., p. 176.

[36]*Public Papers of the Presidents: Richard Nixon, 1970* (Washington, D.C.: Government Printing Office, 1971), p. 659.

[37]Quoted in Senator Jackson's letter to the president March 8, 1974, protesting Nixon's change in position.

[38]*Public Papers of the Presidents: Richard Nixon, 1973*, p. 98.

[39]Ibid., p. 772.

[40]See, for example, William K. Reilly, ed., *The Use of Land: A Citizen's Policy Guide to Urban Growth* (New York: Thomas Y. Crowell Co., 1973), the task force report of the Citizens Advisory Committee on Environmental Quality which had been established by presidential executive order in

May 1969 under chairmanship of Laurance Rockefeller. See also James C. R. Graham's testimony for the Chamber of Commerce of the United States before a House interior subcommittee, April 24, 1975, p. 4 of a Chamber of Commerce release.

[41]Udall's press release of Feb. 26, 1974. Also, Senator Jackson's press release of March 13, 1974.

[42]Interior Department press release, June 12, 1974.

[43]*Washington Post*, June 13, 1974.

[44]U.S., Congress, House, *Congressional Record*, 93d Cong., 2d sess., June 11, 1974, p. H5024.

[45]Ibid., p. H5029.

[46]U.S., Congress, House, Committee on Interior and Insular Affairs, Subcommittee on Energy and the Environment, *Land Use and Resources Conservation: Hearing on H.R. 3510 and Related Bills*, 94th Cong., 1st sess., March 18, 1975, p. 122.

4. THE FALL OF ALBERT B. FALL

[1]This chapter draws upon journalist Mark Sullivan's popular *Our Times: The United States, 1900–1925*, vol. 6, *The Twenties* (New York: Charles Scribner's Sons, 1935), chap. 14, pp. 272–349, and other contemporary accounts, including stories by Paul Y. Anderson in the *St. Louis Post-Dispatch*. For a detailed and documented account, see Burl Noggle, *Teapot Dome: Oil and Politics in the 1920s* (Baton Rouge: Louisiana State University Press, 1962). Of Sullivan, it was once said he was "probably too good a journalist to be a good historian." A basic source is the hearings presided over by Senator Walsh of Montana; see U.S., Congress, Senate, Committee on Public Lands and Surveys, *Leases upon Naval oil Reserves: Hearings . . .* , 67th Cong., 4th sess., 1923, and 68th Cong., 1st sess., 1924, paooim.

[2]See E. Louise Peffer, *The Closing of the Public Domain* (Stanford: Stanford University Press, 1951), pp. 115–119.

[3]U.S., *Statutes at Large*, 41:437.

[4]Robert W. Swenson, "Legal Aspects of Mineral Resources Exploitation," in *History of Public Land Law Development*, by Paul W. Gates (Washington, D.C.: Government Printing Office, 1968), chap. 23, p. 741.

[5]Noggle, *Teapot Dome*, p. 36.

[6]Sullivan, *Our Times*, vol. 6, chap. 14, pp. 272 ff.

[7]Noggle, *Teapot Dome*, pp. 36–38, 47.

[8]Theodore Roosevelt knew and admired Fall. They were fellow veterans of the Spanish-American War, and both were enthusiastic supporters of American involvement in World War I. Senator Fall placed Roosevelt's name in nomination at the Republican National Convention in 1916. In thanking Fall for this, Roosevelt wrote to him on June 17, 1916: "You have been the kind of a public servant of whom all Americans should

feel proud." (*Letters of Theodore Roosevelt*, sel. and ed. Elting Morison [Cambridge: Harvard University Press, 1954], 8:1065). In the same work may be found Roosevelt's telegram to Fall of October 30, 1918, defending the senator against an effort by President Woodrow Wilson to unseat Fall in the upcoming election (pp. 1383–1384). Roosevelt told Fall: "No American Representative in either House of Congress during the last five years has a more absolutely straight American and war record than yours." See *New York Times*, November 2, 1918.

9Noggle, *Teapot Dome*, p. 79.

10Sullivan, *Our Times*, 6:329. However inflamed the public judgment of Fall's actions may have been in the 1920s, and however time may soften that judgment, one must conclude that the unfortunate secretary would have been wise to look beyond his oil friends for solutions to his personal financial problems.

11Ibid., p. 333. See also Francis Russell, *The Shadow of Blooming Grove* (New York and Toronto: McGraw-Hill, 1968), p. 615. Russell's book, which deals with Warren G. Harding, lists the Wilson cabinet officers whom Doheny had employed, in addition to McAdoo, as Secretary of War Lindley M. Garrison, Attorney General Thomas W. Gregory, and Secretary of the Interior Franklin K. Lane.

12Paul Y. Anderson, *St. Louis Post-Dispatch*, April 21, 1928.

13Ibid., October 25, 1929. Paul Y. Anderson won a Pulitzer Prize in 1929. His vivid, intense coverage reflects the high public interest in the Fall case.

14Naval Petroleum Reserves Production Act of 1976, Public Law 94-258, U.S., *Statutes at Large*, 90:303.

15Department of Energy Organization Act of 1977, Public Law 95-91, Title III, U.S., *Statutes at Large*, 91:581.

5. THE FEDERAL SENTINELS

1See Charles E. Wallace, *Creation of the Department of the Interior: March 3, 1849*, Office of Communications, U.S. Interior Department (Washington, D.C.: Government Printing Office, 1976), pp. 1–14. Also see Norman O. Forness, "The Origins and Early History of the United States Department of the Interior" (Ph.D. diss., Pennsylvania State University, 1964).

2U.S., Interior Department, *Annual Report of the Interior Department*, in *Appendix to the Congressional Globe*, 31st Cong., 1st sess., December 3, 1849, 22:20–23.

3Ibid., p. 23.

4U.S., Congress, House, Committee on Interior and Insular Affairs, Subcommittee on Indian Affairs, *Alaska Native Land Claims: Hearings on H.R. 3100 . . .*, 92d Cong., 1st sess., May 3, 1971, p. 105.

5U.S., Congress, Senate, *Confirmation Hearings on Nomination of Walter J. Hickel to be the Secretary of the Interior*, 91st Cong., 1st sess., January 18, 1969, p. 397.

⁶Ibid., January 16, 1969, p. 153, wherein Sen. Gaylord Nelson, Wisconsin Democrat, questions Hickel about a Washington, D.C., press conference of December 18, 1968, and Hickel is quoted as saying: "I think we have had a policy of conservation just for conservation purposes." In Hickel's subsequent book, *Who Owns America?* (Englewood Cliffs, N.J.: Prentice Hall, 1971), Hickel quotes himself as having said, "I think we have had a policy of conservation for conservation's sake" (p. 11).

⁷Hickel, *Who Owns America?*, pp. 279–280. Hickel was interviewed at the Interior Department by Mike Wallace of the Columbia Broadcasting System, and the interview was carried on "60 Minutes" November 23, 1970.

⁸See William Safire, *Before the Fall: An Inside View of the Pre-Watergate White House* (Garden City, N.Y.: Doubleday, 1975).

⁹U.S., Congress, Senate, Committee on Interior and Insular Affairs, *Hearings on Nomination of Rogers C. B. Morton to be Secretary of the Interior*, 92d Cong., 1st sess., January 26, 1971, pp. 111–134.

¹⁰U.S., Congress, House, Subcommittee of Committee on Appropriations, *Hearings on Interior Department Appropriations for Fiscal 1973*, 92d Cong., 2d sess., p. 54.

¹¹Author's interview of Interior Department official, 1972.

¹²Interior Department press conference transcript, November 25, 1975.

¹³Conversation with author, 1975.

¹⁴Message to the Congress, Water Resource Projects, February 21, 1977, *Public Papers of the Presidents: Jimmy Carter, 1977* (Washington, D.C.: Government Printing office, 1978), p. 207. Carter listed nineteen projects—the famous "hit list"—that were to be removed from the budget "on economic, environmental and/or safety grounds." Andrus made no secret of his feeling that White House handling of this matter was inept.

¹⁵Author's interview of former Secretary Udall in his Washington, D.C., law office August 16, 1979.

¹⁶Francis Russell, *Shadow of Blooming Grove* (New York and Toronto: McGraw-Hill, 1968), p. 615.

¹⁷See H. Duane Hampton, *How the U.S. Cavalry Saved Our National Parks* (Bloomington and London: Indiana University Press, 1971), passim. Hampton notes that all the military acting superintendents of Yellowstone National Park were members of the Boone and Crockett Club, which had been founded in New York by Theodore Roosevelt, George Bird Grinnell, and others.

¹⁸John Ise, *Our National Park Policy*, (Baltimore: Johns Hopkins Press, 1961), p. 27.

¹⁹Interior Department press release, December 13, 1972.

²⁰See *Public Land Statistics, 1976*, U.S. Interior Department, Bureau of Land Management (Washington, D.C.: Government Printing Office, 1976), p. 1.

²¹Butz's appointment as counselor for natural resources was announced by Nixon in a January 1973 statement.

[22]The Federal Land Policy and Management Act of 1976, Public Law 94-979, U.S., *Statutes at Large*, 90:2743.

6. WINNOWING THE LAWS

[1]*One Third of the Nation's land*, the 1970 report of the Public Land Law Review Commission (Washington, D.C.; Government Printing Office), p. 1. In plainer language, the report says in its second paragraph, "We urge reversal of the policy that the United States should dispose of the so-called unappropriated public domain lands."

[2]U.S., Congress, House, *Report of the Public Land Commission*, in *House Executive Documents*, 46th Cong., 2d sess., 1880, 22, no. 46 (serial no. 1923). See also Paul W. Gates, *History of Public Land Law Development* (Washington, D.C.: Government Printing Office, 1968), pp. 422–434.

[3]Gates, *Public Land Law*, p. 434.

[4]U.S., *Statutes at Large*, 20:89.

[5]Gates, *Public Land Law*, pp. 468–477.

[6]U.S., Congress, House, *Report of the Commissioner of the General Land Office* [William A. J. Sparks], in *House Executive Documents*, 49th Cong., 1st sess., October 22, 1885, 2:(serial no. 2378) 202–203. Earlier in the report, Sparks expressed in his own words the same idea put forward by Inspector Greene. "It seems," Sparks said, "that the prevailing idea running through this office and those subordinate to it was that the government had no distinctive rights to be considered, and no special interests to protect hence, as between the government and the spoilers of the public domain, the government usually had the worst of it" (p. 155).

[7]Third annual message to Congress, December 7, 1903, *Messages and Papers of the Presidents*, ed. James D. Richardson (New York: Bureau of National Literature, 1897—), 14:6800–6801.

[8]Jerry A. O'Callaghan, *The Disposition of the Public Domain in Oregon*, a doctoral dissertation at Stanford University printed for the use of the Senate Committee on Interior and Insular Affairs (Washington, D.C.: Government Printing Office, 1960), pp. 89–92 and passim.

[9]U.S., Congress, Senate, *Report of the Public Land Law Review Commission*, in *Senate Documents*, 58th Cong., 3d sess., March 7, 1904, 4, no. 189 (serial no. 4766):xv and passim. The report reflects a sensitivity to the harmful implications of land monopoly and the spread of a tenant system not often encountered in the 1970s. "Nearly everywhere," the report warned, "the large landowner has succeeded in monopolizing the best tracts whether of timber or agricultural land. There has been some outcry against this condition. Yet the lack of greater protest is significant. It is to be explained by the energy, shrewdness, and influence of the men to whom the continuation of the present condition is desirable" (p. xxiv).

474

[10]Hoover's message to the Western Governors' Conference at Salt Lake City, August 27, 1929, *Public Papers of the Presidents: Herbert Hoover, 1929* (Washington, D.C.: Government Printing Office, 1930), no. 185, p. 262. See also E. Louise Peffer, *The Closing of the Public Domain* (Stanford: Stanford University Press, 1951), pp. 203 ff.

[11]Gates, *Public Land Law*, p. 524.

[12]Hoover's message to the Western Governors' Conference, p. 264.

[13]Report to the president of the Committee on the Conservation and Administration of the Public Domain, January 16, 1931, reprinted in U.S., Congress, Senate, *Hearings before the Committee on Public Lands and Survey* on bills proposing to grant vacant unreserved, unappropriated lands to accepting states, 72d Cong., 1st sess., March–April 1932, pp. 333–371. At the hearings, Gifford Pinchot testified against transfer to states (p. 298).

[14]Gates, *Public Land Law*, p. 528.

[15]U.S., *Statutes at Large*, 48:1269.

[16]For example, in "Sacred Cows and Public Lands," *Harper's Magazine*, July 1948, reprinted in Bernard DeVoto, *The Easy Chair* (Cambridge: Houghton Mifflin Co., Riverside Press, 1955), pp. 257–281.

[17]Marion Clawson, *The Bureau of Land Management* (New York, Washington D.C., and London: Praeger Publishers, 1971) pp. 32–33.

[18]Ibid., p. 41.

[19]Telephone conversation with the author at Washington, D.C., Dec. 23, 1975.

[20]Ibid.

[21]The National Forest Multiple Use and Sustained Yield Act of 1960, U.S., *Statutes at Large*, 74:215.

[22]The Public Lands Classification and Multiple Use Act of 1964, U.S., *Statutes at Large*, 78:986.

[23]The commission's organic act, U.S., *Statutes at Large*, 78:982.

[24]The Federal Advisory Committee Act of October 6, 1972 (Public Law 92-463). Metcalf's law acknowledged that advisory committees frequently are useful and beneficial but provided that they should be "advisory only" and should be "fairly balanced" in membership. Minutes of meetings were to be kept and, normally, made public. The meetings themselves were to be open. Some advisory groups found means of circumventing the spirit of the law, on one ground or another. See Robert Engler, *The Brotherhood of Oil* (Chicago and London: University of Chicago Press, 1977), pp. 181–182.

[25]The Wilderness Preservation Act of 1964, U.S., *Statutes at Large*, 78:980.

[26]*Report of the Public Land Law Review Commission*, 1970, p. iii.

[27]Ibid., p. 2.

[28]Author's interview with Clark in Tucson, 1971.

[29]Ibid.

[30]*Report of the Public Land Law Review Commission*, 1970, p. 44.

[31]*What's Ahead for Our Public Lands?*, a summary review of the activities and final report of the Public Land Law Review Commission, compiled for

the Natural Resources Council of America by Hamilton K. Pyles (Washington, D.C.: Natural Resources Council of America, 1970), p. 11 and passim.

[32]U.S., Congress, House, *Hearings before a Subcommittee of the Committee on Appropriations*, 93rd Cong., 1st sess., March 26, 1973, pt. 1, pp. 748 ff.

[33]Ibid., p. 754.

[34]In August 1966, after leaving the Bureau of Land Management, former BLM Director Charles H. Stoddard made a twenty-four-page "report and summary" of actions in the BLM during his directorship. The quoted paragraph is on p. 1.

[35]The Federal Land Policy and Management Act of 1976, U.S., *Statutes at Large*, 90:2743.

[36]Author's interview in Gregg's office, Interior Department Building, June 19, 1979.

7. THE BOWELS OF THE EARTH

[1]The Mining Act of 1872, U.S., *Statutes at Large*, 17:91. This rounded out and superseded two earlier laws approved by Congress in 1866 and 1870. The earlier laws were an Act Granting the Right of Way to Ditch and Canal Owners over the Public Lands, and for Other Purposes, U.S., *Statutes at Large*, 1866, 14:251, and an amendment thereto, U.S., *Statutes at Large*, 1870, 16:217.

[2]Frank J. Barry, Jr., *Basic American Mining Law* (Tucson: College of Mines, 1966), p. 3. Barry first delivered this address to a symposium sponsored by the College of Mines and College of Law, University of Arizona, Tucson, on March 21–23, 1966. He was then solicitor of the Interior Department.

[3]Secretary Udall's letter to the chairman and members of the Public Land Law Review Commission, dated January 15, 1969, urges complete replacement of the 1872 law. The passage quoted is on p. 1 of the four-page, single-spaced letter. It was accompanied by a draft of a leasing bill.

[4]Text of Overton's address, made available by the American Mining Congress.

[5]U.S., Congress, House, Committee on Interior and Insular Affairs, Subcommittee on Mines and Mining, *Mining Law Reform: Hearings on H.R. 5831 and H.R. 9292*, 95th Cong., 1st sess., October 13, 14, and 18, 1977 (serial no. 9528).

[6]Ibid., p. 121.

[7]Surface Mining Control and Reclamation Act of 1977, Public Law 95-87, U.S., *Statutes at Large*, 9:445.

[8]*Public Land Statistics, 1976*, U.S. Interior Department, Bureau of Land Management (Washington, D.C.: Government Printing Office, 1976), pp. 100–101.

9*One Third of the Nation's Land,* the 1970 report of the Public Land Law Review Commission (Washington, D.C.: Government Printing Office), p. 121.

10Polk's annual message to Congress, December 5, 1848, *Messages and Papers of the Presidents,* 4:629. Also quoted by Robert W. Swenson, "Legal Aspects of Mineral Resources Exploitation," in *History of Public Land Law Development,* by Paul W. Gates (Washington, D.C.: Government Printing Office, 1968), chap. 23, p. 708.

11See William S. Greever, *The Bonanza West: The Story of the Western Mining Rushes, 1848–1900* (Norman: University of Oklahoma Press, 1963), p. 54. The total California yield for the first ten years, through 1859, has been put at about $595 million.

12U.S., Congress, Senate, *Congressional Globe,* 36th Cong., 1st sess., 1860, p. 1754. Also see Swenson, "Legal Aspects," p. 713.

13Ibid., p. 1772.

14U.S., Congress, House, *Congressional Globe,* 39th Cong., 1st sess., 1866, pp. 4049–4054. Also see Swenson, "Legal Aspects," pp. 716–721; and George W. Julian, *Political Recollections: 1840 to 1872,* reprint ed. (Miami, Fla.: Mnemosyne Publishing Co., 1969), chap. 13.

15*Congressional Globe,* 39th Cong., 1st sess., 1866, p. 4050.

16The "prudent man" doctrine was articulated by the secretary of the interior in a landmark 1894 case called *Castle* v. *Womble,* a contest between a homesteader and a miner. In this case, the miner prevailed.

17Barry to author, April 4, 1979.

18See Greever, *The Bonanza West,* and C. B. Glasscock, *The War of the Copper Kings: Builders of Butte and Wolves of Wall Street* (Indianapolis and New York: Bobbs-Merrill Co., 1935), passim.

19Atlantic Richfield's annual report for 1977. Anaconda was merged into a wholly owned subsidiary of Atlantic Richfield on January 12, 1977. The purchasing company said its investment was about $700 million. In its annual report for 1979, Atlantic Richfield noted there had been a "vigorous recovery" in the world copper market in the last year, with copper reaching $1.30 a pound by early 1980.

20Gustavus Myers, *History of the Great American Fortunes* (New York: Modern Library, 1936). Note Pt. III, chap. 1, "The Seizure of the Public Domain," p. 213–238.

21Gene M. Gressley, introduction to *Bostonians and Bullion: The Journal of Robert Livermore, 1892–1915,* ed. Gressley (Lincoln: University of Nebraska Press, 1968), p. xiii.

22Ibid., chap. 9, "Camp Bird, Telluride, and the Smuggler-Union." Labor strife involving the Western Federation of Miners was bitter in the Rockies in the early 1900s.

23W. A. Swanberg, *Citizen Hearst: A Biography of William Randolph Hearst* (New York: Charles Scribner's Sons, 1961), p. 20 and passim.

24Ibid., p. 36.

[25]See Harvey O'Connor, *The Guggenheims: The Making of an American Dynasty* (New York: Covici, Friede, 1937), chap. 6, "Shaking Down the Smelter's Trust."

[26]Ibid., chap. 15, "Silver Prince in the Senate," pp. 241, 246. Guggenheim joined eighteen other millionaires in the Senate, O'Connor notes.

[27]For details about Arizona copper mining over the years, see Charles H. Dunning with Edward H. Peplow, Jr., *Rock to Riches: The Story of Arizona Mines and Mining* (Pasadena: Hicks Publishing, 1966). Clark's heirs sold the United Verde to Phelps Dodge in 1935.

[28]Viewed when the author visited the Twin Buttes operations in November 1971.

[29]Mining and Minerals Policy Act of 1970, Public Law 91-631. U.S. *Statutes at Large* 84:1876.

[30]Charles F. Barber, testifying on July 9, 1969, U.S., Congress, Senate, *Hearing before the Subcommittee on Minerals, Materials, and Fuels of the Senate Committee on Interior and Insular Affairs*, 91st Cong., 1st sess., p. 45. The hearing concerned S. 719, a bill to establish a national mining and minerals policy.

[31]National Materials Policy Act of 1970, Title II of the Resource Recovery Act, Public Law 91-512. U.S. Statutes at Large 84:1234.

[32]*Material Needs and the Environment Today and Tomorrow*, final report of the National Commission of Materials Policy (Washington, D.C.: Government Printing Office, 1973), p. 1–5.

[33]Gary Bennethum and L. Courtland Lee, "Is Our Account Overdrawn?" *Mining Congress Journal*, September 1975. Bennethum was staff assistant to the assistant secretary for land and water resources. Lee was a geologist with the Division of Mineral Resources, Bureau of Land Management.

[34]William K. Wyant, *St. Louis Post-Dispatch*, December 18, 1971. Reprinted as part of a series on mining in U.S., Congress, Senate, *Congressional Record*, March 28, 1972, pp. S4933–4934.

[35]U.S., Congress, House, Subcommittee on Mines and Mining, *Mining Law Reform*, October 13, 1977, p. 111.

[36]Ibid., October 14, 1977, pp. 137–143.

[37]Ibid., October 14, 1977, p. 180. This was Russell Chadwick of Spokane, Washington, chairman, Legislative Committee, Northwest Mining Association.

8. PENNSYLVANIA, TEXAS, AND BIG OIL

[1]Nixon's address to the nation about policies to deal with the energy shortage, November 7, 1973, *Public Papers of the Presidents: Richard Nixon, 1973*, (Washington, D.C.: Government Printing Office, 1974), no. 323, pp. 916–922.

[2]Nixon's special message to the Congress on energy policy, April 18, 1973, *Papers of the Presidents*, no. 128, pp. 302–319. Deregulation of natural gas was proposed on pp. 305–306.

[3]U.S., Congress, Senate, Current Energy Shortage Oversight Series, 6 pts., December 14, 1973–April 10, 1974, *The Major Oil Companies: Hearings before the Permanent Subcommittee on Investigations, Government Operations Committee*, 93d Cong., 2d sess., January 21, 1974, pt. 2.

[4]Ibid., January 23, 1974, pt. 4, p. 473. When a senior Exxon USA official said he could not supply information on the company's dividends offhand, Jackson responded, "I am flabbergasted."

[5]Noting that bills had been introduced in both the Senate and the House to break up oil companies into "functional sectors" and keep them from developing coal, uranium, and other nonoil energy sources, the American Petroleum Institute, which represents the oil industry, sent to the news media in August 1977 copies of a book by John R. Coyne, Jr., and Patricia S. Coyne, *The Big Breakup: Energy in Crisis* (Kansas City: Sheed Andrews & McMeel, 1977).

[6]Ruth Sheldon Knowles, *The Greatest Gamblers: The Epic of American Oil Exploration* (New York, Toronto, and London: McGraw-Hill, 1959), p. 9.

[7]See Thomas Lloyd Miller, *The Public Lands of Texas, 1519–1970*, with a foreword by Ralph W. Yarborough, former Democratic senator from Texas (Norman: University of Oklahoma Press, 1972), passim.

[8]Ibid., p. 32.

[9]Ibid., p. 160.

[10]Ibid., p. ix.

[11]James A. Clark and Michel T. Halbouty, *Spindletop* (New York: Random House, 1952), passim.

[12]Ibid., p. 139.

[13]Richard O'Connor, *The Oil Barons* (Boston and Toronto: Little, Brown & Co., 1971), pp. 139–143.

[14]James A. Clark and Michel T. Halbouty, *The Last Boom* (New York: Random House, 1972), passim.

[15]Joseph Stanley Clark, *The Oil Century: From the Drake Well to the Conservation Era* (Norman: University of Oklahoma Press, 1958), pp. 96–98, and Samuel B. Pettengill, *Hot Oil: The Problem of Petroleum* (New York: Economic Forum Co., 1936), p. 75. The frequently cited case, involving a gas lease, is *Westmoreland and Cambria Natural Gas Co. v. Dewitt et al.*, 130 *Pennsylvania State Reports* 235 (1889).

[16]The Railroad Commission of Texas has had the duty of conserving oil and gas in the state since about 1919. Clark's *The Oil Century* describes the waste of the early years on pp. 147–165. Efforts by oil-producing states to limit production tend to keep prices up, of course, and bear some resemblance to policies later adopted with spectacular success by the Oil Producing and Exporting Countries (OPEC). Despite the "hot oil" trou-

479

bles of the 1930s, some oilmen were not enthusiastic about putting their heads under a federal yoke. The brash Harold L. Ickes, secretary of the interior, addressed the American Petroleum Institute at Dallas in November 1934, urged federal action to curb waste, and said: "I have no doubt that facing me in this audience today are men who readily join in the general acclaim of business men generally in the United States that private industry, no matter how badly managed, is better managed than it would be by government. Again, if I were not as polite as I really am, I might remark that if private initiative is so wonderful and so self-sufficient, how did it happen that the oil industry got into such a mess and why did it ever think of appealing to the federal government for help?" (quoted in Pettengill, *Hot Oil*, p. 253).

[17]*American Petroleum—Supply and Demand*, a report of the American Petroleum Institute published in 1925. A summary signed by API President J. Edgar Pew and ten other oilmen ended with this statement: "Waste in the production, transportation, refining and distribution of petroleum and its products is negligible" (quoted in Pettengill, *Hot Oil*, pp. 212–214).

[18]An Act to Regulate Interstate and Foreign Commerce in Petroleum . . . , February 22, 1935, U.S., *Statutes at Large*, pt. 1. 49:30.

[19]Clark and Halbouty, *The Last Boom*, pp. 266–271.

[20]Tax Reform Act of 1969, U.S., *Statutes at Large*, 83:487.

[21]Tax Reduction Act of 1975, U.S., *Statutes at Large*, 89:26.

[22]See *A Time to Choose: America's Energy Future*, Energy Policy Project of the Ford Foundation (Cambridge, Mass.: Ballinger Publishing Co., 1974); *Energy in America's Future: The Choices before Us*, a study by the staff of the Resources for the Future National Energy Strategies Project (Baltimore and London: Johns Hopkins University Press, 1979); and Robert Stobaugh and Daniel Yergin, eds., *Energy Future*, report of the Energy Project at the Harvard Business School (New York: Random House, Ballantine Books, 1979).

[23]The $90 billion figure was mentioned by George Fumich, Jr., assistant secretary for fossil energy, U.S. Department of Energy, in remarks prepared for delivery October 13, 1980, at a conference on synthetic fuels at San Francisco.

[24]*The Report of the Platform Committee to the 1980 Democratic National Committee*, chap. 4, "Energy, Natural Resources, Environment and Agriculture."

[25]See *Environmental Quality—1979*, tenth annual report of the Council on Environmental Quality (Washington, D.C.: Government Printing Office, 1979), pp. 318.

[26]Crude Oil Windfall Profit Tax Act of 1980, Public Law 96-223, U.S., *Statutes at Large*, 94:611.

[27]Energy Security Act, Public Law 96-294.

[28]*Washington Post*, January 29, 1981.

[29]*Congressional Quarterly*, November 1, 1980, p. 3286.

9. TIDELANDS AND THE OUTER SHELF

[1]Ernest R. Bartley, *The Tidelands Oil Controversy: A Legal and Historical Analysis,* reprint ed. (New York: Arno Press, 1979). See this book for a thorough discussion of the tidelands issue. The Ickes letter to Proctor is dealt with on pp. 128 ff.

[2]*Energy Resources and National Policy,* report of the Energy Resources Committee to the National Resources Committee (Washington, D.C.: Government Printing Office, 1939), p. 29.

[3]*Public Papers of the Presidents: Harry S. Truman, 1946* (Washington, D.C.: Government Printing Office, 1947), no. 189, pp. 371–372.

[4]*U.S.* v. *California,* 332 *U.S. Reports* 19, p. 32.

[5]Ibid., p. 38.

[6]339 *U.S. Reports* 707.

[7]Rear platform and other informal remarks in Texas, September 27, 1948, *Public Papers of the Presidents: Harry S. Truman, 1948,* no. 212, p. 582.

[8]Address at the National Convention Banquet of the Americans for Democratic Action, May 17, 1952, *Public Papers of the Presidents: Harry S. Truman, 1952,* no. 129, p. 345.

[9]Veto of bill concerning title to offshore lands, May 29, 1952, ibid., no. 146, pp. 379–384.

[10]Statement by the president upon issuing order setting aside submerged lands of the Continental Shelf as a naval petroleum reserve (Executive Order 10426), January 16, 1953, *Public Papers of the Presidents: Harry S. Truman, 1953,* no. 379, pp. 1202–1203.

[11]U.S., Congress, Senate, *Congressional Record,* 83d Cong., 1st sess., April 1, 1953, 99, pt. 2:2611. The "little band of liberals," as Senator Morse called them, put on a vivid forensic display and seemed to enjoy themselves even though they considered defeat inevitable. They took on themselves the role of defenders of the public lands, frequently invoking the memory of the great Republican conservationists Theodore Roosevelt and Gifford Pinchot. The tidelands bill, they charged, was a "giveaway" of $50 to $100 billion in public assets. It amounted to a classic Senate debate, worth reading in 1980 as background for the so-called Sagebrush Rebellion in western states.

[12]Malone's effort came on May 4, 1953, the day before the final vote. *Congressional Record,* pp. 4334 ff.

[13]Submerged Lands Act of 1953, U.S., *Statutes at Large,* 67:29.

[14]Outer Continental Shelf Lands Act, U.S., *Statutes at Large,* 67:462.

[15]*Environmental Quality—1980,* eleventh annual Report of the Council of Environmental Quality (Washington, D.C.: Government Printing Office, 1980), pp. 279–281.

[16]U.S., Department of Energy, Energy Information Administration, *Annual Report to Congress, 1979* (Washington, D.C.: Government Printing Office), 3:122.

[17]*Overview: Energy in Transition, 1985–2010,* final report of the Committee on Nuclear and Alternative Energy Systems, National Research Council, National Academy of Sciences (Washington, D.C.: Government Printing Office, 1979), pp. 21–22.

[18]*Environmental Quality—1980,* p. 280.

10. THE PUBLIC'S COAL, NATURAL GAS, AND OIL SHALE

[1]U.S., Congress, Senate, Committee on Interior and Insular Affairs, Subcommittee on Minerals, Materials, and Fuels, *Federal Coal Leasing Amendments Act of 1975: Hearings on S.391 . . . ,* 94th Cong., 1st sess., May 7–8, 1975.

[2]Ibid., pp. 276 ff.

[3]Ibid., p. 279.

[4]Surface Mining Control and Reclamation Act, U.S., *Statutes at Large,* 91:445.

[5]*Where We Agree: Report of the National Coal Policy Project,* released under sponsorship of the Georgetown University Center for Strategic and International Studies, Washington D.C., February 9, 1978. On the same date, the Environmental Policy Center issued a press release criticizing the project's recommendations.

[6]U.S., *Statutes at Large,* 17:607.

[7]See Robert W. Swenson, "Legal Aspects of Mineral Resources Exploitation," in *History of Public Land Law Development,* by Paul W. Gates (Washington, D.C.: Government Printing Office, 1968), chap. 23, pp. 726–730.

[8]U.S., *Constitution,* Art. IV, sec. 3.

[9]Theodore Roosevelt, *An Autobiography* (New York: Macmillan Co., 1913), p. 393. See also Everett Dick, *The Lure of the Land* (Lincoln: University of Nebraska Press, 1970), p. 328.

[10]James Penick, Jr., *Progressive Politics and Conservation: The Ballinger-Pinchot Affair* (Chicago and London: University of Chicago Press, 1968), passim.

[11]Natural Gas Act of 1938, U.S., *Statutes at Large,* 52:821.

[12]U.S., Congress, Senate, Subcommittee of the Committee on Interstate and Foreign Commerce, *Hearings on Reappointment of Leland Olds to the Federal Power Commission,* 81st Cong., 1st sess., September 27–29 and October 3, 1949. The Texas congressman was Rep. John E. Lyle, Democrat, who had been wounded at Anzio (see p. 28).

[13]*Phillips Petroleum Co.* v. *Wisconsin,* 347 *U.S. Reports* 672.

[14]Veto of bill to amend the Natural Gas Act, February 17, 1956, *Public Papers of the Presidents: Dwight D. Eisenhower, 1956* (Washington, D.C.: Government Printing Office, 1957), no. 41, pp. 256–257. Eisenhower cited evidence of "highly questionable activity" and spoke of conduct he described as arrogant and in defiance of acceptable standards of propriety.

[15]The National Energy Act, passed by Congress on October 15, 1978, and signed into law by President Carter November 9. "We have declared to ourselves and the world," the president said, "our intent to control our use of energy, and thereby to control our own destiny as a nation."

16*North Central Power Study: Report of Phase I*, 2 vols. (Billings, Mont.: 1971). The Bureau of Reclamation, Interior Department, had overall responsibility for the study, which was launched by Smith at Omaha on May 26, 1970.

17The Clean Air Amendments of 1970, Public Law 91-601, U.S., *Statutes at Large*, 84:1676. The National Environmental Policy Act of 1969, Public Law 91-190, U.S., *Statutes at Large*, 83:852.

18*Sierra Club* v. *Ruckelshaus*, affirmed by an equally divided U.S. Supreme Court June 11, 1973. 412 *U.S. Reports* 541. Bruce J. Terris argued the case for the conservationist side. Also present was James W. Moorman, who later became assistant attorney general under President Carter.

19*Sierra Club* v. *Morton*, 44 U.S.L.W. 5104(U.S. June 28, 1976).

20*NRDC* v. *Hughes*, 10 E.R.C. 1717 (D.D.C. 1977).

21U.S., General Accounting Office, *Improvements Needed in Administration of Federal Coal-Leasing Program*, March 29, 1972.

22Ibid. See also the GAO's report, *Further Action Needed on Recommendations for Improving the Administration of Federal Coal-Leasing Program*, April 28, 1975, appendix I, p. 19.

23*Leased and Lost*, report of the Council on Economic Priorities, New York, 1974. In September 1976, the council in its *Newsletter* reviewed western coal development again, noting that the Interior Department's three-year leasing moratorium had been lifted. It reported plans for rapid expansion of western coal production. See also U.S., General Accounting Office, *Rocky Mountain Energy Resource Development: Status, Potential, and Socioeconomic Issues*, July 13, 1977.

24U.S., Congress, House, Appropriations Subcommittee, *Hearings for 1979*, 95th Cong., 2d sess., p. 548.

25See *Andrus* v. *Shell Oil Co. et al.*, in which the U.S. Supreme Court on June 2, 1980, affirmed the Tenth Circuit Court of Appeals in holding that the federal government could not invalidate pre-1920 oil shale claims by imposing a "present marketability" requirement. The Supreme Court was divided six to three. The Justice Department, which argued unsuccessfully that the claims were not valid, had asserted that an adverse decision might require the United States to patent more than five million acres of federal land for $2.50 an acre under the old 1872 Mining Law.

26Special message to the Congress on energy resources, June 4, 1971, *Public Papers of the Presidents: Richard Nixon, 1971*, p. 709.

27U.S., Interior Department, *Final Environmental Statement for the Prototype Oil Shale Leasing Program* (Washington, D.C.: Government Printing Office, 1973).

28Ibid., 1:1–42.

29*Environmental Quality—1975*, sixth annual report of the Council on Environmental Quality (Washington, D.C.: Government Printing Office, 1975), pp. 436–438.

[30]President Ford visited the Paraho site by helicopter from Vail, Colorado, on August 18, 1975. For a discussion of oil shale problems, see Chris Welles, *The Elusive Bonanza: The Story of Oil Shale—America's Richest and Most Neglected Resource* (New York: E. P. Dutton & Co., 1970).

[31]U.S., Department of Energy, Energy Information Administration, *Annual Report to Congress—1979* (Washington, D.C.: Government Printing Office), 3:134–135.

[32]U.S., Department of Energy, *Reducing U.S. Oil Vulnerability: Energy Policy for the 1980s*, an analytical report to the secretary of energy prepared by the assistant secretary for policy and evaluation, November 10, 1980, p. 23.

[33]*Environmental Quality—1980*, eleventh annual report of the Council on Environmental Quality (Washington, D.C.: Government Printing Office, 1980), pp. 263–264.

[34]Ibid., p. 263. See also Sierra Club, *National News Report*, August 31, 1979, April 28, 1980, and July 10, 1980.

11. FALLEN TIMBERS

[1]Ralph W. Hidy, Frank Ernest Hill, and Allan Nevins, *Timber and Men: The Weyerhaeuser Story* (New York: Macmillan Co., 1963), pp. 212–213 and passim.

[2]F. K. Weyerhaeuser, *Trees and Men* (Princeton, N.J.: Newcomen Publications, 1951), p. 23.

[3]Statistics on operations of the major timber companies are drawn largely from their annual reports for 1973.

[4]Brock Evans, Washington representative of the Sierra Club, to author, April 18, 1979.

[5]See *The Outlook for Timber in the United States*, Forest Service Report no. 20, Department of Agriculture, July 1974.

[6]Paul W. Gates, *History of Public Land Law Development* (Washington, D.C.: Government Printing Office, 1968), pp. 546 ff.

[7]Philip Hyde and Francois Leydet, *The Last Redwoods* (San Francisco: Sierra Club, 1963). See also Kramer Adams, *The Redwoods: The Larger-than-Life Story of the Noblest Plants on Earth* (New York: Popular Library), passim.

[8]President Johnson's annual message to Congress on the state of the Union, January 17, 1968, *Public Papers of the Presidents: Lyndon B. Johnson, 1968–69* (Washington, D.C.: Government Printing Office, 1970), no. 14, p. 31.

[9]Redwood Park Act, Public Law 90-045, U.S., *Statutes at Large*, 82:931.

[10]Over the years since this quip was attributed to the future President Reagan, doubt has arisen as to precisely what was said. He contends he was misquoted. Reagan, then a candidate for governor of California, was addressing the Western Wood Products Association, an industry group, on March 12, 1966, at the St. Francis Hotel. Bob Adams, of the *St. Louis Post-Dispatch* Washington Bureau, listened to a tape of the program that was found among Reagan's gubernatorial papers at the Hoover Institution at

Stanford University. Adams reported in the *Post-Dispatch* August 3, 1980, that Reagan was asked at a question-and-answer session what he thought of the proposed Redwood National Park and made a response that wound up: "You know, a tree's a tree—how many more do you need to look at?"

This was in the context of Reagan having told the audience he had not studied the federal park proposal but was inclined toward an industry plan that would bring to 115,000 the total acreage in the state's redwood parks.

Adams's version of the Reagan remark corresponds with the version given by California's former Democratic Gov. Edmund G. ("Pat") Brown in his book, *Reagan and Reality: The Two Californias* (New York: Praeger, 1970).

[11]Redwood Park Act of 1978, Public Law 95-250, March 27, 1978, U.S., *Statutes at Large*, 92:163.

[12]Gates, *Public Land Law*, p. 558.

[13]The 1897 forest law was tucked into an appropriations bill in the first session of the Fifty-fifth Congress. It said no forest reservations were to be established "except to improve and protect the forest within the reservation, or for the purpose of securing favorable conditions of water flows, and to furnish a continuous supply of timber." (U.S., *Statutes at Large*, 30:35).

[14]The National Forest Multiple Use and Sustained Yield Act of 1960, U.S., *Statutes at Large* , 74:215.

[15]The Public Lands Classification and Multiple Use Act of 1964, U.S., *Statutes at Large*, 78:986.

[16]The Wilderness Preservation Act of 1964, U.S., *Statutes at Large*, 78:980.

[17]U.S., Congress, House, Subcommittee on Public Lands, Interior Committee, *Wilderness Preservation System: Hearings on Bills to Establish . . .* , 87th Cong., 1st sess., November 6, 1961, p. 890.

[18]U.S., Congress, Senate, Committee on Interior and Insular Affairs, Subcommittee on Public Lands, *Hearings on Eastern Wilderness Areas*, 93rd Cong., 1st sess., February 21, 1973, p. 262.

[19]See the Wilderness Society's press release of June 15, 1978, on the publishing of the RARE-II draft environmental impact statement by the Forest Service, and the Sierra Club's *National News Report* of May 18, 1979, after President Carter had passed the Forest Service's recommendations along to Congress.

[20]Brock Evans to author, April 18, 1979.

[21]See Sierra Club, *National News Report*, May 9, 1980.

[22]U.S., Congress, House, Committee on Agriculture, Subcommittee on Forests, *National Timber Supply Act of 1969: Hearings on H.R. 10344 . . .* , 91st Cong., 1st sess., May 21–23.

[23]Ibid., p. 9.

[24]Author's interview with Brandborg, January 9, 1975.

[25]U.S., Congress, House, *Congressional Record*, 91st Cong., 2d sess., 116, pt. 4:5099–5117. Rep. Wayne Aspinall, Democrat of Colorado, supported the timber bill. His Republican counterpart, the conservation-minded Rep. John Saylor of Pennsylvania, denounced it and spoke of the "disgraceful performance of two Cabinet secretaries dancing to the industry's tune." He referred to George Romney of housing and urban development and Clifford M. Hardin of agriculture.

[26]Nixon's statement about the report of the Task Force on Softwood Lumber and Plywood, June 19, 1970, *Public Papers of the Presidents: Richard Nixon, 1970*, no. 194, p. 510. The full timber report was printed in the *Weekly Compilation of Presidential Documents*, 6:788. President Nixon called on the Agriculture and Interior departments for an increased timber harvest.

[27]*One Third of the Nation's Land*, 1970 report by the Public Land Law Review Commission (Washington, D.C.: Government Printing Office), pp. 50, 97.

[28]Author's interview with Brandborg, January 9, 1975.

[29]Nixon's statement about the report of the Advisory Panel on Timber and the Environment, September 24, 1973, *Public Papers of the Presidents: Richard Nixon, 1973*, no. 271, pp. 821–822.

[30]*Sierra Club, NRDC, et al.* v. *Butz* was filed in June 1972. The plaintiffs obtained a preliminary injunction in August 1973.

[31]Natural Resources Defense Council press release, February 25, 1974.

[32]U.S., Congress, Senate, Committee on Interior and Insular Affairs, Subcommittee on the Public Lands, *"Clear-cutting" Practices on National Timberlands: Hearings*, 92nd Cong., 1st sess., April 5–6, 1971, pt. 1, "Management Practices on the Public Lands."

[33]*A University View of the Forest Service*, prepared for the Committee on Interior and Insular Affairs, U.S. Senate, by a select committee of the University of Montana at the request of Senator Metcalf, 91st Cong., 2d sess., December 1, 1970, p. 13.

[34]Senator McGee testified at the Church Senate subcommittee hearings on clear-cutting April 5, 1971. See U.S., Congress, Senate, *"Clear-cutting" Practices*, pp. 2–9.

[35]Ibid., p. 22.

[36]Ibid., April 6, 1971, p. 158.

[37]Ibid., May 7, 1971, pt. 3, pp. 829–830.

[38]Ibid., May 7, 1971, pt. 3, p. 939.

[39]Ibid., April 6, 1971, pt. 1, p. 198.

[40]Forest and Rangeland Renewable Resources Planning Act of 1974, U.S., *Statutes at Large*, 88:476.

[41]*Izaak Walton League* v. *Butz*, 5 E.L.R. 20573 (4th Cir. August 21, 1975).

[42]National Forest Management Act of 1976, U.S., *Statutes at Large*, 90:2958.

[43]Gifford Pinchot, *Breaking New Ground* (Seattle and London: University of Washington Press, 1972), p. 284.

12. COME BLOW YOUR HORN

[1]Walter Prescott Webb, *The Great Plains* (New York: Ginn & Co., 1931), pp. 291–298. Webb's book has many merits, one of which is that the author takes the trouble to define his terms and explain what he is talking about.

[2]Theodore Roosevelt, whom some westerners called "Old Four Eyes" because of his spectacles, was looked upon as something of a renegade when he made vigorous efforts to stop illegal fencing. He had been a rancher himself, and it was thought he should have been sympathetic.

[3]Mari Sandoz, *The Cattlemen* (New York: Hastings House, 1958), p. 453.

[4]Paul W. Gates, *History of Public Land Law Development* (Washington, D.C.: Government Printing Office, 1968), and E. Louise Peffer, *The Closing of the Public Domain* (Stanford: Stanford University Press, 1951), p. 80.

[5]Elting E. Morison, ed., *The Letters of Theodore Roosevelt*, 8 vols. (Cambridge: Harvard University Press, 1951-1954), 4:1217–1218. Quoted in Gates, *Public Land Law*, p. 488.

[6]Wyant, *St. Louis Post-Dispatch*, September 7, 1972.

[7]T. A. Larson, *History of Wyoming* (Lincoln: University of Nebraska Press, 1965), pp. 180 ff. Also see Gates, *Public Land Law*, p. 477.

[8]Larson, *History of Wyoming*, p. 382.

[9]Ibid., p. 270. See also Harry Sinclair Drago, *The Great Range Wars: Violence on the Grasslands* (New York: Dodd, Mead & Co., 1970), pp. 260 ff.

[10]This lamentable disorder was known as the Rock Springs Massacre, occurring September 2, 1885. See Larson, *History of Wyoming*, pp. 141–144. Although sixteen men were arrested, a county grand jury failed to indict.

[11]Paul H. Roberts, *Hoof Prints on Forest Ranges: The Early Years of National Forest Range Administration* (San Antonio: Naylor Co., 1963), pp. 68–77. See also Gifford Pinchot, *Breaking New Ground* (Seattle and London: University of Washington Press, 1972), p. 272.

[12]*U.S. v Grimaud et al.*, a California case, 220 *U.S. Reports* 506, and *U.S. v. Light*, a Colorado case, 220 *U.S. Reports* 523. In both cases, decided in early May 1911, the Supreme Court held that regulations made by the secretary of agriculture as to the grazing of sheep on forest reserves have the force of law and that violations are punishable.

[13]Taylor Grazing Act of 1934, U.S., *Statutes at Large*, 48:1269.

[14]Wesley Calef, *Private Grazing and Public Lands: Studies of the Local Management of the Taylor Grazing Act* (Chicago: University of Chicago Press, 1960), p. 43.

[15]Roberts, *Hoof Prints on Forest Ranges*, p. 102.

[16]Gates, *Public Land Law*, p. 607.

[17]Ibid., pp. 614–615. See also Marion Clawson, *Bureau of Land Management* (New York: Praeger, 1971), pp. 35–36.

[18]After his federal career, Carpenter served as a spokesman for the ranching community of which he was a part. He was considered an eloquent advocate. See Phillip O. Foss, *Politics and Grass: The Administration of Grazing on the Public Domain* (Seattle: University of Washington Press, 1960), particularly chap. 6, "Home Rule on the Range."

[19]Clawson, *Bureau of Land Management*, p. 172.

[20]Bernard DeVoto, "The West against Itself," in *The Easy Chair* (Boston: Houghton Mifflin Co., 1955), p. 250.

[21]Special message to the Congress transmitting Reorganization Plan 3 of 1946, May 16, 1946, *Public Papers of the Presidents: Harry S. Truman, 1946* (Washington, D.C.: Government Printing Office, 1947), no. 118, pp. 262–263.

[22]William Voigt, Jr., *Public Grazing Lands: Use and Misuse by Industry and Government* (New Brunswick, N.J.: Rutgers University Press, 1976), p. 6. Voigt was associated with the Izaak Walton League of America.

[23]DeVoto, "The West against Itself," in *The Easy Chair*, p. 251.

[24]Barrett's hearings were held in the spring and summer and early fall of 1947, reaching a climax at Grand Junction, Colorado, on September 5. U.S., Congress, House, Committee on Public Lands, *Hearings . . .*, 80th Cong., 1st sess. At Rawlins, Wyoming, on September 2, and later at Grand Junction, Forest Service officials were accused of stirring up public sentiment against ranchers. Barrett saw an "attempt to make scoundrels and crooks of the stockmen of the West."

[25]DeVoto's "Sacred Cows and Public Lands," written in July 1948, provided a lively account of the Barrett "Wild West Show" and chided Barrett for his attempt to abolish the Jackson Hole National Monument. The Izaak Walton League observer's complaint is in *The Easy Chair*, p. 273.

[26]Voigt, *Public Grazing Lands*, p. 207. On the western effort against federal ownership, see also Gates, *Public Land Law*, pp. 622–632, and Foss, *Politics and Grass*, p. 190.

[27]See U.S., Congress, Senate, Committee on Interior and Insular Affairs, Subcommittee on Public Lands, *Review of the Taylor Grazing Act: Hearings . . .*, 88th Cong., 1st sess., January–March 1963, 3 pts., passim.

[28]The tangled grazing fee situation at the change of administrations from Johnson to Nixon was promptly explored by both the Senate and House. On the House side, Rep. Wayne N. Aspinall, of Colorado, was not happy with the increase in fees announced by the outgoing administration on Jan. 14, 1969. See U.S., Congress, House, Committee on Interior and Insular Affairs, Subcommittee on Public Lands, *Review of Grazing Fees: Hearings . . .*, 91st Cong., 1st sess., March 4–5, 1969.

[29]U.S., Congress, Senate, Committee on Interior and Insular Affairs, Subcommittee on Public Lands, *Grazing Fees on Public Lands: Hearings . . .*, 91st Cong., 1st sess., February 27–28, 1969.

[30]Ibid., p. 204.

[31]Ibid., p. 399.

[32]Ibid., p. 146.

33See U.S., Congress, Senate, *Congressional Record*, 91st Cong., 1st sess., September 17, 1969, pp. 25767–25770.

34*The Nation's Range Resources: A Forest-Range Environmental Study*, U.S. Department of Agriculture, Forest Service, Forest Resources Report no. 19 (Washington, D.C.: Government Printing Office, 1972).

35*Range Condition Report Prepared for the Senate Committee on Appropriations*, U.S. Interior Department, Bureau of Land Management (Washington, D.C.: Government Printing Office, 1975), p. vi.

36Federal Land Policy and Management Act of 1976, Public Law 94-579, U.S., *Statutes at Large*, 90:2743.

37*Study of Fees for Grazing Livestock on Federal Lands*, a report from the secretary of the interior and the secretary of agriculture (Washington, D.C.: Government Printing Office, 1977).

38Public Rangelands Improvement Act of 1978, Public Law 95-514, U.S., *Statutes at Large*, 92:1803.

39U.S., Congress, House, Subcommittee of Appropriations Committee, *Hearings on Department of the Interior and Related Agencies, Bureau of Land Management*, 95th Cong., 2d sess., March 13, 1978, pp. 594–597.

13. TO HAVE AND TO HOLD

1Morris K. Udall, "Land Speculation: Investment in the Future . . . or Downpayment on Dust?" *Field and Stream*, December 1972. Also, reprint issued as press release by Udall's office.

2Sinclair Lewis, *Babbitt* (New York: Harcourt, Brace & Co., 1922).

3Colorado River Compact of 1922, Colorado River Commission, signed at Santa Fe, New Mexico, November 24, 1922.

4Wallace Stegner, *Beyond the Hundredth Meridian*, pp. 138–139.

5See *Dictionary of American Biography* (New York: Charles Scribner's Sons, 1961), 6:114–115.

6For a concerned view, one may turn to the General Accounting Office's report of May 4, 1979, *Colorado River Basin Problems: How to Reduce Their Impact* (Washington, D.C.: Government Printing Office, 1979). "The Colorado River Basin is in trouble," this study warned. The system functioned despite the 1977 dry year, the report said, but soon after the year 2000 the prospect is that there will not be enough water to serve the region's booming population, sustain its rapid industrial development, and support its fertile farmlands (see p. 7). For the year ending September 30, 1978, the Reclamation Bureau reported that 8,229,000 acre-feet of water passed the compact point at Lees Ferry.

7John A. McPhee, *Encounters with the Archdruid* (New York: Farrar, Straus & Giroux, 1971), p. 173.

8Lynn Bowman, *Los Angeles: Epic of a City* (Berkeley, Calif.: Howell-North Books, 1974), p. 250.

9*The Story of Hoover Dam*, U.S. Interior Department Bureau of Reclamation (Washington, D.C.: Government Printing Office, 1971), passim.

[10]Boulder Canyon Project Act of 1928, U.S., *Statutes at Large*, 45:1057.

[11]Upper Colorado River Basin Compact of 1948, Harry W. Bashore (Washington, D.C.: Government Printing Office, 1949).

[12]*Arizona* v. *California*, 373 *U.S. Reports* 546. Decided June 3, 1963.

[13]Colorado River Storage Project Act of 1956, U.S., *Statutes at Large*, 70:105.

[14]Eliot Porter, *The Place No One Knew: Glen Canyon on the Colorado* (San Francisco: Sierra Club, 1963).

[15]U.S., Congress, House, *Congressional Record*, 84th Cong., 2d sess., February 29, 1956, pp. 3619–3621.

[16]See *The Central Arizona Project: Hearings before the House Committee on Interior and Insular Affairs*, 82nd Cong., 1st sess., February–April 1951.

[17]Morris K. Udall, *Education of a Congressman: The Newsletters of Morris K. Udall, Member of Congress, Second District of Arizona*, ed. Robert L. Peabody (Indianapolis and New York: Bobbs Merrill Co., 1972). See "Tapping Arizona's Last Water Hole," May 21, 1963, pp. 145–147.

[18]McPhee, *Encounters with the Archdruid*, p. 166. See also the *Sierra Club Handbook* of 1971, which has the following on p. 55: "Following the Club's ads in major newspapers on behalf of Grand Canyon protection, the Internal Revenue Service ruled that contributions to the Sierra Club were no longer tax-deductible because of its substantial legislative effort," an event set forth in the organization's chronology for 1966.

[19]Udall, *Education of a Congressman*, p. 155. Udall's Town Hall speech, a lengthy one, was inserted in the record of the House Interior Committee's *Hearings on the Colorado River Basin Project*, 90th Cong., 2d sess., January 30, 1968, pt. 2, pp. 810–820.

[20]Colorado River Basin Project Act (Central Arizona Project), Public Law 90-537, September 30, 1968.

[21]Udall, *Education of a Congressman*, p. 157.

[22]Skillfully organized by the Jackson committee's excellent staff, the Southwest power hearings provided useful information on what was going on. See U.S., Congress, Senate, Committee on Interior and Insular Affairs, *Problems of Electrical Power Production in the Southwest: Hearings . . . ,* 92d Cong., 1st sess., May–November 1971.

[23]Ibid., Albuquerque, New Mexico, May 24, 1971, pt. 1, p. 1.

[24]Ibid., Las Vegas, Nevada, May 25, 1971, pt. 2, p. 710.

[25]U.S., Congress, House, Committee on Interior and Insular Affairs, *Colorado River Basin Project: Hearings . . . ,* 90th Cong., 2d sess., 1968, pp. 886–888.

[26]Ibid., p. 888.

[27]The establishment of the Interior Department task force was announced in a press release May 7, 1971. A press release on the Southwest Energy Task Force study followed on December 19, 1972.

[28]Secretary Morton's rejection of the Kaiparowits project and Senator Moss's reaction were described in press releases from the Interior Department and Senator Moss's office. The rejection was announced June 13, 1973.

[29]*Sierra Club* v. *Ruckelshaus*, June 11, 1973.

[30]*Sierra Club* v. *Morton*, finally decided in June 1976.

[31] Telephone interview of Southern California Edison spokesman by author at the time of the Kaiparowits combine's decision not to go ahead with the project.

[32] See, for example, *Westwide Study Report on Critical Water Problems Facing the Eleven Western States,* Interior Department, April 1975 (Washington, D.C.: Government Printing Office, 1975). This study was mandated by Congress in the Colorado River Basin Project Act of 1968. It warned that the Colorado River, on which more than half the West's population is directly dependent, may face future water shortages.

[33] In an interesting but confusing change of pace, the General Accounting Office took an encouraging new direction in a report issued January 24, 1980. Whereas in 1979 the GAO had warned that the Colorado River Basin was in trouble, with a prospect for water shortages after the year 2000, the January 1980 GAO study—*Water Supply Should Not Be an Obstacle to Meeting Energy Development Goals*—was much more encouraging. Challenging the view that the energy industry would create severe shortages throughout the West, the report said that recent evidence indicates such predictions are outdated and that "adequate water is available for energy development through at least the year 2000."

[34] U.S., National Water Commission, *Water Policies for the Future,* final report to the president and to the Congress (Washington, D.C.: Government Printing Office, 1973). See also U.S., Congress, Senate, Committee on Interior and Insular Affairs, Subcommittee on Water and Power Resources, *National Water Commission Report: Hearing...,* 93rd Cong., 1st sess., June 28 and July 17, 1973.

[35] When the Water Resources Congress met in Washington, D.C., shortly after the president's "hit list" came out, a speaker explaining the Carter water policy was Kathy Fletcher, who had been a staff scientist for the Environmental Defense Fund in Denver before becoming an assistant director on Carter's Domestic Policy Staff. Fletcher, a young Phi Beta Kappa from Harvard and Radcliffe and the owner of a pet cat named NEPA, apparently made a capable presentation but incurred the wrath of some of the water-project enthusiasts.

[36] White House press release on President Carter's water policy message, June 6, 1978.

[37] "The Pork Barrel Runneth Over," an editorial in the *Los Angeles Times,* October 4, 1978.

[38] For background on the Reclamation Act and the complaints about its enforcement, two Senate inquiries are helpful. See U.S., Congress, Senate, *Farmworkers in Rural America, 1971–1972: Hearings before the Subcommittee on Migratory Labor of the Committee on Labor and Public Welfare,* 92d Cong., 1st and 2d sess., and *Will the Family Farm Survive in America? Joint Hearings before the Select Committee on Small Business and the Committee on Interior and Insular Affairs* (Federal Reclamation Policy, Westlands Water District), 94th Cong., 1st sess., July 1975–February 1976.

[39] 71 I.D.D. 496.

[40]Pleadings and relevant documents in the Imperial Valley case, *Bryant et al. v. Yellen et al.,* are on file in the Justice Department, Washington, D.C., and were inspected by the author under a Freedom of Information letter in the summer of 1979.

[41]*Bryant et al.* v. *Yellen et al.,* certiorari to the United States Court of Appeals for the Ninth Circuit, no. 79-421. Argued March 25, 1980; decided June 16, 1980.

14. A PILGRIM'S PROGRESS

[1]The Paley Commission report and the quoted paragraph were mentioned in chap. 1 of this volume, along with reference to the Boyd study of the Nixon administration. They are mentioned again for the sake of emphasis.

[2]Lynton K. Caldwell, *Environment: A Challenge to Modern Society* (Garden City, N.Y.: Doubleday & Co., Anchor Books, 1971), p. 32.

[3]Ibid., p. 35.

[4]John C. Whitaker, *Striking a Balance: Environment and Natural Resources Policy in the Nixon-Ford Years* (Washington, D.C.: American Enterprise Institute for Public Policy Research, 1976). Whitaker's 1974 speech and the subsequent book have similar themes. On p. 45, Whitaker speaks of the "iron triangle" that, as he says, really runs the federal government. The triangle consists of the vested interest involved, select members of Congress, and the middle-level bureaucracy.

[5]Maurice H. Stans, "Wait a Minute," address delivered before the National Petroleum Council, July 15, 1971. Commerce Department press release, July 15, 1971, p. 13.

[6]It was Fairfield Osborn, we may recall, who wrote *Our Plundered Planet* (Boston: Little, Brown & Co., 1948).

[7]William Frederick Bade, *Life and Letters of John Muir* (Boston and New York: Houghton Mifflin Co., 1924), 2:255–256. In a letter to Robert Underwood Johnson, one of Muir's friends who joined in urging formation of the Sierra Club, Muir wrote, "The love of nature among Californians is desperately moderate, consuming enthusiasm almost totally unknown."

[8]Background information about the origins and management of the NEPA legislation was obtained by the author in part from conversations with Van Ness and Dreyfus of the Senate Interior Committee staff and from correspondence with Caldwell at Indiana University. See the account in Caldwell's book, *Environment: A Challenge to Modern Society;* also see *A Report on Presidential Action to Meet Emerging Issues of Environmental Policy* (October 1968), prepared for Russell E. Train, then president of the Conservation Foundation, and, also, *Public Policy and the Natural Environment: An Opportunity for National Leadership,* a report to the Citizen's Advisory Committee on Recreation and Natural Beauty (November 21, 1968), pre-

pared for Chairman Laurance Rockefeller. The two documents were drawn up as advice to the incoming President Nixon.

[9]U.S., Congress, Senate, *Congressional Record*, 91st Cong., 1st sess., July 10, 1969, pp. S7813–7819.

[10]Ibid., September 23, 1969, pp. H8263–8286.

[11]Ibid., December 20, 1969, pp. S17450–17462 (Senate passage of the conference report), and December 23, 1969, pp. H13091–13096 (House passage).

[12]Ibid., December 20, 1969, p. S17451. Jackson referred on the following page of the *Congressional Record* to what he described as "a new kind of revolutionary movement underway in this country."

[13]Ibid., December 20, 1969, p. S17452. Senator Jackson's handling of the NEPA's passage through Congress was considered very adroit.

[14]See Luther J. Carter's series on environmental law in *Science*, beginning in the March 23, 1973, issue. See also Mark J. Green, "The Perils of Public Interest Law," *The New Republic*, September 20, 1975. The *Scenic Hudson* case of 1965 was a lawsuit in which the U.S. Second Court of Appeals ordered the FPC to take another look at its decision to license a power installation at Storm King Mountain.

[15]*Ford Foundation Grants in Resources and the Environment* (New York: Ford Foundation, Office of Reports, 1978).

[16]*The Washington Post*, Business and Finance Section, September 14, 1979.

[17]See *Annual Report*, Pacific Legal Foundation, Sacramento, California, for various years. Also, see "More Freedom Fighters: Some Public Interest Law Firms Oppose Big Government," *Barron's National Business and Financial Weekly*, August 15, 1977. Late in 1980, President-elect Ronald Reagan's nominee as secretary of the interior was James G. Watt, president and chief legal officer of the Mountain States Legal Foundation in Denver, a PLF affiliate.

15. OIL, ICE, AND POLITICS

[1]See Ernest Gruening, *The State of Alaska* (New York: Random House, 1968), pp. 142 ff.

[2]Ibid., p. 536.

[3]U.S., Congress, Senate, Committee on Interior and Insular Affairs, *Oversight of Oil Development Activities in Alaska: Hearings . . .* , 91st Cong., 1st sess., August 12, 1969, p. 17.

[4]U.S., Congress, Senate, Committee on Interior and Insular Affairs, *Trans Alaska Pipeline: Hearings . . .* , 91st Cong., 1st sess., October 16, 1969, pt. 2, p. 125.

[5]"The Forgotten American," Special Message to the Congress on the Problems of the American Indian, March 6, 1968, *Public Papers of the Presidents: Lyndon B. Johnson, 1968* (Washington, D.C.: Government Printing

Office, 1969), no. 113, pp. 335–344. The reference to native claims is on p. 343.

⁶U.S., Congress, Senate, Committee on Interior and Insular Affairs, *Alaska Native Land Claims: Hearings . . .* , 90th Cong., 2d sess., July 12, 1968, pp. 524 and 536.

⁷Ibid., p. 544.

⁸Alaska Native Claims Settlement Act of 1971, U.S., *Statutes at Large*, 85:688.

⁹The House considered and passed its version of the native-claims bill October 19–20, 1971. The Senate approved its own amended version November 1, and the House and Senate agreed to a conference report on December 14, 1971. U.S., Congress, *Congressional Record*, 92nd Cong., 1st sess., 1971, vol. 117.

¹⁰See Arthur H. Lachenbruch, *Some Estimates of the Thermal Effects of a Heated Pipeline in Permafrost*, United States Geological Survey Circular no. 632 (Washington, D.C.: Government Printing Office, 1970). See also *St. Louis Post-Dispatch*, December 6, 1969, and January 16, 1970.

¹¹*St. Louis Post-Dispatch*, April 2, 1970.

¹²*Wilderness Society et al.* v. *Morton et al.*, nos. 72-1796, 72-1797, 72-1798, United States Court of Appeals for the District of Columbia Circuit. The appellate court decision in favor of the environmentalists on February 9, 1973, set the stage for Congress's action to alter the right-of-way law and enable the pipeline to be approved.

¹³Author's interview with Russell E. Train, chairman of the Council on Environmental Quality, in 1970.

¹⁴*St. Louis Post-Dispatch*, April 25, 1970.

¹⁵U.S., Congress, Senate, *The Nomination of Rogers C. B. Morton to be Secretary of the Interior: Hearings . . . before the Senate Committee on Interior and Insular Affairs*, 92d Cong., 1st sess., January 25–26, 1971, p. 74.

¹⁶*Trans Alaska Pipeline Hearings*, Bureau of Land Management, Interior Department (Washington, D.C.: Hoover Reporting Co., 1971), February 16, 1971, 1:18. These hearings were held at the Department of Commerce Auditorium in the national capital.

¹⁷Ibid., p. 214.

¹⁸Ibid., pp. 214–215.

¹⁹*St. Louis Post-Dispatch*, February 17, 1971.

²⁰*Trans Alaska Pipeline Hearings*, U.S., Interior Department, 1:215.

²¹Ibid., p. 5.

²²*Final Environmental Impact Statement: Proposed Trans-Alaska Pipeline*, U.S. Interior Department (Washington, D.C.: Government Printing Office, 1972).

²³There was great concern among environmentalists that Congress's action to speed the Alaska oil pipeline might do harm to the NEPA law, with the result that it might easily be overridden. In July 1973, the Alaska Public Interest Coalition warned that the proposed bill "would gut NEPA."

²⁴See U.S. Senate, Committee on Interior and Insular Affairs, *Rights-of-Way across Federal Lands: Transportation of Alaska's North Slope Oil: Hearings . . .* ,

93rd Cong., 1st sess., May 2–3, 1973, pt. 3. Midwestern senators made a strong plea for consideration of the trans-Canadian alternative. See Charles J. Cicchetti, *Alaskan Oil: Alternative Routes and Markets,* published by Resources for the Future (Washington, D.C.: Johns Hopkins Press, 1972).

[25]Interior Department press release, January 23, 1974.

16. CARVING THE LAST MELON

[1]"Administration Asks That United States Protect 92,000,000 Alaska Acres for the Future," Interior Department press release, September 15, 1977. See also Andrus's testimony on January 19, 1978, before the Senate Committee on Energy and Natural Resources.

[2]"Alaska and Interior Agree to Settlement of State's Land Selection Lawsuit," Interior Department press release, September 5, 1972.

[3]Transcript of Press Conference of Secretary of the Interior Rogers C. B. Morton, September 13, 1972 (Washington, D.C.: Hoover Reporting Co., 1972). See pp. 17–21 and 28–29 for Morton's views on avoiding the errors of land disposal in the lower 48 western states and regenerating a spirit of conservation in Alaska.

[4]"Secretary Morton Completes Withdrawal of Almost 79,000,000 Acres for Study as Potential Additions to National Park, Forest, Refuge, and River Systems," Interior Department press release, September 13, 1972.

[5]"Secretary Morton Proposes Doubling Areas of Park, Wildlife Systems, and Boosting National Forests and Wild River Systems in Alaska," Interior Department press release, December 18, 1973.

[6]Robert Cahn, "Alaska: A Matter of 80,000,000 Acres," *Audubon,* July 1974. See pp. 11–12 for a discussion of Morton-Butz trade-offs. To grasp the size of the tracts involved in the Alaskan controversy, it is useful to keep in mind that Texas, the second largest state, has a total of 171,096,-320 acres, while California has 101,563,520.

[7]President Ford's Remarks at Yellowstone National Park, August 29, 1976, *Public Papers of the Presidents: Gerald R. Ford, 1976* (Washington, D.C.: Government Printing Office, 1977), no. 743, pp. 2188–2191. See also *St. Louis Post-Dispatch* coverage of Ford's visit to Yellowstone. "There's something about the wide open spaces that is a necessity for Americans," the president said.

[8]Secretary Andrus's testimony before the Subcommittee on General Oversight and Alaska Lands, in U.S., Congress, House, Committee on Interior and Insular Affairs, *Inclusion of Alaska Lands in National Park, Forest, Wildlife Refuge, and Wild and Scenic Rivers Systems: Hearings . . . ,* 95th Cong., 1st sess., September 15, 1977, pp. 2 ff.

[9]President Carter's Environmental Message to Congress, *Public Papers of the Presidents: Jimmy Carter, 1977,* pp. 967 ff.

[10]Andrus's testimony on September 15, 1977, before House Subcommittee on General Oversight and Alaska Lands, cited in no. 8 above, pp. 4–5.

[11]CMAL's Washington office on Capitol Hill was run by Tony Motley of Anchorage, a former real estate dealer and former member of Governor Hammond's staff. See the CMAL brochure *Alaska, the Land of Challenge, Opportunity, Conflict* for information about the organization and its objectives. See also *The Future of Alaska: For What and for Whom*, an illustrated booklet prepared and printed by the American Mining Congress, Alaska Miners Association, and CMAL. In January 1978, the conservationist Alaska Coalition held a press conference on Capitol Hill to protest what it called "a slick media and lobbying campaign" by a state-financed Alaska agency, the Steering Council for Alaska Lands. Led by Celia Hunter, an Alaskan then heading the Wilderness Society, the coalition objected to a twelve-minute propaganda film called *Not Man Alone* (*St. Louis Post-Dispatch*, January 31, 1978).

[12]Alaska Natural Gas Transportation Act of October 22, 1976, U.S., *Statutes at Large*, 90:2903.

[13]The future President Ford's remarks on Canada were intended to buttress the argument that an oil pipeline route across Alaska, rather than through Canada, would be more secure from the American standpoint. See U.S., Congress, *Congressional Record*, 93d Cong., 1st sess., August 2, 1973, p. H27642.

[14]Stevens was interested in bringing gas to southern Alaska for industrial and other purposes, but he later appeared not too unhappy with the approved gas route across Canada.

[15]Joint statement by Prime Minister Pierre Elliott Trudeau and President Jimmy Carter, White House press release, September 8, 1977.

[16]See the Sierra Club's *National News Report* for May 19, 1978. Charles ("Chuck") Clusen, then chairman of the Alaska Coalition campaign, said: "This vote proves that the momentum is still with us, and that we have been getting stronger at every stage of the legislative process, culminating in a vote of historic proportions." Udall and Seiberling termed the vote an "incredible victory."

[17]President Carter took action December 1, 1978, to protect some fifty-six million acres of Alaska by designating them as national monuments under the 1906 Antiquities Act. As Representative Udall later noted, on February 1, 1979, at a meeting of the House Committee on Interior and Insular Affairs for a briefing on the Alaska lands, there had been a danger that the expiration on December 16 of interim protection under the Native Claims Act might damage Congress's options on Alaska. Therefore, Udall and some 129 other House members wrote to Carter asking him to use his protective authority, which he did. See also the White House press release of December 1, consisting of a presidential statement in which he recalled that President Theodore Roosevelt had used the Antiquities Act to preserve the Grand Canyon. For details of Carter's actions, see U.S., Congress, House, Committee on Interior and Insular Affairs, *Alaska National Interest Lands Conservation Act of 1979: Hearings . . .*, 96th Cong., 1st sess., February 1, 6, 7, 8, and 13, 1979.

[18]Sierra Club, *National News Report*, May 18 and May 28, 1979. The victory was seen as an encouraging turnaround.

[19]*Alaska National Interest Lands*, report of the Committee on Energy and Natural Resources, U.S. Senate, together with additional views to accompany H.R. 39, 96th Cong., 1st sess., November 14, 1979, no. 96-413. See Sierra Club, *National News Report*, November 5, 1979.

[20]Sierra Club, *National News Report*, August 26, 1980.

[21]Ibid., November 24, 1980.

[22]"Remarks of the president at signing ceremony for the Alaska National Interest Lands Conservation Act," White House Press release, December 2, 1980.

EPILOGUE: LOOKING TO THE FUTURE

[1]Alexander Hamilton, James Madison, and John Jay, *The Federalist* (Cambridge, Mass.: Harvard University Press, Belknap Press, 1961), no. 10, pp. 129–136.

[2]G. O. Trevelyan, *Life and Letters of Lord Macaulay* (New York: Harper & Bros., 1875), 2:452.

[3]John Locke, *Of Civil Government*, bk. 2, *Of Property* (London and New York: J. M. Dent & Sons, Everyman's Library, 1924), "An Essay Concerning the True Original, Extent, and End of Civil Government," p. 132.

[4]Theodore Roosevelt, *An Autobiography* (New York: Macmillan Co., 1919), p. 438.

[5]U.S., Department of Agriculture, *Status of the Family Farm*, Second Annual Report to the Congress, September 1979, p. 2. By a new, official definition of a farm instituted by the Agriculture Department in 1979, requiring a place to have $1,000 minimum sales of farm products to be counted as a farm, the 1978 farm numbers were even smaller, dropping to 2,370,000.

[6]*Another Revolution in U.S. Farming? A Summary Analysis of the Structure of U.S. Farming*, Agricultural Information Bulletin no. 433 (Washington, D.C.: U.S. Department of Agriculture, 1980), p. 1. Also see Gene Wunderlich, *Facts about U.S. Land Ownership*, Agricultural Information Bulletin no. 422 (Washington, D.C.: U.S. Department of Agriculture, 1979), and *Who Owns the Land? A Preliminary Report of a U.S. Land Ownership Survey* (Washington, D.C.: U.S. Department of Agriculture, September 1979). See also James A. Lewis, *Land Ownership in the United States, 1978.* Economics, Statistics and Cooperative Service, Agriculture Information Bulletin no. 435 (Washington D.C.: Government Printing Office, April 1980), pp. 1, 38, appendix table 2.

[7]*Where Have the Farm Lands Gone?*, a pamphlet published by the National Agricultural Lands Study, a federal interagency study initiated in 1979 under cochairmanship of the secretary of agriculture and the chairman of the Council on Environmental Quality (Washington, D.C.: U.S. Department of Agriculture, 1979), p. 4.

[8]Walter Prescott Webb, *The Great Plains* (New York: Ginn & Co., 1931), p. 498.

[9]Ibid., p. 500.

[10]Aldo Leopold, *A Sand County Almanac, 1949* (New York: Oxford University Press, 1966), p. 218.

[11]*Environmental Quality—1979*, tenth annual report of the Council on Environmental Quality (Washington, D.C.: Government Printing Office, 1979), pp. 1–16.

[12]Ibid., p. iii.

[13]*Environmental Quality—1980*, eleventh annual report of the Council on Environmental Quality (Washington, D.C.: Government Printing Office, 1980), p. iii.

[14]Ibid., p. iv.

[15]Ibid., p. 297.

BIBLIOGRAPHY

HISTORY, GENERAL AND REGIONAL

Abernethy, Thomas P. *The South in the New Nation, 1789–1819.* Littlefield Fund for Southern History of the University of Texas. Baton Rouge: Louisiana State University Press, 1961.

Athearn, Robert G. *In Search of Canaan: Black Migration to Kansas, 1879–80.* Lawrence: University Press of Kansas, 1978.

Beard, Charles A. *The Supreme Court and the Constitution.* 1912. Reprint. With an introduction by Alan F. Westin. Englewood Cliffs, N.J.: Prentice-Hall, 1962.

Beard, Charles A., Mary R. Beard, and William Beard. *The Beards' New Basic History of the United States.* Garden City, N.Y.: Doubleday & Co., 1960.

Beard, Charles A., and Mary R. Beard. *The Rise of American Civilization.* New York: Macmillan Co., 1930.

Bowers, Claude G. *The Tragic Era: The Revolution after Lincoln.* Cambridge, Mass.: Houghton Mifflin Co., 1929.

Coulter, Ellis M. *A Short History of Georgia.* Chapel Hill: University of North Carolina Press, 1947.

———. *The South during Reconstruction, 1865–1877.* Littlefield Fund for Southern History of the University of Texas. Baton Rouge: Louisiana State University Press, 1947.

DeVoto, Bernard. *Across the Wide Missouri.* Boston: Houghton Mifflin Co., 1947.

———. *The Year of Decision: 1846.* New York: Little, Brown & Co., 1943.

Goldman, Eric F. *Rendezvous with Destiny:A History of Modern American Reform.* 1952. Paperback reprint. New York: Vintage Books, 1955.

Hofstadter, Richard. *The Age of Reform: From Bryan to FDR.* 1955. Paperback reprint. New York: Vintage Books.

———. *Social Darwinism in American Thought.* 1944. Rev. ed. Boston: Beacon Press, 1964.

Matloff, Maurice, general ed. *American Military History.* U.S. Army, Office of the Chief of Military History, Army Historical Series. Washington, D.C.: Government Printing Office, 1969.

Morison, Samuel Eliot, and Henry Steele Commager. *The Growth of the American Republic.* 4th ed. 2 vols. New York: Oxford University Press, 1950.

Nevins, Allan, and Henry Steele Commager. *The Pocket History of the United States.* New York: Pocket Books, 1956.

Parrington, Vernon Louis. *Main Currents in American Thought: An Interpretation of American Literature from the Beginnings to 1920.* 1927. Reprint (3 vols. in 1). New York: Harcourt, Brace & Co., 1930.

Rossiter, Clinton. *Conservatism in America: The Thankless Persuasion.* 1955. Reprint. New York: Vintage Books, 1962.

Smith, Henry Nash. *Virgin Land: The American West as Symbol and Myth.* Cambridge, Mass.: Harvard University Press, 1950.

Stampp, Kenneth M. *The Era of Reconstruction, 1865–1877.* New York: Alfred A. Knopf, 1970.

Stegner, Wallace. *Beyond the Hundredth Meridian: John Wesley Powell and the Second Opening of the West.* With an introduction by Bernard DeVoto. Boston: Houghton Mifflin Co., 1954.

——. *The Gathering of Zion: The Story of the Mormon Trail.* New York, Toronto, London: McGraw-Hill, 1964.

Webb, Walter Prescott. *The Great Plains.* Boston and New York: Ginn & Co., 1931.

——. *The Great Frontier.* Austin: University of Texas Press, 1964.

——. *The Texas Rangers: A Century of Frontier Defense.* Austin: University of Texas Press, 1935.

HISTORY OF THE PUBLIC LANDS

Carstensen, Vernon. *The Public Lands.* Madison: University of Wisconsin Press, 1962.

Clawson, Marion. *Uncle Sam's Acres.* New York: Dodd, Mead & Co., 1951.

Dick, Everett. *The Lure of the Land.* Lincoln: University of Nebraska Press, 1970.

Donaldson, Thomas C. *The Public Domain: Its History with Statistics.* 1880. 3d ed. *House Executive Documents,* 47th Cong., 2d sess., 1884, 19, pt. 4, no. 45.

Gates, Paul W. "Federal Land Policy in the South, 1866–88." *Journal of Southern History* 6 (August 1940):303–330.

——. *History of Public Land Law Development.* With a chapter by Robert W. Swenson. Public Land Law Review Commission. Washington, D.C.: Government Printing Office, 1968.

——. "Research in the History of the Public Lands." *Agricultural History,* January 1974, pp. 31–50.

Hibbard, Benjamin Horace. *History of the Public Land Policies.* New York: Peter Smith, 1939.

Nathan, Harriet, ed. *America's Public Lands: Politics, Economics, and Administration.* Berkeley: University of California Institute of Governmental Studies, 1972.

O'Callaghan, Jerry A. *The Disposition of the Public Domain in Oregon.* Ph.D. dissertation, Stanford University, printed for the use of the Senate Committee on Interior and Insular Affairs. Washington, D.C.: Government Printing Office, 1960.

Okada, Yasuo. *Public Lands and Pioneer Farms, Gage County, Neb.—1850–1900.* Tokyo: Keio Economic Society, 1971.

Peffer, E. Louise. *The Closing of the Public Domain: Disposal and Reservation Policies, 1900–1950.* Stanford: Stanford University Press, 1951.

Robbins, Roy M. *Our Landed Heritage: The Public Domain, 1776–1936.* Princeton: Princeton University Press, 1942.

Bibliography

Rohrbach, Malcolm J. *The Land Office Business: The Settlement and Administration of American Public Lands, 1789–1837.* New York: Oxford University Press, 1968.

Other historical works will be mentioned under appropriate headings below.

EARLY SETTLEMENT—ORIGINS AND OVERVIEW

Beatty, Charles. *The Journal of a Two Months Tour with a View of Promoting Religion among the Frontier Inhabitants of Pensylvania [sic].* 1766. Reprint. Chicago: Scholarly Press, 1972.

Burnet, Jacob. *Notes on the Early Settlement of the Northwestern Territory.* Cincinnati: Derby, Bradley & Co., 1847.

Burnett, Edmund C., ed. *Letters of Members of the Continental Congress.* 1936. 8 vols. Reprint. Gloucester, Mass.: Peter Smith, 1963.

DeCrèvecoeur, Hector Saint John. *Letters from an American Farmer.* 1784. New York: Albert & Charles Boni, 1925.

———. *Journey into Northern Pennsylvania and the State of New York.* 1801. Ann Arbor: University of Michigan Press, 1964.

DeVoto, Bernard, ed. *Journals of Lewis and Clark.* Boston: Houghton Mifflin Co., 1953.

Fitzpatrick, John C., ed. *Writings of George Washington.* 39 vols. Washington, D.C.: Government Printing Office, 1931.

Freeman, Douglas Southall. *George Washington.* Vol. 6. New York: Charles Scribner's Sons, 1954.

Hanna, Charles A. *The Scotch-Irish, or the Scot in North Britain, North Ireland, and North America.* 1902. 2 vols. Reprint. Baltimore: Genealogical Publishing Co., 1968.

Harris, Thaddeus Mason. *The Journal of a Tour into the Territory Northwest of the Alleghany Mountains: Made in the Spring of the Year 1803.* Boston: Manning & Loring, 1805.

Hildreth, S. P. *Biographical and Historical Memoirs of the Early Pioneer Settlers of Ohio.* Cincinnati: H. W. Derby & Co., 1852.

Journals of the Continental Congress, 1774–1789. 34 vols. Reprint. New York and London: Johnson Reprint, 1968.

Koch, Adrienne. *The Philosophy of Thomas Jefferson.* New York: Columbia University Press, 1943.

Koch, Adrienne, and William Peden. *The Life and Selected Writings of Thomas Jefferson.* New York: Random House, Modern Library, 1944.

Locke, John. *Of Civil Government.* Reprint of 1924 ed. Everyman's Library, no. 751. London and New York: J. M. Dent & Sons, E. P. Dutton & Co., 1943.

Madison, James, Alexander Hamilton, and John Jay. *The Federalist.* Cambridge, Mass.: Harvard University Press, Belknap Press, 1961.

Malone, Dumas. *Jefferson the Virginian.* Boston: Little, Brown & Co., 1948.

National Park Service Series. Washington, D.C.: Government Printing Office, various years.

———. *Explorers and Settlers.* 1968.

———. *Founders and Frontiersmen.* 1967.

———. *Lewis and Clark.* 1975.

———. *The Presidents.* 1977.

———. *Prospector, Cowhand, and Sodbuster.* 1967.

———. *Signers of the Constitution.* 1976.

———. *Signers of the Declaration.* 1975.

———. *Soldier and Brave.* 1971.

Ogg, Frederick Austin. *The Old Northwest.* Chronicles of America Series, vol. 19. New Haven: Yale University Press, 1919.

Ogilvie, William. *Birthright in Land.* 1782. Reprint. New York: Augustus M. Kelley, 1970.

Parkman, Francis. *The California and Oregon Trail.* New York and London: G.P. Putnam, 1849. For a more recent edition, see *The Oregon Trail.* Madison: University of Wisconsin Press, 1969.

Perkins, James Handasyd. *Memoir and Writings.* Edited by William Henry Channing. Cincinnati: Trueman & Spofford, 1851.

Public Land Statistics. U.S. Interior Department, Bureau of Land Management. Washington, D.C.: Government Printing Office, published annually.

Public Papers of the Presidents. Washington, D.C.: Government Printing Office, published annually in recent decades.

Richardson, James D., ed. *Messages and Papers of the Presidents.* New York: Bureau of National Literature, 1897–.

Stewart, Lowell O. *Public Land Surveys.* 1935. Reprint. New York: Arno Press, 1979.

Trollope, Frances. *Domestic Manners of the Americans.* Edited, with a history of Mrs. Trollope's adventures in America, by Donald Smalley. New York: Alfred A. Knopf, 1949.

The Writings of Thomas Jefferson. Washington, D.C.: Thomas Jefferson Memorial Association of the United States, 1903.

THE GILDED AGE, BEFORE AND AFTER

Athearn, Robert G. *Westward the Briton.* New York: Charles Scribner's Sons, 1953.

Bellamy, Edward. *Looking Backward.* 1887. Reprint. New York: Random House, Modern Library, 1951.

Birkbeck, Morris. *Letters from Illinois.* 1818. Reprint. New York: DaCapo Press, 1970.

———. *Notes on a Journey in America, from the Coast of Virginia to the Territory of Illinois.* New York: Augustus M. Kelley, 1971.

Bishop, Abraham. *Georgia Speculation Unveiled.* 1797. March of America Facsimile Series, no. 55. Ann Arbor: University Microfilms, 1966.

Brown, Dee. *Bury My Heart at Wounded Knee.* New York: Holt, Rinehart, and Winston, Bantam Books, 1971.

Bibliography

Busch, Noel F. *TR: the Story of Theodore Roosevelt and His Influence on Our Times.* New York: Reynal & Co., 1963.

Carrington, Charles. *Rudyard Kipling.* London: Macmillan & Co., 1955.

Clemens, Samuel L. [Mark Twain]. *Roughing It.* 2 vols. in 1. New York and London: Harper & Bros., 1871.

Clemens, Samuel L. [Mark Twain], and Charles Dudley Warner. *The Gilded Age.* 1873. Reprint. With an introduction by Justin D. Kaplan. New York: Trident Press, 1964.

Crawford, J. B. *The Credit Mobilier of America: Its Origin and History: Its Work of Constructing the Union Pacific Railroad and the Relations of Members of Congress Therewith.* Boston: C. W. Calkins & Co, 1880.

Dickens, Charles. *American Notes for General Circulation, 1842.* London: Penguin Books, 1972.

————. *Life and Adventures of Martin Chuzzlewit. 1844.* Reprint. Oxford University Press, 1951.

Durant, Mary, and Michael Harwood. *On the Road with John James Audubon.* New York: Dodd, Mead & Co., 1980.

Garland, Hamlin. *Prairie Folks; or, Pioneer Life on the Western Prairies.* 1899. Reprint. New York: Garrett Press, 1969.

————. *A Son of the Middle Border,* 1917. New York: Macmillan Co., 1962.

George, Henry. *The Land Question: What It Involves and How Alone It Can Be Settled.* New York: Doubleday, Page & Co, 1906.

————. *A Perplexed Philosopher: Being an Examination of Mr. Herbert Spencer's Various Utterances on the Land Question, with Some Incidental References to His Synthetic Philosophy.* Garden City, N.Y.: Doubleday, Page & Co., 1911.

————. *Progress and Poverty: An Inquiry into the Cause of Industrial Depressions and of Increase of Want with Increase of Wealth. . . .* 1879. Reprint. New York: Robert Schalkenbach Foundation, 1979.

Goetzmann, William H. *Exploration and Empire.* New York: Alfred A. Knopf, 1966.

Gonzalez, Manuel Pedro. *José Marti: Epic Chronicler of the United States in the Eighties.* Chapel Hill: University of North Carolina Press, 1953.

Hearst, William Randolph. *Selections from the Writings and Speeches of William Randolph Hearst.* San Francisco: Published Privately, 1948.

Holbrook, Stewart H. *James J. Hill.* New York: Alfred A. Knopf, 1955.

Howard, Robert West. *The Great Iron Trail: The Story of the First Transcontinental Railroad.* New York: G. P. Putnam's Sons, 1962.

Josephson, Matthew. *The Robber Barons.* New York: Harcourt, Brace & Co., 1934.

Kinney, Jay P. *A Continent Lost—A Civilization Won: Indian Land Tenure in America.* New York: Farrar, Straus & Giroux, Octagon Books, 1975.

Kipling, Rudyard. *From Sea to Sea.* Garden City, N.Y.: Doubleday, Page & Co., 1918.

Laut, Agnes C. *Romance of the Rails.* New York: Tudor Publishing Co., 1936.

Lavender, David. *The Great Persuader.* Garden City, N.Y.: Doubleday & Co., 1970.

McCabe, James D. *Behind the Scenes in Washington: Being A Complete and Graphic Account of the Credit Mobilier Investigation.* 1873. Reprint. New York: Arno Press, 1974.

Mangam, William D. *The Clarks: An American Phenomenon.* New York: Silver Bow Press, 1941.

Marsh, George Perkins. *Man and Nature.* 1864. Reprint. Cambridge, Mass.: Harvard University Press, 1965.

Martin, Harold H. *Georgia, a History.* Bicentennial Series. New York: W. W. Norton & Co., 1977.

Mintz, Morton, and Jerry S. Cohen. *America, Inc.: Who Owns and Operates the United States.* New York: Dial Press, 1971.

———. *Power, Inc.: Public and Private Rulers and How to Make Them Accountable.* New York: Viking Press, 1976.

Moore, Thomas. *Moore's Melodies and American Poems.* With a biography and a critical review of lyric poets by Dr. R. Shelton MacKenzie. New York: International Publishing Co., 1871.

Myers, Gustavus. *History of the Great American Fortunes.* 1907. Reprint. New York: Random House, Modern Library, 1936.

O'Connor, Richard. *Iron Wheels and Broken Men: The Railroad Barons and the Plunder of the West.* New York: G. P. Putnam's Sons, 1973.

Parmet, Herbert S. *Eisenhower and the American Crusades.* New York: Macmillan Co., 1972.

Porter, William Sidney [O. Henry]. *The Best Stories of O. Henry.* Selected and with an introduction by Bennett A. Cerf and Van H. Cartwell. New York: Random House, Modern Library, 1945.

———. *Heart of the West.* Garden City, N.Y.: Doubleday, Page & Co., 1920.

———. *Stories of the Old Texas Land Office.* Austin: Daughters of the Republic of Texas, Museum Committee, 1964.

Raaen, Aagot. *Grass of the Earth: Immigrant Life in the Dakota Country.* Northfield, Minn.: Norwegian-American Historical Association, 1950. Reprint. New York: Arno Press, 1979.

Rolvaag, Ole Edvart. *Giants in the Earth: A Saga of the Prairie.* 1927. Reprint. New York: Harper & Row, Harper Torch Books, 1964.

Roosevelt, Theodore. *The Letters of Theodore Roosevelt.* 8 vols. Selected and edited by Elting E. Morison. Cambridge, Mass.: Harvard University Press, 1951-1954.

Sakolski, A. M. *The Great American Land Bubble.* New York and London: Harper & Bros., 1932.

Seligman, Ben B. *The Potentates: Business and Businessmen in American History.* New York: Dial Press, 1971.

Stearn, Gerald Emanuel, ed. *Broken Image: Foreign Critiques of America.* New York: Random House, 1972.

Stewart, William Morris. *Reminiscences of Senator William M. Stewart of Nevada.* Edited by George Rothwell Brown. New York and Washington, D.C.: Neale Publishing Co., 1908.

Bibliography

Swados, Harvey, ed. *Years of Conscience: The Muckrakers.* Cleveland and New York: World Publishing Co., 1962.

Whitaker, John C. *Striking a Balance: Environment and Natural Resources Policy in the Nixon-Ford Years.* Washington, D.C.: American Enterprise Institute for Public Policy Research, 1976.

CONGRESS

Bancroft, Frederic, ed. *Speeches, Correspondence, and Political Papers of Carl Schurz.* 6 vols. New York and London: G. P. Putnam's Sons, 1913. Includes Schurz's address, "The Need of a Rational Forest Policy," 5:22–23.

Dick, Everett. *The Sod-House Frontier, 1854–1890.* New York: D. Appleton-Century Co., 1937.

Galloway, George B. *The Legislative Process in Congress.* New York: Thomas Y. Crowell Co., 1955.

Hoyt, Edwin P., Jr. *The Guggenheims and the American Dream.* New York: Funk & Wagnalls, 1967.

Ise, John. *Sod and Stubble: The Story of a Kansas Homestead.* New York: Wilson-Erickson, 1936.

Johnson, Virginia Weisel. *The Unregimented General: A Biography of Nelson A. Miles.* Boston: Houghton Mifflin Co., 1962.

Journal of Southern History. Southern Historical Association. Baton Rouge: Louisiana State University Press, published quarterly.

Kerr, Robert S. *Land, Wood, and Water.* New York: Fleet Publishing, 1960.

Marti, José. *Obras completas: edition commemorativa del cincuentenario de su muerte.* With a prologue and biographical notes by M. Isidro Mendez. Havana: Editorial Lex, 1946.

Mencken, H. L. *A Mencken Chrestomathy: 1916–1949.* New York: Alfred A. Knopf, 1949.

O'Connor, Harvey. *The Guggenheims. The Making of an American Dynasty.* New York: Covici-Friede, 1937.

Powell, John Wesley. *Report on the Arid Region of the United States, with a More Detailed Account of the Lands of Utah.* 1878. Reprint. Cambridge, Mass.: Harvard University Press, Belknap Press, 1962.

Prochnau, William W., and Richard W. Larsen. *A Certain Democrat: Senator Henry M. Jackson, a Political Biography.* Englewood Cliffs, N.J.: Prentice-Hall, 1972.

Sherrill, Robert. *Gothic Politicians in the Deep South.* New York: Grossman Publishers, 1968.

Swanberg, W. A. *Citizen Hearst.* New York: Charles Scribner's Sons, 1961.

Taylor, Theodore W. *The States and Their Indian Citizens.* U.S. Interior Department, Bureau of Indian Affairs. Washington, D.C.: Government Printing Office, 1972.

Thayer, George. *Who Shakes the Money Tree?* New York: Simon & Shuster, 1973.

Trevelyan, G. O. *The Life and Letters of Lord Macaulay.* 2 vols. New York and London: Harper & Bros., 1875.

Tyler, S. Lyman. *A History of Indian Policy.* U.S. Interior Department, Bureau of Indian Affairs. Washington, D.C.: Government Printing Office, 1974.

TEAPOT DOME

Democratic Campaign Book, 1924. Democratic National Committee and Democratic Congressional Committee. Washington, D.C.: Government Printing Office, 1924.

Fall, Albert B. *The Memoirs of Albert B. Fall.* Edited with annotations by David H. Stratton. Monograph no. 15, vol. 4, no. 3. Southwestern Studies. El Paso: Texas Western Press, 1966.

Murray, Robert K. *The Harding Era.* Minneapolis: University of Minnesota Press, 1969.

Noggle, Burl. *Teapot Dome: Oil and Politics in the 1920s.* Baton Rouge: Louisiana State University Press, 1962.

O'Keane, Josephine. *Thomas J. Walsh: A Senator from Montana.* Francestown, N.H.: Marshall-Jones Co., 1955.

Ravage, Marcus E. *The Story of Teapot Dome.* 1924. Reprint. New York: Burt Franklin Reprints, 1974.

Russell, Francis. *The Shadow of Blooming Grove: Warren G. Harding in His Times.* New York and Toronto: McGraw-Hill, 1968.

St. Louis Post-Dispatch, news reports on the Teapot Dome case by Paul Y. Anderson, various dates.

Sullivan, Mark. *Our Times.* Vol 6, The Twenties. New York: Charles Scribner's Sons, 1935.

U.S., Congress, Senate, Committee on Public Lands and Surveys. *Leases upon Naval Oil Reserves: Hearings...*, 67th Cong., 4th sess., 1923, and 68th Cong., 1st sess., 1924.

THE FEDERAL AGENCIES

Adams, Ansel. *The National Parks.* With three photographic portfolios. *The American West* 6, no. 5 (September 1969).

Bade, William Frederick. *Life and Letters of John Muir.* Boston and New York: Houghton Mifflin Co., 1924.

Clawson, Marion. *The Bureau of Land Management.* Library of U.S. Government Departments and Agencies. New York, Washington, and London: Praeger Publishers, 1971.

Everhart, William C. *The National Park Service.* Library of U.S. Government Departments and Agencies. New York, Washington, and London: Praeger Publishers, 1972.

Forness, Norman O. "The Origins and Early History of the United States Department of the Interior." Ph.D. dissertation, Pennsylvania State University, 1964.

Bibliography

Frome, Michael. *The Forest Service.* Library of U.S. Government Departments and Agencies. New York, Washington, and London: Praeger Publishers, 1971.

Haines, Aubrey L. *Yellowstone National Park: Its Exploration and Establishment.* Washington, D.C.: Government Printing Office, 1974.

Hampton, H. Duane. *How the Cavalry Saved Our National Parks.* Bloomington and London: Indiana University Press, 1971.

Hickel, Walter J. *Who Owns America?* Englewood Cliffs, N.J.: Prentice-Hall, 1971.

Ickes, Harold L. *The Secret Diary of Harold L. Ickes.* 3 vols. New York: Simon & Shuster, 1953–1954.

Ise, John. *Our National Park Policy: A Critical History.* Resources for the Future. Baltimore: Johns Hopkins Press, 1961.

Malek, Frederic V. *Washington's Hidden Tragedy: The Failure to Make Government Work.* New York: Macmillan Co., Free Press, 1978.

Manners, William. *TR and Will: A Friendship That Split the Republican Party.* New York: Harcourt, Brace & World, 1969.

Pennick, James L., Jr. *Progressive Politics and Conservation: The Ballinger-Pinchot Affair.* Chicago and London: University of Chicago Press, 1968.

Runte, Alfred. *National Parks: The American Experience.* Lincoln and London: University of Nebraska Press, 1979.

Shankland, Robert. *Steve Mather of the National Parks.* 2d ed., rev. and enl. New York: Alfred A. Knopf, 1954.

Trani, Eugene P. *The Secretaries of the Department of the Interior, 1849–1969.* 2 vols. Washington, D.C.: National Anthropological Archives, 1975.

Wallace, Charles E. *Creation of the Department of the Interior: March 3, 1849.* U.S. Interior Department, Office of Communications. Washington, D.C.: Government Printing Office, 1976.

Warne, William E. *The Bureau of Reclamation.* Library of U.S. Government Departments and Agencies. New York, Washington, and London: Praeger Publishers, 1973.

THE NATION'S LAND LAWS

Baldwin, Sidney. *Poverty and Politics.* Chapel Hill: University of North Carolina Press, 1968.

Bosselman, Fred, and David Callies. *The Quiet Revolution in Land Use Control.* Washington, D.C.: Government Printing Office, 1972.

Bosselman, Fred, David Callies, and John Banta. *The Taking Issue.* Council on Environmental Quality. Washington, D.C.: Government Printing Office, 1973.

Clawson, Marion. *America's Land and Its Uses.* Baltimore and London: Johns Hopkins Press, 1972.

Farb, Peter. *Face of America.* New York and Evanston, Ill.: Harper & Row, 1963.

Douglas, Louis H. *Agrarianism in American History.* Lexington, Mass.: D. C. Heath & Co., 1969.

Hofstadter, Richard. *Anti-Intellectualism in American Life.* New York: Alfred A. Knopf, 1963.

Lewis, James A. *Landownership in the United States, 1978.* U.S., Department of Agriculture, Economics, Statistics and Cooperatives Service. Agriculture Information Bulletin No. 435. Washington, D.C.: Government Printing Office, April 1980.

McGovern, George, ed. *Agricultural Thought in the Twentieth Century.* American Heritage Series. Indianapolis: Bobbs-Merrill Co., 1967.

Natural Resources Council of America. *What's Ahead for Our Public Lands?* Washington, D.C.: Natural Resources Council of America, 1970.

"The People Left Behind"—Four Years Later. Report on the effectiveness of implementation of the recommendations of the Presidential Commission on Rural Poverty. Prepared by Economic Research Service, U.S. Department of Agriculture. Printed for use of the Senate Committee on Agriculture and Forestry. Washington, D.C.: Government Printing Office, 1971.

Public Land Law Reviews.

———. 1879. *Report of the Public Land Commission, House Executive Documents,* 46th Cong., 2d sess., 1880, 22, no. 46 (serial no. 1923).

———. 1903. *Report of the Public Land Commission, Senate Documents,* 58th Cong., 3d sess., March 7, 1904, 4, no. 189 (serial no. 4766).

———. 1929. *Report of the Committee on Conservation and Administration of the Public Domain.* 1931. Reprinted in U.S., Senate, *Hearings Before the Committee on Public Lands and Survey on Granting Remaining Unreserved Public Lands to States,* 72d Cong., 1st sess., March 15–April 5, 1932.

———. 1964. *One Third of the Nation's Land.* Report by the Public Land Law Review Commission to the president and to the Congress. Washington, D.C.: Government Printing Office, 1970.

Reilly, William K., ed. *The Use of Land: A Citizen's Policy Guide to Urban Growth.* Task force report of the Citizens Advisory Committee on Environmental Quality. Published under sponsorship of the Rockefeller Brothers Fund. New York: Thomas Y. Crowell Co., 1973.

Where Have the Farm Lands Gone? Pamphlet published by the National Agricultural Lands Study, a federal interagency effort begun in 1979 under cochairmanship of the U.S. secretary of agriculture and the chairman of the Council on Environmental Quality. Washington, D.C.: U.S. Department of Agriculture, 1979.

Who Owns the Land? U.S. Department of Agriculture, Land Ownership Survey, Preliminary Report ESCS 70. Washington, D.C.: U.S. Department of Agriculture, 1979.

Wunderlich, Gene. *Facts about U.S. Landownership.* Agriculture Information Bulletin no. 422. Washington, D.C.: U.S. Department of Agriculture, 1979.

Bibliography
MINING AND MINERALS

Barry, Frank J., Jr. "Basic Statutory Mining Law and Leading Cases." *Symposium on American Mineral Law Relating to Public Land Use, 1966*. J. C. Dotson, ed. Tucson: University of Arizona, College of Mines, 1966. Pp 1–29.

Copper Camp: Stories of the World's Greatest Mining Town, Butte, Montana. Compiled by workers of the WPA writing program in the state of Montana. Books, Inc., New York: Hastings House, 1943.

Dunning, Charles H., with Edward H. Peplow, Jr. *Rock to Riches: The Story of Arizona Mines and Mining*. Pasadena, Calif.: Hicks Publishing, 1966.

Federal Materials Reviews.

——. *Material Needs and the Environment Today and Tomorrow*. Final report of the National Commission on Materials Policy, June, 1973. Washington, D.C.: Government Printing Office.

——. *Resources for Freedom*. Report to the president by the President's Materials Policy Commission, June 1952. Washington, D.C.: Government Printing Office.

Glasscock, C. B. *The War of the Copper Kings*. New York: Grosset & Dunlap, 1935.

Greever, William S. *The Bonanza West: The Story of the Western Mining Rushes, 1848–1900*. Norman: University of Oklahoma Press, 1963.

Julian, George W. *Political Recollections, 1840–1872*. 1884. Reprint. Miami, Fla.: Mnemosyne Publishing Co., 1969.

Livermore, Robert. *Bostonians and Bullion: The Journal of Robert Livermore, 1892–1915*. Edited by Gene M. Gressley. Lincoln: University of Nebraska Press, 1968.

Marcosson, Isaac F. *Anaconda*. New York: Dodd, Mead & Co., 1957.

Murdoch, Angus. *Boom Copper: Story of the First U.S. Mining Boom*. New York: Macmillan Co., 1943.

O'Farrell, P. A. *Butte: Its Mines and Copper Kings*. New York: Printing House of James A. Rogers, 1899.

Park, Charles F., Jr. *Minerals and the Political Economy*. San Francisco: Freeman, Cooper & Co., 1968.

Park, Charles F., Jr., and Roy A. MacDiarmid. *Ore Deposits*. San Francisco: W. H. Freeman & Co., 1964.

Parker, Watson. *Gold in the Black Hills*. Norman: University of Oklahoma Press, 1966.

Paul, Rodman W. *California Gold: The Beginning of Mining in the Far West*. Cambridge, Mass.: Harvard University Press, 1947.

——. *Mining Frontiers of the Far West, 1848–1880*. New York: Holt, Rinehart & Winston, 1963.

Powell, Lawrence Clark. *Arizona, a Bicentennial History*. Bicentennial Series. New York: W. W. Norton & Co., 1976.

Senzel, Irving. "Administration of the Mining Laws in Areas of Conflict."

509

Symposium on American Mineral Law Relating to Public Land Use, 1966. J. C. Dotson, ed. Tucson: University of Arizona, College of Mines, 1966. Pp. 239-262.

Spence, Clark C. *Montana, a Bicentennial History.* Bicentennial Series. New York: W. W. Norton & Co., 1978.

Taylor, Raymond W., and Samuel W. Taylor. *Uranium Fever.* New York: Macmillan Co., 1970.

Whitaker, J. Russell, and Edward A. Ackerman. *American Resources.* New York: Harcourt, Brace & Co., 1951.

Wolle, Muriel Sibell. *The Bonanza Trail: Ghost Towns and Mining Camps of the West.* Bloomington: Indiana University Press, 1953.

OIl AND ENERGY

Abels, Jules. *The Rockefeller Billions.* New York: Macmillan Co., 1965.

Adelman, M. A. *The World Petroleum Market.* Resources for the Future. Baltimore: Johns Hopkins Press, 1972.

Bartley, Ernest R. *The Tidelands Controversy.* Austin: University of Texas Press, 1953.

Carr, Albert Z. *John D. Rockefeller's Secret Weapon.* New York: McGraw-Hill, 1962.

Clark, James A., and Michel T. Halbouty. *Spindletop.* New York: Random House, 1952.

―――. *The Last Boom.* New York: Random House, 1972.

Clark, J. Stanley. *The Oil Century.* Norman: University of Oklahoma Press, 1958.

Coyne, John R., and Patricia S. Coyne. *The Big Breakup: Energy in Crisis.* Kansas City: Sheed, Andrews & McMeel, 1977.

Dolson, Hildegarde. *The Great Oildorado: The Gaudy and Turbulent Years of the First Oil Rush, Pennsylvania, 1859-1880.* New York: Random House, 1959.

Dye, Lee. *Blowout at Platform A: The Crisis That Awakened a Nation.* Garden City, N.Y.: Doubleday & Co., 1971.

Engler, Robert. *The Brotherhood of Oil: Energy Policy and the Public Interest.* Chicago and London: University of Chicago Press, 1977.

―――. *The Politics of Oil.* Chicago and London: University of Chicago Press, Phoenix Books, 1961.

Giddens, Paul H. *The Birth of the Oil Industry.* New York: Macmillan Co., 1938.

―――. *Standard Oil Co. (Indiana).* New York: Appleton-Century-Crofts, 1955.

Hersh, Burton. *The Mellon Family: A Fortune in History.* New York: William Morrow & Co., 1978.

Johnson, Arthur M. *Petroleum Pipelines and Public Policy, 1906-1959.* Cambridge, Mass.: Harvard University Press, 1967.

Knowles, Ruth Sheldon. *The Greatest Gamblers.* New York: McGraw-Hill, 1959.

Marcosson, Isaac F. *The Black Golconda.* New York and London: Harper & Bros., 1924.

Bibliography

McFarland, Andrew S. *Public Interest Lobbies: Decision-Making on Energy*. Washington, D.C.: American Enterprise Institute, 1976.

Miller, Thomas Lloyd. *The Public Lands of Texas, 1519–1970*. Norman: University of Oklahoma Press, 1972.

Mosley, Leonard. *Power Play: Oil in the Middle East*. New York: Random House, 1973.

O'Connor, Harvey. *The Empire of Oil*. New York: Monthly Review Press, 1955.

O'Connor, Richard. *The Oil Barons: Men of Greed and Grandeur*. Boston and Toronto: Little, Brown & Co., 1971.

The Oil Import Question. Report on the relationship of oil imports to the national security by the Cabinet Task Force on Oil Import Control. Washington, D.C.: Government Printing Office, 1970.

Pettengill, Samuel B. *Hot Oil: The Problem of Petroleum*. New York: Economic Forum Co., 1936.

Presley, James. *A Saga of Wealth: The Rise of the Texas Oilmen*. New York: G. P. Putnam's Sons, 1978.

Studies on Energy Policy.

————. 1972. *U.S. Energy Outlook*. Report of the National Petroleum Council's Committee on U.S. Energy Outlook. Washington, D.C.: U.S. Interior Department, National Petroleum Council.

————. 1974. *A Time to Choose: America's Energy Future*. Final report by the Energy Policy Project of the Ford Foundation. Cambridge, Mass.: Ballinger Publishing Co. (Lippincott), 1974.

————. 1979. *Energy in America's Future: The Choices before Us*. Study by the staff of the Resources for the Future National Energy Strategies Project. Baltimore and London: Johns Hopkins Press.

————. 1979. *Energy Future*. Edited by Robert Stobaugh and Daniel Yergin. Report of the Energy Project at the Harvard Business School. New York: Random House, Ballantine Books.

Tugendhat, Christopher. *Oil. The Biggest Business*. New York: G. P. Putnam's Sons, 1968.

Welles, Chris. *The Elusive Bonanza: The Story of Oil Shale*. New York: E. P. Dutton & Co., 1970.

FORESTS AND TIMBER

Adams, Kramer. *The Redwoods*. New York: Popular Library, n.d.

Clawson, Marion, ed. *Forest Policy for the Future*. Papers and discussions from a forum held May 8–9, 1974. Washington, D.C.: Resources for the Future, 1974.

————. *The National Forests: A great national asset is poorly managed and unproductive*. Reprinted from *Science*, 191, 4227, February 20, 1976, 762–767. Reprint 127 Washington, D.C.: Resources for the Future, 1976.

————. "Forests in the Long Sweep of American History," *Science*, 204, 4398, June 15, 1979, 1168–1174.

Bibliography

Current, Richard Nelson. *Pine Logs and Politics: A Life of Philetus Sawyer, 1860–1900.* Madison: State Historical Society of Wisconsin, 1950.

Dodds, Gordon B. *Oregon, a Bicentennial History.* Bicentennial Series. New York: W. W. Norton & Co., 1977.

Eckholm, Eric P. *Losing Ground: Environmental Stress and World Food Prospects.* Worldwatch Institute, with the support and cooperation of the United Nations Environment Program. New York: W. W. Norton & Co., 1976.

Frome, Michael. *Whose Woods These Are: The Story of the National Forests.* Garden City, N.Y.: Doubleday & Co., 1962

Hidy, Ralph W., Frank Ernest Hill, and Allen Nevins. *Timber and Men: The Weyerhaeuser Story.* New York: Macmillan Co., 1963.

Lillard, Richard G. *The Great Forest.* New York: Alfred A. Knopf, 1947.

McFarland, N. C. *Instruction to Special Agents of the General Land Office Appointed to Prevent Timber Depredations upon Government Lands and to Protect the Public Timber from Waste and Destruction.* U.S. Interior Department, General Land Office. Washington, D.C.: Government Printing Office, 1883.

Nixon, Stuart. *Redwood Empire.* New York: E. P. Dutton & Co., 1966.

The Outlook for Timber in the United States. U.S. Department of Agriculture, Forest Service Report no. 20. Washington, D.C.: Government Printing Office, 1974.

Pinchot, Gifford. *Breaking New Ground.* New York: Harcourt, Brace & Co., 1947.

———. *The Fight for Conservation.* Seattle and London: University of Washington Press, American Library, 1910.

Pinkett, Harold T. *Gifford Pinchot: Private and Public Forester.* Urbana: University of Illinois Press, 1968.

Robinson, Glen O. *The Forest Service: A Study in Public Land Management.* Resources for the Future. Baltimore and London: Johns Hopkins Press, 1975.

Stone, Christopher D. *Should Trees Have Standing?* Los Altos, Calif.: William Kaufmann, 1974.

A University View of the Forest Service. Prepared for the Committee on Interior and Insular Affairs, U.S. Senate, by a select committee of the University of Montana. 91st Cong., 2d sess., December 1, 1970.

U.S., Senate, Interior Department, Committee on Interior and Insular Affairs, *"Clear-Cutting" Practices on National Timberlands: Senate Hearings before the Subcommittee on the Public Lands,* 92d Cong., 1st sess., April 1971.

Weyerhaeuser, Frederick K. *Trees and Men.* New York, San Francisco, and Montreal: Newcomen Society, 1951.

THE WESTERN RANGE

Blacker, Irwin R. *The Old West in Fact.* New York: Ivan Obolensky, 1962.

Brown, Mark H., and W. R. Felton. *Before Barbed Wire.* New York: Henry Holt & Co., 1956.

Bibliography

Calef, Wesley. *Private Grazing and Public Lands.* Chicago: University of Chicago Press, 1960.

DeVoto, Bernard. *The Easy Chair.* Boston: Houghton Mifflin Co., 1955.

———. *Forays and Rebuttals.* Boston: Little, Brown & Co., 1936.

Drago, Harry Sinclair. *The Great Range Wars: Violence on the Grasslands.* New York: Dodd, Mead & Co., 1970.

Dresden, Donald. *The Marquis de Mores: Emperor of the Bad Lands.* Norman: University of Oklahoma Press, 1970.

Fletcher, Robert H. *Free Grass to Fences.* New York: University Publishers, 1960.

Henry, Stuart. *Conquering Our Great American Plains.* New York: E. P. Dutton & Co., 1930.

Howard, Joseph Kinsey. *Montana: High, Wide, and Handsome.* New Haven: Yale University Press, 1959.

Foss, Phillip O. *Politics and Grass: The Administration of Grazing on the Public Domain.* Seattle: University of Washington Press, 1960.

Jonas, Frank H. *Western Politics.* Salt Lake City: University of Utah Press, 1961.

Josephy, Alvin M., Jr. *The Great West.* New York: American Heritage Publishing Co., 1965.

Larson, T. A. *History of Wyoming.* Lincoln: University of Nebraska Press, 1965.

———. *Wyoming, a Bicentennial History.* Bicentennial Series. New York: W. W. Norton & Co., 1977.

Laxalt, Robert. *Nevada, a Bicentennial History.* Bicentennial Series. New York: W. W. Norton & Co., 1977.

Morgan, H. Wayne, and Anne Hodges Morgan. *Oklahoma, a History.* Bicentennial Series. New York: W. W. Norton & Co., 1977.

Rister, Carl Coke. *The Southwestern Frontier, 1865–1881.* Cleveland: Arthur H. Clark Co., 1928.

Roberts, Paul H. *Hoof Prints on Forest Ranges.* San Antonio: Naylor Co., 1963.

Roosevelt, Theodore. *An Autobiography.* New York: Macmillan Co., 1919.

———. *Stories of the Great West.* New York: Century Co., 1909.

———. *The Winning of the West.* New York: Hastings House, 1963.

Russell, Charles M. *Good Medicine: Memories of the Real West.* Garden City, N.Y.: Garden City Publishing Co., 1929–1930.

———. *Trails Plowed Under.* Garden City, N.Y.: Garden City Publishing Co., 1941.

Sandoz, Mari. *The Cattlemen.* New York: Hastings House, 1958.

Sprague, Marshall. *Colorado, a Bicentennial History.* Bicentennial Series. New York: W. W. Norton & Co., 1976.

Stegner, Wallace. *The Uneasy Chair: A Biography of Bernard DeVoto.* Garden City, N.Y.: Doubleday & Co., 1974.

Voigt, William, Jr. *Public Grazing Lands: Use and Misuse by Industry and Government.* New Brunswick, N.J.: Rutgers University Press, 1976.

THE ARID WEST

Adams, Henry. *The Education of Henry Adams.* 1918. Reprint. New York: Modern Library, 1931.

Baldwin, Malcolm. *The Southwest Energy Complex: A Policy Evaluation.* Washington, D.C.: Conservation Foundation, 1973.

Berkman, Richard L., and Kip Viscusi. *Damming the West.* Nader task force report on the Bureau of Reclamation. Washington, D.C: Center for Study of Responsive Law, 1971.

Bowman, Lynn. *Los Angeles: Epic of a City.* Berkeley, Calif.: Howell-North Books, 1974.

Darrah, William Culp. *Powell of the Colorado.* Princeton: Princeton University Press, 1951.

Dasmann, Raymond F. *The Destruction of California.* New York: Macmillan Co., 1965.

———. *The Last Horizon.* New York: Macmillan Co., 1963.

Johnson, Vance. *Heaven's Tableland: The Dust Bowl Story.* New York: Farrar, Straus & Co., 1947.

Jones, Holway R. *John Muir and the Sierra Club: The Battle for Yosemite.* San Francisco: Sierra Club, 1965.

King, Clarence. *Mountaineering in the Sierra Nevada.* 1872. Reprint. Unabridged and with an introduction by Thurman Wilkins. Keystone Western Americana Series. Philadelphia and New York: J. B. Lippincott Co., 1963.

Lavender, David. *California, a Bicentennial History.* Bicentennial Series. New York: W. W. Norton & Co., 1976.

Mann, Dean E. *The Politics of Water in Arizona.* Tucson: University of Arizona Press, 1963.

McPhee, John A. *Encounters with the Archdruid.* New York: Farrar, Straus & Giroux, 1971.

Moss, Frank E. *The Water Crisis.* New York: Frederick A. Praeger, 1967.

Paulson, Morton C. *The Great Land Hustle.* Chicago: Henry Regnery Co., 1972.

Politics of Land. Ralph Nader's study group report on land use in California. Robert C. Fellmeth, project director. New York: Grossman Publishers, 1973.

Porter, Eliot. *The Place No One Knew: Glen Canyon on the Colorado.* San Francisco: Sierra Club, 1963.

Riegel, Robert E., and Robert G. Athearn. *America Moves West.* New York: Holt, Rinehart & Winston, 1964.

Svobida, Lawrence. *An Empire of Dust.* Caldwell, Idaho: Caxton Printers, 1940.

Tannehill, Ivan Ray. *Drought, Its Causes and Effects.* Princeton: Princeton University Press, 1947.

Udall, Morris K. *Education of a Congressman: The Newsletters of Morris K. Udall.* Edited by Robert L. Peabody. Indianapolis and New York: Bobbs-Merrill Co., 1972.

Bibliography

U.S., Senate, Committee on Interior and Insular Affairs. *Problems of Electrical Power Production in the Southwest: Hearings. . . .* 92nd Cong., 1st sess., May–November 1971.

Westwide Study. Report on critical water problems facing the eleven western states. U.S. Interior Department, Bureau of Reclamation. Washington, D.C.: Government Printing Office, 1975.

Wilkins, Thurman. *Clarence King: A Biography.* New York: Macmillan Co., 1958.

Wolff, Anthony. *Unreal Estate.* San Francisco and New York: Sierra Club, 1973.

Wright, Jim. *The Coming Water Famine.* New York: Coward-McCann, 1966.

CONSERVATIONISTS AND NATURALISTS

Anderson, Frederick R. *NEPA in the Courts: A Legal Analysis of the National Environmental Policy Act.* Washington, D.C.: Resources for the Future, 1973.

Anderson, Frederick R., et al. *Environmental Improvement through Economic Incentives.* Washington, D.C.: Resources for the Future, 1977.

Baldwin, Malcolm, and James K. Page, Jr. *Law and the Environment.* New York: Walker & Co., 1970.

Brown, Harrison. *The Human Future Revisited: The World Predicament and Possible Solutions.* New York: W. W. Norton & Co., 1978.

————. *The Next Hundred Years.* New York: Viking Press, 1957.

Brown, Lester R. *The Twenty-ninth Day.* Worldwatch Institute. New York: W. W. Norton & Co., 1978.

————. *In the Human Interest: A Strategy to Stabilize World Population.* Aspen Institute for Humanistic Studies, Overseas Development Council. New York: W. W. Norton & Co., 1974.

Burroughs, John. *John Burroughs' America: Selections from the Writings of the Hudson River Naturalist.* Edited by Farida A. Wiley. New York: Devin-Adair Co., 1951.

Cahn, Robert. *Footprints on the Planet: A Search for an Environmental Ethic.* New York: Universe Books, 1978.

Caldwell, Lynton K. *Environment: A Challenge to Modern Society.* Garden City, N.Y.: Doubleday & Co., Anchor Books, 1971.

Carson, Rachel. *Silent Spring.* Boston: Houghton Mifflin Co.; The Riverside Press, Cambridge, 1962.

Carter, Luther J. *The Florida Experience: Land and Water Policy in a Growth State.* Resources for the Future. Baltimore and London: Johns Hopkins University Press, 1974.

Chase, Stuart. *Rich Land Poor Land: A Study of Waste in the Natural Resources of America.* New York and London: McGraw-Hill, Whittlesey House, 1936.

Conservation Directory. Washington, D.C.: National Wildlife Federation, published annually.

515

Coyle, David Cushman. *Conservation.* New Brunswick, N.J.: Rutgers University Press, 1957.

Ekirch, Arthur A., Jr. *Man and Nature in America.* New York: Columbia University Press, 1963.

Emerson, Ralph Waldo. *America the Beautiful: In the Words of Ralph Waldo Emerson.* Waukesha, Wis.: Rand McNally & Co., Country Beautiful.

Evans, Rowland, Jr., and Robert D. Novak. *Nixon in the White House: The Frustration of Power.* New York: Random House, Vintage Books, 1971, 1972.

Green, Fitzhugh. *A Change in the Weather.* New York: W. W. Norton & Co., 1977.

Hayes, Denis. *Rays of Hope: The Transition to a Post-Petroleum World.* Worldwatch Institute. New York: W. W. Norton & Co., 1977.

Hicks, John D. *The American Nation.* Boston: Houghton Mifflin Co., 1962.

Jacoby, Erich H. *Man and Land: The Essential Revolution.* New York: Alfred A. Knopf, 1971.

Leopold, Aldo. *A Sand County Almanac: With Other Essays on Conservation from Round River.* New York: Oxford University Press, 1966.

Leuchtenburg, William E. *The Perils of Prosperity, 1914–32.* Chicago and London: University of Chicago Press, 1958.

Lowenthal, David. *George Perkins Marsh: Versatile Vermonter.* New York: Columbia University Press, 1958.

Marsh, George Perkins. *Man and Nature.* 1864. Reprint. Cambridge, Mass.: Harvard University Press, 1965.

Meadows, Dennis L., et al. *The Limits to Growth: A Report for the Club of Rome's Project on the Predicament of Mankind.* New York: Universe Books, 1972.

Mitchell, John G., with Constance L. Stallings, eds. *Ecotactics: The Sierra Club Handbook for Environmental Activists.* With an introduction by Ralph Nader. New York: Sierra Club, Trident Press, 1970.

Muir, John. *John of the Mountains: The Unpublished Journals of John Muir.* Edited by Linnie Marsh Wolfe. Boston: Houghton Mifflin Co., 1938.

———. *The Wilderness World of John Muir.* With introduction and interpretive comments by Edwin Way Teale. Boston: Houghton Mifflin Co., 1954.

Osborn, Fairfield. *Our Plundered Planet.* Boston: Little, Brown & Co., 1948.

Phillips, John C. *American Game Mammals and Birds: A Catalog of Books, 1582 to 1925—Sport, Natural History, and Conservation.* With approval of Boone and Crockett Club. Boston and New York: Houghton Mifflin Co., 1930.

Ridgeway, James. *The Politics of Ecology.* New York: E. P. Dutton & Co., 1970.

Roosevelt, Nicholas. *Conservation: Now or Never.* New York: Dodd, Mead & Co., 1970.

Sax, Joseph L. *Defending the Environment: A Strategy for Citizen Action.* With an introduction by George McGovern. New York: Alfred A. Knopf, 1971.

Smith, Frank E. *The Politics of Conservation.* New York: Random House, Pantheon Books, 1966.

Smith, Herbert F. *John Muir.* New Haven: College and University Press Publishers, 1965.

516

Bibliography

Swift, Hildegarde Hoyt. *From the Eagle's Wing: A Biography of John Muir.* New York: William Morrow & Co., 1962.

Teale, Edwin Way. *The Wilderness World of John Muir.* Boston: Houghton Mifflin Co., 1954.

Thoreau, Henry David. *Walden and the Famous Essay on "Civil Disobedience."* New York and Toronto: New American Library, Signet Classic, 1960.

White, Gilbert. *The Natural History of Selborne.* 1789. Reprint. London and New York: John Lane, 1900.

Udall, Stewart L. *The Quiet Crisis.* With an introduction by John F. Kennedy. New York: Holt, Rinehart & Winston, 1963.

Zurhorst, Charles. *The Conservation Fraud.* New York: Cowles Book Co., 1970.

ALASKA

U.S., Senate. *Alaska National Interest Lands.* Report of the Committee on Energy and Natural Resources. 96th Cong., 1st sess., November 14, 1979. Washington, D.C.: Government Printing Office, 1979.

Alaska Natives and the Land. U.S., Federal Field Committee for Development Planning in Alaska. Chairman, Joseph H. FitzGerald; Natural Resources Officer, David M. Hickok; Consultant, Arlon R. Tussing, etc. Washington, D.C.: Government Printing Office, 1968.

Cicchetti, Charles J. *Alaskan Oil: Alternative Routes and Markets.* Resources for the Future. Baltimore and London: Johns Hopkins Press, 1972.

Final Environmental Impact Statement: Proposed Trans-Alaska Pipeline. U.S. Interior Department. Washington, D.C.: Government Printing Office, 1972.

Gruening, Ernest. *The Battle for Alaska Statehood.* Seattle and London: University of Alaska Press, 1967.

———. *The State of Alaska.* New York: Random House, 1968.

Gruening, Ernest, ed. *An Alaska Reader, 1867–1967.* New York: Meredith Press, 1966.

Johnson, Hugh A., and Harold T. Jorgenson. *The Land Resources of Alaska.* Conservation Foundation study published for the University of Alaska. New York: University Publishers, 1963.

McPhee, John. *Coming into the Country.* New York: Farrar, Straus & Giroux, 1977.

Trans-Alaska Pipeline Hearings. Bureau of Land Management, U.S. Interior Department. Washington, D.C.: Hoover Reporting Co., 1971.